ReJoycing

New Readings of *Dubliners*

Rosa M. Bollettieri Bosinelli
and Harold F. Mosher Jr.
Editors

THE UNIVERSITY PRESS OF KENTUCKY

Publication of this volume was made possible in part
by a grant from the National Endowment for the Humanities.

Editorial and Sales Offices: The University Press of Kentucky
663 South Limestone Street, Lexington, Kentucky 40508-4008

98 99 00 01 02   5 4 3 2 1

Library of Congress Cataloging-in-Publication Data

ReJoycing : new readings of Dubliners / Rosa Maria Bollettieri
Bosinelli and Harold F. Mosher, Jr., editors.
    p. cm. — (Irish literature, history, and culture)
    Includes bibliographical references and index.
    ISBN 0-8131-2057-8 (acid-free paper). — ISBN 0-8131-0949-3 (pbk.
: acid-free paper)
    1. Joyce, James, 1882-1941. Dubliners. 2. City and town life in
literature. 3. Dublin (Ireland)—In literature. I. Bosinelli
Bollettieri, Rosa Maria. II. Mosher, Harold Frederick, 1930.
III. Series
PR6019.09D8774   1998
823'.912—dc21   97-47260

37993217

This book is printed on acid-free recycled paper meeting
the requirements of the American National Standard
for Permanence of Paper for Printed Library Materials.

Manufactured in the United States of America

To the memory of Bernard Benstock

Contents

Preface

The ever-increasing number of books and articles on James Joyce testifies not only to his popularity and eminent place in twentieth-century literature but also to the diversity of his work, aspects of which become evident with each new study. Probably Joyce's most celebrated and experimental novels are *Ulysses* and *Finnegans Wake,* but *Dubliners,* begun in 1904 and published as a book in 1914, remains the most widely read. In this collection of short stories, one can observe Joyce experimenting with the familiar modes of his day—realism and symbolism—and with the very form of the novel itself, for *Dubliners* exhibits many features of this genre and anticipates some of the peculiarities of Joyce's writing strategies that will be fully developed in his later works.

The idea for this collection of essays on Joyce's *Dubliners* originated at two James Joyce International Conferences in Copenhagen and Monaco in 1986 and 1990, respectively. Harold F. Mosher Jr., the editor of *Style,* invited two Joyce specialists, Rosa Maria Bollettieri Bosinelli and Christine van Boheemen, along with the coeditor of *Style,* John V. Knapp, to assemble essays for a special issue of the journal on *Dubliners.* That issue appeared in volume 25, number 3, in the fall of 1991. Favorable reviews in the *James Joyce Quarterly,* the *James Joyce Literary Supplement,* and the *James Joyce Broadsheet* encouraged the editors to conceive of expanding the original number of nine essays by five newly commissioned ones for an augmented collection suitable for book publication. The present volume is the result of these efforts. *ReJoycing: New Readings of* Dubliners includes nine updated articles, which originally appeared in *Style,* and adds five new ones commissioned expressly for this volume. All the contributions were written by internationally known Joyce specialists from the United States, Canada, Italy, Switzerland, Croatia, and Germany.

These essays reveal a Joyce very much abreast of literary, cultural, and political developments of his time but also questioning them. He may have used many of the techniques of nineteenth-century symbolism and realism—for example, narrative objectivity, free indirect discourse, and even the titles of his stories—but he often subverted them to impede or defer the reader's interpretations. At other times, he combines realistic and symbolist methods for their mutual enrichment. In the traditions of still other literary devices, the etymology of certain key words or allusions to a Dantean intertext or even foreign language translations will reveal the complexity of Joyce's writing. In one of the essays here, this complexity is made evident by a fresh look at the geometric figure of the gnomon, which appears on the first page of *Dubliners*. We learn that Joyce may have worked by augmentation rather than by the usually understood gnomonic way of subtraction.

Many of the essays in *ReJoycing* discover subtle thematic and stylistic conflicts, perhaps reflecting Joyce's own conflict with Ireland. British colonization turns out to be not only political but also linguistic: the Irish who submit to British institutions, including British English, participate in their own oppression. Joyce, though, can imply his awareness of such a submissive posture by infiltrating the narrator's authoritative voice into a sentence that also imitates British speech. On other occasions, the imperceptive narrator, in a switch of power, can become the victim of a revolt by the characters. Still another pervasive conflict, one between the real and the ideal, is suggested by the discordance resulting from the difference between romantic or poetic aspirations and the repetitive and hackneyed language used to express them. Finally, an opposition between the sexes may take the form of how memory serves or fails men and women, of how women characters struggle for the right to speak in direct discourse, and of how falling and rising stylistic rhythms reflect respectively opposition and harmony in this confrontation of genders.

This wide-ranging collection—investigating themes; style; the significance of titles; the intertextual element; etymology; translations; geometric structures; political, linguistic, narrative, and gender conflicts—offers a representative sampling of contemporary criticism on *Dubliners* and should appeal to advanced undergraduates and graduate students alike as well as to Joyce scholars.

The editors are deeply indebted to Bernard Benstock, who first suggested submitting an enlarged edition for book publication. Berni's enthusiasm was a deciding factor in the editors' decision to proceed with this project. It is with a deep feeling of loss and regret for his premature passing away that the editors dedicate this volume to his memory.

The editors also wish to express their gratitude to a number of friends and colleagues without whose help this book would not have been produced. Karen Blaser's long and faithful dedication to the processing of the text has allowed work to progress promptly and accurately. At an earlier stage, Phillip Ronald Stormer contributed similar help. Lisa Chase Bywater's assistance in securing permissions and answering technical questions has accelerated work in the face of deadlines. Nita Challgren has proved to be a valuable liaison between a fallible editor and infallible computers. During the editorial work on the *Style* issue on *Dubliners,* John V. Knapp provided acute commentary on submitted manuscripts. James Mellard, the current editor of *Style,* has shared his experience and advice on strategies of manuscript preparation for publication. Special thanks must go to James I. Miller, chair of English at Northern Illinois University, for his effective intercession in regard to financial and personnel contributions and to Shari Benstock for her friendly encouragement and intelligent comments. During indexing, Raffaella Baccolini came to our rescue with fitting advice and generous participation.

Finally, we recognize the continual support, especially during difficult times, of our spouses, Nicole Marie-Josèphe Mosher and Marino Bosinelli, whose attentions over the years of this book's gestation have resulted in a more serene offspring.

Last but not least, Rosa Maria Bollettieri Bosinelli wishes to express her gratitude to Harold Mosher not only for his encouragement and understanding when she was acting as guest editor for the special issue of *Style* but also for his generous collaboration during their joint venture as coeditors living on different sides of the ocean, having a different mother tongue, belonging to a different culture, and accustomed to different editorial traditions.

Harold Mosher, in turn, wishes to acknowledge Rosa Maria Bollettieri Bosinelli's valuable contributions to this project in soliciting manuscripts and providing so successfully the essential liaison between the "home" office in the United States and the various residences of our European colleagues. Her "translations" enabled effective communication between diverse cultures. Nevertheless, *vivent les différences!*

ROSIA MARIA BOLLETTIERI BOSINELLI
HAROLD F. MOSHER JR.

Introduction

Patrick A. McCarthy

James Joyce began *Dubliners* in 1904 as a short story sequence for George Russell's agricultural journal *The Irish Homestead,* which published versions of "The Sisters," "Eveline," and "After the Race" before complaints from readers offended by the stories' caustic treatment of Irish life led Russell to suspend publication of the stories. By then, however, Joyce was already planning to recast his series of discrete narratives into a book of stories linked by their common concern with Catholic middle-class life in Dublin as well as by various overlapping themes, images, and situations. *Dubliners* was published in 1914, after numerous delays and complicated negotiations with the English publisher Grant Richards (who canceled a 1906 contract but issued a new one eight years later and finally brought out the volume) and with the Dublin firm of Maunsel and Company, whose printer raised objections to the stories both because of their alleged obscenity and because he feared lawsuits by people and businesses named in them.[1] When it was published the book attracted none of the legal actions feared by Joyce's publishers and printers; on the other hand, it received mixed reviews, and its sales were meager, as Joyce noted in a letter to Richards in which he expressed regret that "neither you nor I have gained anything" from the book's publication (*D* 292; *Letters* 2:340-41). For Joyce, the lack of royalties was less disappointing than the fact that the book had done little to stimulate interest in his new projects or to establish him as a major author.

The publication of *Dubliners* thus proved anticlimactic, an event easily overshadowed by the appearance of *A Portrait of the Artist as a Young Man* (serialized in *The Egoist,* 1914-15; first book publication, December 1916) and, far more spectacularly, by the 1922 publication of *Ulysses,* after which Joyce was widely recognized as a central modernist writer—indeed, as one of the most important avant-garde artists of his time. In retrospect, however, 1914 stands out as an important year in the history of the modernist short story and modern fiction in general. Several reasons for the importance of *Dubliners* are suggested by Joyce's own description of his aims and methods in a May 1906 letter to Grant Richards:

My intention was to write a chapter of the moral history of my country and I chose Dublin for the scene because that city seemed to me the centre of paralysis. I have tried to present it to the indifferent public under four of its aspects: childhood, adolescence, maturity and public life. The stories are arranged in this order. I have written it for the most part in a style of scrupulous meanness and with the conviction that he is a very bold man who dares to alter in the presentment, still more to deform, whatever he has seen and heard. [*D* 269; *Letters* 2:134]

Here, in capsule form, are Joyce's defenses of the collection on the bases of its subject matter (a critique of Dublin society as "the centre of paralysis"), its comprehensive organization, its "style of scrupulous meanness," and above all its realism and adherence to the truth. Setting himself against "the indifferent public," Joyce implies that by portraying the "paralysis" at the heart of Dublin's public life he will force readers out of their apathy. A similar note appears in a letter to Richards written seven weeks later, in which Joyce argues that "the odour of ashpits and old weeds and offal" emanating from his stories is a necessary part of his depiction of the city and grandly declares that Richards's failure to publish *Dubliners* would "retard the course of civilisation in Ireland by preventing the Irish people from having one good look at themselves in [his] nicely polished looking-glass" (*D* 286; *Letters* 1:63-64).

In these and other letters concerning *Dubliners,* Joyce provided models for two distinct lines of inquiry that have been followed by critics of the book. There is, on the one hand, an emphasis on its form, which has led to stylistic and structural studies, including analyses of image patterns and other readings of the stories in relation to one another. At the same time there is Joyce's insistence that the stories accurately portray Dublin itself, not only the physical city but the political and cultural milieu in which the narratives are enacted. These two emphases might lead to different forms of scholarly inquiry: a concern with aesthetic form underlies New Critical readings, symbolic interpretations, and studies of the book's "unity," whereas an emphasis on Joyce's subject matter may be discerned in writings by Marxist, feminist, and postcolonial critics, among others. In practice, however, these two main areas of critical emphasis are hard to separate precisely because the style and structure of *Dubliners* are both the means by which Joyce presents his subject and an integral part of that subject. Thus, for example, Hugh Kenner argues that in Joyce's works generally "the usual criterion of style, that it disappear like glass before the reality of the subject, doesn't apply to his pages. The language of Dublin *is* the subject" (12). In this reading, and in countless others that consider ways in which Joyce's language carries an implicit critique of his characters and their world, Joyce becomes the supreme example of a modernist writer in whose works it is virtually impossible to distinguish form from content.[2]

As a contribution to the art of the short story, *Dubliners* is noteworthy for several reasons. Its sparse yet economical style, its use of suggestive details that at times seem to have a symbolic meaning, its refusal of any sort of neat conclusion have all influenced the shape of the modern short story.[3] Equally important is the fact that *Dubliners* is a coherent collection of related stories, a sort of novel with a collective rather than an individual protagonist. A few earlier collections had included stories with common locations, themes, and images—George Moore's *The Untilled Field* (1903) is the outstanding example in Ireland—but *Dubliners* is the most fully realized, and most influential, volume of the kind. Apart from the first few stories that Joyce wrote, all of the *Dubliners* narratives were composed with book publication in mind, and the stories often take on different meanings when read within the context of the collection than they do in isolation. Sometimes the connections between stories are made by small touches, as when Eveline's "holding her black leather purse tightly in her hand as she elbowed her way through the crowds" (*D* 38) ironically undercuts the more romantic version of this image in "Araby," where, as he makes his way through a similar crowd, the narrator imagines himself bearing a "chalice" rather than a purse (*D* 31). Some of the book's forms of repetition are obvious enough—the conclusions of several stories involve darkness, tears, or both, and the desperate attempt of the boy at the end of "Counterparts" to avoid a beating by saying a Hail Mary for his father is immediately followed by "Clay," the story of a Maria whose attempts at peacemaking are generally ineffectual—while others are more subtle, but they all contribute to the economy of *Dubliners*.

As an example of a significant recurrent element in Joyce's portrayal of Dublin we might cite the emphasis on absence. The theme is introduced on the first page of "The Sisters," whose narrator associates the key word *paralysis* with two other words whose contexts he specifies: "*gnomon* in the Euclid and . . . *simony* in the Catechism" (*D* 9). These three italicized words connect Joyce's themes of passivity (*paralysis*), corruption (*simony*), and absence (*gnomon*).[4] Absence and negation frame "The Sisters," a story that begins with the narrator's recognition that "there was no hope" left for Father Flynn, concludes with his listening for a sound from the dead priest's coffin (and, predictably, not hearing it), and includes a strikingly large number of ellipses in its dialogue. Absence, for Joyce, is a kind of presence, exerting pressure on what remains, as we see from the examples of dead people who continue to influence the living: Eveline Hill's mother in "Eveline," Mrs. Sinico at the end of "A Painful Case," Charles Stewart Parnell in "Ivy Day," Michael Furey in "The Dead." Characters who are alive but absent, like Joe's brother Alphy in "Clay" and Farrington's wife at the end of "Counterparts," play their own parts in the stories, as do any number of missing items: the two missing pages of correspondence in

"Counterparts" point to a void in Farrington's life, for example, and in "Clay" the plumcake, the nutcracker, a corkscrew, the clay itself (after it is thrown away), and the second verse of Maria's song are as conspicuously absent as Alphy.

Joyce's original plan for a series of ten stories had been expanded to twelve by the time he sent the manuscript to Richards at the end of 1905, with two more—"Two Gallants" and "A Little Cloud"—following in 1906. Had the book been published as it then stood, a collection of fourteen stories beginning with "The Sisters" and ending with "Grace," it would have been very different from the book we now have: opening with a story of a priest whom the boy associates with simony and concluding with another whose treatment of God as an accountant implies a related corruption of the spiritual realm by materialism, *Dubliners* would have been a more insistently ironic portrayal of Dublin's "paralysis," focusing on the characters' inability to escape or improve their stagnant lives. The addition of "The Dead" in 1907 not only gave the book a very different—a more ambiguous as well as a more symbolic and more stylistically powerful—conclusion; it also balanced Joyce's criticism of Dublin with a display of its hospitality. In other ways as well, the scope of the collection was enlarged by "The Dead," which has a far broader vision of the human condition than any other story in *Dubliners*. That scope is especially evident in the final apocalyptic vision of "all the living and the dead," which is strikingly unlike the abrupt, minimalist conclusions of the earlier stories.

While "The Dead" may be read in isolation, some of its effects are lost if we do not recognize that it was the only story Joyce wrote with the rest of the collection in mind, a fact that led Joyce to incorporate into the story many coda-like echoes of other *Dubliners* stories. When the narrator says of Gabriel's mother, "thanks to her, [his brother] Constantine was now senior curate in Balbriggan and, thanks to her, Gabriel himself had taken his degree" (*D* 186-87), the repeated phrase "thanks to her" ironically echoes a similar statement about Mrs. Kearney in "A Mother": "thanks to her, everything that was to be done was done" (*D* 139). Gabriel's insistence that Lily take a coin from him might be regarded as a form of unwitting compensation for the coin that Corley took from the slavey in "Two Gallants," and Gabriel's refusal of a candle at the hotel (*D* 216) parallels similar refusals by Father Keon in "Ivy Day" and by Tom Kernan in "Grace" (*D* 126, 171-72). Moreover, in insisting that he and Gretta have no need of a candle, Gabriel insures that the only light in their hotel room will come from the street. The result is that at the end of the story when he stands in the darkened room looking out a window that is lighted on the other side, Gabriel exchanges positions with the boy who stands at night in the street studying a "lighted square of window" at the outset of "The Sisters." While recapitulating themes, images, situations, and verbal motifs from earlier

Dubliners stories, however, "The Dead" also serves as a turning point in Joyce's fiction, for it is the story whose mundane materials are most fully transformed, even redeemed, by their incorporation within its grand human vision.

Just as the stories of *Dubliners* may be read in isolation or as part of the collection, the book may be read by itself or as an integral part of Joyce's major work, which, apart from *Dubliners*, consists primarily of *A Portrait of the Artist as a Young Man* (1916), *Ulysses* (1922), and *Finnegans Wake* (1939). Each book could be regarded as the unique product of a phase in Joyce's career, an experiment in literary form that he never repeated: *Dubliners*, a realistic collection of short stories, was followed by *A Portrait*, an impressionistic novel, based on Joyce's early life, that describes the growth of an artist's imagination; by *Ulysses*, a stylistic and narrational tour de force filled with innumerable allusions and based in part on an analogy between the epic world of *Odyssey* and the modern Dublin traversed by a humane advertising canvasser; and by *Finnegans Wake*, a fantastic dream vision narrated in an obscure but often hilarious punning language. Thus the pattern of Joyce's career is one of incessant internalization, moving from realism toward a concern with the mind and the language through which the mind attempts to come to terms with the world and with itself. At the same time, *Dubliners* gives us fine examples of several important recurrent features of Joyce's work, including its intricate craftsmanship, its careful attention to all aspects of style, its concern with the relationship between individual characters and the cultural and historical environment in which they live, and its exploration of the relationship between art and politics.

Apart from perfunctory discussions in critical studies devoted mainly to the later Joyce, *Dubliners* received relatively little attention during the first few decades of Joyce criticism, in part because the book's apparently straightforward style gave critics few clues to the stories' artistry and because the short story form provided Joyce with a narrower canvas than the ones he used in *A Portrait of the Artist, Ulysses,* and *Finnegans Wake.* Much of the criticism of *Dubliners* from the 1940s through the 1960s was stimulated by critics' interest in such features of the later works as their use of mythic parallels, highly developed symbolic patterns, and symbolic complexity, an interest that led to hopes of discovering the same qualities in *Dubliners.*[5] Still, most criticism during that time focused on individual stories rather than on the structure or themes of the collection, a strategy encouraged by the New Critical emphasis on autonomous works of art. Even today, most studies involve close or theoretical readings of individual stories.

The first four critical volumes devoted entirely to *Dubliners* did not appear until the late 1960s. Two of these—Peter K. Garrett's collection of essays on *Dubliners* in the Twentieth-Century Interpretations series (1968) and the critical handbook edited by James R. Baker and Thomas F. Staley (1969)—consisted mainly of reprinted material, but significant new views appeared in *Joyce's* Dubliners: *Substance, Vision, and Art* by Warren Beck (1969) and in *James Joyce's* Dubliners: *Critical Essays,* edited by Clive Hart (1969). Beck's book argued strongly against overly ingenious symbolic interpretations while Hart's contributors engaged in what remain some of the best close readings of the stories. The range of critical and scholarly materials available to students of *Dubliners* has increased considerably in recent years. Three books that concentrate on factual information are Don Gifford's *Joyce Annotated* (1982), a set of glosses on *Dubliners* and *A Portrait of the Artist* that also comments on the social and political backgrounds to the early works;[6] *The Joycean Way* by Bruce Bidwell and Linda Heffer (1982), which provides essential information about places referred to in *Dubliners* and the *Portrait;* and Donald T. Torchiana's background study of *Dubliners* (1986).

The growing stature of *Dubliners* as part of the Joyce canon is also reflected in the appearance of four important book-length critical studies. Craig Hansen Werner's Dubliners: *A Pluralistic World* (1988) is both a solid introduction to *Dubliners* for general readers (containing, among other things, an excellent review of previous criticism) and a highly original study focusing on the many critical perspectives from which the stories may be read. Two major studies that examine *Dubliners* through the psychoanalytic theories of Jacques Lacan are Garry M. Leonard's *Reading* Dubliners *Again* (1993) and Earl G. Ingersoll's *Engendered Trope in Joyce's* Dubliners (1996). Less overtly theoretical but equally valuable in its finely nuanced close readings of the text is Bernard Benstock's *Narrative Con/Texts in* Dubliners (1994), which moves confidently through *Dubliners,* aided by a set of critical terms suggested by the stories themselves.

Although I have emphasized book-length studies, much of the best *Dubliners* criticism has appeared in journals, including the fall 1991 issue of *Style,* a special number devoted to *Dubliners* that serves as the core of the present collection.[7] Five previously unpublished essays have been added to the original nine, and the result is a set of diverse perspectives spanning the range of critical issues that are central to contemporary Joyce scholarship with particular attention to language, gender, and political and cultural power. The essays are grouped into five sections according to their subjects. In "Symbolism, Realism, and Style," Sonja Bašić, Thomas Jackson Rice, Harold F. Mosher Jr., and Jolanta W. Wawrzycka investigate aspects of the narrative and stylistic techniques through which *Dubliners* generates meaning. Approaches to "Language and Power" by Trevor L. Williams, Claire A. Culleton, and John Paul Riquelme show in different ways that the book's language is deeply implicated in its examination of political and narrative control. Raffaella Baccolini,

Marlena G. Corcoran, and David Leon Higdon approach the issue of power from another perspective in "Gender and Control," while in "Meaning Deferred and Revealed" Ulrich Schneider, Michael Brian, and Lucia Boldrini examine thematic aspects of the stories through their titles or through etymological or Dantean references. Finally, Fritz Senn, whose work stands alone in the "New Directions" section, considers anew the narrative implications of Joyce's gnomonic style. Approaching the stories from different angles, concerning themselves either with particular stories or with the collection as a whole, these representative contemporary readings of *Dubliners* demonstrate once again the rich artistry masked by the "style of scrupulous meanness" in Joyce's fascinating stories.

Notes

1. For more detailed accounts of the composition of *Dubliners* (hereafter cited with page numbers as *D*) and the disputes involved in its publication, see Morris Beja 32-39; Richard Ellmann 207-11, 219-22, 231-32, 267, 290-91, 310-11, 313-15, 323-24, 328-38, 348-54; Michael Groden 78-84; Florence L. Walzl 160-64; and "The Evidence of the Letters" (*D* 257-93). See especially "A Curious History" (*D* 289-92). Joyce satirized Maunsel and Company and the Dublin printer John Falconer in his 1912 broadside "Gas from a Burner" (*Critical Writings* 242-45).

2. This principle was stated most strikingly by Samuel Beckett in a 1929 essay on Joyce's *Work in Progress* (*Finnegans Wake*): "Here form *is* content, content *is* form. . . . His writing is not *about* something; *it is that something itself*" ("Dante" 14). Two years later, Beckett said much the same thing about Marcel Proust, who "makes no attempt to dissociate form from content. The one is a concretion of the other, the revelation of a world" (*Proust* 67).

3. The most thorough examination of Joyce's relationship to earlier short story writers remains that of Marvin Magalaner and Richard M. Kain.

4. "Simony," so called after the example of Simon Magus (see Acts 8:18-19), refers to attempts to buy or sell pardons or other spiritual things; "gnomon," as the term is used in Euclidean geometry, denotes the irregular geometrical figure created by removing a parallelogram from one of the corners of a larger parallelogram. Other meanings of the *gnomon* image have been explored in Joyce criticism, most recently (and interestingly) by David Weir in *Joyce's Art of Mediation* and by Fritz Senn in the essay printed in this volume. For discussions of Joyce's "gnomonics" in terms related to those I have touched on here, see Bernard Benstock's chapter 2 and Phillip F. Herring's argument that the gnomon image "suggests that certain kinds of absence are typical of the whole of Dublin at a significant *time* in its history. . . . In effect, a *gnomon* may be a key synecdoche of absence, part of a political rhetoric of silence within a larger framework of language" (4).

5. Influential examples of these types of critical focus include the works by Richard Levin and Charles Shattuck, Brewster Ghiselin, and William York Tindall listed in my works cited section. The limitations of these studies are apparent today,

but they all played a significant role in shaping criticism of *Dubliners* during their time, and the articles by Levin and Shattuck and by Ghiselin were especially useful in calling attention to *Dubliners* as a work that carried patterns from one story to another.

6. *Joyce Annotated* is a revised and corrected version of Gifford's 1967 book *Notes for Joyce.*

7. The essay by Lucia Boldrini in this volume has been substantially revised from the one that appeared in *Style.*

Works Cited

Baker, James R., and Thomas F. Staley, eds. *James Joyce's* Dubliners*: A Critical Handbook.* Belmont: Wadsworth, 1969.

Beck, Warren. *Joyce's* Dubliners*: Substance, Vision, and Art.* Durham, N.C.: Duke Univ. Press, 1969.

Beckett, Samuel. "Dante . . . Bruno. Vico . . . Joyce." In *Our Exagmination Round His Factification for Incamination of Work in Progress,* 1-22. Paris: Shakespeare and Company, 1929; New York: New Directions, 1972.

———. *Proust.* London: Chatto, 1931; New York: Grove, 1957.

Beja, Morris. *James Joyce: A Literary Life.* Columbus: Ohio State Univ. Press, 1992.

Benstock, Bernard. *Narrative Con/Texts in* Dubliners. Urbana: Univ. of Illinois Press, 1994.

Bidwell, Bruce, and Linda Heffer. *The Joycean Way: A Topographic Guide to* Dubliners *and* A Portrait of the Artist as a Young Man. Baltimore: Johns Hopkins Univ. Press, 1982.

Ellmann, Richard. *James Joyce.* Rev. ed. New York: Oxford Univ. Press, 1982.

Garrett, Peter K., ed. *Twentieth-Century Interpretations of* Dubliners. Englewood Cliffs, N.J.: Prentice-Hall, 1968.

Ghiselin, Brewster. "The Unity of *Dubliners.*" *Accent* 16 (spring 1956): 75-88, (summer 1956): 196-213 (reprinted in Baker and Staley 35-62 and Garrett 57-85).

Gifford, Don. *Joyce Annotated: Notes for* Dubliners *and* A Portrait of the Artist as a Young Man. 2d ed. Berkeley: Univ. of California Press, 1982.

Groden, Michael. "A Textual and Publishing History." In *A Companion to Joyce Studies,* ed. Zack Bowen and James F. Carens, 71-128. Westport, Conn.: Greenwood, 1984.

Hart, Clive, ed. *James Joyce's* Dubliners*: Critical Essays.* New York: Viking Press, 1969.

Herring, Phillip F. *Joyce's Uncertainty Principle.* Princeton, N.J.: Princeton Univ. Press, 1987.

Ingersoll, Earl G. *Engendered Trope in Joyce's* Dubliners. Carbondale: Southern Illinois Univ. Press, 1996.

Joyce, James. *The Critical Writings of James Joyce.* Ed. Ellsworth Mason and Richard Ellmann. New York: Viking, 1964.

———. Dubliners*: Text, Criticism, and Notes.* Ed. Robert Scholes and A. Walton Litz. New York: Viking, 1969.

———. *Letters of James Joyce.* Ed. Stuart Gilbert and Richard Ellmann. 3 vols. New York: Viking, 1966.

Leonard, Garry M. *Reading* Dubliners *Again: A Lacanian Perspective.* Syracuse, N.Y.: Syracuse Univ. Press, 1993.

Kenner, Hugh. *Dublin's Joyce.* Bloomington: Indiana Univ. Press, 1956.

Levin, Richard, and Charles Shattuck. "First Flight to Ithaca: A New Reading of Joyce's *Dubliners.*" *Accent* 4 (winter 1944): 75-99 (reprinted in *James Joyce: Two Decades of Criticism,* ed. Seon Givens, 47-94. Rev. ed. New York: Vanguard, 1963).

Magalaner, Marvin, and Richard M. Kain. *Joyce: The Man, the Work, the Reputation.* New York: New York Univ. Press, 1956.

Tindall, William York. *A Reader's Guide to James Joyce.* New York: Noonday, 1959.

Torchiana, Donald T. *Backgrounds for Joyce's* Dubliners. Boston: Allen, 1986.

Walzl, Florence L. "*Dubliners.*" In *A Companion to Joyce Studies,* ed. Zack Bowen and James F. Carens, 157-228. Westport, Conn.: Greenwood, 1984.

Weir, David. *Joyce's Art of Mediation.* Ann Arbor: Univ. of Michigan Press, 1996.

Werner, Craig Hansen. Dubliners*: A Pluralistic World.* Boston: Twayne, 1988.

Symbolism, Realism, and Style

CHAPTER ONE

A Book of Many Uncertainties

Joyce's *Dubliners*

Sonja Bašić

"Oui, la bêtise consiste à vouloir conclure."
("Yes, stupidity consists in wanting to conclude.")
Gustave Flaubert

One of the problems presented by the existing critical approaches to James Joyce's *Dubliners* is overinterpretation or too literal interpretation. On the whole, there has been too much "irritable reaching" after verifiable facts and incontrovertible conclusions, not only among the critics who consider *Dubliners* preeminently as a realist work but even among those who give precedence to its symbolist complexities. The "realists" have tended to rely too much on the reputation of *Dubliners* as the simplest, most accessible of Joyce's works, forgetting that this work is also revolutionary in a particularly underhand way. And the "symbolists" have in turn neglected the specifically subversive nature of Joyce's symbols.[1]

Some of this critical confusion has resulted from the fact that while seemingly following realist/naturalist conventions and also using symbolist devices even at that very early stage in his career, Joyce subverted both. Treacherously, *Dubliners* simultaneously invites and undermines categorization and sense making. In this respect it is quite unique, and this uniqueness has not been sufficiently acknowledged. The simplicity of *Dubliners* is a trap: led on by the deceptive transparency of the stories, the critics rush to conclusions about facts instead of patiently studying the infinitely tenuous and often imperceptible uncertainties and indeterminacies of the fiction.[2]

One indicator that *Dubliners* seems to be particularly at odds with certainties can also be demonstrated a posteriori by pointing out the sheer contradictory diversity of existing critical interpretations, which with respect to some characters, situations, and events or even entire stories are quite astounding.[3] I cannot in fact think of any modern novel, let alone a collection of stories, that

Original version published in *Style* 25.3 (1991).

has been accorded such a number of contradictory interpretations. A good example of this is the particularly striking divergences in the moral and psychological motivation and evaluation of characters. Maria, Eveline, and Gabriel, for example, are submitted to a gamut of moral critical judgments running from complete sympathy to downright disgust. Some critics empathize with them and like them; others consider them sadly deficient and often responsible for their deficiencies (Eveline is unable to love; Gabriel's love is worthless; Maria's little illusions are the result of despicable moral blindness, and so on). This type of criticism strikes me as particularly unsuitable with respect to Joyce's characters, who are superbly presented as human figures but also demand to be seen as Genettian *figures*.[4]

The very fact that "normal" referential or allegorical readings of Joyce's stories seem to encounter the stubborn resistance of his text, causing great critical confusion, should act as a warning to the reader. On the surface these stories appear extremely transparent. As a rule, particularly at first glance, nothing sounds simpler than a sentence in *Dubliners;* nothing seems closer to that accurate mimeticism that is associated with realism or with that particular brand of objective documentation of the sordid, which is often called naturalism. *Dubliners* seems to offer its readers too few discernible warnings that they are surrounded by Roland Barthes's *espace littéraire.* The warnings are therefore overlooked or ignored much more easily than in *Ulysses,* where the writerly aspects of the text are so conspicuous. Moreover, Joyce himself said he wanted to write "the moral history" of his country and allow the Irish people to have "one good look at themselves" in his looking glass (*Selected Letters* 88, 90), so why should the reader not take him at his word and proceed to be as referential, earnest, and moralizing as he feels?

The symbol hunters have been guilty of the same interpretive "earnestness," regardless of whether they believed that "from first to last, Joyce was primarily a symbolist writer" (Magalaner and Kain 67) or simply saw symbolism as a prominent feature of the book. Prevailing among the symbolist readings of *Dubliners* are those concentrating on Christian allusions; the Homeric and Irish references have also received much critical attention. Images and symbols along with their allusive indirection certainly play a very important role in the structuring of these stories and, along with Joyce's scrupulous reconstruction of the Dublin atmosphere, contribute to the unity of the collection. However, symbolist readings also abound in exaggeration, exclusiveness, and arbitrariness. Perhaps a careful look at what has been considered as realist and symbolist in *Dubliners* will reveal to us that Joyce has used both strategies with a twist, a twist that has been ignored or insufficiently appraised by too many critics and calls for a reappraisal and redefinition of these strategies in the light of their subversive functions.

Joyce has frequently been compared to Flaubert particularly as a modern realist-cum-symbolist. The writing of both authors produces a subversive quality, impeding or reducing the effects or functions of certain literary strategies or conventions that have been sanctioned by tradition and producing this effect in a covert rather than overt way.[5]

In his study *Flaubert: The Uses of Uncertainty,* Jonathan Culler points out that for Flaubert realism was a mode of "self-protection." "'I never pose as a man of experience,' said Flaubert, 'that would be too foolish; but I observe a great deal and never conclude—an infallible way of avoiding error'" (53). Never concluding, Culler suggests, meant writing "against the novel as an institution," the Balzacian novel, for example, which presupposed the existence of a "nice fit between the world and language" (93). I propose that this "nice fit" between world and language, this illusion on which realism seems to rely, was made problematic by Joyce as early as *Dubliners.* This can be observed in several strategies undermining the narrative authority that "guarantees" the existence of the fit.

In attempting to characterize the kind of realism we find in *Dubliners* and the type of subversion generated by its strategies, one should bear in mind that the collection was originally to conclude with "Grace."[6] "The Dead" was first planned in Rome in 1906-7, and, as suggested by Ellmann, it also seems to have been written in a different spirit from that of the rest of the stories (*Selected Letters* 35). In spite of the thematic unity of the stories in *Dubliners* as it stands today, *including* "The Dead,"[7] the last story is the product of somewhat different narrative strategies, as I shall argue later on in this essay.

From "The Sisters" to "Grace," *Dubliners* is the work of an artist working ostensibly in the manner of "modern realism" and/or naturalism. Some of the basic qualities of realism relevant for this study are (1) a striving for objectivity[8] and (2) transparency, usually seen as a contrast to opaqueness, as these terms are defined in formalist structuralist critical theory. Tzvetan Todorov has argued—and this is also very relevant for poststructuralist critical theory—that no literary discourse can be a "docile reflection of events" nor are words "simply the transparent names of things" (80). Thus all literary discourse is opaque, and transparency is an illusion. However, it still seems useful to use these two terms conditionally and see transparency as a formal aspect of realism also often attached to the notion of its stylistic (linguistic) simplicity as, for example, in David Lodge's definition of realism as "the representation of experience in a manner which approximates closely the descriptions of similar experience in non-literary texts of the same culture" (25).

Realism thus offers us a code of interpretability based on the assumption (illusion) that mimesis is viable, that language is referential, and that in analogy with science, including the sciences of man (biology and psychology) and the science of language, literature can observe and study the human personality as an entity individually and as part of another larger entity, society, both entities describable, their actions and words imitable, and their meaning communicable. Or if one is inclined to doubt that this assumption is possible, one can see realism as a literary convention resting on verisimilitude as defined for example by Michael Riffaterre: "an artifact, . . . a verbal representation of reality rather than reality itself" (xv).

The concept of verisimilitude presupposes narrative authority and the notion of "fictional truth." However, in his search for objectivity, the modern realist has divested himself more and more of narrative authority. In the English tradition it was probably in Henry James that readers first began to miss the author: the meddling Thackeray, the moralizing George Eliot, the copiously interfering Dreiser. And yet, although he did not directly offer us many of his own opinions, James gave us such exhaustive figural presentations of experienced and reflected life that he was still functioning as a kind of guide. Even when the meddling was silenced, most modern realists found ways of encoding their guidance to the reader. In *Dubliners,* however, these codes seem to be much sparser and, in addition, more mysterious and confusing. As the role of authors as persons involved with the story has shrunk, so has the presence and coloring of their voices. The general tone of *Dubliners* seems ironic, but often we cannot be quite sure. (How far are we to empathize with Eveline's fear? Are we to take at its face value the boy's feeling in "Araby" that he was "a creature driven and derided by vanity"? [*D* 35]; how sorry are we expected to feel for Little Chandler?) As early as *Dubliners* Joyce already seems to be asking us not to listen for personal narrators giving or implying their opinions and leading us, even if covertly, to conclusions. And this is not what the realists asked of us or, rather, this is not what traditional novel readers thought the realists were asking of them.

Dubliners is a fiction where the impersonality and restraint of the text can ideally accommodate narratology, which sees narrative told in the third person as stemming from a disembodied source called the narrator (divorced from the notion of author as a matter of principle) and called by Genette even more impersonally the "narrating instance" (31). In *Dubliners* Joyce's narrator refuses to give us much guidance. Most of the time we are not sure what to make of the protagonists, and the exceptions seem to be there only to prove the rule. Thus we know what to make of Mrs. Mooney, who "dealt with moral problems as a cleaver deals with meat," because it is the narrator who tells us this ("The Boarding House" *D* 61); and we know that in characterizing the "gratefully oppressed" Dublin crowds in "After the Race" (*D* 42), Joyce is letting the narrator "speak" because Jimmy, who often participates in the free indirect style of this story, could not be the source of that phrase. However, in most examples of characterization in *Dubliners* Joyce seems to tell us that knowing what to "make of a character" is not the point of his writing at all. His writing all too often avoids "coming to the point" because there is no point to come to. Joyce's plots are never well-made, and his endings are inconclusive. For example, no amount of character analysis, psychological or moral, will give us an answer to questions such as: Was Eveline capable of love? Were Frank's intentions honest, or was he a good-for-nothing who would leave her in the first port? What exactly did the boy in "An Encounter" see? We do not know, but Joyce also seems to indicate that we need not know the precise answers or even ask such questions, because in literature characters, events, and motivations are fluid and finally unfathomable just as they are in life.

In *Dubliners* Joyce has installed a narrator who seems to create opaqueness out of the very fact of objectivity pushed to the very limit. As Karen Lawrence has pointed out, "Paradoxically, the lack of authorial intrusion seems, at times, to be an announcement of a narrative feat: with his hands tied behind his back, the author seems to say, he will wrestle with and pin down his city and his characters" (17). Lawrence's remark bears on the kind of subversion that Joyce's realism seems to generate out of itself as it were: using so many devices spelled out in realism's book, then foregrounding them as devices, or finding other ways of subverting mimesis or verisimilitude, thereby unsettling its code of interpretability. The lack of narrative intervention and guidance creates not a positive sense of objectivity but a "negative" sense of uncertainty unsettling the realist convention. With its insistence on observation and documentation and on the "scientific" method, this convention tacitly wished to add to the readers' knowledge and awareness of life in its material, biological, social, and psychological manifestations (a wish that is seen today in more sophisticated terms as inscribed in the structure of the text), thus creating the code of realism's "interpretability." In the course of this essay I will also deal with the "interpretability" of symbolism, arguing as we go along that both are subverted by Joyce.

In the area of narrative meditation, an unsettling effect is created simply by the narrator's absence, his refusal to mediate. This refusal can take several forms. One of them is the strategy used in "Grace," where indeed the perspective seems to be that of an (ironical and Irish) God sitting somewhere above and beyond his creation, paring his fingernails. Descriptions of characters' thoughts and emotions are conspicuously sparse, and, quite surprisingly, there is hardly any focalization. The story consists of three scenes connected by one protagonist who remains almost a completely closed book. All description is external. We only see the bare surfaces of the setting and hear the bare "surfaces" of the talking. All the rest is left to the reader to work out. Similar strategies are used, for example, in "Ivy Day in the Committee Room."

Another and in fact quite opposed strategy of narratorial "invisibility" is to achieve restriction of field through focalization: having the character "see" and thereby making it unnecessary for the narrator to *tell* us what the character sees. However, focalization often hides as much as it reveals. For example, the transparency of the focalized narratives of "Eveline" and "Counterparts" is quite deceptive. In "Eveline" especially, her traumas and fears remain deeply hidden and unformulated under her simple (and evasive?) thoughts. When focalization passes into free indirect style, *Dubliners* can also be antirevelatory, often preventing us from finding out who speaks.

Joyce has been praised by countless critics for his use of free indirect style, in *A Portrait of the Artist as a Young Man* in particular. However, only a few critics have pointed out that along with drawing us into the figural perspective through focalization and letting us hear the figural voice, Joyce also often invalidates the notion of focalization and free indirect style. He does this by preventing the easy recuperation of personalized sources of discourse, obscuring the interpretability of character motivation, and more generally posing obstacles to psychological and moral character analysis, which nevertheless still constitutes the bulk of criticism elicited by *Dubliners*.

"Eveline" is probably the classical example of focalization and free indirect style in *Dubliners*, its narration rather closely attuned to the girl's perspective and vocabulary. At the very end of the story, however, Joyce interrupts her musing and completely withholds from us information about what takes place in her mind between her twilight vigil and her final momentous refusal to leave. We will never know what causes her intense panic, just as in "An Encounter" we are never told what Mahony sees simply because the protagonist/narrator never looks! In "Eveline" the subversion results mainly from the abrupt and arbitrary gap created in the focalized presentation. This gap undercuts our expectation, established by the first pages of the text, that we shall go on sharing Eveline's "vision."

Uncertainty also prevails in the free indirect style used in one of the earliest and least sophisticated stories, "After the Race." This story bears some strong authorial statements, remnants of narrative strategies mainly discarded by Joyce even at this very early stage. For example, Jimmy is certainly not aware of the "channels of poverty and inaction" (*D* 42) and the notion of the "gratefully oppressed" (*D* 42) Irish people. Halfway through the story the point of view shifts to Jimmy, which is indicated by "classic" syntactic markers: the use of questions and exclamations. In many places, however, we cannot be sure who is seeing and speaking. How much of the awareness of Dublin "wearing the mask of a capital" (*D* 46) and of the beauty of its "pale globes of light" (*D* 45) hung above it is shared by Jimmy? The extent of this sharing is rather crucial for our interpretation of the protagonist. Jimmy would, perhaps, be a more significant character if he were able to verbalize these phrases, if they were his thoughts rendered in free indirect style rather than narratorial renderings.

The undecidability of free indirect style is particularly prominent in "A Little Cloud," a later and very carefully crafted story in which Joyce certainly knew clearly what he was doing and perhaps therefore obfuscated more thoroughly some of its vital points. In this story the reader is obviously allowed to share many of Little Chandler's delusions and some of his insights in classical free indirect style fashion. However, sometimes the text holds contradictory statements that may or may not be colored by free indirect style: for example, Chandler first sees the children of the poor as vermin and mice, giving them "no thought" (*D* 71); then, two pages later, he is described as pitying "the poor stunted houses" (*D* 73) in which they live, suggesting that he does give them some thought after all. Then he is shown remembering "richly dressed ladies" in a series of impressions recognizable as free indirect style, but when they are described alighting from their cabs like "alarmed Atalantas" (*D* 72), a stylistic register is struck that seems somewhat out of Chandler's depth. Chandler is shown elsewhere as sticking to set phrases: he feels that "it was useless, useless! He was a prisoner for life" (*D* 84). And sometimes the clichés in his free indirect discourse are piled up as if parodying his "style": "There was always a certain . . . something in Ignatius Gallaher that impressed you in spite of yourself. Even when he was out at elbows [1] and at his wits' end for money [2] he kept up a bold face [3]" (*D* 72). The ellipsis and the "you" are certainly marks of free indirect style. The three clichés (which I have marked with numbers) indicate that Little Chandler is to be taken ironically as a poor thinker and bad writer. They are stylistically out of tune with the "alarmed Atalantas," which therefore seem closer to the authorial vocabulary. Here the sources of the free indirect style voices are blurred, destabilizing character consistency and unity of style. This prevents us from making firm characterizations and blurs the overall "solidity of specification" extolled (and yet so often forsaken) by Henry James.

It is rather paradoxical that the greatest opacity should occur in "The Sisters," a story told in the first person and therefore having a narrator in full view (like "Araby" and "An Encounter"). This first-person internal narrator is very reticent: we are only offered some of his observations and memories along with snippets of overheard conversations, which overtly at least he is not trying to make sense of. Thus of the four narrative modes used in *Dubliners*— unfocalized and focalized narration in the third person, free indirect style, and first-person narration—in "The Sisters" Joyce chose (rather perversely) to make the last seem most opaque. However, in "The Sisters" this is just one aspect of the indeterminacy that is created by a variety of other devices discussed in this essay.

One specific form of subversion in *Dubliners* undermines certain thematic and structural aspects that are not directly related to narrative mediation: such aspects are thematic unity and the notion of closure as a final "wrapping up" of a plot. Speaking of Flaubert's treatment of theme, Culler writes: "When one attempts to explore these themes in greater detail one encounters a curious indeterminacy: as if Flaubert had set out to frustrate, by the construction of the novels, the working out of those themes which are explicitly posed and carried by the general movement of the plot. Attention is deflected from the problems which the novels raise and we find ourselves drawn into a puzzling inconclusiveness as soon as we try to take them seriously as thematic statements" (136).[9]

In *Dubliners* one finds comparable thematic strategies. An exception can perhaps be found in "A Painful Case," a story where the theme—the rejection of life and love—is not only clearly outlined but also firmly related to character motivation. We are not surprised by the ending of the story: it seems to have been encoded in the protagonist. Culler's description seems to apply very felicitously to "Grace" and "The Sisters." In both stories the thematic indeterminacy is of course also related to the question of narrative authority outlined in my discussion of focalization.

"Grace" begins ironically and most dramatically with perhaps the most shocking description in the whole book: "Two gentlemen who were in the lavatory at the time tried to lift him up: but he was quite helpless. He lay curled up at the foot of the stairs down which he had fallen. They succeeded in turning him over. His hat had rolled a few yards away and his clothes were smeared with the filth and ooze of the floor on which he had lain, face downwards. His eyes were closed and he breathed with a grunting noise. A thin stream of blood trickled from the corner of his mouth" (*D* 150). For all we know, the "gentleman" may have had a stroke and may be dying. His face is suffused by a "grey pallor." When he speaks, he does so with a very thick voice. However, we soon learn that the gentleman, Mr. Kernan, a taster of tea, tripped on the stairs because he was drunk and speaks thickly because he has bitten his tongue. What began ominously turns into cold and trivial farce with a huge policeman, who is not very nimble with his pencil, a young "medical man" in a bicycle suit, and finally a colleague, Mr. Powers, who takes Mr. Kernan home in a cab. In the middle part of the story, which takes up four-fifths of its entire length, Mr. Kernan receives his friends at home. We get only a few general glimpses of him. Because he lies in bed and speaks very little, the reader loses interest in him, realizing after all that the theme is not based on him and on the possibly dramatic consequences of his alcoholism as the opening section of the story intimated.

The entire middle section of the story is written in the form of a very rambling and diffuse dialogue, and it is not easy at first to discern its underlying theme. His friends have decided to trick Kernan into going to a retreat with them, but the subject is approached with great lack of seriousness, and many questions remain dangling. (Do any of them believe that it will help them? Are they going there only because of Kernan? and so on.)

We also wonder if the theme is religious, and in the final segment of the story we find out that religion is indeed the subject of the story, particularly religion as practiced in public. Frank O'Connor mentions Stanislaus's comments about the story's tripartite structure's imitating the *Divine Comedy* (310). However, the Dantean pattern seems to be emptied out, subverted by the humor of the first part and the coziness of the purgatory with porter and whiskey at Kernan's bedside. The middle section is all filled by talk. Discontinuous and incredibly uniformed and banal as it is, this talking, much of it in clichés (e.g., the Jesuits are referred to as "the boyos" [*D* 163] who have most influence), seems to be at the center of the writer's attention. The dialogue is nearly meaningless in its rambling discontinuity as Joyce wanted it to be. We know from his letters that during his stay in Rome he went to the library expressly to check the details concerning the dogmas of the infallibility of the pope and of immaculate conception discussed in the story (*Selected Letters* 130) and could have given us a very lucid exposition. Instead, Joyce seems to be more interested in dim minds and the clichés of discourse. Perhaps the dialogue in "Grace" already expresses his awareness, reflected so amply in *Ulysses*, that randomness and banality are a legitimate and human aspect of language and literature.

Where does this leave us in respect to the story's theme? In the last section the Jesuit preacher is talking to an audience conspicuously and ironically studded with pawnbrokers and moneylenders. He takes a very practical attitude to religion, however, eschewing all its mystery and its power to bestow divine "grace." The sermon itself—or the portion we are offered by Joyce, who cuts it off abruptly in the strangest, most inconclusive of closures—has been seen by critics as an epiphany, shocking us into awareness of its meretricious banality.

In accordance with this view, one might conclude that the theme of the story is the very lack of what is mentioned in the title but is pointedly absent from the text and mentioned verbatim only once, in the last paragraph of the story. However, trying to validate the thesis that lack of grace is the theme of the story, we encounter further difficulties. First, the characters in the story, although rather disreputable and petty, are not shown to be particularly despicable or depraved, that is, particularly in need of grace. Moreover, in spite of the satirical tone, the characters are not caricatures. Their humanness undercuts any serious metaphorical extension of the purgatory theme and makes us appreciate their stubborn resilience and concreteness, which are positive qualities. It is as if Joyce's youthful anger against those who "betrayed" him was being washed away and the scene was slowly being set for a character like Bloom, so conspicuously free of anger. Thus the story can be seen *both* as a presentation of lowly but in no way depraved humanity and a demonstration of religion being sold in the Irish marketplace.

We must be aware, however, that these presentations follow no firm thematic development. Thematically the story begins at one point and ends up at another rather arbitrarily. In other words, A does not lead to B; B (vulgarized religion) just insinuates itself while A (Kernan's drunkenness) becomes peripheral. The narrative refuses to engage in figural psychological and moral analysis, finally leaving us stranded in the middle of a sermon, entertaining possibilities that we cannot easily relate to either the characters in the story or Joyce himself. Joyce was not a religious writer, not overtly at least, and grace in his books does not have the meaning it has in the works of Eliot or Paul Claudel. On the realist side, Joyce has created in "Grace" a number of sketchily drawn but convincing characters along with three perfect cameos of the Dublin scene: the pub, a lower-middle-class home, and a religious ceremony. However, the elaboration of theme and plot, as I have tried to show, remains deliberately ambiguous and inconclusive. The transparency of this story functions on the level of accurate, even if restrained, realistic observation. However, on another level the title of the story establishes a kind of ironic allegorical relation with the crass meretriciousness of the sermon, establishing a semblance of symbolism, a theme I shall return to later in this essay.

Even more than "Grace," Joyce forces us to read "The Sisters" in a new, less confident way. Told in the first person, the story takes us automatically into the mind of the protagonist, limiting our horizon of knowledge to his own. Here, however, we encounter at least two sets of obstacles in trying to make sense of the story on a realistic factual and psychological basis. The first set is the things related to the priest's former life that the boy himself does not know or only catches glimpses of through the veiled and stunted talk of the elders. The second set of obstacles derives from the author's perversely arbitrary suppression of what the boy might be expected to know but does not tell us: for example, his feelings for the priest or the reason why he continued to visit him in the first place in spite of the obvious repulsiveness of the old man. So much of the boy's psychology is missing that the recuperation of facts and emotions, usually available in realistic texts, cannot bear fruit in this instance and can only amount to distorting guesswork marring a lot of *Dubliners* criticism. In this story Joyce is obviously not interested in psychology, at least not in psychology as most often found in realistic fiction, bent on exploring cognitive processes, emotional growth or transformation, motivating actions, and so on and thus a psychology also actively contributing to the development and movement of the theme.

"The Sisters" is particularly misleading because again its text seems to stick only to facts and nothing but facts and to give accurate description of physical details—the booties in the shop window, the old woman's worn heels (another of the distasteful images this story abounds in)—and yet the facts stubbornly refuse to fall into a pattern recognizable within the realistic convention. I will try to show a little later that the story offers an equally wobbly basis for symbolic elaboration (paradoxically, it is too stubbornly and literally factual for that). This story can therefore be seen as the very embodiment of the "uncertainty principle," indicating that experience is unfathomable (the boy is confused; he does not know what his feelings are particularly in respect to the shocking fact of death including the sense of liberation it brings) and, more important, that the powers of narrative (of language) itself are limited in their attempt to represent the experience of the world. Thus the narrator only lets us see the priest from the boy's incomplete memory or the confused and probably slanted remarks of his primitive sister and the innuendos of old Cotter and his aunt. (The things the narrator decides not to tell us may be arbitrarily selected, but the uncertainty they convey seems genuine.)

This does not mean that the story has no theme but that a modernist rather than realist strategy is being used to convey what Joyce in his early essay "A Portrait" has himself called "the curve of an emotion" (Scholes and Kain 60). In numerous instances in *Dubliners* the details are offered not only to document and describe Dublin and Ireland but also to render the author's emotion about his city and native country. One might thus see "The Sisters" as a departure from realist aims, an attempt to use language as "experiential" activity. By reproducing the "curve" of the boy's confusion and its concomitant gaps, the writer creates a general feeling of unease, blockage, perhaps cunning withdrawal invading the boy without his necessarily even being aware of it, feelings shared by the writer who is "troping a mood."

We can thus trace the general thematic contours of this story around the unease of childhood, also an Irish childhood, faced with the facts of its immediate physical surrounding (Dublin) and the more general facts of life (sickness, old age, and death), which, however, are not "nicely fitted" together or interpreted for us. We see the individual segments of the story as indicators of confusions, moods, and emotions and are discouraged from determining in every detail what our particular child knew, did, or thought. Even when looking for other types of patterning and sense making, such as the symbolic strategies of indirection discussed below, our search will be similarly inconclusive. Especially when reading "The Sisters," we should not forget all those modern theorists stressing the gap between word and thing and warning us that no "going back" to the text for "reinterpretation" can ever close this gap completely.[10]

Very different, yet close to "The Sisters" in recreating an emotion national and political this time, is "Ivy Day in the Committee Room." Harold Bloom has praised Hemingway's "Old Man at the Bridge" for "permanently troping a historical mood" (4), and this exactly is what Joyce has done in "Ivy Day." The canvassers are as mercenary as the politicians they work for. They engage in a conversation of sublime banality, referring among other topics to the tragic end of Parnell. The story concludes with the reciting of a mediocre but sincerely felt poem in Parnell's praise. The narrative authority is again lacking, owing to the equivocal character of both the protagonists and the poem and the even more equivocal character of the reaction elicited by the poem—the "pok!" of a cork ejected from a bottle of beer, the questionable motion of a feckless young man, and the narrator's poker-faced report of an opinion, the sincerity of which we shall never be able to gauge: "Mr. Crofton said that it was a very fine piece of writing" (*D* 135).

The strategies applied in the story "A Mother" are very similar. I do not think that Mrs. Kearney, although aptly characterized by Joyce, is worthy of all the critical ink spent on the psychological or moral analysis of her behavior. This story tropes a political mood in which all the participants are given the same mean social and moral coloring; their individual importance (depth) is therefore weakened in proportion to their (paltry) public role. The scheming mother and daughter are no worse than the shady and clownish "patriots" and their entourage: "Hoppy" Holohan, "assistant secretary of the *Eire Abu* Society," walking up and down Dublin with dirty pieces of paper in his pocket, organizing the patriotic concerts (*D* 136); the faded soprano (*D* 143); the "first item" shaking "like an aspen" (*D* 147); and the dignified baritone, who is above it all probably because he has been paid in advance. This story is a triumph of little details and banalities and is comparable to Chekhov's masterpieces.[11]

Closures in *Dubliners* deserve special attention because every single story (except perhaps "The Dead") seems to end in a subversive way. The closures are either inconclusive or elided by gaps and sudden interruptions. They are also undermined by puzzles and inconsistencies as well as surprises that are anticlimactic as a rule and should be rigorously distinguished from the "surprises" of the well-made story.

In this respect "The Boarding House" and "Counterparts" are particularly interesting because they would represent the most absolutely and perfectly executed specimens of modern naturalism in Joyce's canon in each and every one of their aspects if this effect were not unexpectedly yet I feel irreversibly undermined by their very last sentences. In "Counterparts" all the motivation can be reduced to a combination of biological, social, and psychological factors. Farrington is the *homme moyen sensuel* of every writer's dream. He suffocates in the office and finds solace in drink; incensed by his superiors and frustrated by circumstances, he takes it out on his little son by flogging him. "The Boarding House" contains superb realistic characterization. Mrs. Mooney is a butcher's daughter who "dealt with moral problems as a cleaver deals with meat" (*D* 61). The transparency of the objective description and the spare but unerring psychological touch—for example, Polly and Mrs. Mooney conniving without ever admitting it to one another or even to themselves—along with the occasional precise sordid detail (the sugar and butter safely locked away, the broken bread saved for the Tuesday bread pudding) are high points of modern realism and naturalism.

However, the endings of these two stories seem to be out of tune (even if ever so slightly) with their exemplary naturalist transparency and are sprung at us as if out of ambush. They seem to belong to other strategies and are discreetly but insidiously unsettling. James's *The Wings of the Dove,* for example, also ends with a mysterious sentence. Densher's plea that Kate and he continue as they were is answered by Kate's "We shall never be again as we were" (510). This is a plurisignificant modernist ending, indicating a change in their relationship but refusing to tell us in plain words whether Kate and Densher will stay together or not. However, the author has been preparing us for this. The ambiguity of "as we were" rests on four hundred pages of plotting and preparation. The little boy's promise that he will say a Hail Mary for his pa, on the other hand, is quite arbitrary and irrelevant for our understanding of Farrington, who from beginning to end is the sole protagonist of this story. Seen from this angle the prayer is completely out of context and is therefore subversive of more traditional conventions of consistent plotting and closure. It introduces several new possibilities of interpretation but sanctions none. For example, it can be seen as striking a tone of Christian helplessness, suggesting that prayers are to no avail. It can also indicate a faint glimmer of possible salvation. It is of course also plainly funny in its inadequacy. Whatever its meaning, one thing is certain: structurally, the theme of the immemorial Christian prayer appended to the end of this story has unsettled its topological purity and realistic transparency, pervading it with a modernist touch. James's and Joyce's closures are both ambiguous, but Joyce's is more subversive.

Ambiguously, at the end of the "The Boarding House," after literally everything has been "explained" and motivated to our satisfaction—the bridegroom safely cornered by a perfectly plausible fear of scandal and feeling of guilt and the mother feeling righteously satisfied—Polly still remains quite a mystery. For example, we are never told whether she is pregnant. We do not know what she feels for her future husband. We do not know how cold-blooded her maneuvers were. And at the very end we see her falling into a reverie whose content is rendered rather obliquely. She looks at the pillows, and they awaken "secret, amiable memories," probably of a sensual nature. However, her memories then gradually give place to "hopes and visions of the future . . . so intricate that she no longer saw the white pillows on which her gaze was fixed or remembered that she was waiting for anything" (*D* 68). Up to this point we have seen Polly as a sensual little animal, a scheming female, and are not prepared for a situation that could—why not?—also be seen as containing elements of an ecstatic, trance-like state. (She forgets where she is and why she is there; she does not see what stands before her.) Polly's reverie is wrapped up by the last sentence of the story: "Then she remembered what she had been waiting for" (*D* 69).

This last sentence may of course refer to an anticlimactic triviality: after her reverie, Polly is called back to the "reality" of her mother having successfully caught a husband for her. However, if we are aware of the pattern of Christian references in the collection as a whole and of Polly herself being compared earlier on, as if in passing, to "a little perverse madonna" (*D* 62-63), could the voice she hears after "waiting" not be seen as an ironic Annunciation? This symbolic possibility cannot be asserted irrefutably because it is too tenuous. And yet, might not Joyce be suggesting here that this is the only Annunciation Polly, being only human, can have? With this suggestion Joyce might also be exposing the pretentiousness of those smug readers and critics who tend to look down at all these poor Dubliners from superior moral heights. Certainly, this "Annunciation" is neither an attempt to elevate the sanctity of a Christian ideal through opposition to "sinful" love nor to debunk it as an ideal in itself. Rather, if we decide to see it there, it shimmers like a chimera before our eyes, eons away from the symbolic solidity of the albatross hung about the Mariner's neck or the rich poetic effect of Yeats's rose upon the rood of time. The text reverberates with possible meanings, starting a slight and ambiguous subterranean (subtextual) tremor and unsettling the solid realist bedrock of this story.

I will indicate below that the closure of "Araby," although psychologically attuned to the very young, sensitive protagonist, also must be seen by the reader as ironically discrepant as must that of "A Little Cloud." However, while the boy seems to feel too much, Little Chandler reveals too little. His tears may be "tears of remorse" (*D* 85), but this is not all that they express, or at least not all the reader feels they should. On that day he has been disillusioned in a "friend" and shocked by the realization that he is in a trap, married to a woman with "cold eyes," with no chance to pursue his literary interests however unjustified they may be. His cup is full, and the child's crying is just the last drop. It is obvious from the context that what makes him cry is frustration and exasperation for which "remorse" is an incomplete substitute, covering up for much more including the resentment for being "a prisoner for life" (*D* 84). The word "remorse" therefore might be seen as a "misnomer" placed there deliberately by the author, perhaps in order to suggest the confusion in Little Chandler's mind, while washing his hands of any direct moral/psychological reflection on his protagonist including any comment on his ability to grasp or face his entrapment.

The enigmatic closures in *Dubliners* are truly various in type. It is difficult to find two that are alike in structure or identical in their narrative strategy although they nearly all have the same function: subversion through indeterminacy. Sometimes a discrepancy is small and difficult to pin down as, for example, in "After the Race." Something in that disastrous and drunk card game is in sharp dissonance with the way in which daybreak is announced. The narrator does not try to harmonize this dissonance. Instead, he leaves us with the image of the Hungarian standing at the door "in a shaft of grey light" (*D* 48) almost like a messenger. In its isolation this very concrete "image" brings vague associations (discordant and perhaps irrelevant) with religious paintings (El Greco's, for example) where figures of saints stand flooded by shafts of heavenly light. The closing sentence seems to point vaguely toward some other perhaps more meaningful world, incommensurable with the one described in the story, while at the same time remaining a common remark that could have been made during a comparable scene in "reality."

It seems easier to pin down the closure of "An Encounter." This story also ends on a "false" note; it does so by foregrounding a motif of secondary importance. The story, whatever it is about, surely is not about the relationship between the protagonist and Mahony. And yet it ends with a comment on this relation, a comment justified in part by the fact (also ironical) that simple Mahony is still to be preferred to the pervert. On the other hand, Mahony is a screen for the obviously central event, as if the shock of the encounter with a disgusting adult (and the abysses of potential sexual and moral disgust opened by his behavior) had to be surrounded by a ring of silence and therefore replaced by any substitute that was at hand. However, this substitute then also gets obfuscated by the use of a religious term, "penitent" (*D* 28), whose potential inadequacy is transcended by the author's irony. Fritz Senn has suggested (34) that this word contributes to the story's pattern of symbolic religious imagery. I agree but would like to add that the image must also be seen in an ironic light because the word is simply too strong for whatever the boy-narrator might feel about Mahony after realizing he had despised him "a little." Thus, just as Joyce intended, the word "penitent" reverberates in our mind while we grope for its justification. Motivationally tangential, on the level of the text the word, however, remains solidly present as a formal element of the religious pattern, a potential symbol reduced to a sign, a marker like the word "grace" in the final paragraph of "Grace" or the mention of "Hail Mary" in "Counterparts." In these stories, which are studded with pedestrian events, the symbolic words often seem even playful, allowing very little depth, their possible religious transcendences muted, discontinuous, subdued, and somewhat arbitrary, both there and not there like the smile of the Cheshire cat.

As for "Grace," Garrett has suggested that its closure is clear in its "apparent arbitrariness and actual completion . . . in the midst of Father Purdon's sermon, epiphanizing the sterility of his secularized religion by giving formal emphasis to his commercial metaphor" (13-14). This seems a very reasonable interpretation if we agree that all the strands of this story are harmoniously subsumed under the theme of religious vulgarization. However, I have suggested earlier that some other themes have been left pending in the curiously unrelated parts of this "tripartite" story structure, and this fact in my opinion prevents a tidy closure. The closure remains surprisingly unconventional, resembling the truncated sentences in *Ulysses*, the sermon cut off "with a cleaver" just like a sausage, at the point where the reader may be safely expected to have grasped what kind of sausage it was.

In "The Sisters" the conversation that takes up the second half of the story resembles on one level the dialogue in the middle section of "Grace" and could be seen as the paradoxical apotheosis of reproducing mimetically the inconclusiveness and rambling quality of ordinary speech. This conversation is transparent in its seemingly transcribed faithfulness yet completely opaque because the reader lacks the fillers usually offered by context as well as other indicators of a living dialogue (gestures, intonation); the writer, who obviously refuses to help the reader, does not offer him any of the immemorial narrative sense-making tricks. The dialogues are contrived, of course, but the writer pretends they are not. In "The Sisters" we have the bad luck of seeing every new piece of information, which "normally" might be used as material leading toward plot clarification, crumble between our fingers. The aunt's remarks, like those offered by Old Cotter, seem to indicate that there was more to the priest's story than the sister was capable or ready to admit. However, the episode with the chalice remains insufficiently explained. The sister's remarks remain cryptic. Why were the duties of the priesthood too much for him? Only because he broke the chalice? And how "nervous" was he? Why did he laugh in the confessional? How could the boy learn so much from the priest if he was disturbed and demented?

The closure of the story seems equally imponderable. It is quite inconceivable, for example, that the priest's loving sisters should place in his poor hands the very reason for his downfall: the chalice, of all things. Joyce, the inveterate mystifier, did not choose some other, much more acceptable possibilities—such as a cross or a rosary—but opted for the truly outrageous variant, which is one of the most subversive choices he made in the entire collection. Further, the extraordinary revelation that the old priest had been found laughing in the confessional is repeated in the penultimate sentence but not at all clarified. The final, closing sentence is unfinished and also contains a rephrased statement, another repetition without clarification. ("There was something gone wrong with him" [*D* 18] echoes "That affected his mind" [*D* 17].) Thus the last two unfinished sentences are repetitions of things said before about the old priest, one verbatim and the other rephrased, absurdly redundant and subversive owing to their repeated refusal to illuminate the reader as to why and what had "gone wrong with him." Of course, in spite of the psychological, factual, and moral imponderables, a measure of determinacy is still retained: the story can be understood as a metaphor of the unease and mystery of sickness and death as well as of the boy's lonely struggle to come to terms with experience, lost in a sea of provincial triviality as well as a sea of words including mysterious and menacing ones such as "paralysis," "gnomon," and "simony." The latter have been interpreted as symbols of his situation, just as the old priest can be seen as standing for Ireland and its church, to whom the boy (and Joyce himself) is fettered in a love-hate relation. And yet, "The Sisters" remains for me one of the most indeterminate narratives in English literature, a text "which poses fundamental questions about the nature of meaning and the functions of literature" (Graff 163).

In his book on *Ulysses* Stuart Gilbert offers a description of this novel that can also be applied to *Dubliners:*

> Its true significance does not lie in problems of conduct or character. After reading *Ulysses* we do not ask ourselves: "Should Stephen Daedalus have done this? Ought Mr Bloom to have said that? Should Mrs Bloom have refrained?" . . . The meaning of *Ulysses,* for it has a meaning and is not a mere photographic "slice of life"—far from it—is not to be sought in any analysis of the acts of the protagonist or the mental make-up of the characters; it is, rather, implicit in the technique of the various episodes [or stories in *Dubliners*], in nuances of language, in the thousand and one correspondences and allusions with which the book is studded. Thus *Ulysses* is neither pessimist nor optimist in outlook, neither moral nor immoral in the ordinary sense of these words; its affinity is, rather, with an Einstein formula, a Greek temple, an art that lives the more intensely for its repose. [19-20]

Gilbert's paragraph—the last sentence in particular—reflects a belief in the autonomy of art, a stance that has become dated. On the other hand, being allegedly so close to Joyce's pulse, its warning against a positivistic realistic reading should be seriously considered. This warning can also be applied to symbolist readings, which, as I have indicated, paradoxically also often become too literal in the hands of critics.

Gilbert sees the function of Joyce's symbolism as Solomon's seal representing the unity of all creation as well as of all the elements composing a book. This may well have been the gist of Joyce's philosophical views. His fiction, however, seems to present many obstacles to a sense of unity particularly in matters of narration, the reading process stumbling against fragmentation, discontinuity, irony, parody, and other forms of subversion including the functioning of symbols. As Clive Scott suggests, Mallarmé still seemed to believe that a symbol has "dimensions enough to repossess all the ideas which, as the occasion of the poem, it engendered" (210), although his poetics was ironic, lacking full belief in the communicability of words. Joyce seems to have gone one step further in denying his symbols the power of significant repossession.

As Gilbert points out (55-60), in *Ulysses,* for example, Stephen associates the Martello Tower with the Delphic oracle, the world's omphalos; Joyce connected 7 Eccles Street to the island of Ogygia, where Calypso dwelt; Molly is seen as Calypso as well as Penelope; and Ogygia is connected to the omphalos theme because, Gilbert tells us, Homer called it "the navel of the sea" (58). Such combinatorics requires a new notion of symbolism, which also has a flat and abstract side depending on Joyce's reading, on his factual and literary knowledge, on information. In addition to its possible poetic translucence, as posited by Coleridge, Joyce's omphalos symbol is based on various references, culled mainly from books. In addition, it is a kind of quotation, something superimposed or preimposed on the pattern of the novel, the result of willed artificiality. The same symbol is also stretched by Joyce to include subversion into ludicrous irony (e.g., the line to Edenville via navel telephone). Certain potentially symbolic images are thus often reduced to mere markers: the porter bottle in "Proteus," called "island of dreadful thirst" mainly as a verbal reference to the "island of dreadful hunger," repossessing no significant meaning, used as word play.

The parodic and discrepant aspect of the *Ulysses* symbolism is already clearly prefigured in *Dubliners.* This anticipation can, for example, be demonstrated by the stories' religious symbolism whose existence cannot be denied but which requires an assumption of indecidability, possibly reducing its significance but certainly underscoring its existence as a literary device. Let us consider for a moment some religious symbols in "Clay" and "Two Gallants" in this light. Maria has been associated with the Virgin Mary and so has the servant girl in "Two Gallants" (the critics have pointed out that she is wearing Mary's colors, a blue skirt and white blouse). The symbolic reference could be seen as ironic: both Maria and the servant girl are most unsuitable symbols of the Mother of God. One is old and sterile; the other is far from being a virgin. Thus, we could interpret in terms of contrasts: instead of saintliness, corruption; instead of youth, dessicated old age. However, even this ironic contrast is not to be taken too seriously, for nowhere in *Dubliners* has Joyce showed us his firm belief in the validity of Christian symbolism, nor is there any indication in his books or his life that he set any special value on virginal women. We therefore have no grounds to assume that Joyce expects us to recuperate fully here the idea of Christianity either as an ideal or a moral norm of behavior. Instead, he often cuts short all significant transcendence. With the Virgin as a possible, but strictly limited, religious metaphorical extension, Maria and the servant girl remain in the last analysis stubbornly themselves. They are therefore to be taken "literally" in the spirit of Gilbert's instructions, probably on Joyce's authority, to read the "Homeric correspondences" in "Sirens," as "generally speaking, rather literal than symbolic" (220).

The reader should also be particularly aware in *Dubliners* of certain symbols that may be seen as lures or traps: for example, the (Irish) color green. Some critics have pointed out that the pervert in "An Encounter" has been given green eyes, which may indicate that he is a symbol of Ireland. Perhaps this possibility should be excluded in the first place. However, characters' eyes *are* green more than once in this collection, and this trait may have been ascribed on purpose. The crucial distinction here is not between treating green eyes as symbolic or not but between, on one hand, traditional, "in depth" symbolism and, on the other, Joyce's allegorical pattern, which often seems to be "horizontally" dispersed on the surface of the text where it functions self-referentially without reaching for "significant repossession." The important thing is to see this kind of symbolic transfer as never fully realized and therefore to regard it as a rather arbitrary sign, comparable to something like a car sticker or conference tag. Joyce's use of such symbolism must also be seen as a kind of game. The author seems to be saying, "Okay, readers, green is the color of Ireland; let's play around with this!" One might therefore be tempted to conclude that these symbols are functioning at least in part as antisymbols.

Indeed, we often can and must seriously entertain an image or situation as a symbol in *Dubliners* provided we do not take that symbolic meaning too seriously. Another one of the many innovations introduced by Joyce and one that has not been sufficiently underlined by critics is the changed, new impact and function of symbolism in his texts. Along with more traditional uses, Joyce's symbols are often emptied of much of their potential force, truncated, stunted, and cut off from any chance of radiating too much or too far.

Two examples of different types of symbols can be found in "Two Gallants." One is traditional and needs little further elucidation: the harp. The harp is a unifying, cohering element, bringing in a reference to a sadly debased yet, through its music (which Joyce knew and loved), potentially beautiful Ireland. The function of the harp is primarily thematic. The function of the other image, the gold coin, is primarily structural. It reveals to us what the story is about on the literal level of the plot: with the full connivance of Lenehan (who must therefore never be compared to Joyce as some have done), Corley is planning to "touch" the girl in more than one sense and succeeds in the attempt. Shocking in itself, the revelation is even more shocking because the poor girl has given him a *gold* coin. The value of this coin seems out of proportion to everything the story has so firmly established as its paltry social background. Thus the symbolic function of the gold coin is more difficult to determine than that of the harp. The immediate "drama" of the two gallants revolves about a setting of pubs and cheap eating places. Thus, on the level of verisimilitude, a silver coin would have been more likely. The unexpected gold forces us to readjust our (naturalistically) formed assumptions and see the whole story in a new, more arbitrary light. Moreover, gold has a long symbolic history, and some of this is probably woven into the final impact of the story although it is difficult to say precisely what. Abstract, disembodied symbolism we may call it but symbolism nevertheless. The ironic and hateful final revelation has a ritual air about it, as if a miracle were being performed by the master before an adoring disciple, strongly reminiscent of another betrayal involving coins performed long ago; however, the other betrayal had been performed by the "disciple," not by the master, and that time the coins were silver.

There has been much conjecturing about the symbolism of "Araby." Ben L. Collins has proposed, for example, that the dead priest's bicycle pump could be considered symbolic of the serpent in the Garden of Eden: "The rusty bicycle pump, peeping out from under an adjacent bush like the Serpent in the Garden, suggests that like it love and religion which could once inflate (raise and elate) are inoperative and relates directly to its late owner, the dead priest" (95). The pump may indeed perhaps be seen as a reference to the serpent; the central apple tree in the yard is a rather obvious reference, and, once established, it allows Mangan's sister to play Eve opposite the serpent (it is difficult to resist the temptation of embroidering the possible metaphorical extensions of "raising" and "inflating" as connected to this phallic implement).

Further, it can be interesting and rewarding to explore the possibility of seeing (as critics have done) Mangan's sister as the temptress, the clink of coins at the bazaar as the sinful work of the changers at the Temple, and the boy's experience of the train and the resounding bazaar space as a kind of "season in hell." However, one must simultaneously also be aware of the discrepancies in scale produced by the juxtaposition of elevated biblical and Dantean symbolic references with the basically innocent desire of the very young protagonist to buy a present for a girl at the fair. The function of these "symbols" is not to point to any possible "evil" the boy has done but, on the contrary, to create an ironical and amusing interplay of incompatible levels of vision. The biblical analogies here also may have the function of obliquely embodying the boy's great sensitivity, by paralleling his childish tendency to magnify a trivial occasion, and thus increasing our sympathy for his innocence, which is in no way diminished by the awakening of his hormones. In fact this interpretation is a basic requirement for an understanding of this text. "Araby" is, namely, consistently pervaded by a delicate, empathetic humor unmatched in the entire collection. Any literal application of the heavy biblical analogies blots it out like a daisy crushed under a clumsy boot sole.

To sum up, the use of these symbols does not imply that the boy is a sinner in any serious biblical sense. The symbols are the vehicle through which Joyce is probably ironically and with an unusually light touch indicating that as women are men's perdition, in due time the boy will also let them "ruin" him. Beyond that the symbols simply add new elements to the "horizontal" allegorical pattern.

The same also applies to the closure of the story. I cannot see the boy in any way as a creature driven and derided by "vanity." This is how he sees himself but not how *we* should see him. This boy will perhaps become an artist, and he possesses strong emotions as well as a child's and artist's tendency to magnify whatever happens to him. Typically Christian and Irish are his way and style of thinking (including its pernicious dwelling on moral guilt) inculcated into an entire nation by religious education. Thus, the closure of this story is as subversive as its symbolism: the final realization of the boy reflects a convincingly agonizing reaction, but it must also be seen by the reader as gently ironical of the exaggerated, blown-up nightmares of childhood. The greatness of this story lies in its holding together in suspension so many different thematic and structural elements, overlaid by symbolic suggestions, which however must never be allowed to achieve a complete and solemn transformation of bicycle pump into biblical serpent.

In Joyce's use of symbols we thus must allow for a new arbitrariness, a formal assigning of symbolic properties that likens symbols to puzzles and riddles, not to be taken completely outside the limits of game playing. The chalice on the dead priest's breast, the gold coin revealed to the awed "disciple," the prayer offered as "bribe," a girl "waiting," the colors of eyes, someone standing in a "shaft of light"—these images emerge suddenly from seas of realist/naturalist renderings of details and scenes, which in the conventions we know cannot support the full development of a symbolic reference. Some of the allegorical gold seems to rub off at times, but the possible depths of symbolic transcendences are arrested on the flat surface of the text or at least are not allowed to travel too far. Maria bearing the name of the Virgin, the rusty bicycle pump under the apple tree, "penitence," and "grace"—these symbols partake of the properties of references and citations, of mathematical signs, of the patterns of parody. They should not be fully spelled out either at their face or reverse value. The girl in "Two Gallants" may be wearing Mary's colors, but she is not to be seen as a debased negation of Christian values. In *Dubliners* the transfer toward traditional symbolic meanings is rarely complete because in spite of its indeterminacy this world is still too stubbornly material. Rather, it remains incomplete, stamped by the opaqueness of Joyce's "a-thousand-and-one" literary arrangements and rearrangements.

Finally, something must be said about "The Dead," without the beauty of which *Dubliners* would not be the great collection we know although it would be a more consistent narrative structure. It may sound blasphemous to say that "The Dead" is less interesting as narrative experiment than most of the other *Dubliners* stories. It is certainly less subversive, marked by greater emotional richness and generosity of inspiration, in spite of the incontrovertible fact that numerous thematic links connect it strongly to the setting and background of *Dubliners*. These thematic links have been admirably elaborated by a number of critics. However, some of its narrative strategies give it a very special place but a place apart in this collection.

The specialness of "The Dead" begins with the presentation of its protagonist, Gabriel Conroy, and his relationship with his wife. Gabriel is in fact quite unique in the entire Joyce opus. In his yearnings and frustrations, Gabriel comes closest to the spirit and themes of Joyce's extraordinary letters to his wife. So uncharacteristic of any of Joyce's other writing, these letters expressed the wish for a love no human wife could offer. Apart from their very human longing, they also reveal an artist's imperious and "inhuman" pitiless perfectionism. Aside from the titillating aspect of these letters, they give us a picture of Joyce that we can literally get nowhere else: not in the documents, the facts, or the fiction. They probably express Joyce's "true feelings" at a certain point of his relationship to Nora. However, in their stylization of a perennial theme—ideal love—these letters are also fictions, revealing a great affinity with the love theme of "The Dead." "Do you remember the three adjectives I have used in 'The Dead' in speaking of your body?" he wrote. "They are these: 'musical and strange and perfumed'" (*Selected Letters* 163). I see this sentence and its emotional content as emblematic of the departure of "The Dead" from the other stories and as suggestive of its different narrative strategies.

The story of "The Dead" is more easily recoverable and more fully and completely motivated than most of the other stories, and so, in spite of its ambiguities, is its closure. (Of course, this greater degree of completion is also partly due to the fact that it is four times the length of the longest among the other stories.) Like the boy in "Araby," Gabriel is oversensitive, and he overreacts by calling himself a "ludicrous figure . . . orating to vulgarians and idealizing his own clownish lusts, the pitiable fatuous fellow he had caught a glimpse of in the mirror" (*D* 220). We must not concur with Gabriel's feeling that his love is inferior to that of the young man from Gretta's youth, who stood singing under that dripping tree. Without arguing with other critics, we should simply remember Gabriel's tender pity for his sleeping wife and his memory of her while drying her rich copper hair by the fire a few days before in order to see that his love is presented by Joyce as a good, human (and humanly limited) love. There is no indication in the text that this love needs to be reformed although it might gain from Gabriel's deepened awareness. The passion implied by the memory of the boy who died of love is not to be contrasted to Gabriel's "inadequate" love but to be seen as an impossibly ideal and not necessarily desirable thing. Gabriel may blame himself in his humility, but we as readers cannot think for a moment that Joyce expected Gabriel to place himself beneath some "dripping trees" and die of pneumonia. Both Gretta and Gabriel are in fact deluded and mocked by the idealized image of the dead lover, but so are we all, Joyce implies, mocked by unattainable dreams. There is a depth of unalloyed and unsubverted moral insight and emotional involvement in Joyce's portrait of Gabriel, which gives him quite a unique place not only in *Dubliners* but in Joyce's entire oeuvre.

Structurally, Gabriel's self-critical thoughts, prompted by his all too human lust and disappointment, are not the closing "epiphany." The true closure is his meditation/reverie on passion and death with the image of snow blending over into the half-consciousness of sleep. The ambiguity and indeterminacy of the symbolism of the snow mentioned in the closing sentence make it difficult to assign to it a clear meaning. The difficulty here is one of modernist poetic ambiguity rather than of an ironical undercutting of the symbolization process or of parodic subversion. "His soul swooned slowly as he heard the snow falling faintly through the universe and faintly falling, like the descent of their last end, upon all the living and the dead" (*D* 224). (Perhaps this mode is not Joyce's absolute forte, but it is effective enough and, above all, distinctive in the context of *Dubliners*.) Apart from other possible symbolic analogies, the snow here seems analogous to sleep and perhaps death.

After all the recalcitrant effects and subversions of the other stories, in this closure the book has unexpectedly received a grand finale: in the sweeping quality of its setting—the central plain, the distant hills, the dark and mutinous Shannon waves, the bond of the living with the dead achieved in Gabriel's revery, and the harmony of the images, sounds, and rhythms—the closing paragraphs seem to reach for the all-encompassing moral and symbolist quality of the wings of James's dove or the whiteness of the whale. Different from the rest of Joyce's great collection, where every word seems to have fought its way through a crucible before the author grudgingly allowed it to appear on the page, in its final part this story achieves a generous breadth, a richly (perhaps too richly?) and fully patterned and realized poetic allusiveness as well as a unique kind of Joycean closure, somewhat related to that of "Ithaca," enveloping the irksome particularities of Dublin in the all-encompassing softness and generality of sleep and dream.

In this essay I have attempted to show some of the reasons why *Dubliners* should be assigned a very special place in Joyce's subversive modernist funhouse, a place higher and decidedly different from the place it has traditionally held in the Joycean canon. I believe it was as early as *Dubliners* that Joyce began to subvert the strategies of historical stylistic formations such as realism and symbolism and the properties of fiction as a genre—thematic unity, logic of plot, closure, all of which made critical interpretation more problematic.

If realism and symbolism are the two principal sources of modernism,[12] then the fact alone that they coexist and mutually interact in *Dubliners* places this work in the modernist orbit. However, modernism often travels the road of richness and excess, creating what the New Critics loved to call "ambiguity." In the closure of "The Dead" and often in the earlier chapters of *Ulysses*, Joyce uses indirection and poetic symbolic patterning to achieve that effect and elicit the empathy and involvement of the reader.

In the later chapters of *Ulysses* there is great richness and excess of another, parodic/hypertextual kind that is subversive by definition[13] and produces a distancing kind of opaqueness as well as indeterminacy. In this essay I have tried to show that, unlike in *Ulysses*, in *Dubliners* the main manifestation of indeterminacy is not excess but a mock transparency never repeated in his subsequent work, subversive because it either withholds from us some vital information or springs at us some new element or unexpected new angle of vision, unsettling our confidence as readers. The opaqueness of *Dubliners* is not created by those "screens of language" that Kenner describes as the principal feature of *Ulysses*. Instead, its opaqueness is one of gaps and reticences, of what often seems a perverse (because nearly invisible) twisting of conventions and codes, of a game of hide and seek with the reader, played by a text that seems to be what it is not. It is thus owing to a series of specific strategies which I have tried to outline here that *Dubliners* should be seen not just as a realist/naturalist masterpiece but as a significant stepping-stone integrated into the modernist structure of Joyce's mature work.

Notes

1. This neglect marks almost all of the more traditional collections of *Dubliners* criticism, some of which are included in the bibliography. Much of the more recent criticism of *Dubliners* (hereafter cited with page numbers as *D*) also strikes me as too positivistic.

2. John Fletcher and Malcolm Bradbury see one result of modernism as "a progressive fading of that realism which has long been associated with the novel; language ceases to be what we see through, and becomes what we see" (401). Speaking of the chapters of *Ulysses* after "Sirens," Hugh Kenner says: "For no longer do we see the foreground postures directly, in order to see past them perhaps to Homer. Our immediate awareness now is of screens of language, through or past which it is not easy to see. The Language is what we now confront, as in *Dubliners* we had confronted the characters" (*Joyce's Voices* 41). It is my opinion that even as early as *Dubliners* Joyce prevents us from confronting anything "directly," alerting us to the indeterminacies of his writing.

3. Florence L. Walzl comments: "Conflicting elements in Maria, the heroine of James Joyce's 'Clay' in *Dubliners,* have led to contradictory interpretations of the character: as saint . . . ; as thematically disunified combination of laundress, witch and Virgin Mary figure . . . ; and as unconsciously selfish troublemaker" (107).

4. Among Gérard Genette's most outstanding works are three volumes entitled *Figures* (1966), *Figures II* (1969), and *Figures III* (1972), all published by Editions du Seuil. A portion of the last "Discours du récit" first appeared in English translation as *Narrative Discourse* in 1980. Genette's French titles refer to the meaning of the word *figure* as used in "figure of speech."

5. I see the Joycean subversive strategies as related to the notion of indeterminacy. I try to use the latter term without theoretical rigidity, rather in the sense given to it by Gerald Graff, who points out that theorists use this notion to show that in literature "language attempts to build up positions of authority which language itself calls into question" (170). It is thus possible to challenge "the truths and values" of "traditional interpretations" of even the greatest books of the past. "Read against the grain, what these works prove to be about is not the truths and values that traditional interpretations have found in them, but rather the uncertain, indeterminate nature of their own status as interpretations" (171). Although I accept Graff's warning that "indeterminacy could hardly pose itself as a problem unless it could be seen against a background of partial determinacy that makes it stand out" (174), I believe that the notion has special relevance in regard to Joyce's work which, incidentally, may have contributed to the critical prominence of the notion in the first place.

6. Richard Ellmann remarks that by autumn 1905 "Joyce had not yet thought of writing 'Two Gallants,' 'A Little Cloud,' or 'The Dead'" (78 n. 1).

7. The thematic unity of the collection has been ingeniously elaborated by Kenner (*Dublin's Joyce*). Ulrich Schneider points out, for example, that nearly all of the protagonists of *Dubliners* are "imprisoned," a clear thematic pattern. Other patterns are seen by him as woven out of frustrated love or artistic ambition.

8. See George Becker (3-38) for a classical discussion of realism and Michael Riffaterre for a more recent theoretical approach. Kenner offers an excellent discussion of objectivity and its reliance on sense experience (*Joyce's Voices* 1-14).

9. Culler also points out that "Flaubert's characters are poor reflectors in that they do not compose the world for us, do not organize it in ways that reveal new possibilities of feeling and perception. When they do attempt to order it, they do so in ways which are undercut by the obviousness of the cultural models they are using or by the failure of their images of the world when they try to live in accordance with them" (129). I believe that "Grace," for example, is a story that greatly profits by such a reading.

10. Phillip Herring proposes to deal with a theme that is also central for this essay. He makes useful and interesting observations particularly in his introduction that are pertinent for my approach. In dealing with the individual stories, however, there is much close reading of the traditional kind. In opposition to his title, Herring seems to rely too strongly on interpretation and the belief in the recuperation of meaning.

11. However, after Joyce's much publicized pronouncements on Irish paralysis and corruption, the reader is surprised to find that his writing pulsates with vitality, offering us a less negative and less subversive picture of Irish life than he professed he would. Indeed, perhaps no city that can name a fellow "Hoppy Holohan" with such a happy feeling for assonance can be quite damned, and a writer who with a few strokes can create suave Mr. O'Madden Burke, led to the drinks in an upstairs room "by instinct" and using his "magniloquent western name" as the "moral umbrella upon which he balanced the fine problem of his finances" (*D* 145), cannot be motivated in his writing only by disgust.

12. According to Malcolm Bradbury and James McFarlane, "Those who value in Modernism its pursuit of raw experience, its primitivism even, and who see Impressionism as the common denominator of the movements current round the turn of the century, may side with Hauser who . . . calls Impressionism [as an outcrop of realism] the 'last universally valid *European* style.' Those others who esteem modernist literature as a liberation of the text, of the word, will probably point to symbolism as the source of the self-subsistent work that lives among the multiple privacies of its language, and side rather with Edmund Wilson who in *Axel's Castle* saw the foundations of modern literature in 'the development of Symbolism and its fusion or conflict with Naturalism'" (206).

13. This type of subversion can be associated with Jean-François Lyotard's notion of writing "au trop de livre" (329-41). "But in Joyce," he says, "it is the identity of writing which is the victim of an excess of the book (*au trop de livre*) or of literature" (339). We might thus see the subversion of *Dubliners* as an undermining of the identity of writing by an "excess" that is masked as a refusal.

Works Cited

Baker, James R., and Thomas F. Staley, eds. *James Joyce's* Dubliners: *A Critical Handbook*. Belmont: Wadsworth, 1969.

Beck, Warren. *Joyce's* Dubliners: *Substance, Vision, and Art*. Durham, N.C.: Duke Univ. Press, 1969.

Becker, George. "Introduction: Modern Realism as a Literary Movement." In *Documents of Modern Literary Realism,* ed. George Becker, 3-38. Princeton, N.J.: Princeton Univ. Press, 1963.

Bloom, Harold, ed. Introduction to *Modern Critical Views: Ernest Hemingway,* 1-5. New York: Chelsea, 1985.

Bradbury, Malcolm, and James McFarlane, eds. *Modernism 1890-1930.* New York: Penguin, 1976.

Collins, Ben L. "'Araby' and the 'Extended Simile.'" In *Twentieth-Century Interpretations of* Dubliners: *A Collection of Critical Essays,* ed. Peter Garrett, 93-99. Englewood Cliffs, N.J.: Prentice-Hall, 1968.

Culler, Jonathan. *Flaubert: The Uses of Uncertainty.* Ithaca, N.Y.: Cornell Univ. Press, 1974.

Ellmann, Richard, ed. *Selected Letters of James Joyce.* New York: Viking, 1975.

Fletcher, John, and Malcolm Bradbury. "The Introverted Novel." In *Modernism 1890-1930,* ed. Malcolm Bradbury and James McFarlane, 394-415. New York: Penguin, 1976.

Garrett, Peter, ed. *Twentieth-Century Interpretations of* Dubliners: *A Collection of Critical Essays.* Englewood Cliffs, N.J.: Prentice-Hall, 1968.

Genette, Gérard. *Narrative Discourse: An Essay in Method.* Ithaca, N.Y.: Cornell Univ. Press, 1980.

Gilbert, Stuart. *James Joyce's* Ulysses: *A Study.* 1930. New York: Penguin, 1969.

Graff, Gerald. "Determinacy/Indeterminacy." In *Critical Terms for Literary Study,* ed. Frank Lentricchia and Thomas McLaughlin. Chicago: Chicago Univ. Press, 1995.

Hart, Clive, ed. *James Joyce's* Dubliners: *Critical Essays.* New York: Viking, 1969.

Herring, Phillip. *Joyce's Uncertainty Principle.* Princeton, N.J.: Princeton Univ. Press, 1987.

James, Henry. *The Wings of the Dove.* 1902. New York: NAL, 1964.

Joyce, James. Dubliners: *Text, Criticism, and Notes.* Ed. Robert Scholes and A. Walton Litz. New York: Viking, 1969.

———. *Selected Letters of James Joyce.* Ed. Richard Ellmann. New York: Viking, 1975.

Kenner, Hugh. *Dublin's Joyce.* Boston: Beacon, 1962.

———. *Joyce's Voices.* London: Faber, 1978.

Lawrence, Karen. *The Odyssey of Style in* Ulysses. Princeton, N.J.: Princeton Univ. Press, 1981.

Lodge, David. *The Modes of Modern Writing: Metaphor, Metonymy, and the Typology of Modern Literature.* London: Arnold, 1977.

Lyotard, Jean-François. "Answering the Question: What Is Postmodernism?" In *Innovation/Renovation: New Perspectives on the Humanities,* ed. Ihab Hassan and Sally Hassan, 329-41. Madison: Univ. of Wisconsin Press, 1983.

Magalaner, Marvin, and Richard M. Kain. *James Joyce: The Man, the Work, the Reputation.* New York: New York Univ. Press, 1956.

O'Connor, Frank. "Work in Progress." In Dubliners: *Text, Criticism, and Notes,* ed. Robert Scholes and A. Walton Litz, 304-15. New York: Viking, 1969.

Riffaterre, Michael. *Fictional Truth.* Baltimore: Johns Hopkins Univ. Press, 1990.

Schneider, Ulrich. *James Joyce:* Dubliners. Munich: Fink, 1982.

Scholes, Robert, and Richard Kain. *The Workshop of Daedalus*. Evanston, Ill.: North-western Univ. Press, 1965.

Scholes, Robert, and A. Walton Litz, eds. Dubliners: *Text, Criticism, and Notes*. New York: Viking, 1969.

Scott, Clive. "Symbolism, Decadence and Impressionism." In *Modernism 1890-1930*, ed. Malcolm Bradbury and James McFarlane, 206-27. New York: Penguin, 1976.

Senn, Fritz. "An Encounter." In *James Joyce's* Dubliners: *Critical Essays*, ed. Clive Hart, 26-38. New York: Viking, 1969.

Todorov, Tzvetan. *The Poetics of Prose*. Ithaca, N.Y.: Cornell Univ. Press, 1977.

Walzl, Florence L. "'Clay': An Explication." In *Twentieth-Century Interpretations of* Dubliners: *A Collection of Critical Essays*, ed. Peter Garrett, 107-9. Englewood Cliffs, N.J.: Prentice-Hall, 1968.

CHAPTER TWO

The Geometry of Meaning in *Dubliners*
A Euclidian Approach

Thomas Jackson Rice

In December 1921, two months before the publication of James Joyce's *Ulysses* in book form, the French critic Valéry Larbaud established himself as the first Joycean to recognize a structural correspondence between Joyce's forthcoming novel and his first prose work, *Dubliners* (1914): "This is still the society of *Dubliners*, and the eighteen parts of *Ulysses* can provisionally be considered as eighteen tales with different aspects of the life of the Irish capital as their subjects." Larbaud proceeds, however, to distinguish what he has earlier described as Joyce's more traditional naturalism in *Dubliners* from his symbolic method in *Ulysses*:

> Although each of these eighteen parts differs from all the others in form and language, the whole forms none the less an organism, a book. . . . [A]ll sorts of coincidences, analogies, and correspondences between these different parts come to light. . . . We begin to discover and to anticipate symbols, a design, a plan, in what appeared to us at first a brilliant but confused mass . . . and we realise that we are before a much more complicated book than we had supposed, that everything which appeared arbitrary and sometimes extravagant is really deliberate and premeditated; in short, that we are before a book which has a key. [259-60]

For Larbaud this key was not hard to find ("It is the title: *Ulysses*" [260]), and one immediate consequence of Larbaud's essay was an onslaught of "symbolic" readings of *Ulysses*, such as Paul Jordan Smith's optimistically titled monograph *A Key to the* Ulysses *of James Joyce*, culminating in Stuart Gilbert's schematic analysis of the "thousand and one correspondences and allusions with which the book is studded" in his *James Joyce's* Ulysses (9).[1]

Larbaud clearly discriminates between what he sees as Joyce's predominantly naturalistic approach to his subject matter in *Dubliners* and his symbolic

Original version published in Style 25.3 (1991).

method in *Ulysses*. All too many later critics, however, enthused by Larbaud's idea of a hidden symbolic agenda in *Ulysses*, extended the search for the "key" to interpreting submerged meanings back to the earlier fiction, initially turning their attention to Joyce's anticipations of his symbolic method in *A Portrait of the Artist as a Young Man* and, inevitably, arriving at this interpretive strategy for *Dubliners*.[2] Thus, there now exists a considerable body of criticism on the underlying symbolic meanings of individual stories as well as of *Dubliners* as a whole. Remarkably, despite all reasonable reservations against the practice of reading an author's early works in terms of his later techniques—implicitly denying that any development of technique has taken place—and despite a strong tradition of viewing *Dubliners*, as does Larbaud, as essentially naturalistic in conception, the quantity and quality of symbolic readings of *Dubliners* convince the reader that Joyce may well have meant these stories to be read *both* for their indirect suggestion of "deeper" symbolic significance and for their direct treatment of slices of Dublin life. What these readings routinely lack, however, is anything like Larbaud's justification for seeing a symbolic pattern within surface detail ("It is the title"); they consistently fail to demonstrate from the text itself that Joyce intended that his stories be read for their symbolism, as Larbaud has done for *Dubliners*. A critic such as William York Tindall, for example, takes his cue from elsewhere in Joyce, from Stephen Dedalus's definition of the "epiphany" in *Stephen Hero,* and justifies intensive symbolic readings of the stories on the assumption that Joyce's aesthetic is Stephen's, in *Dubliners* as much as in *Ulysses*.[3]

Yet, to this reader at least, Larbaud's reservations cannot be simply countered by such a jump to another (unpublished) text to support an assumption about Joyce's presumed symbolic method in an earlier work. The reader's "decision to interpret," as Tzvetan Todorov has remarked, which sometimes, as in Joyce criticism, approaches a "form of paranoia" ("interpretive delirium"), is invariably motivated by cues found *within* the text (38). A major question in *Dubliners* criticism, thus, remains unanswered: if a kind of symbol-hunting reading, the search for what Todorov calls the "geometry of meaning" (14), is invited by the stories in *Dubliners,* how is this patterned symbolic interpretation justified or validated by the stories themselves?

It is tempting to seek the answer to this question, as has Larbaud, in the first element of the text that the reader encounters, its title.[4] Such an argument would hold that Joyce is characteristically playing on the double entendre of *Dublin,* "doubling" his fifteen disparate, naturalistic stories with a patterned substratum of meaning: each story has its double or doubles within the collection, as established by thematic links and symbolic clusters, and each action or character has its counterpart or double in the symbolic (one might almost say "spiritual") world of its substratum.[5] The experienced Joycean might find such an argument convincing, looking at *Dubliners* (again) from the perspective of the later work, but the "uninitiated" reader must suspect mostly whimsical ingenuity in the correlation, say, of the Pigeon House in "An Encounter" with the Holy Ghost or of the "rusty bicycle pump" in the garden of "Araby" with an atrophied soul (a "decayed spiritual apparatus") or of the name of Dublin with the idea of doubling.[6]

There are two serious obstacles here to seeing Joyce's title as a validation of his presumed symbolic method. First, *Dubliners* is a perfectly adequate and apt title for merely describing fifteen slices of Dublin life as experienced by its inhabitants. Further, *Dubliners*, as a title, expresses the naturalist's thesis that the systematically frustrated lives described have been determined by the stultifying environment of Dublin. A second major objection to finding a key to Joyce's symbolic intentions in the title *Dubliners* is that it is concrete and specific, referring to actual people in a real place, whereas the remaining titles of his major works are increasingly abstract and suggestive: *A Portrait* (a representation), *Exiles* (a condition), *Ulysses* (a mythic figure), and *Finnegans Wake* (a variety of archetypal suggestions). Yet, I would argue that a convincing defense can be made for seeing the title of *Dubliners* as a key to, and a validation of, Joyce's correlation of discrete naturalistic accounts of Dublin life with sustained patterns of symbolism to create a "geometry of meaning." This defense can be made, moreover, as it must be, from within the work itself.

Joyce corroborates the assumption that two parallel worlds of the real and the symbolic are coexistent and related in his text in a way that can be graphically illustrated by the (appropriately) *geometrical* figure of the gnomon, the incomplete parallelogram, alluded to in the opening paragraph of the first story in *Dubliners*, "The Sisters."[7] If the realistic and symbolic levels of the collection be visualized as the parallel, horizontal lines of the gnomon, then the unbroken diagonal line connecting the two horizontals, a vector projecting the reader from the level of the real to the level of the symbolic, can be compared to the emphatic invitation to seek symbolic significance in the real data of the first story's opening paragraph, an invitation made by the italicized terms *paralysis, gnomon,* and *simony.* As geometry students are challenged to see the completed parallelogram by a small extrapolation from the gnomon, if they know the propositions and corollaries governing lines and angles, so are Joyce's readers challenged to complete the figure, finding the missing angle and lines that connect the symbolic level back again to the real, justifying the "double" reading of *Dubliners.* And this does in fact happen, almost so easily as not to be noticed, significantly in the last "corner" of the collection in the concluding paragraph of the latest written and final story, "The Dead."

If it be demonstrated, moreover, that the symbolic interpretation of these stories is in some way authenticated by Joyce himself, a second, similarly important issue must be considered: how far is this pursuit of symbols allowed to go before it becomes, in Todorov's terms, a kind of "interpretive delirium" (38)? Does Joyce's symbolic method give readers a license to freely associate meanings in the text, as sometimes seems the case in Joyce criticism? This is not a new question, although it rarely has been asked about the symbolic interpretation of *Dubliners*.[8] Joyce implicitly addresses this issue throughout the collection, encouraging readers to develop a kind of tact, an ability to distinguish between what is really being communicated and what they might wish were implied. To do this, readers must suppress their impulse to interpret and attain a clear perception, or apprehension, of the author's statements. Gretta Conroy, for example, is not always thinking only of Gabriel, though he presumes she is, nor is Joyce necessarily saying what the readers would like to imagine. I would argue, therefore, that Joyce develops the interrelated themes of communication and egoism (in its most extreme form of solipsism) throughout *Dubliners* (hereafter cited with page numbers as *D*) and especially in his final story, "The Dead," as an implied warning against readers allowing their creative imaginations to supersede the author's intentions.

Successful communication depends on a balance of articulateness and perception in both the communicator and the audience. Many of Joyce's Dubliners are inarticulate for a variety of reasons. Old Cotter in "The Sisters" speaks in broken phrases. Apprehensiveness makes the title character of "Eveline" dumb. Farrington, though he stumbles into wit on one occasion in "Counterparts," is too ignorant to speak other than with his fists. Joe Donnelly in "Clay" can only express his melancholy by asking for a corkscrew. And Mr. Kernan in "Grace" can hardly speak at all, for he has bitten his tongue. Those Dubliners who can speak are so blinded by egoism that they are unable to perceive their audience, and their communication rebounds upon themselves: Corley of "Two Gallants" "spoke without listening to the speech of his companions. His conversation was mainly about himself" (*D* 51).

As audience, Joyce's Dubliners suffer from a variety of limitations, chiefly their inability to hear or to understand correctly what they do hear (for example, Nannie and the boy in "The Sisters"). Even more prominent are the Dubliners' failures to *see* what lies before them. Much has already been said about the failure of vision as symptomatic of the Dubliners' disease and about Joyce's repeated references to blindness or darkened vision (for example, in "Araby"). Little notice has been paid, however, to Joyce's systematic correlation of the failure in vision with the failure in communication. Consider the boy and Mahony in "An Encounter." When the "queer old josser" briefly departs to do his unspecified thing, presumably some act of depravity, the boy narrator averts his eyes while Mahony, who watches, is unable to describe what he is seeing: "—I say! Look what he's doing! As I neither answered nor raised my eyes

Mahony exclaimed again:—I say . . . [a significant ellipsis, suggesting Mahony's inability either to understand or to verbalize what he sees, other than by lapsing into the inexpressive conclusion] He's a queer old josser!" (*D* 26).

Joyce attributes these related limitations in perception and communication either to ignorance and innocence or, more disturbing, to an essential egoism that progressively moves the growing Dubliner toward solipsistic self-enclosure. In "Araby" he portrays the inarticulate and uncommunicated love of the figuratively "blind" boy for Mangan's sister. Although the boy possesses the intellectual and perceptual sophistication to "interpret [the] signs" (*D* 33) in what he hears, rightly construing the sounds of his uncle's movements upon arriving home on the night of the fair as symptoms of drunkenness, he concludes his story in silence, darkness, and isolation. His culminating vision is a pseudoenlightenment, contaminated by his unaltered egoism: "Gazing up into the darkness I saw *myself* as a creature driven and derided by vanity" (*D* 35; emphasis mine). That the boy has seen something in himself is incontestable, but he is still only seeing himself. Perhaps he can be forgiven, for he is young.

Much later in the volume Joyce presents the middle-aged Mr. James Duffy of "A Painful Case" as a less forgivable counterpart to the boy of "Araby." The egoistic Duffy initially responds to the news of Mrs. Sinico's "commonplace vulgar death" as a reflection on himself. His self-image has been tarnished by association with her: "Not merely had she degraded herself; she had degraded him" (*D* 115). On maturer consideration, however, Duffy seems to move toward an altruistic recognition of his own responsibility for her demise: "Why had he withheld life from her? Why had he sentenced her to death? He felt his moral nature falling to pieces" (*D* 117). Mr. Duffy fails to realize that his taking a perverse "credit" for a decline in Mrs. Sinico is, in fact, a sublime form of egoism. She "began to be rather intemperate in her habits" only "two years ago," the newspaper report of the inquest tells us (*D* 115); since Mr. Duffy reads this account "Four years" after his break with Mrs. Sinico (*D* 112), her decline must date from events quite unconnected with him, occurring at least two years after the end of their brief relationship. Mr. Duffy's recognition of responsibility is nothing but self-pity: "No one wanted him." He sees only himself, an "outcast from life's feast." He returns from his false moment of vision, the narrator notes, still in the darkness, "the way he had come" (*D* 117). Thus, those Dubliners who can see, such as Mr. Duffy, see only mirror images of themselves. Those who can speak and hear listen only to the sound of their own voices: Mr. Duffy's union with Emily Sinico "exalted him, wore away the rough edges of his character, emotionalised his mental life. Sometimes he caught himself listening to the sound of his own voice. He thought that in her eyes he would ascend to angelical stature" (*D* 111).

Such a self-preoccupied and sterile Dubliner as Mr. James Duffy seems re-markably like Gabriel Conroy in his relationships with himself, his wife, and his world in Joyce's final story "The Dead." Yet, unlike Duffy or the boy of "Araby," Gabriel appears to progress toward a genuine act of communication and an uncontaminated moment of vision in the conclusion of his story, much as he ascends "from the dark" to the light (of the "heavy chandelier") in the opening two sections of the story (*D* 177, 186). This progress is accompa-nied by an escape from egoism and a new acuity of perception. Gabriel truly comes to hear his wife for the first time. But even more important, at the con-clusion of the story Gabriel sees clearly for the first time (even though he cer-tainly has taken his glasses off when going to bed). What Gabriel sees is what the perceptive reader of *Dubliners* has seen all along: the simultaneous rela-tionship of the world of reality and the world of symbolic meaning.

The examples of Mr. Duffy and the boy of "Araby" earlier in the collection help the reader better understand the distance Gabriel must travel during his evening. Like Duffy, Gabriel relishes the sound of his own voice, seeing him-self as a gifted public speaker or the designated raconteur of the family's fa-vorite story of Grandpa Morkan's "Never-to-be-forgotten Johnny." He too assumes that he has mounted to the stature of an angelic Gabriel in the eyes of his wife, Gretta, until shaken by the discovery of a rival angelic presence, Michael Furey. He too regards only himself throughout the story, from his early anxieties about the effectiveness of his after-dinner speech and the two significant occasions of his seeing himself in the mirror to the supreme egoism of his catastrophic leading question, "Gretta dear, what are you thinking about?" (*D* 218). Of course he presumes she is thinking of him, not "The Lass of Aughrim" sung earlier in the evening by Bartell D'Arcy.

Gabriel's solipsistic self-preoccupation and limited vision are repeatedly correlated through "The Dead" as we witness his several failures in communi-cation. Gabriel is skilled at speaking at people, not communing with them. He sees his audience but does not apprehend them. Near the beginning his shell is punctured by Lily's misconstruction of his apparently genuine interest in her. The breach is quickly repaired by Gabriel's reassertion of their social separate-ness, by his giving Lily a tip, but not before Joyce inserts a pointed reference to his limited perception: "On his hairless face there scintillated restlessly the pol-ished lenses and the bright gilt rims of the glasses which screened his delicate and restless eyes" (*D* 178). As an audience Gabriel is equally lacking: "Gabriel could not listen while Mary Jane was playing her Academy piece." At the same time we are told that "Gabriel's eyes, irritated by the floor, which glittered with beeswax under the heavy chandelier, wandered to the wall above the piano" (*D* 186).

These episodes are reinforced by Gabriel's inept response to Miss Ivors's perhaps ill-timed but nonetheless genuine attempt at communication. The subject of her remarks, Gabriel himself, would seem to guarantee his interest. Yet "Gabriel tried to cover his agitation. . . . He avoided her eyes" (*D* 190). Miss Ivors, presumably an outspoken "New Woman," wants to discuss issues, not the nice music or pretty dresses that Gabriel would probably consider appropriate topics for a formulaic dance conversation. He cannot buy Miss Ivors off as he has Lily. She is his social and intellectual equal. As the narrator remarks, he cannot even "risk a grandiose phrase with her" (*D* 188). He plans his payback in his after-dinner speech when no response will be possible.

Gabriel escapes from Miss Ivors more immediately in his amusingly inconsequential conversation with Mrs. Malins. As his eyes moved earlier from Mary Jane at the piano to the wall, Gabriel triggers the stuttering Mrs. Malins's monologue concerning her "beautiful crossing," her daughter's "beautiful house" and "nice friends," and her son-in-law's "beautiful big big fish," and "[w]hile her tongue ramble[s] on," he turns inwardly to the more important business of banishing "from his mind all memory of the unpleasant incident with Miss Ivors" (*D* 190-91). Gabriel's ideal conversation, therefore, is one he does not have to listen to in great part because he already knows, or thinks he knows, what will be said.

The final section of "The Dead" continues this patterned juxtaposition of conversation, flawed perception, and egoism, but a significant development takes place. In a disastrous series of leading questions, provoking increasingly unexpected replies, Gabriel is forced into a communication with Gretta, a different kind of communion with her than he had anticipated, resulting in his recognition of her otherness. The facts alone that she can think of someone or even something other than him, that she exists independently of him, that she has had a life before she ever met him, and that she had received the attentions, however innocent, of another male do not annihilate Gabriel's self-absorption though they seriously undermine his self-possession: "A shameful consciousness of his own person assailed him. He saw himself as a ludicrous figure, acting as a pennyboy for his aunts, a nervous well-meaning sentimentalist, orating to vulgarians and idealising his own clownish lusts, the pitiable fatuous fellow he had caught a glimpse of in the mirror. Instinctively he turned his back more to the light lest she might see the shame that burned upon his forehead" (*D* 219-20). At this point Gabriel has turned his back on enlightenment as well. He remains turned away from the light, which enters the darkened hotel room from the lamplight outside until the concluding paragraph of the story.

Gabriel fully comes to terms with the otherness of Gretta when he recognizes his failure to communicate to her the equivalent of the self-denying love of a Michael Furey, which she has deserved: "He had never felt like that himself towards any woman but he knew that such a feeling must be love" (*D* 223). His position is precisely analogous to that of the boy in "Araby," who has truly loved only himself in darkness. Gabriel's recognition of this could be considered just as self-pitying as Duffy's final vision of himself "outcast from life's feast" had Joyce not prefaced it by noting that "*Generous* tears filled Gabriel's eyes" (emphasis mine) and followed it with a significant moment of perception, assisted by the altruistic, generous tears that both blur and create Gabriel's vision: "The tears gathered more thickly in his eyes and in the partial darkness he imagined he saw the form of a young man standing under a dripping tree. Other forms were near. His soul had approached that region where dwell the vast hosts of the dead. He was conscious of, but could not *apprehend*, their wayward and flickering existence" (*D* 223; emphasis mine). For Gabriel's perception of these "wayward and flickering" existences to progress toward a full apprehension, his ego must be suspended, as it shortly will be. Put another way, Gabriel must grasp what these "flickering" apparitions actually are as well as what he, in his imagination, conceives them to be. Gabriel here is looking at a reflection, as Joyce will soon suggest, but at least the reflection now is not of himself.

Gabriel, an English professor, has cultivated a tendency to see symbols in reality. Earlier in the evening he has stood at the foot of the stairs "gazing up at his wife. There was a grace and mystery in her attitude as if she were a symbol of something." Gabriel follows this observation with the quintessential question of literary interpretation: "He asked himself what is a woman standing on the stairs in the shadow, listening to distant music, a symbol of" (*D* 210).[9] Gabriel does not answer his own question at this point. In light of later events, he might interpret the visual signs in this scene as symbolic of the unknown and perhaps ultimately unknowable otherness of Gretta. At the foot of the stairs, however, Gabriel turns his attention to how, were he an artist, "he would paint her in that attitude. . . . *Distant Music* he would call the picture if he were a painter" (*D* 210). The reader might well associate Gabriel's vision here with Little Chandler's egoistic fantasy about the reviews his never-to-be-written poetry might receive in "A Little Cloud." In his reverie Chandler misses his turn to Corless's; for Gabriel, it takes a few moments to realize that the woman on the stairs ("He could not see her face") is in fact his wife (*D* 209). But his final symbolic vision of the "vast hosts of the dead" in the hotel room is less self-conscious. Gabriel is clearly moving beyond self-fixation: "His own identity was fading out into a grey impalpable world: the solid world itself which these dead had one time reared and lived in was dissolving and dwindling" (*D* 223). Of course, what the reader realizes is that Gabriel is literally falling asleep.

But note what this realization means: "Gabriel is *literally* falling asleep." At this moment in the story and in the collection Joyce has reversed the reader's relationship to his text. To this point the reader, so inclined, has been speculatively assigning symbolic meanings to factual information presented. At times Joyce's insistence on certain words, ideas, or motifs has encouraged this, but nowhere, as I observed at the beginning, has he validated this presumptive search for symbolic meaning. Now, however, the reader is placed in the region of purely symbolic statement. Gabriel is not a "fading identity"; he is just an unsatisfied husband in a Dublin hotel, drifting off to sleep, staring at a wall with his back to the window. While reading Gabriel's symbolic vision, the reader is aware of Gabriel in reality lying inertly in bed next to Gretta. The reader's ability to move from the symbolic plane to the real in this passage completes the final vector, or side of the gnomon.

The diagonal line leading the reader from the real to the symbolic levels of the collection in the opening paragraph of "The Sisters" is now complemented by the line leading the reader back from the symbolic to the real. Lest the reader miss this movement, Joyce has Gabriel make an identical move. At the beginning of the last paragraph of "The Dead," Gabriel hears a "few light taps" on the windowpane and turns in his bed toward the window of the hotel room. He returns to reality, emerging briefly from the twilight region of near sleep, but more is involved than simply this. Joyce provides the reader with the information to see the precise correlation between external reality and Gabriel's symbolic vision: "A few light taps upon the pane made him turn to the window. It had begun to snow again. He watched sleepily the flakes, silver and dark, falling obliquely against the lamplight" (*D* 223). What this tells the reader is that Gabriel's vision of the "wayward and flickering existence" of "the vast hosts of the dead" has *literally* been the shadows of snowflakes, projected through the window against an interior wall by an external source of light. What Gabriel has interpreted symbolically has actually been a form of cinematic projection.[10]

Gabriel's vision of the "hosts of the dead" is no fantasy of the dreaming ego (and this is why he is not yet asleep); while an illusion, it is also an accurate reflection of an external reality, as Gabriel sees. Thus, Gabriel is brought to the point of recognizing the interdependencies of the symbolic and the real, the spiritual and the carnal, and the self and the other. As the story ends, it remains for Gabriel to complete his recognitions, to apprehend them in full consciousness, perhaps even to remodel his life upon them. So also has the reader been brought to the point of recognizing the interdependence of symbol and reality in the text and left with the challenge to complete this recognition in the act of interpretation. Crucial to this task is the realization that if there exists by a kind of geometrical logic a real correspondence to the symbolic here at the conclusion of "The Dead," there also exists a symbolic correspondence to the real elsewhere throughout *Dubliners.* Joyce has authenticated the assumption that the real and the symbolic are double, parallel planes in *Dubliners,* intersected by the opening and closing lines of the volume that lead to and from these planes. By an act of extrapolation the gnomon can be fulfilled as a parallelogram by the reader's completion of this last corner of the design. And Joyce assures the reader thematically and technically that both this completion and any symbolic interpretation of *Dubliners* are not to be made fancifully by enthusiastic and free association; rather they are to be made by a careful, self-effacing, objective examination of his text.

Notes

1. As is now well known, Joyce himself assisted and to some extent misled Gilbert on his exposition of the "esoteric theories which underlie the work" (43).

2. Larbaud himself begins the rearward reading of the earlier works by suggesting that a symbolic key can be found for *A Portrait of the Artist as a Young Man* in Joyce's choice of names for his central character, Stephen ("the proto-martyr") and Dedalus ("the architect of the labyrinth") (256). The earliest important attempt to apply the reading strategies of *Ulysses* criticism to *Dubliners* is made by Richard Levin and Charles Shattuck in their essay "First Flight to Ithaca," an exploration of the Homeric parallels in the collection.

3. According to Tindall, "Stephen's theory and this manuscript [*Stephen Hero*] give us a profitable way of approaching Joyce's works, all of which, as Theodore Spencer observed in his Introduction to *Stephen Hero,* may be thought of as epiphanies, *Dubliners* especially" (11).

4. Of course it is equally tempting to cite Joyce's subsequent use of titles to suggest strategies for interpretation, his insistence that *A Portrait* always be referred to by its full title, *A Portrait of the Artist "as a Young Man"* (which validates those interpretations that see a balance of sympathy and irony in his presentation of Stephen), his decision to remove the episode titles from *Ulysses* in order to invest the novel's title alone with the Homeric key found by Larbaud, or his certainty that the jealously guarded title to "Work in Progress," *Finnegans Wake,* would order the apparent chaos of his last novel into clusters of interpretive patterns. But this would lead us again into the use of Joyce's later works to substantiate an assumption about his methods in his earlier fiction.

5. For an argument along these lines, see Albert J. LaValley.

6. See Tindall (17-19) and Harry Stone. Also see Robert ap Roberts's incisive attack on Stone and on symbol mania in Joyce criticism generally.

7. There is nothing novel in this use of the gnomon figure as a key for interpretation in *Dubliners,* though my analysis of the symbolic and structural significance of the gnomon is unique. For recent examples of a reading of "The Sisters" employing both the gnomon figure and the story's title as keys to its meaning, see Leonard Albert and David Weir.

8. The most valuable discussion of the limits of interpretation in Joyce criticism, with particular reference to *Ulysses,* is found in Robert Martin Adams, who writes:

"How far can one look for consistent meaning in [Joyce's freely associated images], and how much of what one finds or creates is really relevant to the novel? Evidently there is some limit beyond which the reader is not justified in imposing *his* private associative ingenuities on the novel" (26). Adams proceeds to argue that a scrupulously close reading of *Ulysses* will enable the critic to distinguish the plausible from the preposterous interpretation of symbolic detail, while I suggest that Joyce embeds in *Dubliners* a caution against the imposition of personal fantasy upon an observed reality. Much the same argument can be made about *Ulysses*.

9. Joyce's use of cadence, convoluted syntax (the suspended preposition), and inappropriate final punctuation in this interrogative sentence wryly suggests both the pomposity and the self-assuredness of Gabriel as the literary critic, as the reader too ready to leap to symbolic meaning. Insufficient attention has been paid to Joyce's verbal humor generally in *Dubliners* and particularly in "The Dead," a story that opens with a malaprop worthy of "Eumaeus": "Lily . . . was *literally* run off her feet" (*D* 175; my emphasis). Hugh Kenner, however, who finds Joyce's language in *Dubliners* "on the whole transparent" (41), briefly examines Joyce's play with words in the maturer stories in the collection and illustrates Joyce's "Uncle Charles Principle" (the impersonal narrator's mimicking of the character's idiom) by the opening sentence of "The Dead" (15-16).

10. Much has been written about the influence of film techniques on Joyce's *Ulysses* and *Finnegans Wake* but nothing about this cinematic quality of the conclusion to "The Dead." It seems clear that Joyce had ample opportunities to consider cinematic techniques in Trieste, which had film theaters several years in advance of Dublin. In fact, two years after the completion of "The Dead" in 1907, Joyce decided to remedy this deficiency by forming a syndicate to open a movie theater, the "Cinema Volta," in Dublin in the fall of 1909 (see Richard Ellmann 300-11).

Works Cited

Adams, Robert Martin. *Surface and Symbol: The Consistency of James Joyce's* Ulysses. New York: Oxford Univ. Press, 1962.

Albert, Leonard. "Gnomonology: Joyce's 'The Sisters.'" *James Joyce Quarterly* 27 (1990): 353-64.

ap Roberts, Robert. "'Araby' and the Palimpsest of Criticism: Or, Through a Glass Eye Darkly." *Antioch Review* 26 (1966-67): 469-89.

Ellmann, Richard. *James Joyce*. Rev. ed. New York: Oxford Univ. Press, 1982.

Gilbert, Stuart. *James Joyce's* Ulysses: *A Study*. 1930. 2d ed. New York: Vintage, 1952.

Joyce, James. Dubliners: *Text, Criticism, and Notes*. Ed. Robert Scholes and A. Walton Litz. New York: Viking, 1969.

———. Stephen Hero, *by James Joyce: Edited from the Manuscript in the Harvard College Library*. 1944. Ed. Theodore Spencer. 2d rev. ed. New York: New Directions, 1963.

Kenner, Hugh. *Joyce's Voices*. Berkeley: Univ. of California Press, 1978.

Larbaud, Valéry. "The *Ulysses* of James Joyce." *Criterion* 1.1 (1922): 94-103 (partially reprinted in *James Joyce: The Critical Heritage*, ed. Robert H. Deming, 1: 252-62.

London: Routledge, 1970).

LaValley, Albert J. "'Doublin Their Mumper': Some Thoughts on the Symbolist Drama of Joyce's *Dubliners.*" In *Literary Studies: Essays in Memory of Francis A. Drumm,* ed. John H. Dorenkamp, 172-90. Worcester, Mass.: College of the Holy Cross, 1973.

Levin, Richard, and Charles Shattuck. "First Flight to Ithaca: A New Reading of Joyce's *Dubliners.*" *Accent* 4 (1944): 75-99.

Smith, Paul Jordan. *A Key to the* Ulysses *of James Joyce.* Chicago: Covici, 1927.

Stone, Harry. "'Araby' and the Writings of James Joyce." *Antioch Review* 25 (1965): 375-410.

Tindall, William York. *A Reader's Guide to James Joyce.* New York: Noonday, 1959.

Todorov, Tzvetan. *Symbolism and Interpretation.* Trans. Catherine Porter. Ithaca, N.Y.: Cornell Univ. Press, 1982.

Weir, David. "Gnomon Is an Island: Euclid and Bruno in Joyce's Narrative Practice." *James Joyce Quarterly* 28 (1991): 343-60.

CHAPTER THREE

Clichés and Repetition in *Dubliners*
The Example of "A Little Cloud"

Harold F. Mosher Jr.

My concern is with repetition in *Dubliners* especially in the form of clichés and hackneyed language, a concern, it would appear, with a surplus of words, but I shall argue that in *Dubliners* Joyce's "gift of gab" paradoxically hides beneath this excessive expression a content of lack much as Flaubert's long but unfinished novel *Bouvard et Pécuchet,* with its accompanying *Dictionnaire des idées reçues,* talks "endlessly" about nothingness, a subject, however, of great importance. This content of lack in *Dubliners* suggests the ultimate significance of Joyce's various forms of repetition of expression and content.[1]

The cliché's signification and value as cliché depends on our recognizing both its perfect imitation, its exact repetition, of the previous occurrences of its own words (to be a cliché, it must be repeatable word for word)[2] and its difference from other possible words that could replace it. It would seem to be the perfect example of the pure (empty) "supplement" in Derrida's terms: it does not represent an original expression; rather it is pure writing referring only to its own system (429). Unlike the fresh metaphor, the cliché, in relying on a repetition of itself for its identity, seems not to draw on difference for its "value" but on sameness. Ostensibly it facilitates conversation, communication, and thus apparently contributes to the progress of discourse and ideas.[3] Looking backward, however, it actually substitutes a lack of originality for creativity. Pretending to be metaphor, it attempts to hide its absence of originality, but, in recalling the metaphor it is not, by this very difference it suggests its own emptiness. Paradoxically, however, many of the stories in *Dubliners* are apparently created out of the emptiness of the clichés that are implied by the stories' content.

The distribution, number, and importance of the acts of omission (a variety of emptiness) throughout *Dubliners* (hereafter cited with page numbers as *D*) are remarkable. In some cases, though the acts are actually committed,

Original version published in *Style* 25.3 (1991).

the narrative distances the reader or the main character from them by only implying them or by narrating them analeptically (by flashback), therefore locating actions in the past and at a metadiegetic (embedded) level as if, in some cases at least, to cover up the shame attached to them. Often the source for distancing may be found to a greater or lesser degree in the character. For example, in "The Dead," Michael Furey's courtship and death are distanced by Gretta's retrospective narrative; by analogy this courtship recalls to Gabriel his lack of romantic passion (*D* 223). In "A Painful Case," Mrs. Sinico's death likewise is narrated analeptically by the newspaper report, creating a distance that implies Mr. Duffy's neglect. In "An Encounter," the boy, who for good reason chooses to remain anonymous, knowingly does not watch the pervert's act at the other end of the field (*D* 26) probably out of shared guilt.[4]

At other times the narrator deliberately omits an explicit identification or narration of the act that had better not have been committed: the identification of the object that Maria touches in "Clay" is not immediately apparent even though the title always holds it before the reader, who is victimized like Maria by the secret (as is the Prefect in Poe's "The Purloined Letter"); in "Two Gallants" and "The Boarding House," the sexual acts are only implied, perhaps out of prudery (or censorship), as in much early cinema, or for shame or because of their routine nature. This last reason might very well motivate the omission of the important conversation between Mr. Doran and Mrs. Mooney at the end of "The Boarding House": the subject and outcome of this dialogue, a marriage that will no doubt shape Polly's and Mr. Doran's lives forever, have already been determined by convention and are self-evident. In other cases the act is actually not performed, thus dramatizing a basic lack usually in the form of insufficient commitment or support from others. This latter reason would seem to be the cause of the boy's failure to buy the gift in "Araby." Perhaps both an absence of self-sufficiency and of external support account for Eveline's refusal to accompany Frank on board the ship in the story that bears her name. In "A Little Cloud," Little Chandler's distraction causes him to forget to buy the coffee; more important, his lack of commitment and talent no doubt prevent him from writing poetry. And the cause for his feeling of self-betrayal to Gallaher, on which the text remains silent, may be his sense of a lack of commitment in his marriage (*D* 81).

One of the most prevalent and well-known motifs in *Dubliners* is the empty promise of escape with its subsequent frustration. Though this motif is often repeated in many different forms, the act of escaping the Dublin condition in an attempt to change one's life is seldom, if ever, accomplished by the main characters. Thus, this nonaction is a lack, but as a repeated one it helps to fill the book's fabula, and, of course, its telling swells the book's discourse. The wish for escape to a better state appears, for example, immediately on the opening page of "The Sisters" in the form of the priest's (hopeful?) prediction, "*I am not long for this world*" (suitably, a hackneyed expression) (*D* 9), continues with Eliza's trite assertion, "he's gone to a better world" (*D* 15), and is echoed in the boy's uncle's recollection that the priest "had a great wish" for the boy (*D* 10), undoubtedly a calling away to the priesthood.[5]

The motif of escape is repeated throughout, recurring in such specific guises as the boy's dream of Persia (*D* 13-14) and its counterpart, the bazaar named Araby; the mysterious "legend" on the "Norwegian vessel" like an invitation from abroad, which the boy fails to "decipher" (*D* 23); Eveline's failure to heed the call from Buenos Aires;[6] the deceitful lure of the continent in "After the Race"; and Lenehan's vain wishes for the comforts of domestic life (*D* 58) in "Two Gallants" about to be granted to others in "The Boarding House" but accepted without great enthusiasm and proven a false hope in "A Little Cloud" and "Counterparts" (not that the nonfulfillment of this domestic adventure is particularly satisfying, as dramatized in "Clay" and "A Painful Case"). In addition to marriage as a way to a supposedly better life, the motif of escape may also take the form of the hope for an improved political situation as in "Ivy Day in the Committee Room" or of a more Christian lifestyle as in "Grace,"[7] neither of which, of course, seems destined for fulfillment. And finally the motif of escape reappears at the end of "The Dead" as Gabriel thinks of setting out "on his journey westward": that is, according to one interpretation, toward death.

In "A Little Cloud," escape by a change to the married state is parodied as it is parodied repeatedly in a number of later stories: "Counterparts," "A Mother," and possibly "The Dead." Gallaher's insincere congratulations to Chandler for having "tasted the joys of connubial bliss" (*D* 78) are rendered ironic by the story's ending and reduced to an economic affair by Gallaher's later cynical remark, "I mean to marry money" (*D* 81). For real adventure and success Gallaher advises those who can to "go away" (*D* 73) "to London or Paris," to the "Moulin Rouge" or "Bohemian cafés" (*D* 76), destinations and activities that reduce the consequence of Chandler's trip to the Isle of Man (*D* 76) or of his entering Corless's bar (which creates an "agitation" almost "overmaster[ing]" him [*D* 74]) for the "adventure of meeting Gallaher" (*D* 80) or ultimately of his "escape from his little house" "to live bravely like Gallaher" by publishing a book of poetry (*D* 83). "A Little Cloud" begins with a summary of Gallaher's escape to London, which has resulted in his having "got on," the ironic, hackneyed signs of which are "his travelled air, his well-cut tweed suit and fearless accent" (*D* 70), just as the earlier "signs of future greatness" had been his drinking and borrowing money (*D* 72).

Other cultural clichés appear frequently in *Dubliners* often with ironic effect. Little Chandler's belief in a saving alternative to his dull marriage through Gallaher's suggestion about "rich Jewesses" takes the form of "dark Oriental eyes ... full ... of passion, of voluptuous longing" (*D* 83), an image repeated in the "large dark brown eyes" of the alluring woman in the bar of "Counterparts" (*D* 95) and in the "big dark eyes" of Michael Furey in "The Dead." Chandler's faith in such conventional notions extends also to literary clichés, expressed in the hope that he might succeed as a poet if his name were more "Irish-looking" (*D* 74) or if he could create a "melancholy tone" (*D* 74), an expression repeated twice later on page 84, or achieve "*The Celtic note*" (*D* 74), also repeated. Ironically, he seems to admire a very English poet, Lord Byron, and his earliest published poem—"Hushed are the winds"—whose romantic melancholy and language have certainly become clichés in early twentieth-century Dublin.

The repetition of such conventional, hackneyed actions and ideas on the plane of content—an abundance ironically revealing the empty routine of adult lives—has its analogue on the plane of expression. *Dubliners'* basic subjects of content provide rich sources for hackneyed language: religion ("God have mercy on his soul" [*D* 10]; "he's gone to a better world" from "The Sisters" [*D* 15]); money ("to play fast and loose" [*D* 45]; "pots of money" from "After the Race" [*D* 45]); drink ("naming their poisons" [*D* 93] or "one little tincture" from "Counterparts" [*D* 94]); sex ("hot stuff" from "A Little Cloud" [*D* 76] or "a bit of a rake" from "Ivy Day in the Committee Room" [*D* 132]) to name a few. The very action of many of the stories suggests that they might have developed from clichés. In "An Encounter," the boy's predilection for the color green combined with the vacant field imply an ironic source in the expression "greener pastures over yonder." In "After the Race," Jimmy's uncomfortable position in the back seat of the speeding automobile and his ultimate victimization could be connected with the saying "to be taken for a ride." In "The Boarding House," seductive Polly and victimized Mr. Doran's sitting or lying in bed suggest "you've made your bed; now lie in it." In "A Painful Case," Mr. Duffy's belated regret for losing Mrs. Sinico may be considered an ironic dramatization of the hackneyed phrase "absence makes the heart grow fonder." The frustration of Mrs. Kearney at the end of "A Mother" could be the ironic result of the truism "mother knows best." And there are others, such as "the spirit moves" ("Grace") or "left out in the cold" (Gabriel in "The Dead"). The more one thinks of the action of the stories, the more easily clichés come to mind, just as the more closely one examines the text of *Dubliners*, the more evident become the clichés.

The same ironic relation between the subject of content and a hackneyed expression may be detected in the title of "A Little Cloud." In calling attention to Little Chandler, the title connects him ironically with the cliché "every cloud has a silver lining": that is, Chandler's hopes, inspired by the drink and talk with Gallaher, to escape from his present straitened circumstances by becoming famous as a poet would seem not to promise fulfillment. What "silver" in the cliché connotes in addition to improvement is, of course, money, and a study of other hackneyed language, repeated words, and their variation by synonyms reveals a fundamental opposition between certain "romantic" ideals and the harsh reality of living, which demands money. The irony of both Chandler's and Gallaher's situations is really a repeated irony as the significance of the cliché evolves into a double irony from what appears to be an original metaphor, to the empty cliché, to a new meaning created by the cliché become metaphor in its context.

For example, we learn apparently from the narrator in the beginning of "A Little Cloud" that Chandler is a melancholy fatalist: "He watched the scene and thought of life; and (as always happened when he thought of life) he became sad. A gentle melancholy took possession of him. He felt how useless it was to struggle against fortune, this being the burden of wisdom which the ages had bequeathed to him" (*D* 71). Since, as we have seen, repetition of content (here Chandler's "always" becoming sad when he thinks of life) doubled by the repetition of the expression "thought of life" may be a sign of the empty, routine life in *Dubliners,* we might be suspicious of the manner in which the narrator uses the word "wisdom." Given Joyce's frequently used "Uncle Charles" principle of "infecting" his narrator's speech with the character's (Kenner, *Joyce's Voices* 18), it is quite possible that "wisdom" is either used ironically by the narrator or is Chandler's word; in either way the comment about the melancholy wisdom of the uselessness of struggle may very well be an unreliable editorial. Certainly the concept is a hackneyed, romantic one and is made to seem more ordinary by the contrasting inflated figure "burden of wisdom," which may sound original for Chandler's thought but is unmasked as at least bordering on the ironically hackneyed if considered as coming from the narrator. (We might well think of such expressions as "rock of ages," "burden of years," "beast of burden," and so on.)

Though Chandler professes belief in such a pessimistic "wisdom" of acceptance, he ironically adopts an optimistic philosophy of hope for his own writing, writing ironically based on his own melancholy, "a melancholy tempered by recurrences of faith and resignation and simple joy" (*D* 73), as Chandler says. In the same paragraph, the word "melancholy" recurs three times, reinforced by its synonym "sadness" (*D* 73-74), and furthermore, it reappears twice at the end of the story as Chandler thinks of Byron's poetry (*D* 84). At this point, however, as if the hackneyed language and repetition of words have exposed the bankruptcy of borrowed romantic ideas, reality in the form of the child's crying destroys Chandler's temporary faith in his future, and his thought returns to the language of the beginning of the story: "useless" appears three times in three lines, accompanied by the exaggerated expression of desperation, "He was a prisoner for life" (*D* 84). Chandler's thought turns from despair to a hope in writing and back again to despair, but throughout, hackneyed language and repetition render his commitment to any stance unconvincing. This ultimate lack of dedication is the increment of meaning that the pervasive cliché and repetition spread in retrospect, if not at first, over all the action.

For example, Gallaher's various stances move through a double irony, if not more. He appears to have succeeded as a bachelor but describes his life in a set of clichés—"I'm going to have my fling first and see a bit of life and the world before I put my head in the sack" (*D* 81)—which, with Chandler's remark on his vulgarity, undercuts his success. Ironically, though, Gallaher congratulates Chandler for "putting his head in the sack" (an expression that Chandler repeats), assuring Chandler that Gallaher's "best wishes" are those "of a sincere friend" (*D* 79). Gallaher's temporary enthusiasm for (Chandler's) married life is then made to seem insincere by his calling that life "stale" (*D* 82). Finally, Gallaher begins to talk about the conditions for his own marriage but in hackneyed terms of another sort, which ultimately reveal that ordinary monetary concerns underlie the "romantic" stances of the melancholy poet on one hand and the high-living journalist on the other. Gallaher belittles married life, then congratulates "sincerely" his friend Chandler for being married, ultimately qualifies that life as "stale," and finally foresees the possibility of his own marriage but in terms that would predict no "connubial bliss" (*D* 78), as he calls it. The words are filled with significance and then emptied by contradictory ones or hackneyed language in one ironic turn after another.

Still this final absence of significance—engendered by the cliché repeating itself, looking back at itself for its identity, instead of anticipating new meaning—ultimately creates meaning, paradoxically, by its contextual relations. The set of hackneyed expressions just referred to, with which Gallaher describes his potential marriage, combined with others reveals an important motivation and thematic conflict in the story, already suggested by the word "silver" in the cliché "every cloud has a silver lining," associated with the title. A series of clichés, repetitions, and synonyms centered on money qualifies Gallaher's idea of marriage: "you may bet your bottom dollar"; "I mean to marry money"; "play my cards properly"; "I mean business" (*D* 81). And the antonymic position (perhaps associated with "connubial bliss") to this stance is expressed in another cliché, "mooning and spooning" (*D* 81). In the same conversation Gallaher repeats the word "money" and multiplies the idea with the synonym "cash" (*D* 81). Retrospectively Gallaher's financial motivation is emphasized if we recall Chandler's earlier memories about Gallaher's being "out at elbows and at his wits' end for money." These clichés appear in company with "money," a word repeated two other times along with its synonymous cliché, "shady affair" (*D* 72). Immediately following Gallaher's words about money at the end of their conversation in Corless's, the narrator associates Chandler with the necessity to save money by hiring no servant (*D* 82). The passage continues, reporting Chandler's thoughts that repeat his monetary obsession in synonymous terms: "cost" (twice), "paying," "penny," "price," "swindle," "ten and elevenpence" (*D* 82-83), and eventually "rich Jewesses" (*D* 83), a repetition of Gallaher's words.

And just as Gallaher's clichés and repetitions about money corrupt the believability of his easy assurances about marrying wealth (he can offer a rich Jewess little more than Corley offers a slavey in "Two Gallants"), so too do Little Chandler's repetitions about money and about the "mean" and "pretty" furniture and eyes of his wife ("mean" appears twice and "pretty" three times on page 83). His wish to escape to the "dark Oriental eyes . . . full . . . of passion, of voluptuous longing" (*D* 83) or to the writing of poetry fails to convince us that he will ever succeed. Little Chandler's repeated act of reading poetry instead of writing it (the positive antonym in this case), cut short by the mundane "sobbing" (repeated with variations of form three times on pages 84 and 85 and amplified with such synonyms as "cry" and "scream" [*D* 84]), becomes an empty gesture; as the narrator remarks early in the story, Chandler "repeated lines to himself and this consoled him" (*D* 71). Ironically, the child's tears might be considered the very sign of melancholy that Chandler is trying in vain to recapture (repeat) for the sake of his unwritten poetry. The repeated reading of poetry is turned into a negative act by repetition (it is a substitute for the positive writing of poetry) and into consolation by its motive; ironically, the repeated (and routine) act of reading poetry is interrupted by the cry of melancholy, which should be the cri de coeur that would enable Chandler to interrupt the repeated chain of reading in favor of the original act of writing. But Chandler's name, we recall, carries with it the epithet "Little," and his smallness of spirit and accomplishment and frustrated promise for the future are reiterated like a refrain at the end of the story by his wife's application of the adjective both literally and figuratively (thus in effect doubling the repetitions) to the small and unfortunate child, creating an ironic comparison to the father. (Irony is also the result of Mr. Henchey's unintended self-characterization by his repetition of the word "little" fourteen times in "Ivy Day" [*D* 123-30], as Michael Brian points out elsewhere in this book.)

According to Saussurean-deconstructionist notions, the meaning and value of words are derived from their similarities to and differences from other terms (Saussure 158-61; Derrida 67).[8] This essay, which so far has emphasized similarities, could continue with a study of differences, although that would seem to lead away from our concentration on clichés, repetition, and synonyms. Actually, this need not be the case. Whereas synonyms and antonyms may be thought of as opposites, according to Saussure they join in serving the same purpose of defining a single sign. In applying an expanded version of this notion to a text, one can think of its words as achieving their significance by their relations to other words both in the text (Saussure's syntagmatic relations [170]) and outside of it (Saussure's associative, or paradigmatic, relations [171]). For the present purpose, I shall only glance at such syntagmatic relations of similarities and dissimilarities in an adaptation of Wolfgang Iser's theory of reading (see chap. 4, especially 96-97).

In many of the stories of *Dubliners,* one might notice sets of synonyms, often established with the aid of repetition, drawing their thematic value from their antonymic relation to another set of synonyms. But these relations between sets are not homogeneous from one story to another. For example, in "Counterparts" there is a subtle modulation, as in a musical composition, from an opening series having as nucleus the concept of anger and moving from "furiously" to "furious" (*D* 86), to "*Blast him*" (*D* 86), to "rage" (*D* 87), to "Blast it" (*D* 90), to "enraged" (*D* 90), to "revel in violence" (*D* 90), to "bitter and violent" (*D* 91), and on to the end with "fury" (*D* 97) and "furiously" (*D* 98). In about the middle of this series a new one begins with "thirst," "drinking," "thirst" (*D* 88) and continues with repetitions of and variations on these words through the narration of the drinking at the bar and the naming of the various drinks consumed (*D* 93-95) to end with "thirsty" (*D* 97).

Here, indeed, is a series of repeated words and synonyms that turns back upon itself, leads nowhere, and as such is a metonymy for Farrington's repetitious job and the vicious circularity of his life: he works at copying and re-copying (*D* 90) the same words in order to earn money to allay his thirst (that is, get drunk) but is still thirsty (that is, he does not get drunk) and must begin all over again the next day to copy in order to earn money in order to get drunk. Farrington's life moves not only from "thirst" to "thirsty" but also from "furiously" (*D* 86) to "furiously" and "viciously" on the last page of the story, which narrates his anger and beating of his son (*D* 98). A repeated variation on this series is that one moving from the description of Mr. Alleyne's head— "like a large egg" (*D* 87), a "polished skull" (*D* 87), an "egg-shaped head" (*D* 91)—to Farrington's desire to "bring his fist down on something violently" (*D* 90), to his doing so (though not on Mr. Alleyne's head) on the table in his own kitchen— "he banged his fist on the table" (*D* 98)—to Mr. Alleyne's own demonstration of anger, "he shook his fist in the man's face" (*D* 91). And still another series connects Farrington's sanguinary nature and face, described as "dark wine-coloured" (*D* 96), to drink and "darkness" (repeated many times throughout the story) as a setting and general condition in the world of *Dubliners,* ultimately to close this story in the dark kitchen where the fire has gone out.

Of course, the resonances of this last image go beyond the story to the "empty fireplace" (*D* 15) in "The Sisters," to the darkness of the hall (*D* 34) in "Araby," to the low-burning fire in "Ivy Day in the Committee Room," and to the pervasive darkness out-of-doors in "The Dead." In this last story, the antonym becomes Gabriel's "tender fires" (*D* 213) (repeated as "tender fire" [*D* 214] and "tender joy" [*D* 213]), which subtly modulates to a value synonymous with that of Farrington's color in Gabriel's "dull anger" and "dull fires of his lust [which] began to glow angrily" (*D* 219). This light modulates more contrastingly to the light associated with Gretta in the hotel room—"colour on her cheeks," the "rich bronze of her hair," her "shining" eyes (*D* 212), and her "fine and brilliant" hair (*D* 217)—and recalls with even greater contrast the light reflecting from Gabriel at the dinner party (*D* 178). Ironically, Gabriel moves from this light to the darkness outside to the muted light of the hotel room with his dull lust and anger at the moment when, finally, light in a figurative sense dawns on him about his relation to Gretta (as light dawns partially on Jimmy in "After the Race" after the night of losing money).

Usually such modulations can be seen as structured more clearly in contrasting sets of values, as in the structure of routine opposing escape in "An Encounter"[9] or reality contrasting with romance[10] in "Araby" or genteelness in opposition to commonness in "A Mother." "A Little Cloud" provides a good example of such a system. Chandler, indeed, feels "acutely the contrast between his own life and his friend's" (*D* 80), and this contrast for the most part manifests itself in an opposition between a set of words governed by the isotopy of romance and another set ruled by reality. For instance, three equivalent phrases appear in the description of setting at the beginning of the story: "kindly golden dust," "gentle melancholy," and "golden sunset" (*D* 71). Here "kindly" and "gentle" pair off, as does the repetition of "golden," and thus "dust," "melancholy," and "sunset" associate with each other and with the other repetitions of "melancholy" later in the story as indicators of Chandler's state of mind and particularly of his attitude toward poetry and the possibility it offers for escape from his "sober inartistic life" (*D* 73).

Of course, "golden" might very well recall the word "silver" in the cliché about clouds and silver linings, and the two words evoke the money that Gallaher finds to be a necessary ingredient for marriage and that is lacking in Chandler's marriage. Such a suggestion is supported by the contrasting set of equivalent words describing Chandler's surroundings, as he sees them, full of noise and squalor: "tiresome," "untidy," "decrepit," "screaming," "grimy," "crawled . . . like mice," "vermin-like" (*D* 71). These "poor stunted houses," this "dull inelegance" (*D* 73), is contrasted with life at Corless's, where "richly dressed ladies [with] powdered faces" and "cavaliers" "eat oysters [and] drink liqueurs" (*D* 72). Chandler's romanticizing then modulates to his "adventure of meeting Gallaher" (*D* 80), to the "voluptuous" Jewesses (*D* 83), to living "boldly" (*D* 80), "stoutly" (*D* 81), and "bravely" (*D* 83), and finally to writing a book of melancholy poetry and is echoed and generated by Gallaher's descriptions of foreign capitals: "gaiety, movement, excitement"; "[h]ot stuff" (*D* 76); "gay"; "spicy" (*D* 77). Gallaher's "romanticizing" continues with comments on these cities' "immorality" (*D* 78) (a repeated word that repeats Chandler's "immoral," itself repeated [*D* 77]) and these cities' "corruption," "vices," and "secrets" and ends with a "story about an English duchess" (*D* 78). This set of terms is meant to be contrasted with "dull," "jog-along Dublin" (*D* 78), but one suddenly realizes that the values identified by these former terms could very well be classed differently and be synonymous with those Chandler uses to denigrate Dublin (that is, physical dirt could be synonymous with moral dirt). The profusion of synonyms repeats the values so often that they eventually become devalued. Indeed, since this evaluation of life in European capitals comes from Gallaher, whose "accent," "gaudy" manner (*D* 77), and "tawdry journalism" (*D* 80) Chandler has just noticed, the two—Gallaher and Europe—could easily modulate out of the "romantic" category to that of unsavory reality, particularly when one recalls that "gaudy" and "tawdry" both relate to the ostentatious display of wealth.

Such a subtle switch of categories, a sort of deconstruction of the system by which a synonym for romance becomes an antonym, occurs perhaps also in regard to money. Money would seem to be connected with the good life of Corless's; it is certainly associated with Gallaher and specifically with his conception of marriage. For him the "joys of connubial bliss" (*D* 78) with or without money can "get a bit stale" (*D* 82), and they obviously have become so for Chandler. Thus romance in marriage is deconstructed, moved from the positive pole of reality to the negative one for reasons of staleness in Gallaher's mind and lack of money in Chandler's. It would seem that money also could undergo this modulation from a positive to a negative category: Gallaher's repetitions of synonyms for money in connection with marriage tend to make money replace the traditional values of marriage and romance, but the values associated with money also modulate from the romantic pole to the negative one of "gaudy" and "tawdry" reality, the latter word actually used by Chandler in connection with Gallaher's journalism (*D* 80).

However, Chandler must forget this association when he later aspires "to live bravely like Gallaher" and "write a book" (*D* 83). Writing a book is apparently opposed to marriage and debt, but the illogical sequence of sentences presenting Chandler's thoughts does not so much oppose it as interpose money in a series that modulates from living bravely like Gallaher in London to writing a book and getting it published. Between these two sentences is the one "There was the furniture still to be paid for" (*D* 83). It is a thought about debt, debt contracted in the past and owed to the future (much like Eveline's stultifying thoughts that prevent her from escaping the confines of her life). Furthermore, money, associated with marriage in abundance by Gallaher and in lack by Chandler, is connected to poetry. Money's absence separates Chandler from poetry: for lack of money, he cannot keep a maid and must mind the child, whose cries, reminiscent of the "screaming" of the "grimy" children in the opening setting, interrupt his reading of melancholy poetry in a clear-cut opposition.

The omission of money in Chandler's life, this absence among many in *Dubliners* (which was mentioned at the outset), is compensated for by his and Gallaher's clichés, repetitions, and associated words in a set of vain substitutions, or intentions, not the least of which is Gallaher's career as a journalist. The repetition of the word "money" and its synonyms, the number of clichés used by Gallaher to describe life and marriage and Chandler's tacit acceptance of their implied values, the cliché about silver suggested by the title—all are forms of empty expression that in their repeated proliferation emphasize the emptiness of the story's content but make the point about the bankruptcy of poetry, perhaps of language, in this fictional world.[11] The hierarchy of writing descends from Chandler's repeated intentions to write poetry, to Gallaher's press reports, to Chandler's copying. Here, too much (writing or talking) yields too little significance, and yet this surplus of words with a lack of content finally produces a full measure of meaning.

Surely, though, this cannot be the last word on *Dubliners* when one considers the intensely poetic style of the last two paragraphs of "The Dead." Here repetition serves other purposes, notably the incantatory one of emphasizing, in the repetition of the word "falling," the pervasiveness of death that unites everyone who, like Gabriel and Gretta, have been separated in life. Certainly one is struck by the singular absence of clichés, and this relative absence suggests another of the cliché's functions that depends on the Russian Formalists' notion of "making strange," of foregrounding certain poetic words against a background of standard language (Mukařovsky 18): in this case, the cliché, acting as nonpoetic language, allows the poetic language to become more evident. Thus, though *Dubliners* begins with a reference to the dead and ends with the words "the dead," its ending rewrites its beginning instead of repeating it. Gabriel thinks of "set[ting] out on his journey westward" (*D* 223), of escaping a condition of which he has become conscious. Though his journey could be thought of as leading to his death, it could also be conceived of as a break with the repeated routine of his eastward trip to the continent. Such a thought cancels the negative in *Dubliner*'s first sentence and makes it read, "There was hope for him this time."

The repeated presence of clichés throughout *Dubliners* thus prepares this positive ending, implied in a poetic style, by an absence of the cliché in the last two paragraphs. Though the content of death is repeatedly evoked, the expression—marked by a significant absence of *Dubliners'* standard, hackneyed language—denies death. In another context when Michael Furey is first mentioned by Gretta, he may appear as a cliché complete with repeated romantic details: his "big dark eyes" with "such an expression in them" (*D* 219), his wish to die, his early death, his dying for love, his separation from his beloved Gretta, his throwing gravel against Gretta's window, the lovers' tryst in the garden, and Gretta's warning with the hackneyed expression that he "would get his death in the rain" (*D* 221). But in Gabriel's final monologue, these hackneyed details are not repeated; Michael Furey is sublimated into the content of death by such forms of expression as "the form of a young man standing under a dripping tree" or "on the hill where Michael Furey lay buried" (*D* 223). A new form of expression changes the content of Michael Furey by changing the context in which he appears and the manner by which he is represented. Art (expression) transforms life (content).

In the end language signals a triumph of the original over the stale, of the romantic spirit of Michael Furey (recalled from the dead) over Gretta's forgetfulness and Gabriel's ignorance of him during all these years. After all, Michael Furey is associated with song, poetry, and love and as such brings something new into Gabriel's life: the spirit of recognition and the power of words, which are so eloquent when contrasted with the clichés and repetitions of his afterdinner speech. The ending does not bring closure but rather openness to Gabriel's westward progress, at least a partial awareness of self, the possibility of an escape from the limits of past routine and of repeated actions and hackneyed language.

Notes

1. Michael Riffaterre requires of the cliché that it be recognized by the reader as hackneyed, banal, and overused and that it be a figure of speech or a rhetorical figure or at least an effect of style (162-64). Ruth Amossy and Elisheva Rosen distinguish (10), as I do, between the cliché, which is strictly speaking a figure of speech, and other stereotyped expressions. Both categories are recognized as hackneyed by their contexts (Riffaterre 164-65), which make clear that their repetitive nature is to be judged derogatorily (Amossy and Rosen 8-9). However, as Riffaterre points out, the disgrace of the literary cliché begins only with the opening of the nineteenth century, and yet since then it has nevertheless been used honorably usually as a renewed form by internal changes or by contrast with its context (169-70, 174-75). Put in the mouths of characters, it has always proved its effectiveness as a characterizing and satirizing device (176). Amossy and Rosen also differentiate between the cliché and the catachre-

sis, which is not considered a figure but is rather perceived as normal usage (12). Nor is the commonplace idea really a cliché for them because it does not depend on its repeated expression for identification: it is a stereotype of thought, not language (13-14). Though accepting this latter distinction, I shall, nevertheless, on occasion deal with hackneyed thought especially, but not exclusively, when it is accompanied by a worn-out expression. In fact, one cannot avoid content because, as Amossy and Rosen point out, hackneyed language refers to a familiar ideological system (20) often for the purpose of calling it into question (65). Anne Herschberg-Pierrot remarks that often gnomic expressions qualify as such clichés ("Problématiques" 342). One might note Laurent Jenny's expansion of the limits of the cliché (one I do not generally treat here) to include literary motifs (499-501), narrative formulas (501-4), rhetorical devices (505-9), and genre signals (509).

2. Amossy and Rosen characterize the cliché as a figure multiplied infinitely (5). It rehearses an earlier expression that is seen as the utterance of society rather than of an individual (16); it is the "already spoken" (67). (Cf. Roland Barthes's use of "écriture" [14-17].) Thus, what is institutionalized (basically the source of Barthes's "écriture") either paradigmatically outside the text or syntagmatically inside the text by its own repetitions becomes a possible generator of the cliché (see Herschberg-Pierrot ["Problématiques" 339] and Jennifer Schiffer Levine's notion of the cliché as repetition of itself and its original context [114]). I do not, however, believe with Françoise Gaillard that all words with a fixed meaning ("toute parole qui agglomère le sens et l'empêche de bouger") are clichés (223). Herschberg-Pierrot identifies two other types of cliché: those signaled ironically and those left undecidable ("Clichés" 90).

3. Amossy lists a number of reading functions of the cliché, among which are its ability to facilitate, speed, and orient reading (36-37).

4. R.B. Kershner notices the boy's complicity, which is emphasized by blending the narrator's speech with the pervert's through indirect discourse (44).

5. Kershner finds that these platitudes function as self-reassurance for the bourgeoisie by its "folk wisdom" (26).

6. Kershner and others interpret Frank's actions as those of a bounder, who is simply repeating romantic clichés to Eveline (62, 71). Kershner cites Hugh Kenner as the originator of this idea ("Molly's Masterstroke" 20-21). Although this alternative is a possibility, the relatively extended account of Frank's apparently long courtship could equally persuade one of the sincerity of his motives. However, Kershner's argument for Joyce's "repetition" of romantic plots in such stories as "Araby" (48-60), "After the Race" (74-79), and "Two Gallants" (81-88) is convincing.

7. Cheryl Herr in her study of the impact of cultural institutions on Joyce's work argues that the church's doctrine represented by Father Purdon's sermon in "Grace" simply repeats the "oppressive economic system" of the business world (245).

8. John Ellis has pointed out that Derrida and the deconstructionists ultimately deform Saussure's idea about specific differences by substituting the notion of free play among signifiers (46-50, 54, 64). I would agree with Ellis's observation.

9. Instead of a simple opposition between imagination and reality in "An Encounter," Kershner prefers to write of the similarity between the mass-produced romances that inspire the boys' minds and the equally mass-produced pornography that

motivates the pervert's speech (46). Both the pervert's speech and pornography are marked by mechanical repetition (44).

10. Kershner finds three sources for the clichés of romance in "Araby": Sir Walter Scott's *The Abbot;* the *Memoirs of Vidocq;* and Alexander Dumas's *The Count of Monte Cristo* (48-60).

11. For other examples of failed narratives and narrators, see Bernard Benstock's account of them in *Dubliners* as instances of emptiness (26-31).

Works Cited

Amossy, Ruth. "The Cliché in the Reading Process." *Sub-Stance* 11.2 (1982): 34-45.

Amossy, Ruth, and Elisheva Rosen. *Le discours du cliché.* Paris: CDU-SEDES, 1981.

Barthes, Roland. *Le degré zéro de l'écriture.* Paris: Gonthier, 1964.

Benstock, Bernard. *Narrative Con/Texts in* Dubliners. Urbana: Univ. of Illinois Press, 1994.

Brian, Michael. "'A Very Fine Piece of Writing': An Etymological, Dantean, and Gnostic Reading of Joyce's 'Ivy Day in the Committee Room.'" *Style* 25 (1991): 466-87.

Derrida, Jacques. *De la grammatologie.* Paris: Minuit, 1967.

Ellis, John. *Against Deconstruction.* Princeton, N.J.: Princeton Univ. Press, 1989.

Gaillard, Françoise. "L'en-signement du réel." In *La production du sens chéz Flaubert,* ed. Claudine Gothot-Mersch, 197-226. Paris: Union Générale d'Editions, 1975.

Herr, Cheryl. *Joyce's Anatomy of Culture.* Urbana: Univ. of Illinois Press, 1986.

Herschberg-Pierrot, Anne. "Clichés, stéréotypie et stratégie discursive dans le discours de Lieuvain." *Littérature* 36 (1979): 88-103.

———. "Problématiques du cliché: sur Flaubert." *Poétique* 43 (1980): 334-45.

Iser, Wolfgang. *The Act of Reading: A Theory of Aesthetic Response.* Baltimore: Johns Hopkins Univ. Press, 1978.

Jenny, Laurent. "Structure et fonctions du cliché: A propos des *Impressions d'Afrique.*" *Poétique* 12 (1972): 495-517.

Joyce, James. *Dubliners.* New York: Viking, 1967.

Kenner, Hugh. *Joyce's Voices.* Berkeley: Univ. of California Press, 1978.

———. "Molly's Masterstroke." *James Joyce Quarterly* 10 (1972): 19-28.

Kershner, R.B. *Joyce, Bakhtin, and Popular Literature: Chronicles of Disorder.* Chapel Hill: Univ. of North Carolina Press, 1989.

Levine, Jennifer Schiffer. "Originality and Repetition in *Finnegans Wake* and *Ulysses.*" *PMLA* 94 (1979): 106-20.

Mukařovsky, Jan. "Standard Language and Poetic Language." In *A Prague School Reader on Esthetics, Literary Structure, and Style,* trans. Paul L. Garvin, 17-30. Washington, D.C.: Georgetown Univ. Press, 1964.

Riffaterre, Michael. "Fonction du cliché dans la prose littéraire." In *Essais de stylistique structurale,* 161-81. Paris: Flammarion, 1971.

Saussure, Ferdinand de. *Cours de linguistique générale.* Ed. Charles Bally, Albert Sechehaye, and Albert Riedlinger. Paris: Payot, 1973.

Works Consulted

(Most of the clichés and hackneyed expressions in this essay appear in one or more of these works.)

Boatner, Maxine Tull, and John Edward Gates. *A Dictionary of American Idioms.* Rev. Adam Makkai. Woodbury: Barron's Educational Series, 1975.

Brewer, Ebenezer. *Brewer's Dictionary of Phrase and Fable.* New York: Harper, 1970.

Chiu, Kwong Ki. *A Dictionary of English Phrases with Illustrative Sentences.* Detroit: Gale, 1971.

Freeman, William, and Brian Phythian, eds. *A Concise Dictionary of English Idioms.* 3d ed. Boston: Writer, 1973.

Henderson, B.L.K., and G.O.E. Henderson. *A Dictionary of English Idioms. Part II: Colloquial Phrases.* London: Blackwood, 1956.

Hornby, A.S., E.V. Gatenby, and A.H. Wakefield, eds. *Idiomatic and Syntactic English Dictionary.* Tokyo: Institute for Research in Language Teaching, 1965.

Ichikawa, Sanki et al., eds. *The Kenkyusha Dictionary of Current English Idioms.* Tokyo: Kenkyusha Press, 1964.

Longman Dictionary of English Idioms. Harbor: Longman, 1979.

Lyell, Thomas R.G. *Slang, Phrase, and Idiom in Colloquial English and Their Use.* Tokyo: Hokuseido, 1931.

MacMillan, M., and A. Barret. *English Idioms, Phrases, Proverbs, Allusions, and Quotations with Their Explanations for Indian Students.* Bombay: Gopal Narayen, 1922.

Oxford English Dictionary. 1933 ed.

Phythian, B.A. *A Concise Dictionary of English Slang and Colloquialisms.* 2d ed. Boston: Writer, 1976.

Stein, Jess, ed. *The Random House Dictionary of the English Language.* Unabridged ed. New York: Random, 1966.

Urdang, Laurence, and Frank R. Abate, eds. *Idioms and Phrases Index.* 1st ed. 3 vols. Detroit: Gale, 1983.

Urdang, Laurence, and Nancy LaRoche, eds. *Picturesque Expressions: A Thematic Dictionary.* Detroit: Gale, 1980.

Vizetally, Frank H., and Leander J. De Bekker. *A Desk-Book of Idioms and Idiomatic Phrases in English Speech and Literature.* New York: Funk, 1923.

Wall, C.E., and E. Przebienda, eds. *Words and Phrases Index.* 4 vols. Ann Arbor: Pierian, 1969-70.

CHAPTER FOUR

Text at the Crossroads

Multilingual Transformations of James Joyce's *Dubliners*

Jolanta W. Wawrzycka

Translation augments and modifies the original which, insofar as it is living on, never ceases to be transformed and to grow. It modifies the original even as it also modifies the translating language. This process—transforming the original as well as the translation—is the translation contract between the original and the translating text.

[Jacques Derrida, *The Ear of the Other 122*]

... real translation is impossible. What passes for translation is a convention of approximate analogies, a rough-cast similitude, just tolerable when the two relevant languages or cultures are cognate. . . .

[George Steiner, *After Babel 77*]

What kind of "Joyce" do foreign readers encounter when they enter *Dubliners* in their native language? What kind of transformations do Joyce's texts undergo in translation? These questions have been asked before; I ask them again in the context of my recent rereading of the Polish translation of *Dubliners*. The Polish version made me realize how much of the Joyce of *Dubliners* could not but be lost in translation, and reflect on the insights into Joyce that Polish critics and academics form based on translations they read. By extension, one has to wonder about the nature of insights formed by any foreign literary scholar who relies on translations. What would Joyce say had he been able to see how some translators had handled his texts? I am reminded here about a shock recorded by Milan Kundera in *The Art of the Novel* in regard to the translations of his Joke. Kundera reports that the French translator rewrote his novel by ornamenting his style and that the English publisher rearranged the whole novel by removing reflective passages and chapters devoted to music. Elsewhere the translator, who did not know a word of Czech, told Kundera that he had translated the Joke "with his heart," carrying Kundera's photo in his wallet and working from the French rewrite. "The shock of the *Joke* translation left a permanent scar on me," confesses Kundera (121). Deciding to put some order into the foreign editions of his books, he devoted himself to reading, checking, and correcting his novels in three or four languages. He reflects, "The writer who determines to supervise the translations of his books finds himself chasing after hordes of words like a shepherd after a flock of wild sheep—a sorry figure to himself, a laughable one to others" (121-22).

Whether sorry or laughable, Joyce, too, was determined to supervise the early translations of his works, especially of *Ulysses*. The existence of such authorized translations can, at least provisionally, guide other translators as to what the author would or would not find acceptable, but the question of such an authorial appropriation of translation is a subject well beyond the scope of this essay. Suffice it to say that Joyce was highly conscious of his works' susceptibility to corruption and adulteration in the process of translation. Already in *Dubliners* (hereafter cited with page numbers as *D* in all translations), his language is a consciously constructed, pedantic language of a "foreign" user of English who is fully aware of language's traps and gaps, power and magic—all the inherent aspects of language that make translation difficult. In this context Stephen's preoccupation with the English language in *A Portrait of the Artist as a Young Man* (hereafter cited as *P*), particularly his question whether the dean of studies came "to teach us his own language or to learn it from us?" (*P* 217), seems particularly poignant. Stephen's comment is not only an indictment of the dean's ignorance about his native tongue but, by extension, an indictment of the ignorance demonstrated by any "language professional"—teacher, writer, translator—of the lexical and semantic subtleties of the very means that he or she claims to profess.

Stood on its head, Stephen's question could also be asked of translators: do they translate to "teach" the translated texts their own languages (i.e., to colonize and appropriate the source text into their culture by altering it), or do they translate to "learn" something from the source text (i.e., to allow the source text to expand their native languages by keeping the source language as close to its original nature as the target language allows)? Perversely enough, there is plenty to be learned about the source text from its (mis)translation into a target language. As I hope to demonstrate here, I do not see "mistranslation" in pejorative terms; rather, I treat it as a "transformation" (as formulated by Jacques Derrida at the beginning of this essay) and thus grant translators in general, and the Polish translator in particular, their due. As a practicing translator, I know of few things more humbling than engaging in a translation. Paul Valéry captured it well when he described the process of translation as "labor of approximation with its little successes, its regrets, its conquests, and its resignations" as one is "making, unmaking, remaking, sacrificing here and there, restoring" (119). In more philosophical terms, for Walter Benjamin the translator was "to release in his own language that pure language which is under the spell of another, to liberate the language imprisoned in a work in his recreation of that work" (80-81).

However tempting it may be to engage in the polylogue on the philosophy of translation, my starting point is a pedestrian, Jakobsonian understanding of translation as an interlingual process of "interpretation of verbal signs by means of signs of some other language" (145), which Jakobson calls "translation proper." In even more general terms, my approach to translation is informed by my belief that no foreign language needs to be involved in transforming, rendering, and approximating the text. Over the years, I have learned just as much about Joyce's works from my students' "translations" of *Dubliners* into their own Englishes as I have from my own readings and rereadings, all of which parallels what Fritz Senn, in the subtitle of his book *Joyce's Dislocutions*, terms "reading as translation."

It is, then, some selected aspects of reading, translation, and transformation of *Dubliners* in Polish that I explore in this essay. Three other translations of *Dubliners*, the French, the Spanish, and the Italian, are employed as "normative" texts, as I look at translators correcting what they think to be errors on Joyce's part, editing Joyce's use of repetition, editing his syntax, and annotating pertinent information not likely to be known to the target-language audiences. The premise of my approach to the Polish *Dubliners* is that knowledge of the English language alone, no matter how perfect, is not necessarily a passport to translating Joyce, just as knowledge of Greek is not a license to translate Homer or of Italian to translate Dante and so on. My working thesis is that Joyce is exceptionally difficult to translate because his texts require translators also to be *scholars* of Joyce, not only fully immersed in the basic facets of Joycean scholarship but also with full access to the Joyce materials such as archives and criticism, published in English. In this essay I will give a few examples of what happens to "Joyce" when the translator is not a Joycean.

Joyce's Malapropisms: Rheumatic General

Most commonly, the translator will *correct* what he or she deems to be an error on Joyce's part. As a case in point, in "Sisters," Eliza tells the mourning guests that Father Flynn had once expressed a desire to go to Irishtown and take her and Nannie with him: "If we could only get one of them new-fangled carriages that makes no noise that Father O'Rourke told him about—them with the rheumatic wheels—for the day cheap . . . " (*D* 17). In all translations under consideration, the phrase "rheumatic wheels" is corrected to "pneumatic wheels" as the context implies. It is creatively rendered as a neologism "roues à pneumoniques" in French (*D* 54) but corrected to "neumáticos en las ruedas" in Spanish (*D* 14) and to "le ruote gommate" in Italian (*D* 49). The Polish rendition of this passage reads: "Gdyby tylko można było wynająć taki powóz, o jakich opowiadał nam ojciec O'Rourke, że nie robią chałasu i mają takie koła co nie trzęsą, dobre dla reumatyków" (*D* 12) ("If it were only possible to rent a carriage, those that Father O'Rourke told us about, which do not make noise and have wheels that do not jolt, good for rheumatics"). Whereas in French, Spanish, and Italian "rheumatic" was simply changed, in the Polish version Joyce's seemingly nonsensical phrase "rheumatic wheels" has undergone a process of semantification, an understandable yet certainly an avoidable step on the part of a translator who is familiar with Joyce's frequent method of allowing his characters to reveal their own shortcomings (e.g., lack of education) through the way they talk. In this case, we encounter Eliza's predilection for malapropisms. Could this particular malapropism function as a Freudian slip of sorts and indicate that Eliza is suffering from rheumatic fever? After all, she is not seen moving around too much; things are done "at her bidding" (*D* 15), as if she were a general, a word she (mis)-uses in another place when she (mis)labels *Freeman's Journal* as *Freeman's General*.

If Eliza's malapropisms are in any way related to her psychosomatic "mal"-being, that possibility is entirely missing from the Polish version of "The Sisters." So is Eliza's unelevated diction: "them flowers and them two candle-sticks" (*D* 16), "them fangled carriages" (*D* 17) are rendered in perfectly correct Polish. In addition, unlike the French, Spanish, and Italian versions, the Polish translation entirely omits the reference to "new-fangled," explained in the *Oxford English Dictionary* (*OED*) as "newly-fashioned" (and present in the *Great English Polish Dictionary*). The phrase is preserved as "fait maintenant" in French (*D* 54), "a la moda" in Spanish (*D* 14), and "moderne" in Italian (*D* 49), but its absence from the Polish translation also erases the fact that Joyce, fascinated as he was by the modern technological inventions, may be showing his character's subconscious contempt for progress, as the tone and the occurrence of malapropism arguably could indicate. If Eliza does indeed suffer from rheumatism, she may not like the idea of the trip to Irishtown, and the very existence of the modern pneumatic tires that would make the ride in the carriage more comfortable takes away the reason why she does not like the idea of the trip in the first place.[1] My rereading of these phrases in Joyce has been influenced by the Polish, French, Spanish, and Italian treatments of Eliza's off-the-scale tone and usage. This is one of the numerous examples of how translation can teach us about the original text.

Censorship(?): Cool Girl

Like Joyce's first publishers, some translators censor his precise vocabulary by opting for euphemisms. A good example of this procedure is the translators' treatment of the word "tart" in "Two Gallants." The Polish rendition of Joyce's "a fine tart" (D 50) reads as "ślicznotka" (D 43) ("a little beauty") and later, "a fine decent tart" (D 54) as "fajna babka" (D 46) ("a swell old girl"). In the French Dubliners "tart" is translated as "une belle poule" (D 103) and "une chouette poule" (D 108); in Spanish as "tipa tan buena" (D 48) and "una tipa muy decente" (D 51); and in Italian as "un bel bocconcino" (D 82; 86), repeated twice in both contexts. Thus the French, Spanish, and Italian versions render "tart" through words that preserve the kind of semantic range that no decent girl, as native speakers inform me, would want to hear addressed to her. The Polish translation opted for fairly harmless euphemisms that suggest compliments more than (as they could in some contexts) derogatory connotations.

In Polish, another censorship-like correction is present in the sentence that in Joyce reads: "I put my arm around her and squeezed her a bit that night" (D 50) but which in Polish is turned into an ellipsis: "Wziąłem ją pod rękę i tak dalej" (D 43) ("I took her arm and so on"). In French, Spanish, and Italian, as in English, the girl does get squeezed, pressed, or held tight but not in Polish.

In this context, it is interesting to take a closer look at the reference to "totties" in "An Encounter" as it is glossed by Robert Scholes and A. Walton Litz in Dubliners and by Don Gifford in Joyce Annotated. Both sources explain "totties" as "high-class prostitutes." Where, in Joyce's phrasing, "Mahony mentioned lightly that he had three totties" (D 25), in the Polish version he "niedbale napomknął, że ma aż trzy sympatie" (D 20) ("mentioned off-handedly that he has three sweethearts"). A multidictionary pursuit of "totties" as "high-class prostitutes" yields no results, but it is Eric Partridge's Dictionary of Slang and Unconventional English that glosses the term as an 1880s word for "high-class whore." The 1993 Jackson-McGinley edition of Dubliners, in addition to supplying Partridge's gloss, adds that the word can mean simply "a little girl," reminding the readers about the 1937 libel case lost by Graham Greene for referring to Shirley Temple as "a little totsie" (Jackson-McGinley 17). The Scholes-Litz gloss explains that "tottie" is a diminutive term for Hottentots.[2] The word "tot" also refers to "a person of disordered brain, a simpleton, a fool," in addition to the familiar meaning, "a very small or tiny child," such as Mahony might have been. Allusions in "Encounter" to Mahony's inferior intelligence suggest that he may have heard and picked up the word "tot"/"tottie" in reference to himself, not only in the sense of a small child (arrested development) but also in the sense of "a simpleton," a synonym for "josser," also in

Mahony's vocabulary. And if Mahony is known among the kids to be even mildly retarded, that would explain why the narrator of "An Encounter" is worried not to appear as "stupid as Mahony" (*D* 25), or why he had always despised Mahony a little, a feeling one might have toward one's perceived inferiors. But these rich lexical possibilities are absent from the Polish text of "Encounter." The Polish translation opts for the contextual meaning of "totties" as "girlfriends" or "sweethearts," giving the Polish readers a fairly straightforward sense of Mahony's inflated boast.

Unlike the Spanish and the Italian, the French translation of the phrase "three totties" seems to have been influenced by the gloss "prostitutes," for it is rendered as "trois poules" (*D* 66), the same phrase used for "tart" in "Two Gallants." The Spanish Mahony refers to "tres chiquitas" (*D* 23) and the Italian one to "tre ragazzine" (*D* 58). The native speakers of Spanish and Italian confirm that the two translations convey no suggestions to girls as "girls" in a demeaning sense. Thus, like the Polish translation, the Spanish and the Italian ones opted for the context to determine the meaning of "totties" as "sweethearts" or "girlfriends," in agreement with dictionaries that render "totties" simply as "little children."

The rereading of Joyce's original text in the light of what does not come through in translation helps to read deeper into the lexical choices made by Joyce and see them as just that: deliberate and careful authorial choices, to be respected by translators.

Repetitions: Very, Very Whipped

In Polish, there are numerous corrections of Joyce's use of lexical repetitions. Almost without exception, they are either substituted by synonyms (where Joyce clearly intended repetition of a given word or phrase) or omitted altogether. One such example is repetition of the word "very" in "Clay" in the description of Maria: she was "a very very small person indeed but she had a very long nose and a very long chin" (*D* 99). Joyce repeats the word "very" four times certainly not because of a paucity of lexical choices before him. That word is, however, entirely absent from the Polish text, which states that Maria "Była niziutkiego wzrostu, ale miała ogromnie długi nos i nie mniej długą brodę" (*D* 87) ("[She] was of tiny height, but she had an enormously long nose and equally long beard").[3] The word "long" is repeated twice in the Polish version, without a single occurrence of "bardzo" (Polish for "very"). The same sentence in French informs the French readers that Maria was "une toute, toute petite personne," who had "un très long nez et un très long menton" (*D* 170). The Italian translation describes Maria as "una personcina piccola piccola" with "un naso molto lungo e il mento molto lungo" (*D* 133). Both

French and Italian translations reduce Joyce's repetition from four to two times two: in French we have "toute, toute" and "très, très" and in Italian, "piccola, piccola" and "molto, molto." The Spanish version struggles with repetition in the following manner: "Maria era una persona minúscula, de veras muy min-úscula, pero tenia una nariz y una barbilla muy largas" (*D* 94), stressing Joyce's "indeed," preserving the repetitive reference to Maria's size, and reducing the occurrence of "muy" to two. Still, in one form or another, repetitions and the word "very" are present in all translated texts but the Polish one, though undoubtedly in each case the translators could have eliminated them for stylistic and/or usage reasons.

If the elimination of Joyce's four "very"s from the Polish version is to be justified on the basis of usage—it might sound a bit too staccato to the Polish ear—it is clear from Joyce's repetition of this word that he, too, had at his disposal lexical means other than the word "very" to render the size of Maria, of her nose, and of her chin, yet he emphatically chose to use that word. Repetitions, in this case "epizeuxis" and "polce," call attention to themselves as nonstandard, poetic uses of language. They underscore moments of vehemence in speech/thought fostered by great emotion and in this context prefigure the refrain-like repetition of Maria's witchlike looks ("the tip of her nose nearly met the tip of her chin" [*D* 101]). For Mukařovsky, it is the violation of standard language that makes the poetic language possible (17).[4] Joyce's "violations" of the standard language are always aimed at rendering his own language artistic or literary, and as such they need to be preserved in translation (Dryden 23; Schleier-macher 44; von Humboldt 56, 58; Ingarden 136-40). In too many places in the Polish *Dubliners,* however, the *literariness* of Joyce's language has been rendered as *standard* language, which poses a poignant question for translation theory: if usage in the source language departs from standard usage, how is the translator to proceed? Joyce's use of repetition is a stylistic and a semantic strategy that partakes in a more widely conceived economy of representation: the linguistic self-referentiality of repetition, besides having incantatory effects, calls attention to Maria and her witchlike looks; witches repeat their spells, and we see Maria do just that with words that run through her mind ("very," "nice") and with the first verse of the song "I Dreamt that I Dwelt." Elimination of repetition can thus eliminate cognitive and aesthetic layers of signification.

A mesmerizing, or "magnetizing," chantlike repetition is present in "Encounter," where the narrator listens to the stranger's talk on "the subject of chastising boys" (*D* 27). The passage is an extended polyptoton in its conglomeration of "whip," "whipping," and "whipped" repeated ten times within the space of twenty-one lines (accompanied by "slap on the hand" and "box on the ear") and qualified by the repetitions of "good," "sound," "nice," and "warm." Whereas the Polish version of this passage preserves eight references to the act of chastising, it does so by using three different lexical units: there are four repetitions of the word "lanie" ("chastising"), two repetitions of "baty" ("whipping"), and two derivatives of the verb "bić" ("to beat up"): "zbiłby" and "biłby" (*D* 21). In other words, because of the use of three different words for "whipping," the impact of the passage is diminished in Polish. The effect of the man's mind circling "slowly round and round its new centre [the whipping] as if magnetised" (*D* 27) is weakened, if not missing, because the figure of polyptoton has been dispersed through semantic equivalents. The French translation preserves all ten repetitions of "le fouet" and its derivatives quite effectively (*D* 68-69). The Italian translation approximates well the effect of the original by rendering eight repetitions of the word "frustati" and its derivatives (*D* 59-60). In Spanish, "la manera de castigar de los muchachos" (*D* 25) is, as in English and French, referred to ten times, but, as in Polish, three different lexical formulations are employed: five times "una buena," three times "una paliza," and two times "azotaría" (*D* 25). Thus, both in Polish and in Spanish an important economy of representation encoded in repetition has been diluted in translation.

Repetitions of Adjectives: Mounting the Staircase

There are some other stylistic departures from Joyce in the Polish *Dubliners* that have to do with repetition. For example, in "Araby," the phrase "the high cold empty gloomy rooms liberated me" (*D* 33) reads in Polish as "W zimnych, pustych pokojach doznałem jakiejś ulgi" (*D* 26) ("in the cold empty rooms I experienced a kind of relief"). Two problems are visible at once. First, out of Joyce's four adjectives, only two, "cold" and "empty," have made it into the Polish version; words "high" and "gloomy" are left out, deflating the young narrator's heightened visual and sensory perception of his surroundings. Adjectival repetitions are common enough in the Polish language for the translator not to be concerned with a possibility of redundant stylistic clumsiness that some repetitions may cause. They are certainly common to Joyce, his trademark almost. One needs only to be reminded of Eileen's "long thin cool white" hands (*P* 49), of "the sad quiet grayblue glow of the dying day" (*P* 145), of "new and soaring, beautiful, impalpable, imperishable" thing that Stephen would create (*P* 150). The French translation keeps three out of Joyce's four adjectives as it describes the rooms to be "froids, vides et sombres" (*D* 77); so does the Spanish, with rooms being "fríos, vacíos, lóbregos" (*D* 31). Only the Italian translation keeps all four adjectives, describing the rooms as "alte, fredde, vuote e oscure" (*D* 65).

The second problem in the Polish rendition of this passage is that Joyce's "liberation" is translated as "relief," which threatens Joyce's innocent, romantic context with unwarranted masturbatory connotations. But are they unwarranted? A look back at Joyce's vocabulary (in the process roughly reminiscent of what Fritz Senn labeled "anagnosis," or "retroactive modification" of what is known, or simply "recognition" [*Anagnostic Probes* 37; 47-48] reveals something. The narrator, irritated by the rhythm of the ticking clock, leaves the room: "I mounted the staircase and gained the upper part of the house. The high cold empty gloomy rooms liberated me and I went from room to room singing" (*D* 33). The boy doesn't "walk up" the stairs or "walk into" the rooms; he mounts and gains, feels liberated and sings. This is no sexually neutral vocabulary; revisited because of transformation in Polish, it reveals new semantic possibilities.

Does the boy's irritation stem from the ticking of the clock that triggers the internal rhythm in him causing him to leave the room and go upstairs to masturbate? As we know, there are times when "a flood from [his] heart seemed to pour itself out into [his] bosom" (*D* 31), confusing his adoration as he tries to love with his heart while his adolescent physiology turns his body into a harp to be strummed with fingers (*D* 31). Also, the boy's rubbing his hands together "until they trembled, murmuring: *Oh love! Oh love!* many times" (*D* 31), indicates, as Brandabur has pointed out, "autoerotic displacement" (53). In this context, Joyce's four adjectival repetitions seem to acquire a masturbatory subtext of "high" erection, of "cold"ness of semen after ejaculation or "empty"ing, and of "gloomy" sadness of postorgasmic solitude. Rhythm (whether lexical, auditory, or visual), heightened sensibility, and onanism seem to go together in Joyce, as exemplified by the behavior of the "queer old josser" or of Bloom on the beach. To miss Joyce's rhythm or to omit his adjectives is to misdirect the reading of Joyce.

Footnotes: Bottle-Colored Eyes

There are certain "givens" in Joyce's works—and in the works of all Irish writers—which in my classes I refer to as "Irelandisms" and by which I mean those highly condensed associative units of knowledge that encapsulate Irish history, legend, and lore. They loom above the surface texts and enhance the richness and Irishness of works by providing the context, the subtext, and the overtext. "Irelandisms" are commonplace for readers of Joyce and of Irish literature, but they are for the most part not readily accessible to foreign-language readers. For example, in "An Encounter," the word "green" in Joyce's phrase "a pair of bottle-green eyes" (*D* 27) is missing in the Polish translation, flattening significantly the symbolic connotations associated with the man that the boys meet in the field. Whereas the French, Italian, and Spanish translations retain that word ("deux yeux vert bouteille" [*D* 69], "un paio d'occhi verde bottiglia" [*D*

60], and "un par de ojos color verde botella" [*D* 25], respectively), the same phrase in Polish speaks of a pair of "oczu koloru butelkowego szkła" (*D* 21) ("eyes of glass-bottle color"), a kind of "empty calorie" piece of nondescription that in old manuals of rhetoric would be listed under the vice of diction called *kakosyntheton,* or a phrase "ill-put-together," for the color of glass and eyes in Polish remains undetermined: clear glass bottle? brown glass bottle? green? Even if the Polish readers were to deduce that the color is to be green, they might not readily know the significance of that color. Retaining the word and footnoting it as relevant to the story would greatly enrich its impact and meaning in Polish.

As the need, at least in the academic environment, for critical, annotated editions of Joyce's texts indicates, annotations are quite indispensable for the English language student/reader. One is reminded here about Nabokov's enthusiastic announcement: "I want translations with copious footnotes, footnotes reaching up like skyscrapers to the top of this or that page so as to leave only a gleam of one textual line between commentary and eternity" (512). But, as Fritz Senn has argued, annotations can spoil the fun of reading ("Annotations" 5-6). They can prematurely give away facts about characters or plot and thus effectively "kill" the pleasure of discovery so essential to the experience of reading in general and to the experience of reading Joyce in particular. Yet, whereas the Anglo-American reading audience will, with relative ease, identify and access the kind of information I call "Irelandisms," the non–Anglo-American audience is much less likely to do so. Annotations, therefore, are of particular importance to the target language audience.

The footnoted information in the Polish version of *Dubliners* is limited to seven glosses and only four of them explicate "Irelandisms" to Polish readers. They are the name of Charles Stewart Parnell and his historical importance, plus a mention of the significance of the ivy leaf in "Ivy Day in the Committee Room" (*D* 108); the reference to "Erin" in Hynes's poem, footnoted as "Ireland; now this name is used only in poetry" (*D* 119); the name "Kathleen" in "A Mother," footnoted as a "genuinely Irish name" (*D* 122); and "banshee" in "Grace," explained as a Celtic fairy who foretells a death in the family (*D* 141). Two other annotations explain that Lothario in "Two Gallants" is a character in Nicholas Rowe's *The Fair Penitent,* a free-thinker and a womanizer (*D* 45), and that "Browne" in "The Dead" means "brown" in English (*D* 181).

Although these six footnotes are relatively harmless, the remaining one, featured in "Grace" in the context of a reference to "penny-a-week" school, represents the type of footnote of which one has to beware. Where Joyce's text reads "—We didn't learn that [i.e., about Pope Leo's strong face and his poems in Latin], Tom, said Mr Power, following Mr M'Coy's example, when we went to the penny-a-week school.—There was many a good man went to the penny-a-week school with a sod of turf under his oxter" (*D* 167), the footnote in Polish explains that "in country schools education was paid for in kind" (*D* 151). First, it is not at all certain that Mr. Kernan refers to "country" schools as conjectured by the translator. Second, "penny-a-week" is translated as "szkola powszechna," or "elementary school," whereas the term refers to National School (also mentioned in "An Encounter," where it is translated into Polish as "szkoła państwowa" [15], or "national school").[5] Having no footnote at all would have left this passage clearer in Polish.

This subject opens up a broad spectrum of textual considerations, especially since all versions of *Dubliners* seem to treat annotations differently: the French translation features by far the largest number of annotations, forty, against only eight in Italian, seven in Polish, and none in Spanish. Obviously, the discrepancy in translators' approaches to Joyce's text, and implicitly to the target language audiences, merits a much closer attention than the scope of this essay allows.

Joyce's Style: Safe/Saved

There are numerous departures from Joyce's phrasing in the Polish version that from the stylistic point of view alter Joyce's painstakingly careful and precise descriptions. For instance, the phrase encoding Eveline's fantasy that Frank "would save her" (*D* 40) is repeated twice by Joyce. The two occurrences are kept in the Polish version as well, but the first time the phrase reads, "Frank ją *ocali*" (*D* 33) ("Frank will *save* her") and the second time, "Będzie przy nim *bezpieczna*" (*D* 33) ("she will be *safe* by his side"). I have highlighted the two words in Polish (*ocali/bezpieczna*) and their translations into English (*save/safe*) to underscore the fact that in spite of semantic overlap in these pairs of words (somebody saved from something may indeed be safe), a careful attention to Joyce's wording reveals that Joyce does not mean Eveline's *security* as the Polish version suggests; it is her *salvation* that he has her think about. Confusing these two words harms Joyce's text and its implications because it fails to convey that whereas Frank may indeed *save* Eveline from the dreariness of life in "Dear Dirty Dublin," we cannot know that she will be *safe* with him. In fact, the opposite may be a more realistic expectation, given the violence of men toward their spouses and children represented or alluded to in most of the stories. Eveline is saved, though certainly not safe, in French ("Franck [*sic*] la sauverait" [*D* 88], repeated twice), in Spanish ("Frank sería su salvacion" [*D* 39], repeated twice), and in Italian ("Frank l'avrebbe salvata" [*D* 72], repeated twice).

Another example of stylistic change can be found at the end of "An Encounter." As the boys flee from the "queer old josser"—reduced in Polish to an old man who "ma bzika" (*D* 21) ("is crazy")—the narrator confesses, "my heart was beating quickly with fear that he would seize me by my ankles" (*D* 28), leaving the readers with the image of a birdlike fright and flight. The Polish version changes the tone dramatically by rendering this phrase as "serce waliło we mnie jak młotem ze strachu, że on mnie schwyci za nogę" (*D* 22) ("my heart was pounding in me like a [sledge] hammer from fear that he will seize my leg"). The French version retains "beating quickly" in the phrase "mon coeur battait vite tant j'avais peur d'être saisi par les chevilles" (*D* 70), as does the Spanish one, "me corazón latía rápido del miedo a que me agarrara por un tobillo" (*D* 25; just one ankle, though), as well as the Italian: "il cuore mi batteva forte per timore che egli mi afferrasse per le caviglie" (*D* 60). And though hearts may beat differently in different languages (which limits translators' choices to a few idiomatic expressions), in most European languages, Polish among them, a heart can "pound" ("walić"), "beat" ("bić"), or "flutter" ("trzepotać"); the translator's careful attention to Joyce's word choice would have preserved the tone of this passage in Polish.

In "A Little Cloud," Annie's sobbing child is tenderly addressed as "Mamma's little lamb of the world" (*D* 85). In Polish the phrase is translated as "moje kociatko" (*D* 75) ("my little kitten"). The transformation of "lamb" into "kitten" is puzzling, especially because the Polish language has two perfect diminutives for "little lamb"—"baranek" and "jagniątko"—both sharing the cuddly and Catholic semantic range implied by Joyce.[6] The French translation preserves Joyce's wording as "Le petit agneau de sa maman" (*D* 151); so does the Spanish one, "¡Corderito divino de mamá!" (*D* 81), as well as the Italian: "agnellino della mamma" (*D* 119).

Scrupulous Meanness: Axed

One of the more significant losses in the Polish translation of *Dubliners* is Joyce's "scrupulous meanness" as a method of characterization and presentation. Joyce, we remember from his famous (and overquoted, but let me not break with tradition) letter to Grant Richards, was very specific as to why he was writing *Dubliners:* "My intention was to write a chapter of the moral history of my country and I chose Dublin for the scene because that city seemed to me the centre of paralysis. . . . I have written it in a style of scrupulous meanness and with the conviction that he is a very bold man who dares to alter in the presentment, still more to deform, what he has seen and heard" (*Letters* 2:134). It is quite disheartening to think that a translator of Joyce (and of *Dubliners* in particular) might not be familiar with the voluminous correspondence, lasting close to a decade, between Joyce and Grant Richards that preceded the publication of the stories in 1914. Such unawareness necessarily leads to inattention, on the one hand, to those aspects of Joyce's style that pre-cipitated his problems with the publisher in the first place and, on the other, to the very gist of what makes Joyce's style so uniquely his.[7]

For example, in "A Boarding House" we learn that Mrs. Mooney, a butcher's daughter, was an appropriately decisive woman: "she dealt with moral problems as a cleaver deals with meat" (D 63). In Polish this sentence reads: "Problemy moralne zwykła traktować podobnie jak mięso które się dzieli toporem" (D 55) ("she treated moral problems similarly to meat that is divided by an axe"). Both the syntax and the rhythm of Joyce's sentence are lost in the Polish version—"cleaver" is rendered as "topór" ("axe") instead of as "tasak"—all of which pretty much butchers for the Polish reader Joyce's poignant, cutting, and "scrupulously mean" simile. The French translation is more faithful in tone and rhythm to Joyce: "Elle traitait les problèmes moraux comme un couperet traite la viande" (D 121); and so is the Spanish version: "Ella lidiaba con los problemas morales como lidia el cuchillo con la carne" (D 61). The Italian version skips the beat but keeps the bite: "Trattava i prob-lemi morali come il macellaio la carne" (D 96).

Similarly, Joyce's exacting sarcasm in "A Mother," expressed in the phrase "the concert expired shortly before ten" (D 140), a sarcasm that encodes Joyce's attitude to the Irish-Renaissance movement, is not expressed in Polish because no attempt is made to preserve Joyce's biting "expired": "Koncert skończył się krótko przed dziesiątą" (D 125) ("The concert ended shortly before ten"). The other translations do Joyce justice by preserving his poignant choice of the word: the French keeps "expira" (D 229), the Spanish employs "extinguio" (D 132), and the Italian opts for "terminò" (D 174), one of whose meanings in-cludes "expired."

Style relies on those peculiarities of word choice and order that are most vulnerable and most likely to be lost in the process of translation. In addition, such figures of thought as irony or "scrupulous meanness" rely on a complex interdependence of modes of presentation (by the author) and modes of per-ception (by characters, by the author, by readers), on lexical multivalence and incongruity, on shifting semantics and shifting contexts, on situations, their development and their outcome. To change these turns of pen is to rewrite rather than to translate. Of course, as one learns from abundant translation criticism, all translations are rewrites. Rosa Maria Bosinelli has demonstrated in her essay "Beyond Translation" that such a text as *Finnegans Wake,* already a "translation" into "jinglish janglage," cannot but be "rewritten into" other lan-guages. But the precision of Joyce's language in *Dubliners,* though by no means easily reproducible in other languages, has to be tended to with utmost care simply because Joyce tended to his writing with utmost care as numerous drafts of *Dubliners'* stories indicate and endless corrections of *Ulysses* and of *Finnegans Wake* confirm.

Winding Down

These are but a few examples of the perils of translating Joyce. As I concluded in another study (Wawrzycka), one has to take note of Fritz Senn's wise warning that "the search for errors in translations, though deeply gratifying to our malevolence and a gleeful pastime of fellow translators, is perhaps the least profitable pursuit" (*Joyce's Dislocutions* 5). I would argue, however, that it is hardly gratifying and certainly far from a gleeful pastime, and to the extent that it is superbly educational as well as a community-forming activity, it is highly profitable. My ongoing immersion in the study of multilingual translations of *Dubliners* has strengthened my conviction that the task of translating Joyce from one language and culture to another carries the highest degree of responsibility to the audience who will read the source text in the target language and therefore requires a scholar translator.

Implicit in the question of target audience is the translator's very raison d'être. To consider the intended reader of a translation helps to illuminate the translator's "workshop," those hidden tools of trade and premise(s) according to which these tools are employed. If translation contains stylistic departures from the original text on lexical and usage levels, yet conveys semantic layers in an attempt to preserve or re-create the "climate" and the general "feel" of the original, then such departures become a part of a translator's programmatic approach and can be explained/justified in terms of the translator's apparatus powered by his or her concern for the target audience. Little of that concern can be discerned from the Polish translation of *Dubliners*. The stories seem to lack that "Joycean" air present in the other three translations where concern for Joyce's idiom comes through in mostly successful and faithful renditions. And if all of these translations are intended for the general audience, it is the French text that in its meticulousness comes close to being also a scholarly, critical translation.

Critical editions of Joyce's works highlight the fact that Joyce's are not "general audience" works anymore: they have become an academic property. Their language is by now removed enough from present-day English to merit footnotes and glosses even for the Anglo-American language readers. A translation of *Dubliners* that aims at re-creating the impact of Joyce's text in the target language would have to strive, impossibly, to preserve *all* of the semantic resonances and ranges that a given word in Joyce carries, even those (especially those) that are now obsolete. This is not to say that I advocate a word-for-word translation; far from it. Like Walter Benjamin, I too believe that "[f]idelity in the translation of individual words can almost never fully reproduce the meaning they have in the original" (79). What I do advocate is scholarly, *philological* attention to Joyce's lexical layer whose structures (repetitions, alliterations, rhythm) inform the semantic layer, which in turn informs all the remaining dimensions of the text: aesthetic, symbolic, historical, political, and so on. And whereas no translation can render all of these layers adequately, to mistreat (change, eliminate) Joyce's text on the *lexical* level is to fail famously on all the remaining levels. I am proposing this sweeping generalization as a supplement to yet another conclusion: critical comparisons of various translations of the same text offer, as I hope to have illustrated here, a fruitful way of reading and *re*reading the original text while heightening one's awareness of the protean intricacies of semantification.

Notes

1. I presented this point for the first time at the 1991 "Miami J'yce Conference." Since then, Garry Leonard arrived at similar conclusion about Eliza's possible rheumatic discomfort. Cf. his *Reading* Dubliners *Again* (46-47).

2. The *OED* describes Hottentots as a South African race "of low stature and dark yellowish-brown complexion who formerly occupied the region near the Cape of Good Hope." In one 1883 account, Hottentots are "a miserable little race, sometimes called 'Totties' in contempt"; their Dutch name "Hottentot" (with variants "Ottentot" and "Hottentoo") means "stutterer" or "stammerer," according to a 1670 source, and is "applied to the people in question on account of their clucking speech." In transferred sense, continues *OED*, the word describes a "person of inferior intellect or culture; one degraded in the scale of civilization, or ignorant of the uses of civilized society."

3. Incidentally, the Polish word "broda" is an unfortunate choice for "chin" in spite of the fact that in Polish it means both "beard" and "chin." A common word in Polish denoting only "chin" is "podbródek," and this word should have been employed here.

4. In his impressive study of translation, *The Poetics of Translation,* Willis Barnstone credits Russian Formalism and the Prague Linguistic Circle with pioneering work relevant to the theory of translation. Recognizing that the influence of Jakobson, Mukařovsky, or Shklovsky on structuralist stylistics is undeniable, Barnstone states that the linguistic-based theories of "literariness," "defamiliarization," and so on are now out of vogue (46). True as it is, some of the vocabulary in this essay clearly indicates that I find it productive to use those theories in the analysis of translation processes. My position, then, is diametrically opposed to Barnstone's, who sees the linguistic approach to the theory and practice of translation as a failure due to "a fundamental misconception of the aims of literary translation, which is not a normative science but, like any form of *original literature,* an art" (46; emphasis added). There is no consensus about how original a translated work is and, for my part, I see no contradiction in tending to both linguistic and aesthetic aspects of translation simultane-

ously. Barnstone's dictum that "art must be translated as art" (47) is precisely what guides me as I analyze translators' treatments of Joyce's language.

5. The Scholes-Litz edition glosses "penny-a-week schools" as the system of government-sponsored schools "feared by Catholic educators, since they pursued an English and nonsectarian theory of education. They were also considered to be socially inferior" (464). Now, to the extent that Polish readers attend nationally run elementary schools, they will not profit from such a footnote, and they will miss the import of Mr. Power's and Mr. Kernan's snide remarks. The gloss supplied by the Jackson-McGinley edition for the English audience does not seem to shed any more light on the significance of penny-a-week schools: "Descended from the hedge-schools of the Penal law period, penny-a-week schools no longer existed by the time this generation was born, though their humble standing was clear enough for the figurative name to be recycled" (149).

6. Although my copy of *Dubliners* in Polish was published in 1991 as a second edition, the Oskar Publishing House gives no indication that it is, in fact, a reprint of the 1958 translation of this work (thanks to Fritz Senn, I was able to confirm this during my research at the Zurich James Joyce Foundation). Would the 1958 communist censors not allow either of the Polish words for "lamb" to appear in print because of its strongly Catholic flavor and force the translator to select a "neutral" kitten?

7. I formulated these statements before I was aware that the 1991 Polish text of *Dubliners* had first appeared in 1958 (see note 6), when the biography of Joyce and most of his letters (other than the 1957 volume 1) had not yet been published. Translators' lack of access to Joyce materials in Communist Poland of the mid-1950s is excusable enough. It is the 1991 reappearance of the very same, unrevised text over thirty years later, when an abundance of Joycean materials had been available for years, that I find difficult to justify.

Works Cited

Barnstone, Willis. *The Poetics of Translation.* New Haven, Conn.: Yale Univ. Press, 1993.

Benjamin, Walter. "The Task of the Translator." In *Theories of Translation,* ed. Rainer Schulte and John Biguenet, 71-82. Chicago: Univ. of Chicago Press, 1992.

Bosinelli, Rosa Maria. "Beyond Translation: Italian Re-writings of *Finnegans Wake.*" *Joyce Studies Annual* 1 (1990): 142-61.

Brandabur, Edward. *A Scrupulous Meanness.* Urbana: Univ. of Illinois Press, 1971.

Derrida, Jacques. *The Ear of the Other: Otobiography, Transference, Translation.* Lincoln: Univ. of Nebraska Press, 1988.

Dryden, John. "On Translation." In *Theories of Translation,* ed. Rainer Schulte and John Biguenet, 17-35. Chicago: Univ. of Chicago Press, 1992.

Gifford, Don. *Joyce Annotated: Notes for* Dubliners *and* A Portrait of the Artist as a Young Man. Rev. ed. Berkeley: Univ. of California Press, 1982.

Humboldt, Wilhelm von. "Introduction to His Translation of *Agamemnon.*" Trans. Sharon Sloan. In *Theories of Translation,* ed. Rainer Schulte and John Biguenet, 55-59. Chicago: Univ. of Chicago Press, 1992.

Ingarden, Roman. "On Translations." Trans. Jolanta W. Wawrzycka. *Analecta Husserliana* 33 (1991): 131-92.

Jakobson, Roman. "On Linguistic Aspects of Translation." In *Theories of Translation,* ed. Rainer Schulte and John Biguenet, 144-51. Chicago: Univ. of Chicago Press, 1992.

Joyce, James. *Dublińczycy.* Trans. Kalina Wojciechowska. Warsaw: Oskar, 1991.

————. Dubliners: *An Annotated Edition.* Ed. John Wyse Jackson and Bernard McGinley. London: Sinclair-Stevenson, 1993.

————. Dubliners: *Text, Criticism, and Notes.* Ed. Robert Scholes and A. Walton Litz. New York: Viking, 1969.

————. *Dublineses.* Trans. Guillermo Cabrera-Infante. Madrid: Alianza, 1974.

————. *Dublinois.* Trans. Jacques Aubert. Paris: Gallimard, 1974.

————. *Gente di Dublino.* Trans. Franca Cancogni. Milan: Mondadori, 1978.

————. *Letters of James Joyce.* Ed. Stuart Gilbert and Richard Ellmann. 3 vols. New York: Viking, 1966.

————. *A Portrait of the Artist as a Young Man.* Ed. R.B. Kershner. Boston: St. Martin's, 1993.

————. *Ulysses.* Ed. Hans Walter Gabler et al. New York: Random, 1986.

Kundera, Milan. *The Art of the Novel.* New York: Harper, 1988.

Leonard, Garry. *Reading* Dubliners *Again: A Lacanian Perspective.* Syracuse, N.Y.: Syracuse Univ. Press, 1993.

Mukařovsky, Jan. "Standard Language and Poetic Language." In *A Prague School Reader on Esthetics, Literary Structure, and Style,* 17-30. Trans. Paul L. Garvin. Washington, D.C.: Georgetown Univ. Press, 1964.

Nabokov, Vladimir. "Problems of Translation: *Onegin* in English." *Partisan Review* 22 (fall 1955): 498-512.

Partridge, Eric. *A Dictionary of Slang and Unconventional English.* London: Routledge, 1951.

Schleiermacher, Friedrich. "On Different Methods of Translating." Trans. Waltraund Bartscht. In *Theories of Translation,* ed. Rainer Schulte and John Biguenet, 36-64. Chicago: Univ. of Chicago Press, 1992.

Scholes, Robert, and A. Walton Litz, eds. Dubliners: *Text, Criticism, and Notes.* New York: Viking, 1969.

Schopenhauer, Arthur. "On Language and Words." Trans. Peter Mollenhauer. In *Theories of Translation,* ed. Rainer Schulte and John Biguenet, 32-35. Chicago: Univ. of Chicago Press, 1992.

Senn, Fritz. "Anagnostic Probes." *European Joyce Studies* 1 (1989): 37-61.

————. "Annotations: A Symposium on Paper." *James Joyce Literary Supplement* 4 (fall 1990): 5-6.

————. *Joyce's Dislocutions: Essays on Reading as Translation.* Ed. John Paul Riquelme. Baltimore: Johns Hopkins Univ. Press, 1984.

Steiner, George. *After Babel: Aspects of Language and Translation.* New York: Oxford Univ. Press, 1992.

Valéry, Paul. "Variations on the *Eclogues.*" In *Theories of Translation,* ed. Rainer Schulte and John Biguenet, 113-26. Chicago: Univ. of Chicago Press, 1992.

Wawrzycka, Jolanta. "Transcultural Criticism: 'jinglish janglage' Joyce in Polish." In *A Collideorscape of Joyce: Festschrift for Fritz Senn,* ed. Ruth Frehner and Ursula Zeller, 1436-43. Dublin: Lilliput, 1997.

Language and Power

CHAPTER FIVE

No Cheer for
"the Gratefully Oppressed"
Ideology in Joyce's *Dubliners*

Trevor L. Williams

This essay examines certain forms of oppression and their effect on consciousness in a few of the stories in Joyce's *Dubliners*.[1] Central to the discussion is the concept of ideology, which I always use with a negative connotation. That is, ideology here is not a neutral term describing a set of ideas held by a group or party. Marxists, in voluminous and often abstruse polemics, have so far failed to define the term satisfactorily. Hence, to reduce an extremely complex debate to one paragraph is simplistic but, for present purposes, necessary.

Marx, in *The German Ideology*, seems to argue that ideology is a form of false consciousness, in which people living under capitalism misperceive the economic contradictions of the system and instead invent abstractions (such as freedom and equality) that superficially serve to justify the system (one is "free" to sell one's labor) but that in fact conceal the system's deeper contradictions ("some are more equal than others"). As Ferruccio Rossi-Landi argues in his *Linguistics and Economics* (from which I quote at length later on), one reason why people fail to perceive the oppression they suffer under is that the means of communication, and thus the available subjects for discussion, are controlled by a few monopolistic corporations whose interests are not served by too close a scrutiny of the economic contradictions they embody. The ideological control of the owning class is aided by, as Louis Althusser put it, the "state apparatuses" (schools, police, the judiciary, the military, churches, and so on), which guarantee the social relations necessary for the reproduction of the state in its present form. Ideology then becomes not so much a particular body of ideas (though it includes that) but the normal, the "natural" way of perceiving and analyzing reality ("common sense," in other words) and at the same time an instrument of oppression. If, however, ideology is so pervasive, guaranteed not only by the state apparatuses but by people's willing complicity in their own

Original version published in *Style* 25.3 (1991).

self-deception and oppression, how does anyone ever manage to step outside such a system to make it the object of criticism? That "oppositional" forces exist (outside the state-sanctioned structure of political parties) is obvious, but how individuals escape "contamination" has not yet been satisfactorily explained. Nor, I hasten to add, does this essay attempt to answer that question.

Even so, Joyce's life and work offer some instructive pointers. His exile from Dublin was precisely a flight from the "net" of church-state ideology, which so suffused his consciousness but which, from a deracinated European standpoint, he could henceforth criticize. Perhaps his most powerful act of demystification at the personal level was his refusal for twenty-seven years to enter into marriage, a legal apparatus embodying for him both (British) state power and religious repression. But one person's *non serviam* does not solve the general problem of ideological domination, and apart from a brief flirtation with Italian socialist and anarchist movements, Joyce distanced himself from any political grouping that may have helped solve the problem.[2] Nevertheless, his work always remained preoccupied with the problem of how to escape from that most ideological of instruments, language itself, in particular the language of the English. To become aware of language as such is the beginning of resistance to the ideological power vested within it. In this light *Finnegans Wake* becomes not a new demystified language, an escape from false consciousness, but a practical demonstration of resistance to ideology, especially the oppression imposed by a unitary, monocular, Cyclopean worldview. Joyce devoted a quarter of his life to this demonstration, an index of the importance he attached to the depth and persistence of linguistic mystification.

It ought never to be forgotten that the Dublin of Joyce's *Dubliners*, besides being a bastion of Roman Catholic faith, was above all an enclave of the British Empire, a colonial serf of London. In this essay I try to point out some of the psychological consequences of this imperial fact. *Dubliners* remains interesting because the problems it poses of rigid, paralyzed, mystified thinking and its associated repression and oppression have not gone away. We are still Joyce's Dubliners. But my analysis must begin with *Ulysses*, whose opening pages clearly spell out these problems.

The first spoken words in *Ulysses* (hereafter cited as *U* followed by chapter and line numbers) are the first words of the Latin mass. The subject of the first dialogue between Stephen and Mulligan is Haines, the "ponderous Saxon" (*U* 1:51). In case we should somehow miss these two points, Joyce, in an unusual concession to the "ponderous" reader of *Ulysses*, has Stephen restate the message:

—After all [Haines says], I should think you are able to free yourself. You are your own master, it seems to me.

—I am the servant of two masters, Stephen said, an English and an Italian.

—Italian? Haines said. . . .

—And a third, Stephen said, there is who wants me for odd jobs.

—Italian? Haines said again. What do you mean?

—The imperial British state, Stephen answered, his colour rising, and the holy Roman catholic and apostolic church.

Haines detached from his underlip some fibres of tobacco before he spoke.

—I can quite understand that, he said calmly. An Irishman must think like that, I daresay. We feel in England that we have treated you rather unfairly. It seems history is to blame. [*U* 1:633-49]

This passage is crucial to an understanding of the driving forces behind Joyce's literary production, the more crucial since such passages (in which there is a confrontation between "England" and "Ireland") are rare. In *Dubliners* there are two: in "After the Race," the Englishman, Routh, cleans out the Irishman, Jimmy, at cards, and in "Counterparts" Farrington is humiliated when he loses at arm wrestling to the young Englishman, Weathers (a possible third occurs at the end of "Araby" between the boy and the young lady, who may be English). In *A Portrait*, the (English) dean of studies confronts Stephen with the Irishman's linguistic subordination, but here in *Ulysses* Joyce makes fully explicit the unequal relationship that exists between the English and the Irish. Haines quickly grasps his role as "English master" and just as quickly moves to suppress what is brought to the surface through Stephen's act of demystification. It is worth concentrating for a moment on the complex act of evasion by which Haines suppresses recognition of his own role as conqueror if only to demonstrate how massive is the task of demystification that confronts Stephen when so much reality can be evaded in so short a passage.

They have been talking desultorily about belief in "a personal God," Stephen sidestepping Haines's direct question about whether he "stands for that" by observing that he is a "horrible example of free thought." In his muddled way, Haines takes up the notion of freedom of thought in a rhetoric of evasion ("After all, I should think" and "it seems to me"), which Stephen immediately politicizes. Only the Englishman, "the seas' ruler" (*U* 1:574), conscious solely of effortless domination, could make so *un*conscious a statement as "You are your own master." By politicizing the statement Stephen is afforded the rare opportunity (at the personal level) of confronting an Englishman with an unmystified view of his country's role in Ireland. Haines, though ponderous, recognizes this and with apparent obtuseness concentrates on elucidation of the "Italian" mystery *only*. Stephen does not allow the evasion, spelling out his subordination to both the English and the Italian master.

Haines's evasion continues at the level of physical gesture as he elaborately removes the tobacco from his lip. Having reestablished conversational dominance by this gesture, Haines concludes by intensifying the evasion of reality. In an attempt to "coopt" Stephen, to draw him into a broad liberal consensus about the Irish past, he expresses understanding and sympathy and then shifts to deflect blame onto the more generalized (and thus unidentifiable) "we." Finally, all the sins of past and present are deprived of all human cause when Haines attributes them to that comforting abstraction, "history." No wonder Stephen refers to history as a nightmare when both Irish and English, from very different angles, use history as a means of avoiding all thought about the present.

It should come as no surprise to any Joycean, certainly not to any student of Irish history, to learn that the Roman Catholic Church and the "imperial British state" have had a profound effect upon Irish consciousness. Yet, it is rare to find criticism of Joyce that takes these negative factors as its starting point.[3] (There is of course no shortage of material explaining at least the Catholicism in Joyce's works.) To take them for granted, however, is to repeat the process of false consciousness that Joyce, starting with *Dubliners*, set out to uncover. In one sense these negative factors can be taken for granted: that is, once they have been foregrounded and their negative effects spelled out, they can thenceforth always be assumed as the ultimately determining causes of most of the events in Joyce's texts. Thus, in analyzing *Dubliners*, I assume that not just Stephen Dedalus but all Dubliners, no matter what, if any, their formal religious or political affiliation, are in some sense servants of these two masters.

I do not wish to argue that Joyce was "correct" in his negative view of church and state: it would be wrong to suggest that there were no emergent positive forces whatsoever in either institution.[4] Rather, I wish to view Stephen's contention that he is serving two masters as a demystifying metaphor that asserts that history is made not by vast impersonal forces but by the actions of specific class-formed groups of men and women. I would then want to ask of *Dubliners* the following questions: granted that the ultimately determining forces within Dublin reside in particular forms of church and state, what are the effects on people's lives of having to serve these two masters? How is it that individuals, far from resisting these forces, actively or passively cooperate in their own enslavement? To what extent are the oppressive tendencies within these forces reproduced in the consciousness of the characters? These questions and my provisional answers are specific to Joyce's *Dubliners*, but I hope I will be understood to be asking through the discussion a more fundamental set of questions: what are the driving forces within our own society, and what are the effects of those forces upon the consciousness of individuals and upon their roles within society?

How do church and state manifest themselves in *Dubliners* (hereafter cited with page numbers as *D*)? Turning first to the church, and leaving aside "The Dead" for a moment, what Joyce originally intended as *Dubliners* began and ended with stories in which the power of the church is foregrounded: "The Sisters" strongly intimates the church's responsibility for paralysis and decay, and "Grace" develops the notion of simony broached in the first paragraph of "The Sisters." In between there is not a single priest who is not somehow morally and intellectually compromised: they are insane (Father Flynn in "The Sisters"); dead (Father Flynn and the "former tenant" in "Araby"); snobbish (Father Butler in "An Encounter" [*D* 20]); "unfortunate" (like the "black sheep" Father Keon in "Ivy Day in the Committee Room" [*D* 126]); prurient (the priest confessing Bob Doran in "The Boarding House" had "drawn out every ridiculous detail of the affair" with Polly [*D* 65]); and above all powerful. In "Eveline" the yellowing photo of an unidentified priest dominates the room, suggesting appropriately a power that transcends time and space (this priest is "in Melbourne now" [*D* 37]; did Joyce intend the black humor of "down under" implied here?). And in "Grace," Father Purdon, the "spiritual accountant" (*D* 174), has the power "to interpret properly" the scriptural texts and thus exercises an authority over his businessman congregation virtually indistinguishable in its social effects from that of the civil administration in Dublin.[5] (Coming as it does at the very end of "Grace," this reference to the interpretation of texts ought to remind us of the terrain on which Joyce the writer was choosing to resist ideological domination: the struggle for a more humane future begins with the "proper" interpretation of the "text" of both the present and the past.)

There are in addition scenes in which the manifestation and the effect of the church seem indistinguishable. In "The Sisters," the chalice, a traditional symbol of the church's power to mediate between God and man, is at best ambivalent. Even when broken it retains the power to paralyze, to suspend all thought, in its function as opiate for "the masses," but perhaps the text also suggests that paralysis is not a permanent state, that the power of the church can be broken. However, the immediate material effect of the broken chalice, if we are to believe the gossip, is to turn the priest insane. In "An Encounter" we learn that Joe Dillon's parents "went to eight-o'clock mass every morning" (*D* 19), but alongside this piety the text remorselessly records the boy's actions and utterances and then provides a comment, a kind of "counterinterpretation" of the church's authority: "He looked like some kind of an Indian when he capered round the garden, an old tea-cosy on his head, beating a tin with his fist and yelling:—Ya! yaka, yaka, yaka! Everyone was incredulous when it was reported that he had a vocation for the priesthood. Nevertheless it was true" (*D* 19).

Here is an example of the Joycean narrator paring his fingernails indifferently as he watches his irony unfold: the overall critical stance toward the church within *Dubliners* tells us that "Ya, yaka" is the language of the church. Thus no one should be "incredulous" that Joe Dillon has a vocation for the priesthood. In "Araby" (*D* 31) as well, language is the site of this duality: the boy's love is his "chalice," and the girl's name springs to his lips in "strange prayers and praises" (just two terms in a paragraph suffused with religious terminology). This example, in which the adolescent boy reaches naturally for religious language to express romantic love, clearly demonstrates the process of mystification as the frustrated boy tries to hold apart two conceptions of reality against the dominant socioreligious pressure to press them into a false unity.

In "Clay" and "A Mother," two exemplars of Catholic piety are described: Maria attends six o'clock mass (*D* 101), while Mr. Kearney "went to the altar every first Friday" (*D* 137). We may infer that Maria's piety is one of the means (perhaps the only one) by which she succeeds in remaining unconscious, in keeping the awful reality of her life at bay. Mr. Kearney, much further up the social scale, derives neither spiritual nor social insight from his piety. Instead, the concentration on mechanical devotion has prevented him from seeing how the Dublin social system works and must be worked, so that, at a crucial moment in the narrative, this intellectual nullity of a man fails to make the decisive intervention that might have prevented his wife from making such a fool of herself. Both characters are paralyzed when put under acute social pressure. When Mr. Holohan appeals to Mr. Kearney to intervene in the argument over the contract, the latter merely "continued to stroke his beard" (*D* 146), his piety helpless to guarantee him either speech or respect. Maria, unable to confront the gap between her own deformed self and the romantic ideal of love held forth in the second stanza of "I Dreamt that I Dwelt," is forced (so out of her own control seems her consciousness) to sing the first stanza again (*D* 106).

Dominic Manganiello sees Maria as "unwittingly a servant of Church and State" and, in her working celibacy, as "a corporal asset of the State" (97). A devout Catholic working in a Protestant institution devoted to the reform of "fallen women," Maria, I would assert, has taken seriously the church's injunction to suppress her sexuality except for the purposes of procreation and thus cannot face even the "allowable" romance of premarital courtship heavily emphasized in the second stanza of Balfe's song. (Don Gifford notes, I think ironically, that the Donlevy *Cathechism* asks the question, "who are the peacemakers?" a title accorded Maria [99]. The answer begins: "Those who subdue their passions . . . well" [79].) More cruelly, however, Maria's unattractive face thoroughly excludes her from the marriage market, while her church, which promises so much in the way of ultimate consolation, fails utterly to "empower" her socially in the face of her hopeless marital prospects. The church (any church) promises "empowerment" in the next life, but a social empowerment in this life is frequently implied, too. Alas, just when characters like Maria, Mr. Kearney, and Farrington's son most need to draw on this social power "guaranteed" by their church, it abandons them as perhaps it must in order to maintain, in Beryl Schlossman's phrase, its "power *over* the community" (xviii; my emphasis).

It is important to stress that this is not a matter of the passive reception of effects, of a simple base/superstructure relationship between (here) the church and human consciousness. The many biological, social, political, educational, juridical, and other factors that mediate between these two poles must be taken into account as well as the capacity of humans both to reproduce actively and to resist their conditions of existence (though there is not much evidence in *Dubliners* of "resistance"). A good example of this complex mediating process occurs at the end of "Counterparts," where it emerges in the last two pages that Farrington lives near the barracks (and thus close to the British presence in Ireland) and that on his return home his wife is "out at the chapel" (*D* 97), having left her five children to the darkness and Farrington. As Farrington prepares to beat his son with the walking stick, the most painful of all the *Dubliners'* endings intervenes, leaving to the reader's imagination the full horror that lies beyond the last ellipsis: "—O, pa! he cried. Don't beat me, pa! And I'll . . . I'll say a *Hail Mary* for you. . . . I'll say a *Hail Mary* for you, pa, if you don't beat me. . . . I'll say a *Hail Mary* . . ." (*D* 98).

Abstracted from their context, these words appear almost farcical, as if the narrator's main point is to satirize the limits of religious consolation. But of course context is all. The full horror of these words derives from the reader's simultaneous awareness of the social degradation Farrington has endured on this day, a degradation whose political dimension is established early and late: Farrington is in the employ of a "North of Ireland" man (*D* 86), and he lives near the barracks, forever in the shadow of the British soldier. Having failed in the politico-economic world, Farrington (in a well-known reversal) imposes his "authority" upon his pathetic domestic world. I want to return to this story, but for the moment I would assert that the narrative, in all its complex interweaving between Farrington's inner and outer world, "accounts for" the ending. The fact remains however that it is the Hail Mary that remains ringing in our ears. We will also have registered that "Ma" was "at the chapel" (repeated twice and italicized).

Three points can be made about this focusing upon the church's role. First, the absent mother's complicity in the reproduction of church power is clear, so that it could as well be said of Mrs. Farrington, as it is of Mrs. Kernan in "Grace," that her "faith was bounded by her kitchen, but, if she was put to it, she could believe also in the banshee and in the Holy Ghost" (*D* 158). Second, the final words demonstrate the endless repetition in Joyce's Dublin of a psychology of dependence. That is, the young boy is searching for the "correct" discourse that will allow him to survive in these social surroundings just as his father has learned that survival in employment depends upon speaking and writing the language of his "oppressor" (symbolized in this instance by Mr. Alleyne, his boss). Third, we witness the pervasive contradiction whereby the boy's consciousness, dominated as well as constructed by the church, imbibes the "power" of the church (the promise of social empowerment again) only to be rendered powerless at a crucial moment in his life.

"Counterparts" provides a useful bridge to the consideration of state power, in practice the manifestation of the British presence in Joyce's Dublin. Unlike the church's, the British presence is muted, perhaps reflecting the reality under colonialism of dominated consciousness. This is a paradox: since British power is the ultimately determining factor upon the forms of Irish economic and political life, one might expect this power to be more insistently manifest than in fact it is in Joyce's literary production. Is it that, in some normative process, British power is taken for granted as if this were the only form of government the Irish could know or possibly aspire to? Historical reality of course suggests that the Irish never took the British presence for granted, yet "historical reality" may mean, for Irish and non-Irish alike, nothing more than our knowledge of important events (such as the Easter Rising or the Phoenix Park murders) when the British presence was most acutely manifested and questioned. However, the daily reality for the mass of dominated people under colonialism may be closer to that described in Joyce's work: the colonial power is always "there" in the background and only occasionally obtrudes itself as in vice-regal cavalcades or in certain people's dependence upon that power for employment.

In "Counterparts," Farrington's boss is an Ulsterman, the mention of which draws upon the subtext of nineteenth-century Irish history: the uneven economic development of Belfast and Dublin under the aegis of British capitalism. Whatever may be Mr. Alleyne's personal origins, his symbolic function in the story is to remind Dubliners of their dependence upon outside agencies[6] and to mock (since he has all the power) their recourse to a bankrupt discourse (Farrington's "witty" response [*D* 91]) as a mode of resistance. Note how all the modifiers in the opening sentence of this story convey the impression of Alleyne's power, a power confirmed in the "imperialism" of the imperative mood: "The bell rang furiously and, when Miss Parker went to the tube, a furious voice called out in a piercing North of Ireland accent:—Send Farrington here!" (*D* 86). There is no hope for Farrington. Later in the story, when his money and the mileage he has extracted from his witticism are about to drain away, he suffers two more defeats at the hands of "outsiders": the woman with "the London accent" (*D* 95) who, he convinces himself, has a "romantic" interest in him but who proves to be scarcely aware of his existence,[7] and the English acrobat who beats him (twice) at arm wrestling. (Ironically, when at the end Farrington reproduces in his relationship with his son the power relations between Mr. Alleyne and himself, the adverb "furiously" reappears: "The man jumped up furiously and pointed to the fire" [*D* 97].)

Few as the manifestations of British presence in *Dubliners* are, they consistently underscore the inequality inscribed within the colonial relationship. For example, Eveline, "a helpless animal" (*D* 41) at the end of that story, lives out the collapse of her romance against a backdrop of milling soldiers leaving for England after completing their tour of garrison duty "guarding" the likes of Eveline. In "After the Race," Jimmy, who has been educated at an expensive Catholic college in England, is comprehensively beaten at cards by the Englishman, Routh. In "A Little Cloud," Little Chandler, a pathetic embodiment of literary exhaustion, dreams only of pleasing the English critics by writing to their expectations of productions that can be labeled "of the Celtic school" (*D* 74). In "Grace," Mr. Kernan, whose abasement on the floor of the pub urinal neatly sums up the degradation so many of Joyce's Dubliners seem to take for granted, works for an English firm as a tea taster (ironically, a job whose very creation bespeaks the expansion of the British Empire),[8] and two of his sons have found work, but in Glasgow and Belfast. Another character in "Grace" (and this leads to the story's central irony) is Mr. Power, who organizes Mr. Kernan's resurrection to social respectability but whose "power" derives entirely from his employment in the Royal Irish Constabulary Office in Dublin Castle. In "Two Gallants," the harp, symbol of Irish nationhood, seems forlorn outside the Kildare Street club, which is redolent of Ascendancy power. All these snapshots are brief but insistent reminders of Irish economic, political, and, above all, psychological dependence, reminders too that the dominated within the colonial relationship are not only exploited but also asked to pay (if only through their psychology of dependence) for the privilege of being exploited. The opening of "After the Race" describes this process exactly: it is "the cheer of the gratefully oppressed" (*D* 52).[9]

The manifestation of state power is easier to quantify than its effects, though in all the above examples an effect is nearly always implied and is sometimes overt. Most criticism of *Dubliners*, as I have said, takes the fact of "paralysis" for granted. I would argue that paralysis is ultimately determined by the particular form of government these characters labor under (though all too many characters labor not at all) and that the church, through its pervasive ideological domination, is complicit with the dominating state force, both having a vested interest in controlling the visions of the future available to the people.[10] Thus the "action" in *Dubliners* (to beg an overwhelming question) is the sum of the effects of these two forces acting in concert. Significantly, character development, an integral part of "action," has for most Dubliners ceased before the narrative begins. Without the possibility of development, without a future, such characters can only flounder in the narrow space allowed to them, all potentiality displaced into false consciousness, petty snobbery, dreams of escape, and fixation upon the past. Not surprisingly, where human relationships are so alienated, images of decay abound.

Above all, there is paralysis: linguistic, sexual, alcoholic, marital, financial; even history itself seems to have stopped. In the first story the numerous ellipses in the women's conversation draw attention to the inability of some characters to control or "possess" their own language as if language is owned (not merely derived from) elsewhere.[11] Some characters, such as Maria in "Clay" and the "queer old josser" in "An Encounter," are truly on the margins of language, doomed not to progress beyond the low level of linguistic achievement implied in the word "nice" (which appears eleven times in "Clay"). Other characters, such as Mr. Duffy and Little Chandler, are unable to write, but in the highly verbal "Ivy Day in the Committee Room," Joe Hynes, with his poem to Parnell, manages to convince his listeners and himself that he has control over the language. The first comment on Hynes's poem after his recitation is the "Pok!" (*D* 135) of the cork flying from the bottle on the hearth, a reminder that for all the fine sentiment evoked by the poem, most of the characters' conversation leading up to this moment has been shallow and venal, fixated upon a past they scarcely believe in any longer. In a sense Hynes's poem, with its undialectical view of the relationship between past and present, is a fitting climax to all that circular, self-deceptive conversation, an index too of the extent to which characters participate in the reproduction of ideology. To hope that "Freedom's reign" will arrive at the "dawning" of some suitable day is a harmless enough activity, so long as the word is taken (as here) for the deed.

Paralysis extends to sexuality and to male-female relationships generally. Sexuality may be repressed (Mr. Duffy) or perversely flaunted (the "queer old josser" in "An Encounter") or commodified (Corley's treatment of the girl in "Two Gallants"). Throughout *Dubliners*, relationships are paralyzed at the commodity level, a lugubrious example being Bob Doran's dalliance with Polly, which is transformed by Mrs. Mooney into a very specific economic relationship: marriage equals "reparation." If Bob Doran is trapped *into* marriage, Little Chandler is trapped *in* marriage. In "Araby" and "Eveline," romance briefly flowers, only to be quickly crowded out by myriad ideological "voices." Alcohol, on the other hand, though paralyzing to mind and body, at least has the virtue of easing the pain of moral and political degradation. It may be significant that the alcoholic haze is thickest in those stories ("Counterparts" and "After the Race") where the narrative pushes the central characters closest to recognition of their economic and political impotence.

In "Counterparts," the narrative immediately stresses Farrington's inferiority (as symbolic "Dubliner") before northern, and ultimately British, power. From this painful reality he seeks refuge in both alcohol and "rhetoric," though the latter, an accidental one-line witticism, proves even less effective than alcohol in keeping the pain at bay. "After the Race" ends in alcoholic stupor, but (or perhaps because) prior to this the narrative has insisted (through the repetition of the word "money") on Jimmy's utterly parasitic status not only in relation to the rich Europeans but in relation to his own past and the (British) source of his wealth. Moreover, though Jimmy is "conscious of the labour latent in money" (*D* 44) and is able "to translate into days' work that lordly car in which he sat" (*D* 45), the allusion is to the labor, not of Jimmy but of his father and his father's employees.

Thus, with wealth no longer (as in Jimmy's case) requiring labor for its generation, history, in the sense of the active reproduction of everyday life or, as Eric Hobsbawm defines it, "the progressively effective utilization and transformation of nature by mankind" (41), has ceased for Jimmy's class (the bourgeoisie), even if it ought not to have done for the "gratefully oppressed" who form the "channel of poverty and inaction" (*D* 42) through which the race passes.[12] But even for them history seems to have stopped, as is demonstrated by the case of Eveline, for whom the voices of an insane past and a brutal present are more potent than any future beckoning across the sea. In "Ivy Day" too, the reference to "Freedom's reign" one day in Erin sounds a false note coming so soon after the dull compulsion of the characters' present and their mystified view of the past. Jimmy wanted everything to "stop" (*D* 48), and so, in *Dubliners*, it has. Even money (in "A Mother") has ceased to circulate: the class-conscious Mrs. Kearney, who had treated her daughter's talent and her daughter as commodities, discovers that life itself almost (but certainly her social well-being) depends on the circulation of money. The gold coin shining in Corley's palm at the end of "Two Gallants" is a fitting tribute to this commodity fetishism that so pervades and paralyzes Joyce's Dublin.

A major manifestation of paralysis is the displacement of human potential into inauthentic consciousness, petty snobbery, and so on. I use the adjective "inauthentic" here rather than "false" to distinguish those infrequent moments in the text when the narrative demonstrates unequivocally that a character's consciousness is secondhand. At such moments we are briefly reminded of ideology's role in the construction of human consciousness. "A Painful Case" (one of the stories discussed in some detail below) yields in Mr. Duffy one of those characters who (like Eveline and Maria at the opposite end of the social scale) is prevented even from speaking, so thoroughly deprived is he of authentic subjectivity (he depends on Nietzsche to confirm his existence and lives "at a little distance from his body" [*D* 108]). The reported monologue in "Clay" ("such was life" [*D* 102]; "even when he has a drop taken" [*D* 103]; the repetition of "nice") suggests that Maria, her mind suffused with clichés, mistaking condescension for kindness, lacks even the most rudimentary intellectual capacity to overcome her near desperate social condition. With Eveline, however, the text is more specific in implying a source for her inauthenticity. Like Gerty MacDowell's, her consciousness appears to be constructed primarily by the world of women's romance: "She was about to explore another life with Frank. Frank was very kind, manly, open-hearted. . . . his hair tumbled forward over a face of bronze. . . . Frank would take her in his arms, fold her in his arms. He would save her" (*D* 38-40).

Briefer examples of this sudden emerging of inauthentic consciousness into full articulation are Ignatius Gallaher's use of French in "A Little Cloud" to address an Irish barman, a conscious attempt to ape the ways of a dominant class, and Mrs. Kernan's acceptance of her husband's alcoholism as natural: "She accepted his frequent intemperance as part of the climate" (*D* 156). Bob Doran abandons all hope of authenticity when he allows himself to transform his flirtation with Polly into the (fully mystified) "sin" (*D* 67). And in "Ivy Day in the Committee Room," the subtext of all the conversation is politics as commodity: whether literally (being paid for canvassing) or metaphorically (the sellout of Parnell). Perhaps it is especially significant that this story, at once one of the most "social" in *Dubliners* and one that raises explicitly the question of Ireland's political past and future, should reveal a collective consciousness so thoroughly inauthentic.

Petty snobbery, yet another articulation of false consciousness, also abounds. No age group, no social institution, is uncontaminated. Father Butler's sneers in "An Encounter" about "National School boys" (*D* 20) are reproduced by the young boy narrator who has always "despised" (*D* 28) his friend Mahony.[13] Bob Doran is offended by Polly's grammar; Little Chandler feels "superior to the people he passed" (*D* 73); Mr. Alleyne calls Farrington an "impertinent ruffian" (*D* 91); Mrs. Kearney's class consciousness is aroused by certain accents (*D* 141); Mr. Power is "surprised" (*D* 154) at the manners and accents of Mr. Kernan's children and does not "relish the use of his Christian name" (*D* 160); Crofton considers his companions in the Committee Room "beneath him" (*D* 130). The litany could go on. Even Eveline, low as she is on the social scale, does not escape this particular taint if, as I believe, the phrase "other people's children" (*D* 36)—why not simply "other children"?—was an attempt by Eveline's family to put some social distance between themselves and their neighbors, an impulse, and this is the common denominator of all these examples, toward reification, the process of fragmentation and objectification both of and between people.

"A Painful Case" is central to the "problem" presented in *Dubliners*: where does one "go" if one's life is dominated by the twin ideological powers of church and state? If socialism is not yet on the horizon, as the story suggests, then one avenue of escape may be cultural nationalism (rejected by Joyce) or (and this is the answer offered repeatedly by *Dubliners*) the cultivation of the self, the displacement of energy into style, the way of paralysis. Mr. Duffy's consciousness is the most thoroughly false of all the Dubliners. Of all the characters he is the most firmly trapped within ideology since he has the necessary qualifications of intellect to penetrate the world around him, yet not only is he unaware of how deeply he himself has been penetrated by ideology but he also consciously labors to sever himself from the world as the very first sentence makes clear: "he wished to live as far as possible from the city of which he was a citizen" (*D* 107). The communal element of "citizen," the notion of shared rights and obligations, is immediately denied.

Mr. Duffy has a respectable middle-class job in a bank but (under what pressure?) is bold enough to step away from his class position to the extent of becoming a member of "an" Irish Socialist Party (*D* 110) or, rather, not a *member* of: he had merely "assisted at the meetings." This is the only example in *Dubliners* (indeed in the whole of Joyce)[14] of a bourgeois character seeking some kind of alignment with the working class. However, by this point in the story, Mr. Duffy, a "unique figure amidst a score of sober workmen in a garret" (*D* 110), has already been firmly established as a bloodless solipsist, so that his right action for the wrong reason must be viewed in the light of the narrative's persuasive irony. To accuse him of solipsism, of a relentless (and ultimately violent) assertion of subjectivity, is to draw attention to the contradiction he embodies by which this extreme subjectivity is maintained only through extreme objectification of himself, of others, and of his relations with others. Just as for Eveline, there is no "escape" for Mr. Duffy, no space in which to develop a healthy subjectivity and an authentic language.

More than anywhere else in *Dubliners*, in "A Painful Case" language calls attention to itself, so much so that it appears to "speak" the character.[15] The narrative style *is* the man. Take this sentence, describing Mr. Duffy's "fellow" socialists: "He felt that they were hard-featured realists and that they resented an exactitude which was the product of a leisure not within their reach" (*D* 111). The language of a man who "lived at a little distance from his body" (*D* 108)—this reifying sentence also illustrates one of the many "theories" Mr.

Duffy pushes upon Mrs. Sinico in exchange for which she sometimes gives out "some fact of her own life" (*D* 110). But her "facts" are never realized except, ironically, in obituary form. Such "facts" are frail manifestations of authenticity, of resistance, amidst this tide of alienated language. But though her facts "emotionalised his mental life" (*D* 111), they are insufficient to counteract the reified consciousness of a man who would compose "a short sentence about himself containing a subject in the third person and a predicate in the past tense" (*D* 108). One of the more bitter ironies is that Mr. Duffy imagines he is in full control of his language, yet his language (both text and subtext) is totally misinterpreted by Mrs. Sinico. For Mr. Duffy the purpose of existence is to refine personality out of existence. As a result, he succeeds only in conveying to her the trace of a more authentic, if deeply suppressed, personality, what the text calls "entanglement."[16]

Clearly Mr. Duffy is wholly unaware of the extent to which his intellectual life is driven by his sexual one, or he would not be so taken aback by Mrs. Sinico's bold move in catching up his hand and pressing it to her cheek. (What indeed has she responded to in him during this "ruined confessional" [*D* 112]?) He has taken the process of objectification so far, however, that he is scarcely aware, now that she is his "confessor," even of their gender difference. The latter was forced upon his consciousness at their very first meeting—how usual is it, even today, for a woman to initiate a conversation with a male stranger?—but despite his surprise at her social confidence and the narrative's insistence on her femininity ("a deliberate swoon of the pupil," "a temperament of great sensibility," "a bosom of a certain fulness" [*D* 110]), Mr. Duffy is immediately at work while they talk, trying "to fix her permanently in his memory" (*D* 109). I take this to mean not simply that he wants to recognize this face if they should chance to meet again, but that he can only "deal with" other people if he can "fix" them, attach labels to them, and thus keep them at a distance. In an unconscious maneuver responsible for the deformation of so many male-female relationships, he uses Mrs. Sinico to confirm his own sense of identity, to assert his own will to power.

In using Mrs. Sinico as a kind of machine to maximize his "profit" (the aggrandizement of his own being), Mr. Duffy acts out the mechanics of a system, capitalism, invented by men, dedicated to the accumulation of profit, whose ethic of competitiveness, though dormant on the economic front even in Mr. Duffy's time, continues to exercise its fascination wherever males are gathered together. The very texture of the prose appears to enact this will to power, for the only "break" away from the pervasively male "voice" of the narrative, the voice that seeks so doggedly to fix meaning, occurs in the two sentences spoken by Mrs. Sinico that establish the relationship. Setting aside the simple question and answer of the juror and the witness in the newspaper report,

Mrs. Sinico's words are the only spoken words in the story. Perhaps this represents one of those few points of "resistance" in *Dubliners*. This virtual exclusion of the female voice, far from being accidental, is essential to the story's realism. If the male characters in *Dubliners* are frequently deprived through colonial dependence of an authentic language, how much more is this true of the females, those "wrecks on which civilisation has been reared" (*D* 115)?[17]

Mr. Duffy, as the ending insists, requires this deprivation as a condition of existence. "A Painful Case" belongs to that minority of stories in *Dubliners* ("An Encounter," "Araby," "The Dead," and perhaps "A Little Cloud" are the others) in which a central character is afforded insight into his psychological dislocation (an insight usually reserved for the reader alone). Mr. Duffy, influenced as always by a written text (here the newspaper report, another object) that sustains his identity (literally almost: he "read the evening paper for dessert" [*D* 112]), is forced to confront his own moral responsibility for Mrs. Sinico's death. The newspaper report ends with the superbly ironic judgment: "No blame attached to anyone" (*D* 115). During the last two pages of the story Mr. Duffy is then shown suppressing this irony, absolving himself from blame. He may be despicable, but he is also tragic because at least he is forced to struggle with his "moral nature" that is "falling to pieces" (*D* 117).

His "moral nature," far from being the gift of the gods, has been produced by a particular social system, one that insists we are all always "alone" (the last word of the story) and that as such our first duty is to ourselves. Yet the story continually signals the opposite message: that only by acknowledging each individual's social production (and thus a responsibility to the collective) can fully human relations hope to develop. This ironic contradiction is the source of the tragedy. Even the title is ironic (since clearly the "painful case" is not Mrs. Sinico the suicide), and thus it aptly introduces the evasions of reality exposed in the story. Mr. Duffy's case is the more painful because he seems actually to be happy at the end: he has restored his ideologically constructed sense of reality. The last two pages reveal a terrible struggle, the end of which might have been the release of Mr. Duffy from his solipsism, a symbolic enactment of the larger social struggle necessary for release from the bondage of false consciousness. But Mr. Duffy struggles only to reinsert himself into ideology, thereby attaining a spurious peace, which is at the same time a kind of moral suicide.

If "A Painful Case" registers the dominance of the male voice, "Counterparts" foregrounds language itself. Here it is no longer a question of whether male voices predominate over female (whether quantitatively or qualitatively),[18] but rather a question of the very ownership of language. Rossi-Landi has written persuasively on linguistic "ownership," a notion he sums up in the following passage:

The ruling class arrogates to itself the control of programs "from a higher social level." It becomes plausible to define "ruling class" as *the class which possesses control over the emission and circulation of the verbal and nonverbal messages which are constitutive of a given community*. . . . Ideology is a social design; the dominant design is precisely that of the class in power. All behavioral programs are submitted, on the part of those who hold power in a given historical moment, to a vaster and more fundamental programming which consists in preserving society just as it is, or in reducing change and absorbing it into the existing system as much as possible. [190-91]

The problem is not simply that language is "possessed." Rather the use to which language is put, the subjects that are publicly discussable (what Rossi-Landi calls "models and programs"), determines an "implicit order" to suppress certain topics that the "competent" speaker, in an act of self-censorship to comply with the dominant code, will obey.

No reader will have difficulty seeing the relevance of this argument to an analysis of the hegemonic forces in Joyce's Dublin. The church and Dublin Castle between them determine the "dominant codes" and ensure what Herbert Marcuse calls the "closing of the universe of discourse" (84). (I have discussed elsewhere ["Resistance" 452-57] the existence of competing or oppositional discourses in *Dubliners*, but they tend to be marginalized. I am thinking of the acts of "resistance" performed by Lily, Miss Ivors, and Gretta in "The Dead.") Nowhere is this subservience to the dominant code more noticeable than in the highly "verbal" stories "Ivy Day in the Committee Room" and "Grace," where conversation either circles and circles as it waits for alcohol to arrive or descends into a kind of *National Enquirer* gossip about the Roman Catholic Church. No amount of low gossip will disturb the power of the church, whereas the efforts of Dubliners to live by a religious code, as Cheryl Herr argues, "perpetuate their willed blindness to the economic and political conditions which guarantee the poor quality of their lives" (245).

One of the less "verbal" stories in *Dubliners*, "Counterparts," nevertheless turns on the question of linguistic ownership, and, as I noted earlier, the twin ideological voices of Dublin establish at the beginning (with the "imperialism" of Mr. Alleyne's "North of Ireland accent") and at the end (with the repetition of the Hail Mary) such large territorial claims that the individual voice is scarcely heard; hence the story's claustrophobia. When Mr. Alleyne asks Farrington if he takes him for "an utter fool," Farrington's tongue replies: "I don't think, sir . . . that that's a fair question to put to me" (*D* 91). Farrington quickly inflates his slip of the tongue into a fully rounded saloon-bar story, confirmed by a fellow worker, Higgins, for which the reward is several rounds of drinks.[19] This gossip, which reveals a remarkable capacity to make a silk purse out of a sow's ear, occupies the middle part of the narrative but fades from memory once the money and the alcohol have run out, thus suggesting its inauthenticity as gossip: it is not sufficient to define personality, to animate, or to confer ownership.

Indeed, language constantly "slips" away from Farrington: he cannot copy even the simplest legal phrase correctly (he writes "Bernard Bernard" instead of "Bernard Bodley" [*D* 90]). To construct meaning he is forced, in this story of repetitions, to repeat himself (Bernard Bernard, the retold story, the reproduction of Mr. Alleyne's power both in his work—he is a "copyist"—and at home). He is not allowed to produce his own linguistic "models" (he has even been caught "mimicking" [*D* 92] Alleyne's Northern Irish accent). Thus Farrington (and his son) are shown using a language that is out of their control, not "theirs." The most he can hope to achieve is the cultivation of style, and even that is debased (he makes a "little cylinder of the coins between his thumb and fingers" [*D* 93]). He is helpless before Alleyne's onslaught when the latter adapts Farrington's own words in order to belittle him: "'*You—know— nothing*. Of course you know nothing'" (*D* 91). This is an accurate statement in the sense that Farrington is so utterly steeped in false consciousness that he cannot construct an accurate picture of reality.

Another obstacle to lucidity is alcohol. More than most stories (the "political" story "Ivy Day in the Committee Room" is, perhaps significantly, a serious contender), "Counterparts" concentrates on alcohol as an obliterator of consciousness and thus of judgment. Like the language Farrington unconsciously manipulates into a temporary rhetorical triumph, alcohol defers the encounter with reality. At the end of the story, Farrington's son, in one of the most poignant moments in Joyce's consistent attack upon the language of Catholic ideology, desperately gropes for the magic language that will spring him from the brutal physical oppression about to descend upon him. But he "knows nothing": the language of the Hail Mary, far from liberating him, enslaves him. That is, the boy has been educated to see the Hail Mary (rich with its promise of spiritual empowerment) as a form of bargaining chip (do this penance and your sins are forgiven) but instead will find, almost certainly, that the words are spiritually bankrupt, have no exchange value, when used in the "real" world in an attempt to ward off oppression.

While Mr. Alleyne exercises real power, the precise nature of their comparison or "counterparting" resides in Farrington's reproduction, in the private sphere, of an ideology of domination and repression. Farrington's defeats on this day are humiliatingly public, while his success (extracting an extra shilling from the pawnbroker) is merely private.[20] Any "success" he has while beating his son will also be private. Farrington's victory over his son reproduces the conditions (the conditions in which his son will come to expect repression as the norm) for the continuing existence of Alleyne's class. Similarly, though he has extracted an extra shilling from the pawnbroker,[21] he acknowledges symbolically what is true actually: time also belongs to the ruling class. In parting with his watch, this vassal of misrule yields up his connection with the world of order and ownership.

The conclusion of "Araby," where "English accents" (*D* 35) predominate, and the following three stories—"Eveline," "After the Race," and "Two Gallants"—all bring to the surface the subject of Ireland's colonial dependence. Indeed, if those three stories are viewed as a group, they can be seen as the political manifestation of the boy's coming to consciousness in "Araby": while the story traces the confusions of "love," its end points to the inferior position of the boy as Irish boy. This break from false consciousness on the boy's part is a move denied to the central characters of the next three stories. In fact the very notion of "central character" is problematic: Eveline is undoubtedly the main focus of narrative attention in her story though her only "action" is one of retreat; Jimmy, the center of attention in "After the Race," is so effete that his disappearance into an alcoholic haze seems the only appropriate conclusion for so indeterminate a character; and in "Two Gallants," it is not clear who or what the central character is. Is it Corley or Lenehan or the girl, or is it the coin for which Corley has labored so parasitically? It is as if under colonialism "character" becomes an irrelevance: for people whose lives are determined outside their own community or country, it is a sham to pretend that they can act freely. Freedom is a luxury (and a contradiction) allowed only to characters in fiction, though Joyce's fiction demonstrates that any such freedom is extremely circumscribed either by the "nightmare of history" or by economic realities. Nowhere does Joyce subscribe to the pernicious myth, so beloved by Hollywood, that the single individual can alone transform society.

"Two Gallants" seems far removed in structure and content from the preceding story, "Eveline": the first paragraph emphasizes movement and process, the free circulation of people within a busy urban environment, while the predominance (compared with "Eveline") of dialogue, of an "unceasing murmur" (*D* 49), suggests that these people do after all, especially in the mass, have a "voice." Yet, as in "Eveline," contradictions exist. The murmur of the crowd may be "unceasing," but it is also "unchanging." And why should the warm air of an August evening bring, at the height of summer, a "memory of summer" (*D* 49)? Does summer's eagerness to decline into fall reflect the city's own loss of vitality? The air "circulates" but does it thereby renew itself or merely go round in circles, like Corley's head and Lenehan's aimless wandering?

Moreover, "Two Gallants" continues, more openly, to hint at a militarized culture. Since Corley is a police informer, this is not surprising. However, the presence of several military metaphors and words with military connotations suggests that the British fettering of Irish consciousness is pervasive. "Eveline" begins with "invade"; the following words or phrases (my italics) appear only in "Two Gallants" and nowhere else in *Dubliners*:

> He was a sporting vagrant *armed* with a vast stock of stories, limericks and riddles. [*D* 50]

> The swing of his burly body made his friend *execute* a few light skips from the path to the roadway and back again. [*D* 51]

> His bulk, his easy pace, and the solid sound of his boots had something of the *conqueror* in them. He approached the young woman and, without *saluting*, began at once to converse with her. She swung her sunshade more quickly and *executed* half turns on her heels. Once or twice when he spoke to her *at close quarters* she laughed and bent her head. [*D* 55]

In their context, words like "armed" and "execute" are innocent enough; they pass unnoticed as one consumes the text. Yet the italicized words are emphatically there, and there (it bears repeating) only in "Two Gallants." What is interesting about these words is not so much their actual presence (Corley's military posture and connections provide sufficient justification) as their role in the ideological process whereby the narrator on behalf of the central characters (and, crucially, the reader also) accepts them as "innocent" in the normal course of reading. Within false consciousness, Lenehan cannot perceive that his only "armour" against the oppression that he vaguely experiences is the clever joke, the deflection (as with Farrington) of a potentially political energy into mere rhetoric. (The contradiction within Lenehan's life is reinforced by the narrator's ironic but damagingly realistic view of the obligations of friendship: "his adroitness and eloquence had always prevented his friends from forming any general policy against him" [*D* 50].)

Contradictions proliferate, always underlining the notion of dependence and paralysis. Lenehan, wearing a yachting cap, his raincoat slung over his shoulder in "toreador fashion" (*D* 50), pretends to romantic heroism in the midst of a desperate passivity betrayed by his "ravaged look" (*D* 50). He uses "foreign" speech ("the *recherché* biscuit" [*D* 50]; "gay Lothario" [*D* 52]) and walks through streets whose names are predominantly English or foreign.[22] The relationships between Lenehan, Corley, and the girl are parasitic, meaningful only in relation to the gold coin, which epiphanically "shows forth" the meaning of life in Dublin: that so much human labor and ingenuity can be devoted to so servile an end.

Perhaps the most telling moment in this litany of dependence is the scene with the harpist outside the Kildare Street club, that symbol of the Protestant

Ascendancy. The harpist plays "Silent, O Moyle," an example, one of hundreds in Joyce's texts, of his radical historicization of literary allusion: the reader is forced out of the immediate fiction toward the text alluded to, only to discover that the latter deals with a specific historical event or with an emotion whose roots can be located in a lived history. The alluded-to text will then almost invariably work ironically, reinforcing the contradictions at the heart of Joyce's texts. Thus, "Silent, O Moyle" contains the following lines:

> Yet still in her darkness doth Erin lie sleeping,
> Still doth the pale light its dawning delay.
> When will that day-star, mildly springing,
> Warm our isle with peace and love?

As Gifford notes, the pillar of the harp is "in the figure of a semi-draped woman; i.e., the harp bears another traditional symbol of Ireland, the Poor Old Woman who metamorphoses into a beautiful young woman ('Dark Rosaleen') in the presence of her true lovers, the true patriots" (58). This moment in "Two Gallants," in all its intertwining of images of Irish "silence" in the midst of "strangers," suggests strongly the inescapable fact of unequal relationships both in the fictional and the real Dublin. Lenehan is inferior to Corley; the "slavey," the lowest class of domestic servant, is inferior to both Lenehan and Corley; the waitress to Lenehan, Lenehan to his usual bar cronies, Corley to his police contacts, and everyone to the shining gold coin.

As in "Eveline," the political and the personal are seen to be inseparable. If relationships in "Eveline" are distorted by the nightmare of colonial history, in "Two Gallants" they are distorted by money itself, though money is merely the symbolic expression of all those reified relationships. Until the conclusion one may be led to believe that the elaborate voyeuristic "delay" in the narrative has to do with Corley's intention to seduce the girl, and indeed it may be that in perpetrating this ambiguity Joyce means to mock the reader's need to consume the text and to participate vicariously in the act of sexual domination. That Corley does intend to seduce the girl seems clear, but the more important point is that the girl must be shown paying for her very own seduction: even the most private personal relationships are invaded by the economic dimension. Corley's position vis à vis the girl is precisely analogous to the political relationship between imperialist power and colonial dependency (it is worth recalling that Ireland, like other dependencies, paid—in taxes, tariffs, and so forth—for the colonial relationship it had not sought), so that "Two Gallants" reproduces at a deeply internalized level the relationship between Britain and Ireland. Moreover, the story provides one of the clearest demonstrations in Joyce of ideology functioning as the reproduction of a distorted reality.

So distorted is this Dublin reality that, at least in this story, no central character can emerge. Corley is merely an instrument, an instrument of the brutality implicit in the unequal colonial relationship. Lenehan is "insensitive to all kinds of discourtesy" (*D* 50): that is, he has no being of his own. And the girl is nameless, voiceless; the description of her (*D* 55) suggests that she is "beef to the heel," mere fodder, certainly not likely to be metamorphosed into a "dark Rosaleen," in fact, likely to end up "on the turf" (*D* 53) like another of Corley's conquests. If she has a symbolic function as a woman, clearly there is little hope for Ireland if its young women can so easily be bought and if they are prepared to pay to be bought. These people are so ultimately cut off from the forces of production that they act like automatons within the hideous process of colonialism and its attendant economic exploitation. Relationships are reified; even language itself (in Lenehan's limericks and riddles) becomes objectified, a weapon or commodity to control the behavior of other people. How appropriate therefore that all these distortions and contradictions should cohere at the last moment in the image of the gold coin, the perfect symbol in history of commodity fetishism and unequal relationships. And, as if to seal these characters' fate, the British sovereign's head, we must assume, nestles comfortably in Corley's palm.

Notes

1. I have discussed several of these issues in an earlier essay, where I also suggested that some of the stories in *Dubliners* (especially "The Dead") show signs of a healthy "resistance" to the prevailing paralysis.

2. See Dominic Manganiello for a comprehensive discussion of Joyce's early "socialism."

3. Cheryl Herr draws attention to Joyce's indictment of the church's cultural function as an economic institution (245); see also note 10.

4. However, much documentary evidence exists to support Joyce's view of Irish life as paralyzed in the period, roughly, of 1904-6 (see Joseph V. O'Brien and Mary Daly).

5. Of course, the alert reader who knows that Purdon Street was the main street in Dublin's red-light district can easily deconstruct Father Purdon's specious "authority" (see Don Gifford 104).

6. In "Eveline," similarly, we learn that Eveline's neighborhood has been developed by a Belfast man, one contributory factor in her spiritual impoverishment.

7. This English girl performs the same function as her compatriot at the end of "Araby": she punctures romantic illusions. Politically, the deflation indicates that the Irish should not look to England, the source of their "troubles," for help, or the dream of absorption into English life is a confession of defeat.

8. Herr makes the further point that Mr. Kernan has been "destroyed not so much by drink as by changes in the economic environment" (241).

9. One further instance of English domination of Irish consciousness is Joe Dillon's adolescent reading matter, *"The Union Jack, Pluck* and *The Halfpenny Marvel"* (*D* 19).

10. Herr makes a similar point when she refers to "the church's intimate ties to the economic system" (239).

11. For the concept of linguistic ownership, see Ferruccio Rossi-Landi.

12. Jimmy's father, who grew rich as a butcher and even richer when he secured the police contracts, is referred to as a "merchant prince" (*D* 43). Most of the characters in *Dubliners* belong to the petty bourgeoisie, the rest dividing into the solid middle class (insofar as anything in Joyce's Dublin can be said to be "solid") and the respectable working class. The lines between the three classes are very thin, and a character's class position can sometimes depend as much on his own estimation of himself as on objective factors such as ownership or employment, income, property, and so forth. Apart from Jimmy, I would assert that the bourgeoisie proper includes Mr. Duffy ("A Painful Case"); Mrs. Kearney and possibly O'Madden Burke ("A Mother"); possibly Martin Cunningham and Mr. Power ("Grace"); and Gabriel Conroy and his aunts. The respectable working class includes Eveline and Maria ("Clay").

13. In 1913 the schoolboys of St. Thomas's National School in Lower Rutland Street joined Larkin's strikers during the Dublin Tramway dispute (O'Brien 231).

14. Two other possible examples are Hynes's defense of Colgan, "the working man" (*D* 121), and Bloom's socialist fantasies in "Circe." Neither, however, involves any active commitment, however minimal, such as Mr. Duffy has shown.

15. The same phenomenon occurs in the hellfire sermons in *A Portrait of the Artist as a Young Man.*

16. "Little by little he entangled his thoughts with hers" (*D* 110) and "Little by little, as their thoughts entangled" (*D* 111).

17. A participant at the 1988 Joyce symposium in Venice, failing to see this realism, berated Joyce for giving men a 2 to 1 speech advantage over women in *Dubliners.*

18. Marilyn French makes an interesting case for the existence of "gender principles" in literature and life. "Masculine literature," she argues, is "linear" and "goal" oriented, appealing to a "cosmic order" that "sanctions the masculine claim to legitimacy and right." "Feminine" literature is "circular and eternal." In feminine literature "cause and effect and chronology may be entirely suspended in favor of psychological, emotional and associational links." Without "goals," it "celebrates flux, the moment, sensation and emotions" (*Shakespeare's* 26). (Incidentally, French's theory nicely illustrates the contradiction of Harlequin Romance: an entirely "masculine" form aimed at an entirely female audience.) Clearly, French's distinction between masculine and feminine literature can be applied fruitfully to the work of Joyce. However, were I a female (especially one involved in political activism), I should be a little uneasy at the notion that the abandonment of a link between cause and effect is reason for celebration.

19. French, in an excellent, though insufficiently politicized, article, sees Farrington's slip as a conscious impertinence stimulated by the presence of the sexually alluring Miss Delacourt ("Missing Pieces" 459).

20. His retort to Alleyne is a public "success," but its ephemeral nature and the fact that it will almost certainly cost him his job make it merely a Pyrrhic victory.

21. For the prevalence of pawnbroking, see O'Brien (162).

22. Terence Brown notes that the names of streets and buildings in "Two Gallants" "toll with the inevitability of exclusion" (14).

Works Cited

Althusser, Louis. *Lenin and Philosophy and Other Essays*. Trans. Ben Brewster. New York: Monthly Review, 1971.

Brown, Terence. "The Dublin of *Dubliners*." In *James Joyce: An International Perspective*, ed. Suheil Bushrui and Bernard Benstock, 11-18. Gerrards Cross, Buckinghamshire: Smythe, 1982.

Daly, Mary. *Dublin: The Deposed Capital*. Cork: Cork Univ. Press, 1984.

French, Marilyn. "Missing Pieces in Joyce's *Dubliners*." *Twentieth Century Literature* 24 (1978): 443-72.

———. *Shakespeare's Division of Experience*. New York: Ballantine, 1983.

Gifford, Don. *Joyce Annotated: Notes for* Dubliners *and* A Portrait of the Artist as a Young Man. Berkeley: Univ. of California Press, 1982.

Herr, Cheryl. *Joyce's Anatomy of Culture*. Urbana: Univ. of Illinois Press, 1986.

Hobsbawm, Eric. "Marx and History." *New Left Review* 143 (1984): 38-47.

Joyce, James. *Dubliners*. Ed. Robert Scholes in consultation with Richard Ellmann. New York: Viking, 1967.

———. *A Portrait of the Artist as a Young Man*. Ed. Richard Ellmann. New York: Viking, 1964.

———. *Ulysses*. Ed. Hans Walter Gabler et al. Harmondsworth: Penguin, 1986.

Manganiello, Dominic. *Joyce's Politics*. London: Routledge, 1980.

Marcuse, Herbert. *One-Dimensional Man: Studies in the Ideology of Advanced Industrial Society*. Boston: Beacon, 1964.

Marx, Karl, and Friedrich Engels. *The German Ideology*. In *The Marxist Reader*, ed. Emile Burns. New York: Avenel, 1982.

O'Brien, Joseph V. *"Dear, Dirty Dublin": A City in Distress, 1899-1916*. Berkeley: Univ. of California Press, 1982.

Rossi-Landi, Ferruccio. *Linguistics and Economics*. The Hague: Mouton, 1977.

Schlossman, Beryl. *Joyce's Catholic Comedy of Language*. Madison: Univ. of Wisconsin Press, 1985.

Williams, Trevor L. "Resistance to Paralysis in *Dubliners*." *Modern Fiction Studies* 35 (1989): 437-57.

CHAPTER SIX

"Taking the Biscuit"
Narrative Cheekiness in *Dubliners*

Claire A. Culleton

What does it mean when a character murmurs "biscuitfully to the dusty windowpane" (*U* 7.237-38)?[1] When Professor MacHugh, a character in episode seven of *Ulysses,* is described in this way, readers must go back to the early *Dubliners* story "Two Gallants" to exact full meaning and amusement from Joyce's adverbial neologism, "biscuitfully." Importantly, when the neologism appears in "Aeolus," Professor MacHugh is busy trying to gather an audience in the newsroom; but other characters continue to interrupt and distract him from his narration. Though Professor MacHugh munches on a biscuit as he softly murmurs to the dusty windowpane, the word "biscuitfully" here also alludes to a similar narrative dilemma first detailed in "Two Gallants," where Lenehan's attempts at breaking into Corley's narrative are punctuated by his enthusiastic exclamation "that takes the biscuit." Because Corley talks incessantly, Lenehan can barely get a word in and can only interrupt his friend's narrative by congratulating him on his cheekiness, saying to Corley, "That takes the biscuit!" "[t]hat takes the solitary, unique, and, if I may so call it, *recherché* biscuit!" and "[t]hat emphatically takes the biscuit" (*D* 50, 51). No doubt, Lenehan's presence in the "Aeolus" chapter of *Ulysses* may account for Joyce's playful biscuit allusion, but it is important to note that not only is the narrator's diction affected by Lenehan's presence, but MacHugh's behavior also is influenced and modulated by the mere presence of Lenehan, Joyce's wistful, biscuitful, *Dubliners* character. Since it is most likely not fortuity but design that links these two examples, an analysis of the biscuit connection Joyce generates via Lenehan can inform a variety of approaches to Joyce's experimental narratology.

Joyce no doubt had a lot of fun exploiting the phrase "taking the biscuit," particularly because the phrase would suggest so many things to his readers. Lenehan employs the phrase in *Dubliners* (and later in *Ulysses*) as an expletive connoting cheekiness. However, it also functions as an ecumenical pun on the taking of the eucharistic wafer, as Joyce suggests in "The Sisters," where the unnamed narrator accepts a "little glass of wine" but declines to "take some cream crackers" (*D* 15), an ecumenical motif that Joyce reinforces later in "Two Gallants" when he describes Lenehan as a "disciple" (*D* 60) who has eaten nothing all day but some biscuits "he had asked two grudging curates to bring him" (*D* 57). The phrase also encodes a sexual "taking" since "biscuit," like "cookie," "cake," and "tart," is early twentieth-century slang for a prostitute (Beale 35, 74, 103, 454-55). The phrase prefigures, as well, Corley's nefarious hustling of the slavey, since "taking the cake" was a particular form of trickery used on passenger railway trains. The trickster, uniformed (like Lenehan and Corley) only by a cap, would tell passengers that he was traveling with the train. Then he would offer to insure their luggage, money, and other valuables, take articles away to be "assessed," and pocket the premium and the valuables (Partridge 713).

Lenehan's phrase "taking the biscuit" touches on all of these interpretations, not least of all those associated with the underworld. But it develops in *Dubliners* into an expression peculiar to the Joycean narrative, since in "Two Gallants" it suggests that a character can take the narrative biscuit—the bread and water of a story—and run with it, stealing the narrative from the implied narrator or from other characters who attempt to usurp the narrator's position, not only inserting himself or herself into the narrative but hoarding it as well, until another character or narrator reclaims it. Nowhere is this sort of theft more evident than in Joyce's *Dubliners*, where characters often interrupt the narrative, preside over their own "objective" descriptions, purloin, maneuver, and manipulate narrative segments, and mutiny aggressively against the stifling reticence imposed by the narrative voice. In doing so, they effectively efface what Gérard Genette calls "the frontiers of [narrative] operation, the conditions of its existence" (127). In *Dubliners*, characters "take the biscuit" in order to empower themselves and to rage against a hierarchy that fetishizes the narrator. It is precisely these changes in the narrative register, where the spectacle of characters' actions manifest diegetic mutiny, that I wish to examine here.[2]

Lenehan's characteristic phrase, "that takes the biscuit," signals his own entry into the narrative discourse of the story and prefaces his attempts to break into the narrative. As such, the phrase "taking the biscuit" becomes a metaphor of narrative control not only here but even in Joyce's later works, where one character's efforts to become engaged in the narrative telling of a story continually are usurped by other characters who jockey in chorus for narrative position, commandeering, supplanting, and straitjacketing the narrative voice in an inventive and subversive transmigration of narrative responsibility. I refer to this narrative stealing as "taking the biscuit" since Joyce introduces the technique so masterfully in *Dubliners*, where Lenehan's characteristic utterances shape the narrative ebb and flow and signal linguistic gaps and semantic holes in the narrative integrity of the short story collection. Because "taking the biscuit" is a narrative strategy that Joyce further develops and exploits in *Ulysses,* it is important to see its nascent counterpart in *Dubliners.*

In an attempt to identify and register the multiple positions in any given story's narrative point of view, Hugh Kenner and Shari and Bernard Benstock have successfully detailed and catalogued Joyce's narrative experimentation across his short stories and novels, referring to stratagem they have termed the "Uncle Charles Principle" (Kenner 15-38) and the "Benstock Principle" (Benstock and Benstock 10-21) and classifying "Joyce's tendency to insert a character's characteristic speech without quote marks into the narrator's discourse" (Mosher 44). Paul van Caspel, in a discussion of the "Scylla and Charybdis" episode of *Ulysses,* for example, further notes that a character's dialogue, too, often is affected by the narrative voice of the episode, and that conversely the narrative voice of an episode often is shaped or affected by one or more of the characters' dialogue (137-39). This technique—so thoughtfully explored by van Caspel—has an early counterpart in *Dubliners,* and because Joyce enlarges this strategy in later works, especially *Ulysses,* it is important to trace its early analogues and to pursue its uncelebrated complements.

Both Kenner and the Benstocks suggest that characters can and do affect, infect, and influence the narrative telling in Joyce, but I argue that characters more often steal it, that they supplant whatever we want to call the "traditional" narrator or narrative voice on duty and straitjacket him, limiting his involvement in the narrative telling, not merely influencing his involvement but aggressively mutinying against the confines and constraints of narrative hierarchy. This narrative paradigm (the Biscuit Principle) relies not only on a weak, limited, and impotent narrator but on strong and commandeering characters as well and as such, differs significantly from the Uncles Charles and Benstock Principles.

Readers have long noticed that one of the particularly interesting elements of the narrative experimentation Joyce uses in *Dubliners* is that the characters often affect the telling of the story. Kenner and the Benstocks argue, for example, that it is the narrator's sensitivity and familiarity that allows him to absorb and approximate the language of his characters. I disagree with their characterization and suggest that it is not the narrator's sensitivity but his lack of control at all levels that allows for mutinous intervention; his sensitivity does not put the narrative at risk so much as does his weak-kneed, Milquetoast personality. These traits, specifically, leave the narrator co-optable and the narrative open to purloinment. Kenner and the Benstocks have not probed far enough into the typical Joycean narrator's character. On closer examination, it becomes clear that this character is a veritable pushover—ripe for the overtaking—a "keep your day job" sort of narrator who allows for and even invites his own periodic (and parodic) overthrows.

Challenging the concept of the conventional "narrative voice," Joyce develops in *Dubliners* a new kind of narrator, one whose voice not only is compromised but co-opted by the thinking and telling minds of the characters whose stories he unfolds, a narrator whose knowledge is more limited than the characters whose action he details. The prototypical *Dubliners* narrator works from a limited vision and characteristically sponges information off the dialogue, passing it off as his own. In "Ivy Day in the Committee Room," for example, the narrator can only describe incoming characters and cannot identify them by name until one of the canvassers salutes them. The narrator displays his ignorance, for example, when Father Keon enters: "A person resembling a poor clergyman or a poor actor appeared in the doorway" (*D* 125). Until Mr. Henchy salutes Keon by name, the narrator remains helplessly unable to identify him, place him, or predict his role in the developing story. The narrator's nominal ignorance is sometimes seen as a deliberate, even covert narrative strategy: the narrator does not identify characters by name in order to impersonalize them or to shroud their entrances with mystery or drama. It is more likely, though, that the narrator is unacquainted with the characters and scrambles to cadge what information he can from the dialogue he also cannot control.

Further into the story, the narrator reveals his greenness again when Crofton and Lyons enter; until they are greeted by the others, the narrator can only describe them as "the fat man" and "the young man":

> Here two men entered the room. One of them was a very fat man, whose blue serge clothes seemed to be in danger of falling from his sloping figure. He had a big face which resembled a young ox's face in expression, staring blue eyes and a grizzled moustache. The other man, who was much younger and frailer, had a thin clean-shaven face. He wore a very high double collar and a wide-brimmed bowler hat.
> —Hello, Crofton! said Mr Henchy to the fat man. Talk of the devil. . . .
> —Where did the boose come from? asked the young man. Did the cow calve?
> —O, of course, Lyons spots the drink first thing! said Mr O'Connor, laughing. [*D* 130]

Once identified by Henchy and O'Connor, Crofton and Lyons become part of the dramatis personae of "Ivy Day" and the narrator immediately refers to them by name in future narrative segments: "Mr Crofton sat down on a box and looked fixedly at the other bottle on the hob," for example, and "Mr Lyons sat on the edge of the table, pushed his hat towards the nape of his neck and began to swing his legs" (*D* 130).

This brand of what has been called selective omniscience on the narrator's part (Mosher 47) continually reminds us that the Joycean narrator typically is not so well-informed as we would have him be; rather, his information characteristically issues from outside sources, and his efforts to disguise his narrative naivete do not go easily unnoticed. Like Lenehan, the narrator too is a "leech" (*D* 50) and feeds off the remarks and comments of the characters whose stories he tells. Even more characteristic, the narrator appears to change dramatically throughout the course of the story's narration, going from a mere denizen of the pub in "Grace," for example, to a knowledgeable raconteur able to fill in detailed background information about Kernan and Power when necessary, just as his narrator counterpart was able to do in "Ivy Day" with characters such as Tierney and O'Connor.

The selective omniscience displayed by Joyce's *Dubliners* narrators reveals something more akin to narrational improvisation than narrational omniscience. Characteristically, they scramble to fill in information, and during their scrambling, they leave themselves open to mutiny. It is not merely that the narrators are weak or that their dilemmas are complicated by the fact that they are narrators of a narrative they cannot control, as Bernard Benstock suggests (12). Rather, the narrator senses his vulnerable position vis-à-vis the characters—that at any moment they will take over—so he expends a great deal of effort to mask his imperfections and to hide detection of the impending mutiny from the reader. Typically, he overinvests the narrative at these moments with physical description, as when he describes Crofton and Lyons's entrances in "Ivy Day" by lingering on their physical attributes. When we find the narrator moving from narration to description, loitering on the attributes of other characters or objects, for example, we discover, as Genette suggests in *Figures of Literary Discourse,* that the narrator's attempts call attention to spectacle, not to story, and allow him "to suspend the course of time and to contribute to spreading the narrative in space" (136). This buys him a little time. However, he cannot keep his eyes or his ears on all of his characters at once. Thus, in his effort to suspend time while scrambling for information to mask his incompetence, he leaves the narrative open to revolt.

With so many new characters making entrances, the narrator's presumed omniscience is impaired by the very characters whose stories he attempts to detail. Caught up in the complexities of the telling, the narrator drops the biscuit, leaving the narrative position vulnerable, ripe for the taking, and teeming as a result with multiple and conflicting points of view. There is never so much omniscience in *Dubliners* that the narrator's position is ever unchallengeable; at best, the narrator works from a position of "functional prescience" (Bernard Benstock 9), but it is his functional prescience that handicaps him.

Disadvantaged by his functional prescience, and arguably functionally *im*prescient or negligible, the narrator invites and even embraces mutiny; when the characters see that the narrator is unable to perform, they take over and direct narrative segments themselves, collating a variety of information unknown and most likely unknowable to the narrator. Sensing and then seizing the opportunity to fill in the gaps, Joyce's Dubliners rise to the occasion, stepping in where the narrator fails to hit the mark. It is as if chance furnishes the narrator what he needs—a claim Joyce made about his own work[3]—and the best the narrator can do is mask his negligence while seeming in control of the narrative. The Uncle Charles and the Benstock Principles buy into the myth of the narrator's presumed control over the narrative, suggesting that most Joycean narrators permit character intervention and encode their characters' desires into the language of the narrative. However, it seems more likely that the narrator gives in to the commotion and ultimately surrenders to his cast of characters instead. Weakened, displaced, and converted into a sidelines player, the narrator relinquishes, vanquished by the clamoring mob, as other characters take the biscuit and redirect the narrative.

Joyce's "Two Gallants" is a good example of this particular narrative strategy. Immediately into "Two Gallants," the reader learns that the streets of Dublin are alive with an "unchanging unceasing murmur" (*D* 49). Aside from that murmur, the two main characters in the story are noted for their own garrulous murmurs: Corley is "just bringing a long monologue to a close" (*D* 49), and Lenehan is tired after "talking all the afternoon in a public-house in Dorset Street" (*D* 50). With loquacious characters such as these vying against each other for their own narrative position, Joyce warns us from the onset of "Two Gallants" that Corley and Lenehan will not only fight to speak and outspeak one another but that the assumed "narrator" of "Two Gallants" is in for a bumpy ride, since he will no doubt be supplanted as storyteller.

Corley dominates the dialogue of "Two Gallants," but Lenehan manages to interrupt Corley's monologue a number of times, each time exclaiming that Corley's tale "takes the biscuit" (*D* 50, 51), each time introducing the biscuit element. Since these are the only times Lenehan interrupts Corley's monologue before the two men part, "taking the biscuit" becomes a linguistic signal or metaphor on Lenehan's part for stealing back the narrative: as soon as Lenehan "takes the biscuit," he becomes the new narrator, displacing Corley, who with his long monologue had displaced the "traditional" narrator of "Two Gallants" to begin with. But Lenehan has no original response to make. Ironically, he steals a narrative position only to use it to fawn over Corley and to reinforce his friend's dubious ego, most often "leaving his flattery open to the interpretation of raillery" (*D* 52): "—You're what I call a gay Lothario, said Lenehan. And the proper kind of a Lothario, too!" (*D* 52), for example, and

"—Ecod! Corley, you know how to take them" (D 53). Vanquished in conversation by Corley's long monologue, and having to compete with the murmuring Dublin streets, Lenehan's only way of getting a word in is by taking the biscuit, by flattering his companion through his servility and by redirecting the narrative's attention to himself.

Lenehan's narrative is indeed a simple one: overcome by his own anxiety about the success of Corley's proposed scheme, Lenehan resorts to the only behavior that has stood him in good stead, obsequiousness, and his uneasiness lends him the impulse to interrupt Corley's monologue at salient points, punctuating his entry into the Symbolic with desperate, stiletto-like refrains. Though described by the narrator as talkative, Lenehan is uncharacteristically muted by Corley; at one point, he decides to "[say] no more" because he does not want to "ruffle his friend's temper" (D 53, 54), for example, and twice emits a mute, noiseless laugh (D 50, 51). Once the two men part—Corley to meet the slavey and Lenehan to wander four and a half miles of Dublin streets—Lenehan goes to the Refreshment Bar and orders a plate of peas because he realizes that biscuits were all he had eaten since breakfast time (D 57). To be sure, Lenehan's hunger stems from the fact that he has only been allowed to "bite" into the present narrative a couple of times. Only in his solitude does Lenehan pick up the biscuit again and narrate the details of his life: just as "the air which the harpist had played began to control his movements" (D 56), Lenehan also feels the pull and restraint of the narrative and steps in to tell his own version of his life, a narrative that encodes an intensely personal look at his social and civic failures. He tries to rewrite his role and considers settling down, envisioning the possibilities of a warm fire, a good job, and a simple-minded girl (D 58). Plaintively, he asks, "Would he never get a good job? Would he never have a home of his own?" (D 58), in appeal to the soothsayer narrator he attempts and desires to dethrone.

The problem of narrative responsibility is further complicated in a short story such as "Eveline," where Eveline involves herself so minimally in the telling that she hardly "takes the biscuit" at all. Although in a self-conscious act to take the biscuit she presumably narrates her story in the letters she leaves for her father and brother (D 39), those letters remain undisturbed; hers is an impulse that is registered but not investigated by the weak-kneed and uncurious narrator she tries to supplant. Like Poe's purloined letter—invisible though in plain sight—Eveline's narratives are as encased as her life has been, anatomically enveloped stories that sit in obvious display but lay undisturbed and unprobed by the narrator who directs her story. The "answer" lies within those envelopes, but the narrator is neither savvy nor sophisticated enough to think of looking there. Eveline's valiant attempt to take the biscuit is thwarted by the narrator if only because it is an effort that is unprobed. To be sure, readers might argue that it is not why Eveline thinks of leaving that remains important to the story but why, at the end, she thinks of staying. Perhaps she senses the futility and sees the narrator's indifference to her motivations as emblematic of her family's and her culture's apathy; she returns to retrieve those very personal narratives. Female characters in Joyce have a unique position in terms of taking the biscuit, in that their attempts are enfeebled by the narrative voice and discredited by the cultural cast of characters with whom they share their fictional lives. Bernard Benstock notes that Joyce's Dublin women "find the way barred to the exposition of [their] own discourse" (23) and seek alternate means of self-expression, resorting with as much aggression as culturally permitted to various stratagem to narrate the suppressed stories of their lives. For example, Mrs. Kearney, Benstock argues, waits two decades before she commandeers the narrative of her life, and "with decanters of whisky, and blush-pink charmeuse, and offers of two-shilling tickets, she [buys] herself an audience" (23). Benstock further argues that disadvantaged by their gender, and as if to "countermand the vow of silence foisted on them," Joyce's women characters "mount a major narrative campaign, especially in the light of masculine inadequacy" (25), describing Maria's telling narrative—"I Dreamt that I Dwelt"— as a narrational confession akin to Aunt Julia's "Arrayed for the Bridal." Because so little narrative attention is lent to the implications of Maria's and Aunt Julia's confessions, the inadequacy Benstock identifies extends as well to the culpable narrators, whose interests remain unpiqued by the women's efforts just as it had in the case of Eveline's confessional letters.

The women try to speak, they try to take the biscuit, but the fault for their inadequate narratives falls on them and not on the narrators whose disingenuous attention encourages their dismissal. As a result, readers characteristically fault the women for their passivity, even though the narrators rely on those culturally endowed traits to distract attention from their own narrational inadequacies. The women's passivity, their seeming nonintervention, provides the perfect alibi for their narrators, and readers remark on the narrators' "functional prescience" instead of on the narrators' incommensurate performance. "Taking the biscuit" is certainly a political act that authorizes and validates hierarchies of gender, class, and status. Not inconsequentially, Father Purdon has little trouble commandeering the narrative at the end of "Grace" and gets the last word in as easily as the sanctimonious O'Madden Burke, who successfully punctuates the ending of "A Mother" by validating Holohan's behavior while at the same time condemning Mrs. Kearney's: "—You did the proper thing, Holohan, said Mr O'Madden Burke, poised upon his umbrella in approval" (*D* 149). The phallic umbrella, like the world of business and accounting alluded to in the closing section of "Grace," symbolizes the stratified male economic world that inhibits and disallows women's easy accessibility to the narrative. More important, O'Madden Burke wields his umbrella as a pike, staving off not only the disempowered women of *Dubliners* but the displaced and castrated narrators as well. Purdon and O'Madden Burke purloin the narrative so that they end up the victors.

This sort of narrative shuffling and narrative substitution becomes evident in "A Little Cloud" as well, where the narrative shifts in style and tone depend upon whether the narrative is purloined by Chandler or by Gallaher, Chandler's antagonistic friend; it is equally dependent upon the way the two men assess themselves and one another, since so much of that story relies upon Chandler and Gallaher's posturings, evaluations, and counterevaluations. When we are told by the presumed narrative voice, for example, "That was Ignatius Gallaher all out; and, damn it, you couldn't but admire him for it" (*D* 73), we might suspect that the colloquial "all out" and "damn it" specifically are generated and inserted by Chandler, since they reflect Chandler's drunken bravado. But the narrative "damn it" signals Chandler's attempt to imitate Gallaher's characteristic bravado, since he had just been thinking of Gallaher's courageous move to London. Thus, when Chandler takes the narrative biscuit, when he tries to manipulate the narrative objectivity, his own thoughts are influenced and further manipulated by the characteristic utterances of Gallaher, making his insertion an unusually ventriloquistic and polyphonic one. His "damn it" reveals his own lust for the bravura that attends adventure, and when he inserts himself into the narrative telling, when he takes the biscuit, he informs the text about the ways in which he wants to be—and insists on being—described, calling attention to attributes in himself or in Gallaher that he most prizes or fears.

We realize, for example, that Chandler wants to be described as "stoutly," since that word describes the way he replies to Gallaher's condescension of connubial bliss (*D* 81). But the word characterizes the way Chandler feels, not the way he acts, when he "stoutly" repeats that Gallaher would "put his head in the sack" like everyone else if he could find the girl (*D* 81). Additionally, we can gauge a dichotomy or tension in the narrative here because while Chandler inserts the word "stoutly" into the narrative, the narrating intelligence undercuts Chandler's insertion and attempts to reestablish its "objectivity" by telling the reader instead that Chandler had only "slightly emphasised his tone" (*D* 81). "Stoutly" cannot accurately describe Chandler because the reader has already been forewarned of Chandler's "under the average" stature and of his fragile, slight frame (*D* 70). Clearly, Chandler's ego invades the narrative here, and at this particular point, the degree of "truth" that marks the difference between the subjective and objective narration reveals Chandler's maneuvering hand within the narrative.

Any character's attempt to "take the biscuit" requires dexterity and keen agility because stealing the narrative even for a moment can be as difficult and as messy as catching the cabbage, a policemen's training technique that Martin Cunningham jokingly describes in "Grace":

> —It is supposed—they say, you know—to take place in the depot where they get these thundering big country fellows, omadhauns, you know, to drill. The sergeant makes them stand in a row against the wall and held up their plates.
> He illustrated the story by grotesque gestures.
> —At dinner, you know. Then he has a bloody big bowl of cabbage before him on the table and a bloody big spoon like a shovel. He takes up a wad of cabbage on the spoon and pegs it across the room and the poor devils have to try and catch it on their plates: *65, catch your cabbage.* [*D* 161]

Kernan and his friends have no doubt heard the story already, since "everyone laugh[s]" when Cunningham alludes to the punchline earlier (*D* 161), but no one dares to take the biscuit from him. Even M'Coy, "who wanted to enter the conversation by any door, pretended that he had never heard the story" (*D* 161), and he punctuates Cunningham's narrative with the self-reflexive comment, "—It's better to have nothing to say to them" (*D* 161). Cunningham commands a respect that even his comrades dare not disrupt. Unlike Professor MacHugh, Cunningham need not speak biscuitfully to this group.

Because Joyce's technique in *Dubliners* lends such resonance to narrative stratagems he exploits later in *Ulysses,* it is useful to examine two short counterparts from the novel that indicate Joyce's development of the Biscuit Principle. The characters' good behavior in "Grace," for example, can be compared with two examples from the Hades episode of *Ulysses*—one that focuses again on Cunningham, and the other on Bloom.

Though Simon Dedalus eagerly interrupts Bloom's narrative concerning Reuben J. Dodd and son, interjecting into Bloom's narrative his own hyperbole and colorful rhetoric, Martin Cunningham subversively takes the biscuit and delivers Bloom's punchline: "—And Reuben J, Martin Cunningham said, gave the boatman a florin for saving his son's life" (*U* 6.286-87). If we compare this narrative maneuvering with the comical narrative delivered by caretaker O'Connell at Dignam's funeral (*U* 6.717-34)—a joke he narrates to Cunningham, Dedalus, Lambert, and Menton, a joke they most likely have already heard since they listen with "vacant smiles" (*U* 6.721)—it is important to realize that no one interrupts O'Connell. Cunningham even acknowledges its intention, saying, "—That's all done with a purpose. . . . To cheer a fellow up. . . . It's pure good-heartedness: damn the thing else" (*U* 6.735-38). Whereas Cunningham commands a certain respect in "Grace" and in *Ulysses,* Bloom clearly does not. His biscuitful attempts at stealing the narrative are quickly suppressed, seditiously undercut, and subversively overpowered by the lot of

Catholic compatriots. Taking the biscuit is related to the power structure and imitates the feeding chain: like wolves, the leaders eat first. Cunningham is a leader, while Bloom is not.

In addition to the many examples Joyce provides in *Dubliners*, the "Hades" episode of *Ulysses* provides other examples of Joyce's large-scale use of the "taking the biscuit" strategy and is a good episode to investigate for narrative polyphony since it is the first chapter in *Ulysses* where a dozen or more characters, each with a distinguishable rhetoric, dip into the narrative and take the biscuit. Bloom does this most often, but the way he manipulates himself into the narrative in "Hades" differs from the way other characters in *Ulysses* insert themselves into the narrative of the first three chapters. Unlike the way Stephen's stream-of-consciousness invades the "Telemachus" episode ("Chrysostomos" and "Old shrunken paps" [*U* 1.26; 1.398]), Bloom's thoughts usually are prefaced by some kind of narrating intelligence. That is, a paragraph or segment usually starts off as "pure" narrative but ends up as stream-of-consciousness. The effect is jarring and anacoluthic, as in the following example where Bloom interjects "always in front of us" into the narrative, causing an abrupt grammatical, syntactical, and semantic change: "After a moment he followed the others in, blinking in the screened light. The coffin lay on its bier before the chancel, four tall yellow candles at its corners. Always in front of us. Corny Kelleher, laying a wreath at each fore corner, beckoned to the boy to kneel" (*U* 6.581-84).

Here, the narrator seems familiar with items associated with the Catholic mass and names the chancel, for example, but Bloom soon takes the biscuit more aggressively and narrates a sizable portion of "Hades." In addition to the personal insertions he injects into the third-person narration, such as "always in front of us," about halfway into the chapter the narrator no longer sounds minimally familiar with the mass but begins to sound as unknowledgeable and innocent of the Catholic burial rites as Bloom is himself. What has happened here is that Bloom has cast himself in the role of narrative figure; he has supplanted the narrator and tries to mask his bravado by feigning what he thinks of as all-important narrative objectivity.

These next two examples, narrated in third-person, reveal how the narrator is ignorant of the names of objects associated with the mass: "A server bearing a brass bucket with something in it came out through a door" (*U* 6.589-90) and "The priest took a stick with a knob at the end of it out of the boy's bucket and shook it over the coffin. Then he walked to the other end and shook it again. Then he came back and put it back in the bucket" (*U* 6.614-16). While these bits are narrated allegedly by a third person, that third person clearly is Bloom himself, who objectively reports much of the action of the chapter while he subjectively comments on it at the same time.

Because he does not know what to call the ritualized objects, he succeeds in reducing the Catholic ritual to absurdity. We know that Bloom tries to remain serious during the service—he had to stop himself from singing "the ree the ra the ree the ra the roo," thinking "Lord I mustn't lilt here (*U* 6.640)—so these examples of Bloom's impersonal, unbiased reporting may be nothing more than exercises to maintain his gravity.

If these are Bloom's attempts at objective narration, it is significant that even his attempts to take the biscuit are rarely sustained, and his narrative segments usually disintegrate into first-person narration though they begin with innocuous objectivity: "The server piped the answers in the treble. I often thought it would be better to have boy servants. Up to fifteen or so. After that, of course . . . " (*U* 6.619-20). He, too, in other words, permits narrative polyphony even in his own "objective" segments and finds it hard to resist taking the biscuit from himself.

Of course, it would be impossible for Bloom not to permit other voices—even his own—to invade his narrative, to take the biscuit, specifically because even his own voice is polyphonic. Just as Stephen's voice in the "Proteus" episode is peppered with traces of his father's voice, Mulligan's voice, Deasy's voice, and Richie Goulding's voice, Bloom's voice also subsumes the language and rhetoric of other characters in the novel, and conversely, the narrator's diction is often affected and co-opted by a character's commanding presence, such as Lenehan's in "Aeolus." Clearly, characters in Joyce seem to practice the same trickery of Lenehan in "Two Gallants": like him, they hold themselves nimbly at the borders of the company until they are included in a round (*D* 50), and when the invitation is slow in coming, they jump right in, maneuver their own narrative segments, and insist on redirecting the narrative's attention on them, on their stories, on their characteristic voices. Though Joyce clearly indicates that multiple characters can feast upon the same biscuit before the narrator ever gets his lunch back, he also encodes his characters' proverbial hunger to tell the story and ushers in a new brand of narrative polyphony that differs in aggressivity from the Uncle Charles Principle and from the Benstock Principle.

Though Lenehan figures as one of the most colorful minor characters in *Ulysses,* he arrives in Joyce's 1922 novel with as much "baggage" as M'Coy, whose disingenuous searches for valises and portmanteaus precede him. Lenehan's characteristic refrain, "that takes the biscuit," influences not only his own gastronomical adventures—he had eaten nothing but a few biscuits since breakfast—but the behavior of the characters with whom he comes in contact. This may be why the murmuring MacHugh chews and whispers "biscuitfully," and why the angry Citizen specifically hurls a biscuit tin in Lenehan's company at the triumphant ben Bloom Elijah as the jarvey rounds the corner. If Lenehan had not literally taken the biscuits from the grudging curates at the pub earlier that morning (*D* 57), he, like so many other narrator-commando-wannabes in Joyce, would have starved just to get a word in edgewise.

Notes

The author wishes to thank Susan Darrah, Brent Fishbaugh, Sean Murphy, and Shawn St. Jean for commenting on early drafts of this essay.

1. Standard abbreviations for Joyce's works are: *U* for *Ulysses,* followed by chapter and line number, and *D* for *Dubliners.*

2. Genette compares changes in the narrative register to the following example, representative of what he calls "the profoundly heterogenous character of the mode of expression to which we are so used that we do not perceive its most sudden changes." He asks us to imagine our surprise "if a seventeenth-century Dutch painter, anticipating certain modern methods, had placed in the middle of a still life, not the painting of an oyster shell, but a real oyster shell" (131). Such recognizable shifts in the narrative register, he argues, disrupt "pure" diegesis.

3. "Why should I regret my talent? I haven't any. I write with such difficulty, so slowly. Chance furnishes me what I need. I am like a man who stumbles along; my foot strikes something, I bend over, and it is exactly what I want" (quoted in Mercanton 213).

Works Cited

Beale, Paul, ed. *Partridge's Concise Dictionary of Slang and Unconventional English.* New York: Macmillan, 1989.

Benstock, Bernard. *Narrative Con/Texts in "Dubliners."* Urbana: Univ. of Illinois Press, 1994.

Benstock, Shari, and Bernard Benstock. "The Benstock Principle." In *The Seventh of Joyce,* ed. Bernard Benstock, 10-21. Bloomington: Indiana Univ. Press, 1982.

Caspel, Paul van. *Bloomers on the Liffey: Eisegetical Readings of Joyce's Ulysses.* Baltimore: Johns Hopkins Univ. Press, 1986.

Genette, Gérard. *Figures of Literary Discourse.* Trans. Alan Sheridan. New York: Columbia Univ. Press, 1982.

Joyce, James. *Dubliners.* New York: Viking, 1967.

———. *Ulysses.* Ed. Hans Walter Gabler et al. New York: Vintage, 1986.

Kenner, Hugh. "The Uncle Charles Principle." In *Joyce's Voices,* 15-38. Berkeley: Univ. of California Press, 1978.

Mercanton, Jacques. "The Hours of James Joyce." In *Portraits of the Artist in Exile: Recollections of James Joyce by Europeans.* Ed. Willard Potts. Seattle: Univ. of Washington Press, 1979. 206-52.

Mosher, Harold F., Jr. "Ambiguity in the Reading Process: Narrative Mode in 'After the Race.'" *Journal of the Short Story in English* 7.1 (1986): 43-61.

Partridge, Eric. *A Dictionary of the Underworld.* Hertfordshire, England: Wordsworth, 1989.

Potts, Willard, ed. *The Hours of James Joyce: Portrait of the Artist in Exile.* Seattle: Univ. of Washington Press, 1979.

CHAPTER SEVEN

Joyce's "The Dead"

The Dissolution of the Self and the Police

John Paul Riquelme

The charge that literature, particularly prose fiction, serves primarily a socially compliant rather than a socially resisting function has been vigorously made in some recent books dealing with nineteenth-and early twentieth-century narratives.[1] The long final chapter of one of these books, Vincent Pecora's *Self and Form in Modern Narrative*, contains a concerted attack on Joyce's "The Dead" as an example of early modernist fictional technique in service to ideological delusions, particularly to a mystification concerning authenticity and generosity that Gabriel Conroy exemplifies.[2] Pecora maintains that both the story's narrating strategies, especially free indirect discourse, and its thematics of generosity are in league with "acquisitive, administrative, deconstructive tendencies" (229) that undermine the potentially resistant autonomy of "the bourgeois individual."

In Pecora's reading, which he clearly seeks to extend to modernist fiction in general, the self in "The Dead" is dissolved into exhaustion and incoherence. The debilitating dissolution renders the self incapable of anything but compliance with the manipulating structures of desire used as forms of administrative control by an imperialistic, capitalistic system. According to Pecora, the compliance and manipulation are not only signaled but also furthered by the difficulty of locating the character's voice in Joyce's version of free indirect style. In this interpretation, Joyce is an ideological writer whose story celebrates bourgeois delusions, particularly in Gabriel's feeling of generosity that is apparently expressed in the closing paragraphs.

The force of Pecora's urgently pressed argument deserves to be recognized but also resisted. His reading objectifies "The Dead" in particular and literature in general by treating both primarily as the result and instrument of social forces. It ignores literature's pragmatic, affective character as the cause of varying responses in readers. "The Dead" can coherently be read as a tale about coercive social forces with which the central character is aligned, but in judging

Original version published in *Style* 25.3 (1991).

the author's, the character's, and our own relations to those forces, we may find good reasons not to accept a description that emphasizes passive complicity. Gabriel Conroy does not just give up in the story in any general, intransitive way. He gives up *something*, his deluded sense of control, superiority, and knowledge. Rather than giving in to administrative control by abandoning the will that might resist, Gabriel begins to leave behind his own willfulness, which has tended to perpetuate social hierarchies of domination.

Social resistance and social complicity are too restrictive a pair of interpretative opposites to account adequately for the shifting implications of "The Dead" and many other prose narratives. As a tale that overtly concerns the effects of death on the living, "The Dead" resists being relegated to mere complicity with the hierarchies that it presents because the presentation exposes delusions about mastery. The exposure of delusion, not the maintenance of hierarchies, is bound up with the dissolution of the self that Pecora excoriates.[3] The death signaled in Joyce's story by the dissolving of the self and by the intensified use of free indirect style tends to reverse rather than to reinforce some conventional attitudes. As the vehicle for communicating and transferring the reversal to the reader, free indirect style is central to the effect that "The Dead" has on the living.

"The Dead" is a text concerned with the sort of social hierarchies that have been increasingly castigated as ideological and exclusionary in recent literary criticism attentive to political concerns. Like the imagined and real presence of snow, the effect of hierarchies, which is general in the story, involves Gabriel Conroy centrally. Gabriel plays a normative and administrative role that verges on policing, understood not neutrally as action designed to maintain order but as action of a manipulative, repressive sort. We learn early in the story that he makes his children eat, do, and wear what he thinks is in their best interest (*Dubliners* 180; hereafter cited with page numbers as *D*). Differently presented, this kind of action might be defended as normal parental solicitude, but his sometimes tactless, high-handed behavior and Gretta's description of his actions make him appear more dominating than concerned. And his reported treatment of the children is, in effect, glossed by his insistence that Gretta wear galoshes for her own good.

That insistence, to which Gretta does not accede, reflects Gabriel's desire to express the superiority of his continental taste and knowledge.[4] Like many other members of the middle and upper classes in his time and in our own, Gabriel has the disposable income and the time to purchase goods and engage in activities intended to promote health, fitness, and longevity. He participates in a cultural mythology about improving and prolonging life that includes a denial of death. More than just a judge of what is good for his family, Gabriel is the main arbiter of taste and action in the story, rendering judgments of praise and blame in his thoughts and in his after-dinner speech. He speaks as one of those in his society empowered to maintain order, tradition, and the status quo.

The numerous interlocking hierarchies that inform the story's social world, particularly those involving class, gender, race, colonialism, nationalism, and regional prejudice, are evident enough. As a young, single, female servant, Lily, the caretaker's daughter, represents the base of a complex social pyramid at whose apex stands Gabriel, a well-off, mature but not yet old, married professional man. A great deal of Gabriel's anxiety in the story concerns his fear of slipping from the pinnacle that he occupies: that is, his fear that others will not see him as he wishes to be seen. His experiences in turn with Lily, with the nationalistic Miss Ivors, and with his wife indicate to Gabriel and to the reader that the views some others hold about him do not in fact conform to his own. The encounters provide perspectives for reassessing his standing and his positions. The sometimes prejudicial language and attitudes with which Gabriel defensively resists the reassessment help make the need for it clear.

When Gabriel finally experiences a dissolution of the self (a state accompanied by increased use of free indirect style), the cause is not his acquiescence to socially administered pressures to conform. (Even if it were, the reader could reasonably be expected to recognize such an acquiescence as a doubtful model for emulation. But the reader is not encouraged to judge Gabriel in such a distanced way.) Instead, the dissolution indicates the undermining of Gabriel's position as judge and model in various hierarchies of conformity. It marks his abdication and his removal from the role of the master that critics such as D.A. Miller align with the police.

At the story's end, Joyce coordinates the dismantling of Gabriel's defenses with Gretta's assumption of the speaker's role. It would be going too far to claim that male speech and the male gaze are displaced by woman's speech and the female gaze at the end of "The Dead," but, at the least, the male's ignorance about the meaning of the woman's perspective is partially overcome in a recognition of shared mortality. When Gabriel discovers his ignorance and achieves certainty about death, the previously unspoken and unspeakable are translated into a style of free indirect discourse that some critics claim is itself "unspeakable."[5] Readily speakable language would be too prone to carry habitual, prescribed meanings. One effect of the language and the situation is to require a reevaluation of our habits. Habit crumbles not in a Paterian experiential moment of multiple, heightened, hedonistic stimulation but in a sober perception about the inevitable, singular end of all stimulation and experience.

When the distinctness of Gabriel's individual voice is submerged in the concluding passages of free indirect style, he loses not his voice per se but only his place as spokesperson for the hierarchy. He becomes instead a means by which voices other than his own, particularly female voices, that have been silenced, slighted, and ignored can begin to be articulated or amplified. As spokesperson for the hierarchy, Gabriel speaks in part to confirm his own self-image and social standing, which he wishes to have echoed back to him. As the catalyst for the nonechoic, unmanipulated speech of others, he experiences in the story's conclusion the displacement of that self-image and a radical, irreversible shift in position. But before he can assume the role of catalyst for a woman's speaking, Gabriel must move beyond being merely the conventional provoker of woman's anger. And he must abandon his automatic, defensive attempts to maintain or regain his mastery.

Women speak in response to Gabriel's provocations throughout the story in ways that he neither anticipates nor intends, and their speech causes him discomfort. In effect, his efforts to hear the confirming echo of his own speech backfire, for the women respond effectively in negative ways to the role he plays as a model of male superiority in an imperialistic, class-structured society. Two moments involving woman's speech in the encounter with Lily can help clarify the meaning of Gabriel's position in a social hierarchy that can be dominating and exploitative.

The first moment includes Lily's pronunciation of Gabriel's surname when she asks, "—Is it snowing again, Mr. Conroy?" Since Joyce renders the statement by standard spelling, the reader has no reason to suspect a nonstandard pronunciation until Gabriel belatedly notes it in thought: "Gabriel smiled at the three syllables she had given his surname and glanced at her" (*D* 177). Unlike the reader, Gabriel has heard not only her individually intended, semantic meaning but the markers of class difference, which are part of a cultural system's intentions rather than merely the individual's. Joyce could easily have presented Lily's dialectal speech at the time of its report rather than leaving the recognition of it to Gabriel, who knows the indexes of social rank within the hierarchy. The insertion of a determinate thought report into the third-person statement of action makes evident the otherwise invisible, hierarchical motivation for Gabriel's smile and glance at someone he sees as an ignorant serving girl. The brief report of thought, coordinated here with Gabriel's position as arbiter of rank, contrasts markedly with the lengthy passage of free indirect style at the story's end, a passage that indicates his removal from that position.

Gabriel's smile and the glance are withdrawn when Lily punctuates their encounter with her remark, "—The men that is now is only all palaver and what they can get out of you" (*D* 178). Since Joyce renders this instance of nonstandard usage explicitly as a matter of grammar, the educated reader does not need Gabriel's assistance this time in placing Lily socially. Gabriel is in no position to assist or even to comment coherently, since he is too taken aback by the vehemence and the semantic content of the statement to register the class difference. Syntactic, semantic, and pragmatic aspects of the statement combine to create a situation that throws Gabriel off balance but not necessarily the reader. The would-be master of ceremonies and speaker is rendered temporarily speechless by the serving girl. His loss of composure initiates a pattern that will be repeated with Miss Ivors and Gretta.

Gabriel recognizes, if only vaguely and defensively, the possibility of a mistake, and the result is not a smile and a look but a blush, a glance away, and the lack of a spoken response, followed by a gift of money as if he felt the money would make up for the gaffe. The exchange, which involves gold and an ungrammatical statement about palaver, indicates again that a hierarchy is in place, but commercial and sexually exploitative elements are evoked that were not evident in the earlier case of dialectal pronunciation. Gabriel's paternalistic view of Lily as a little girl and an ignorant servant finds its negative counterpart, but not its antithesis, in Lily's implied experience as an adult with men. The less than benign character of the hierarchy, including Gabriel's place in it as a man, is communicated implicitly by the word "palaver" and by Gabriel's subsequent gift of the coin. "Palaver" can refer to profuse and idle talk, but the history of the word's use carries other implications.

Neither Lily nor Gabriel appears to know what Joyce almost surely did and the reader can easily discover, the way the word entered the English language. "Palaver" comes from the Portuguese *palavra*, meaning "word," whose Latin and Greek roots also give us the English word "parable." They also give us the word "parley," a kind of talk that involves opposing sides and their relations of power. There is a parable about the connection of imperialism to male chauvinism and to class hierarchies in Joyce's assigning "palaver" to Lily and in her use of it to characterize relations between the sexes. "Palaver" is one normally unspoken "word known to all men" (*Ulysses* 3.435; 15.4192-93; hereafter *U* followed by chapter and line numbers) and to all women in the story's world though not in the sense in which Stephen Dedalus uses that phrase in *Ulysses*.

According to the *Oxford English Dictionary (OED)*, the earliest recorded instance of the substantive refers not just to "a talk, parley, conference, discussion" generally speaking but to a conference "with much talk, between African or other tribespeople, and traders or travellers." As the headnote to the entry in the *OED* explains, "*palavra* appears to have been used by Portuguese traders on the coast of Africa for a talk or colloquy with the natives (quot. 1735), to have been there picked up by English sailors (quot. 1771), and to have passed from nautical slang into colloquial use" (11:90). The *OED* illustrates that colloquial use involving the encounter between invader and native—the kind of encounter frequently alluded to in Joyce's later writing, especially *Finnegans*

Wake—with quotations from the early, the middle, and the end of the nineteenth century. The meaning persisted in published writing about Africa until at least 1897, only a decade before the writing of "The Dead." As the quotations cited in the *OED* make clear, the English exported the word to India as part of imperial culture. There and elsewhere in the Empire, the word was often used as verb or noun to describe in a condescending way native habits of talking. Palaver was predicated of the Indians, the Africans, and, of course, those loquacious Irish.

An Irish writer of Joyce's time sensitive to the hierarchical relations between England and Ireland and to the attendant stereotyping of the Irish might reasonably be expected to use such a word with a wide range of implications. The earliest example cited by the *OED* involves a discussion that concludes with gold changing hands as part of a suit for damages. Lily's statement and Gabriel's gift of the gold coin as inadequate recompense for damages implicitly transfer the imperialistic meanings to the relations between the sexes in "The Dead." Like African traders, men are out to make a profit for themselves by engaging in palaver with supposedly gullible, ignorant, and inferior partners. Like the natives, women are given as recompense in the transaction money or articles of ostensible value, including perhaps jewelry or items of clothing, such as galoshes, intended to brighten up, modernize, or otherwise improve their backward lives. With the help of gold, Gabriel survives his skirmish with the representative of a lower class. He is injured but not disabled for the task of maintaining his place at the top of the social pyramid.

The encounter with Miss Ivors also involves the relations between the sexes and imperial contexts, not trade this time but military action, nationalism, and colonial allegiances. In the story's first part, Gabriel does not dance at the call of "Quadrilles! Quadrilles!" (*D* 183), but he does in the second part when "Lancers were arranged" (*D* 187). According to the *OED*, the word "quadrille" refers to a "square dance, of French origin," but as the headnote to the entry indicates, it derives from French, Spanish, and Italian words that mean "a band, troop, company, 'a Squadron containing 25 (or fewer) Souldiers'" (12:960-61). The name for the kind of quadrille that Gabriel dances, "lancers," makes the military connection explicit for English speakers. By means of "quadrilles" the coordinated movement of soldiers with weapons is domesticated and brought into the drawing room, where it is performed politely and harmlessly to music by noncombatants. The noncombatants, however, are always men and women paired together, as Gabriel and Miss Ivors are in this case. Through the sexual pairing, Joyce undoes the pacification of the dance's origin, in effect revealing the conflictual character of that origin, by turning the man and the woman into antagonists. The dance becomes in "The Dead" the vehicle for a clash that involves national and regional allegiances and gender stereotypes, including the sense of gender identity that depends on those stereotypes.

The coordinated movements unexpectedly become the means by which a joust occurs in which the man is unhorsed. Like Mr. Deasy in the second episode of *Ulysses,* Miss Ivors does not mind breaking a lance with her partner. Gabriel, however, does mind because her looks, speech, and attitudes bring to the fore competing national and regional ties as well as gender expectations in ways that disconcert him. In a partial repetition of the scene with Lily, Gabriel colors, responds to Miss Ivors only "lamely" (*D* 187-88), and avoids her eyes (*D* 190). The pressure directed against the stability of Gabriel's position in the hierarchy has increased considerably over the earlier encounter, however, largely because Gabriel cannot use his class standing as an effective cover. The relatively formal application of the surname to Miss Ivors in the narration concerning Gabriel's encounter with her contrasts with the use of the first name for the servant. The contrast indicates Miss Ivors's higher class standing in Gabriel's eyes. But Gabriel's use of the surname also communicates his male distance and sense of superiority with respect to the woman whom Gretta addresses and refers to simply as "Molly" (*D* 191, 195-96).

Because of Miss Ivor's comparatively unfeminine attire and her frank statements, Gabriel's assumptions about gender, appropriate behavior, and his own identity are all implicitly shaken.[6] As the narrator and, by implication, Gabriel note, "She did not wear a low-cut bodice" (*D* 187). Presumably, a man's eye would respond in a conventional, sexually engaged way to the flesh that a low bodice revealed. In the place of flesh at her throat, Miss Ivors displays the nationalistic emblem that turns the covered bodice into something more aggressive and oppositional than merely a refusal to show flesh. Putting a political symbol where the mark of gender identity should by conventional standards appear reinforces the challenge to Gabriel's composure. His disquiet is keen because Miss Ivors combines unconventional, unfeminine dress and talk with the friendly gesture of a "firmly pressed" hand (*D* 190) and with joking that contains serious criticism of Gabriel's politics. This mixture does not fit neatly into the categories that Gabriel relies on to maintain his sense of identity and decorum; a low-cut bodice would clearly be more comforting.

Gabriel cannot consider her only a girl, as he did Lily, but he also wonders about her being a woman in the way he normally conceives of women. He thinks of her irritably as "the girl or woman, or whatever she was" (*D* 190). Not liking the image of him that he suspects she sees when she is "staring at him," he resists internally by resorting to language that criticizes her looks in the other sense. Her looking at him as she does makes her less than good-looking in his view. Those eyes that have pierced him like a lance become for Gabriel part of an unattractive face that is less than human; they are "rabbit's eyes" (*D* 190).

Gender and politics are conflated in the encounter, with Gabriel emerging as a collaborator whose male identity is threatened and Miss Ivors as his unwomanly nationalist opponent. Since Gabriel finds himself unable to defend his politics easily to her, he resorts to slurs that he refrains from saying aloud but that we hear. Gabriel pays Lily off with a coin. He pays Miss Ivors back silently with the thoughts that she is unattractive physically and, what may be as bad in his view, that she is discourteous (D 203). Her implied failure to meet Gabriel's standards for her gender and her class enables him to keep his sense of himself temporarily intact.

The closing scene with Gretta in the story's third part repeats in heightened and extended ways the two earlier ones. The toppling force exerted against Gabriel's position in the hierarchy is now literally closer to home, and it is impossible for him to ignore the conclusions to be drawn from his talk with Gretta. The views of his spouse are obviously harder to avoid and more intimately bound up with his sense of himself than the views of a servant whom he rarely sees or even those of a colleague. Though Gabriel tries briefly to employ strategies of prejudice with Gretta concerning Michael Furey, whom he considers "a boy in the gasworks" (D 219), they do not protect him in the partially successful way they had earlier in the evening. If Gabriel is not exactly hoisted by his own lance, he at least stumbles badly when he tries to use it. He is "humiliated by the failure of his irony" (D 220). As with Lily and Miss Ivors, he turns away and his face colors, but this time his ability to respond with speech neither disappears temporarily nor turns lame.

His manner of speaking and the implications and effects of that manner are, however, transformed. No longer playing a police-like role, he cannot "keep up his tone of cold interrogation." Instead his voice becomes "humble and indifferent" (D 220). Its indifferent quality implies no lack of feeling, but it does suggest that Gabriel's irony and the motivation to inflict it are gone. Earlier in the conversation, Gabriel wanted to elicit from Gretta certain responses that would have left him feeling satisfied and in charge. Once Gabriel's tone changes, she is no longer the intended object of his potential manipulation. He helps her to speak and to tell her story but not as the subject of an unfriendly interrogation. By posing questions that help her to continue speaking, Gabriel provides only the accompaniment for Gretta's more important performance. Conroy lays down his lance and dispenses with palaver by abetting a woman's speech that tells him things he would rather not hear.

The change in Gabriel's behavior indicates something other than capitulation to socially administered forces. It occurs rather in the wake of his having discovered his own blatant self-delusions about his position as a mortal subject in relation to other mortal subjects. In the three scenes with Lily, Miss Ivors, and Gretta, Gabriel turns away from them in order that they not see the blush that reflects what Gabriel encounters in their views about him. He also averts his eyes in order to avoid seeing reflected in their faces the harsh truth about himself. In the scene with Gretta, Gabriel eventually turns his eyes toward her once she sleeps. When he does, he encounters a fact about her that also applies to himself: "He did not like to say even to himself that her face was no longer beautiful but he knew that it was no longer the face for which Michael Furey had braved death" (*D* 222).

This reflection on her looks differs substantially in tone and implication from Gabriel's vindictive thoughts about Miss Ivors. I say this despite the fact that embedded in the statement may be Gabriel's sense that the young man would have been attracted to Gretta largely for her face. Even if that is part of Gabriel's attitude, it is not the primary part, for Gabriel indirectly expresses as a diminution in beauty both Gretta's aging and their own changed relations. He no longer tries to think delusively of her as the young woman he courted or of their relations as those of young lovers exchanging affectionate letters. His sense of their marriage has changed utterly. That Gabriel sees primarily aging inscribed on her face becomes clear when he recalls almost immediately "that haggard look" on Aunt Julia's face while she was singing. He recognizes in the faces of these two women something that he had failed to see in either Lily or Miss Ivors: the mortality that he shares with them. He sees the equivalent of the snow that will eventually cover their graves and his own.

The women's faces act as mirrors that reverse Gabriel's self-image by reflecting to him an image that he recognizes as his own even though it differs from his expectations and desires. At a moment crucial to the closing dialogue with Gretta, Gabriel literally catches sight of himself in a mirror. At first, the image he sees meets his expectations. But soon he understands the image in the mirror to be other than he wishes. The shift resembles the one that occurred in the talk he had earlier with Lily, in which her nonstandard speech initially occasions a confirmation of his superiority that is subsequently displaced by the unflattering reflection of himself in her statement about "men."

These experiences involving reactions against unwanted representations of the self are related to the passage from Michel Foucault's "Language to Infinity" that Pecora chooses as the epigraph for his discussion of "The Dead": "Headed toward death, language turns back upon itself; it encounters something like a mirror; and to stop this death which would stop it, it possesses but a single power: that of giving birth to its own image in a play of mirrors that has no limits" (214). This is a suggestive statement to juxtapose with a story that literally concerns both death and a character who catches a glimpse of himself in a mirror. The point of Pecora's placement of the passage seems to be that "The Dead" tends toward a self-reflexive play of language that is a denial of death. He has implicitly in view both Joyce's later writing and the frequent celebrations of the free play of language in Joyce by poststructuralists other than Foucault, including Philippe Sollers, Jacques Derrida, and Julia Kristeva. By attacking "The Dead" in the way that he does, Pecora in effect attacks modernism and poststructuralism. But aspects of the story relevant to Gabriel's glimpse in the mirror can be understood in an antithetical way as tending to undo the denial of death that often characterizes modern, bureaucratized, technologized consumer culture.

If we follow Lacan's lead rather than Foucault's, the undoing can be said to involve a momentary reversal of the mirror stage by means of the gaze. But it is only helpful, not absolutely necessary, to invoke Lacan in order to argue against Pecora's suggestion that there is a denial of death in "The Dead." Contrary to his view, "The Dead" is a story about a character who encounters the inevitability of his own death and loses at least temporarily his sense of being at the pinnacle of multiple hierarchies. The displacement reveals rather than reinforces the social conventions supporting the hierarchies that made the now displaced self-representation seem authentic. The curious, uncomfortable position that Gabriel finds himself in at the story's end has one formal counterpart in Joyce's use of free indirect style.[7] Gabriel is neither exactly the teller of his own tale nor exclusively the object of a tale being told by another; he is both teller and tale, representer and representation. His status corresponds to the middle voice in Sanskrit or Greek, which is neither exactly active nor passive but rather somewhere in between. That status also corresponds to Marx's view, formulated in the opening paragraphs of *The Eighteenth Brumaire of Louis Bonaparte,* that when people make history "they do not make it just as they please": they make it always "under circumstances" (595).

What occurs for the reader and for Gabriel is something like a disruption of the conventional realistic perspective in painting. Gabriel Conroy arrives at the position of being neither an autonomous self only nor an administered self (to use Pecora's terminology) through the experience of recognizing himself now as apparently one, now as apparently the other. The oscillation of dominating and dominated selves captured by Joyce's free indirect style and by his narrative signals the simultaneous but mutually transforming reality of both positions. In "The Dead" the mutual interference of the opposing views results not in an experience of undecidability but in Conroy's decidedly unambiguous recognition of eventual death. But the terms "dominating" and "dominated," "autonomous" and "administered," even used together do not capture adequately the effects and implications attending a strong premonition of death, including the "terror" (*D* 220) that can lead to a rethinking of everything from the ground up.

The recognition of what T.S. Eliot called "the skull beneath the skin" is bound up with the reversal that Gabriel experiences when he sees himself briefly in the mirror during the private scene with his wife. The reversal occurs in one way as a felt shift in his position on the social pyramid. Rather than being in charge, he has become a servant, in his own words "a ludicrous figure, acting as a pennyboy for his aunts" (*D* 220). As did Lily earlier, he sees himself now as subject to their whims. He views himself, as he did her, as a child. Like her, he has become the recipient of the largesse of those whom he serves. No longer seemingly independent, he is not just a male working for women but a *boy* running *errands* for *old* women. Many of Gabriel's prejudices obviously contribute to his current negative sense of himself, and the new image counters and reverses the self-representation that Gabriel has struggled to protect.

Rather than displacing the old self-image of something full ("his broad well-filled shirt front" [*D* 218] and his sense of being "full of memories" of a life "full of tenderness and joy and desire" [*D* 219]) with another image of fullness, the new image replaces it with something that is both antithetical and empty. Gabriel reads that opposite as "pitiable," "ludicrous," "fatuous," and devalued, worth a penny, much less than the gold coin he gave to Lily. It is not inconsequential that the emptying out of the previously full image in the mirror occurs in the same scene as do Gabriel's thoughts about his kinship with the moribund and the dead. For the first time he recognizes a basis for comparing rather than contrasting himself with those whom he wanted to dominate. Gabriel's ultimate abasement is to see himself as even lower than a servant, as deader than the dead for having lived less fully than a long dead, young factory worker from the west of Ireland. Gabriel moves from considering himself superior, in effect more sensitive, alive, and valuable than those beneath him in the social hierarchy, to realizing that someone of low birth, country background, and little education has had experiences that he can neither imagine adequately nor hope to have himself. The experience of reading his own image in antithetical ways contributes to the emptying out and the potential transvaluing of all that he thought he knew.

The conjunction of the mirror scene and Conroy's thoughts about death can be formulated in terms of Lacan's mirror stage and the gaze.[8] At the conclusion of his essay on the mirror stage, Lacan implies that psychoanalysis can bring the patient to realize that the self is nothing, that every self-representation is empty because it is always only a representation: a construct rather than something full and present. That realization, which reverses the mirror stage by replacing an apparent fullness with a lack, would seem to involve a return to the prior stage of development, the body in pieces, not yet sufficiently aware of representations of itself to constitute an "I," or unified self. In fact, it is the beginning of a new stage, since the return need not and perhaps cannot be entirely regressive. Instead, it is an adult version of the body in pieces, like Gabriel's premonition of eventual death. In Gabriel's case, it involves the

Fig. 1 Hans Holbein's *The Ambassadors* (1533), reproduced by permission of The National Gallery, London.

recognition that the body in pieces as the body in death is one truth that strenuously resists being eradicated by deluded self-representations and by self-perpetuating social hierarchies. The loss of delusions about one's own immortality is perhaps inevitably dispiriting, but it can also be liberating. Once freed from the constraints of the previous construction, the no-longer-deluded subject has the chance and the obligation to construct something different. Choices become both possible and necessary when past and present are reevaluated in the perspective of the future: that is, in the context of eventual death.

Our own position as readers engaged with the vacillations of free indirect style at the story's end can overlap with Gabriel's suspended position caused by his experience of falling within the socially defined hierarchies of self-representation. We have the opportunity to recognize that ordinary, conventional perspectives—such as apparently reliable, determinate third-person reports of thought or the geometrically defined perspective of realistic painting—can be made visible for what they are, constructions that create only the impression, not the reality, of a well-ordered, intelligible, controllable world. And with that recognition our own stance as the spectator who possesses knowledge and control is destabilized. The reader's deluded sense of stability corresponds to Gabriel's pose of knowing and controlling. Rather than indicating a loss of autonomy, the destabilized position embodies the risks attending the discovery that autonomy is neither absolute nor limited to ourselves. At issue in the closing style of "The Dead" is something like the curiously double or multiple form of the anamorph, a figure that, as the word's etymology suggests, is always forming anew. Joyce's free indirect style is anamorphic in its frequently dialogical character, its simultaneous evocation of two possible sources, the teller and the character. It resembles the anamorph in Hans Holbein's *The Ambassadors* (Fig. 1), which Lacan uses to sketch his concept of the gaze.

The painting includes full-length portraits in conventional perspective of two diplomats with accoutrements apparently relevant to their station in life. But it contains in severely altered perspective beneath their feet a representation of a skull. Once the viewer recognizes the death's head within the depiction of the conventionally presented pair of living diplomats, an interference is set up between two geometrical and interpretative perspectives, neither of which can be ignored. The portrayal of life and achievement has become unexpectedly and indissolubly linked to an image of death. The would-be "normal" perspective of the frontal plane is recognized for its constructed character, as the spectator oscillates between the conventional representation and the skull that is always beneath and always distractingly visible. With a crucial, revealing twist, we see ourselves as dual in the painting understood as a conceptual mirror that reflects the spectator's connection to the ambassadors. The situation resembles that of Dorian Gray, who sees himself always as double and antithetical once he comes into possession of his portrait and it comes into possession of him. As with *The Ambassadors,* the picture of Dorian Gray gazes back at the spectator who recognizes a true but unpleasant self-image in the portrait.

In the frontal plane of Holbein's painting, we recognize something of ourselves in the conventional social beings who are the ambassadors, defined by the trappings that culture provides in order for its members to know and present themselves as conventional. In the angled plane beneath the ambassadors' feet, we see an image that is both ours and the ambassadors'. The monarch that we and these ambassadors serve is death itself. The anamorph undoes more than conventions of realistic geometrical perspective; it undoes temporarily the effect of the mirror stage by giving us the experience of being looked at and controlled rather than being the viewer who occupies the position of control. That experience is one version of what Lacan calls the gaze. Instead of controlling the vanishing point, we experience vanishing and dissolution in the conceptual space projected by the representation's seeming incoherence. The radical, if only temporary, change in our subject position can have a permanent, transvaluing effect. The radical shift and potential effect are captured in Gabriel's recognition of his connection to the dead, his recognition—and ours—that "death" rather than "palaver" is the word known to all men and all women. The snow has begun to look back at Gabriel.

Like the rest of us, no matter what our place in the social hierarchy, Gabriel finally cannot choose to avoid death, though he can choose within limits how he will live until death takes him. For Pecora, however, Gabriel cannot choose even that because everything has already been chosen for him, including his language and his thoughts, especially the word "generous" and the ideological, deluded, self-destructive social tendencies that Pecora claims the word signifies throughout "The Dead" (243-55). He cites as particularly damning the first sentence of the penultimate paragraph: "Generous tears filled Gabriel's eyes" (*D* 223). Pecora identifies the statement as the culmination of a series of apparently generous actions and statements about generosity in the story, including Gabriel's gift to Lily, his remarks in his speech about hospitality (*D* 202-3), and the loan to Freddy Malins that Gretta praises (*D* 217). With good evidence Pecora argues that Gabriel regularly recovers from humiliation through gestures of generosity that are actually self-serving rather than self-sacrificing. In this reading the final mention of the word is merely a habitual, defensive repetition induced by a distorted cultural ethos.

There is a significant pattern of connections pertaining to generosity in "The Dead," a pattern that involves a range of meanings and implications that readers can reasonably attach to the word "generous" as it occurs at the story's end. In this regard, Pecora's reading of the "generous tears" is too univocal. Applying a Nietzschean, genealogical method, he correctly points out that Joyce probably would have known the etymology of the word, that "the Latin *generosus* means, before anything else, 'of noble birth, well-bred'" (243-44). Consequently, every predication of generosity is for Pecora also an assertion of class superiority. Although this etymology is correct, it is also only partial. It conveniently overlooks something that Joyce also probably knew, something that he could have discovered from reading Skeat: the connection of the English word "generous" to the Latin *genus* (stem *gener-*) and to the Indo-European root *genə* or *gen-*. If we go back to this other link and other origin rather than stopping with *generosus*, the English word carries relevant implications that do not involve social hierarchies.

Besides "L. *generōsus,* (properly) of noble birth," Skeat's entry for "generous" includes "L. *gener-*" and sends us to the previous entry, "generic," to find the identification of *gener-* as "decl. stem of *genus*" (210). In his appendix 3, "Select List of Latin Words," Skeat glosses "*gen-us*" as "kin" and lists among the English derivatives not only "genteel," "gentry," and "genuine," which support Pecora's reading, but also "general" (636). That word is, of course, crucial to the story's ending, for it occurs when Gabriel repeats the statement that "snow was general all over Ireland" (*D* 223). "Generous tears" points forward to "general" as much as it does backward to Gabriel's acts of beneficence. In the appendix, Skeat also sends us to his entry for "kin," which he defines as "genus, race" and allies with the Latin *genus* through the root "GEN." In tracing the origin and affiliations of "kin," Skeat lists words that mean "tribe" as well as "kin" (278).

In the entry for "generous," *The American Heritage Dictionary* provides a similar etymology back to "*genus* (stem *gener-*), birth, race, kind" (549) and to the Indo-European root *genə̄*. The dictionary's appendix, "Indo-European Roots," shows that root giving rise both to the word "kin" and the word "king." It is also the origin of the word "kind" in two senses (1516), only one of which supports Pecora's reading. Kind can mean "generous or hospitable," but it also refers to kindred, "a class or category of similar or related individuals" (721). On etymological grounds there is as much evidence for a reversal in the pattern of Gabriel's self-congratulatory and self-protective generosity in the story's end as for its continuance. We can read Gabriel's "generous tears" as linked more with the snow, "general all over Ireland," than with his earlier self-interested magnanimity. In this alternative reading, Gabriel is not merely exercising his habit of dominating solicitude again; he has discovered through a heightened sense of mortality his kinship to a group. His kindred now include the whole tribe or race, and Gretta's story and his thoughts together begin to articulate the "uncreated conscience" of his "race" (*Portrait* 253) that Stephen Dedalus hopes to forge.

There are, in addition, some difficulties of identifying in a univocal way voice and referent in "generous tears" that Pecora does not attend to. Despite the fact that free indirect style regularly raises problems of attribution, problems that Pecora seems to recognize, he assigns the final paragraphs to Gabriel without discussion.[9] This reading assumes that the reader takes the word to be Gabriel's: that is, Gabriel thinks of himself as feeling and acting in a generous way. But the word could instead be the narrator's judgment about Gabriel's feelings rather than a description or rendering of them. Further complicating the reading of "generous" is its dual status as an adjective that can be understood equally well in physical as in psychological terms. The dual reference, to the state of Gabriel's feelings and to the size of his tears, makes determinate attribution difficult.[10] If the physical meaning is accepted (it would be hard to exclude), then the word cannot easily be assigned to Gabriel only, unless we maintain that in the midst of crying he is aware of the size of his own tears.

Given its ambiguous origin in teller or character or both and its dual reference to feelings and size, the word "generous" functions something like the famous drawing resembling both a duck and a rabbit that Wittgenstein and Gombrich discuss (Wittgenstein 194, sec. 2.11; Gombrich 4-6; see the version of this drawing in my *Teller and Tale* [41]). As with other optical illusions, once the perceiver recognizes an alternative to the configuration initially noticed, it is not possible to block out either image entirely and return to a simpler, singular view. Pecora's critical procedure implicitly denies that Joyce's language carries multiple possibilities, even apparently irreconcilable ones, some of which counter the singular meaning that he relies on in his argument. Such a denial of language's sometimes double and antithetical nature removes its antihierarchical potential; it is a denial of language's human, specifically its mortal, character.

As with the gaze in Lacan, the ideological, socially determined aspect of realistic, conventional representation emerges into view when such a double image disturbs the stability of what seemed singular, univocal, and unified. The fluid character of free indirect discourse calls up the self that in speaking tries to take a determinate, comforting shape, but it also undermines the possibility of locating a determinate origin for the speech. Without a sense of origin or stable perspective, the shape becomes protean. It can also become collective, the shape and speech of a group. No longer primarily the passive recipient of shapes that society imposes, this protean subject cannot be contained, though, like the surface of a sphere, it has its limits. As a form of dissolution it recognizes within itself the disintegration that death completes. This side of death, the recognition can dissolve and reform the culturally generated shapes and boundaries of hierarchical difference. The loss of a deluded sense of power over death can displace the false sense of power and authority in other arenas, including especially social relations.

Gabriel repeats in a new context the language of the newspaper already repeated to him by a woman about the snow being general over Ireland. By doing so he begins actualizing a group speech whose content implies the equality of all members of the group. Earlier Miss Ivors berated Gabriel for his contributions to a pro-British newspaper. His relation to a newspaper's language is quite different when he repeats the statement about the snow, a statement that focuses on the weather, something that eludes the power of any political faction to control. His choral speaking involves a blurring of the boundaries of the individual speaking self that has one stylistic counterpart in free indirect discourse. Exploitative palaver and the lancing dance of gender conflict are replaced in the story's ending by speech and actions that carry the meaning of a *danse macabre* in which all the partners are equal.

The discovery that ultimate dissolution is inevitable and always recognizable creates a vacuum where previously there seemed to be a plenitude. A hierarchical culture that denies the reality of death abhors such a vacuum. It does so because the emptiness vigorously and implacably resists being filled by delusions of grandeur, being shackled by the actions of social arbiters, and being controlled by the machinery of culture's representations of itself to itself as intelligible, rational, natural, and benign. The obvious fact that the survival of the individual is limited has potentially significant implications of various sorts for social structure. The attempt to ignore that fact is regularly reflected in hierarchies of rank and domination, such as those within which Gabriel Conroy has functioned. The lack that resists being rationalized by such hierarchies makes possible new arrangements for the subject that need not be motivated by prejudgments that are prejudicial. At the end of "The Dead" those new arrangements are still beyond the horizon of the story's representational limits. They remain to be actualized by the reader as well as by the character when the dissolution of the character's self is communicated and transferred through free indirect style. Rather than putting us under arrest, "The Dead" provides the opportunity for a recognition of human limits that can help make freedom, with all its risks and uncertainties, possible.

Notes

1. The best-known of these is D.A. Miller's *The Novel and the Police,* which deals with nineteenth-century British fiction.

2. See Pecora, chap. 6, "Social Paralysis and the Generosity of the Word: Joyce's 'The Dead,'" 214-59. I provide a more general commentary on *Self and Form* than the one contained in this essay in my review of the book in *Novel.*

3. Pecora's attack on the dissolution of the self in Joyce is largely motivated by the connection he wants to see between it and deconstruction.

4. The history of the words "galoshes" and "guttapercha" (*D* 181) helps clarify the cultural history that is one context for Gabriel's demand that his wife protect her feet from the wet. The word "guttapercha" is derived from the Malay phrase that refers to the substance "gum" derived from the "percha" tree. As the citations in the *Oxford English Dictionary* (6:971) make clear, by the third quarter of the nineteenth century guttapercha, like Indian rubber, had become a significant import into European markets from colonial sources. It made telegraphy possible through its use as an insulating material. The *American Heritage Dictionary* suggests that "galosh" derives ultimately from Latin words referring to Gaul, the part of the continent that includes modern France and Belgium. By recommending galoshes made of guttapercha, Gabriel is supporting a continental fashion that relies on colonial raw materials.

5. This characterization of free indirect discourse is Ann Banfield's.

6. In his recent article, Garry Leonard discusses Gabriel's difficulties with women as threats to masculine subjectivity. Leonard's commentary, which uses Lacanian concepts but not primarily the gaze, is by and large consonant with my own.

7. In suggesting that free indirect style can involve a reversal of manipulative forms of looking on, I am following up an implication of Beth Newman's comment about Virginia Woolf's dispersal of the "narratorial look" (1038). The suggestion is at odds with D.A. Miller's contention that *style indirect libre* involves the subverting of the character's authority and the confirming of the narration's "master-voice" (25). My disagreement with Miller, which I pursue only implicitly in the present essay, extends to his general view of reading as an act of surveillance in which the reader is deluded into feeling free from surveillance (162). Contrary to Miller's reductive characterization of reading, I find that fictional texts can and regularly do provide the reader with an experience that is the equivalent of being looked at, an experience analogous to the one that Gabriel undergoes. They are full of surprises, often surprises that involve cultural history, including the changing meanings of words. Rather than lulling us into a deluded sense of mastery, these surprises can trigger a recognition of our own mortality, our ultimate lack of power over certain things and events.

8. Lacan's best-known discussion of the mirror stage is "The Mirror Stage as Formative of the Function of the I" in *Écrits*. He discusses the gaze in chaps. 6-9, "Of the Gaze as *Objet Petit a*," in *The Four Fundamental Concepts of Psycho-Analysis*.

9. Victor Luftig and Mark Wollaeger discuss this problem in Pecora's argument in their lengthy review of *Self and Form* (681).

10. I discuss this particular problem of attribution briefly in my essay on Joyce's early fiction in *The Cambridge Companion to Joyce* (127) and at greater length in *Teller and Tale* (127). As I mention in *Teller and Tale,* Joyce plays on the double character of "generous" in the tenth episode, "Wandering Rocks," of *Ulysses* when he describes as "generous" (*U* 10.251) Molly's fleshy arm in the act of throwing a coin to the one-legged sailor.

Works Cited

American Heritage Dictionary. 1969 ed.

Banfield, Ann. *Unspeakable Sentences: Narration and Representation in the Language of Fiction.* Boston: Routledge, 1982.

Gombrich, E.H. *Art and Illusion: A Study in the Psychology of Pictorial Representation.* New York: Pantheon, 1960.

Joyce, James. "The Dead." In Dubliners*: Text, Criticism, and Notes,* ed. Robert Scholes and A. Walton Litz. 175-224. New York: Viking, 1969.

———. A Portrait of the Artist as a Young Man*: Text, Criticism, and Notes.* Ed. Chester G. Anderson. New York: Viking, 1968.

———. *Ulysses.* Ed. Hans Walter Gabler et al. New York: Garland, 1984, 1986.

Lacan, Jacques. *Écrits: A Selection.* Trans. Alan Sheridan. New York: Norton, 1977.

———. *The Four Fundamental Concepts of Psycho-Analysis.* 1978. Trans. Alan Sheridan. New York: Norton, 1981.

Leonard, Garry. "Joyce and Lacan: 'The Woman' as a Symptom of Masculinity in 'The Dead.'" *James Joyce Quarterly* 28 (1991): 451-72.

Luftig, Victor, and Mark Wollaeger. Review of *Self and Form in Modern Narrative* by Vincent P. Pecora. *James Joyce Quarterly* 27 (1990): 673-82.

Marx, Karl. *The Eighteenth Brumaire of Louis Bonaparte. The Marx-Engels Reader.* 2d ed. Ed. Robert C. Tucker, 594-617. New York: Norton, 1978.

Miller, D.A. *The Novel and the Police.* Berkeley: Univ. of California Press, 1988.

Newman, Beth. "'The Situation of the Looker On': Gender, Narration, and Gaze in *Wuthering Heights.*" *PMLA* 105 (1990): 1029-41.

Oxford English Dictionary. 1989 ed.

Pecora, Vincent P. *Self and Form in Modern Narrative.* Baltimore: Johns Hopkins Univ. Press, 1989.

Riquelme, J.P. "Complicit Moderns?" a review of *Self and Form in Modern Narrative* by Vincent P. Pecora. *Novel* 24.3 (spring 1991): 331-35.

——. "*Stephen Hero, Dubliners,* and *A Portrait of the Artist as a Young Man:* Styles of Realism and Fantasy." In *The Cambridge Companion to Joyce,* ed. Derek Attridge, 103-30. Cambridge: Cambridge Univ. Press, 1990.

——. *Teller and Tale in Joyce's Fiction: Oscillating Perspectives.* Baltimore: Johns Hopkins Univ. Press, 1983.

Skeat, Walter W. *A Concise Etymological Dictionary of the English Language.* 1882. Reprint, New York: Capricorn, 1969.

Wittgenstein, Ludwig. *Philosophical Investigations.* Trans. G.E.M. Anscombe. 3d ed. New York: Macmillan, 1968.

Gender and Control

CHAPTER EIGHT

"She Had Become a Memory"
Women as Memory in James Joyce's *Dubliners*

Raffaella Baccolini

In my memory are sky and earth and sea, ready at hand along with all the things that I have ever been able to perceive in them and have not forgotten. And in my memory too I meet myself—I recall myself, what I have done, when and where and in what state of mind I was when I did it. In my memory are all the things I remember to have experienced myself or to have been told by others. From the same store I can weave into the past endless new likenesses of things either experienced by me or believed on the strength of things experienced; and from these again I can picture actions and events and hopes for the future; and upon them all I can meditate as if they were present. (St. Augustine, *Confessions* 10:8)

Memory . . . has three different aspects: memory when it remembers things, imagination when it alters or imitates them, and invention when it gives them a new turn or puts them into proper arrangement and relationship. For these reasons the theological poets called Memory the mother of the Muses. (Giambattista Vico, *The New Science* 3:819)

By an epiphany he meant a sudden spiritual manifestation, whether in the vulgarity of speech or of gesture or in a memorable phase of the mind itself. He believed that it was for the man of letters to record these epiphanies with extreme care, seeing that they themselves are the most delicate and evanescent of moments. (James Joyce, *Stephen Hero* 211)[1]

Modernist writers have shown a profound ambivalence toward the past and tradition. If it is true, as Hayden White argues in *Tropics of Discourse,* that the modernists have shown an intense "hostility toward historical consciousness" and toward history itself, it is also true that they have shown a similar obsession with the past, its return and influence on the present (31). James Joyce's Stephen's famous claim that "history . . . is a nightmare from which I am trying to awake" (*Ulysses* 2.377) can be countered by T.S. Eliot's insistence that historical sense is indispensable for the artist and that it "involves a perception, not only of the pastness of the past, but of its presence" ("Tradition" 38). Next to Ezra Pound's modernist imperative "make it new" in canto 53, to Eliot's statement that "novelty is better than repetition" ("Tradition" 38), and to Wyndham Lewis's scornful assessment of the past in the vorticist manifesto, claiming that "our vortex is not afraid of the Past: it has forgotten it's [*sic*] existence" (44), one might juxtapose the pervasive use of the mythic past in Joyce, Pound, Eliot, and H.D., to name only a few prominent modernist writers.

Modernist culture has thus been viewed rightly as a deliberate break with Victorian norms and conventions, but if modernism celebrates the liberation from the past, it is nonetheless true that a critical recovery of tradition and an obsession with the notions of time, memory, and hence identity coexist beside this desire and request for novelty. Modernist art, in fact, openly displays an ambivalent attitude toward the past and tradition, and next to its contempt, at times its hostility, for a certain past, that very same culture recovers what was seen as "the best tradition"—Dante and the *Dolce Stil Novo*, Arnaut Daniel and the troubadour love lyric, to name just a few. Thus, next to Duchamp's penciled-in mustache on the portrait of Mona Lisa, we can also find the recovery of the past by Pre-Raphaelite art and poetry; next to Joyce's inventive play with language and myth in *Finnegans Wake* and *Ulysses*, one finds his borrowing from past tradition, and myth in particular, which is "a way of controlling, of ordering, of giving a shape and a significance to the immense panorama of futility and anarchy which is contemporary history" (Eliot, "*Ulysses*" 177). The consciousness of the past, Eliot reminds us in "Tradition and the Individual Talent," is a necessary step in the progress of an artist and for his or her self-awareness but does not entail a wholehearted admiration for or acceptance of it (37–40); rather, it calls for critical awareness. The modernist critical search for the past displays a search for new values and for identity; it also unveils a fear that only through memory and fragments can we preserve the ruins of modern civilization. Fragments, recollections, and free associations become the structural elements of much modernist writing.[2]

Memory appears then both as a theme and as a structural device. Although the study of memory goes back to Plato and Aristotle, it emerges with renewed emphasis in much literature of the turn of the century. Since memory is a central modernist issue, I believe that a reading of some of Joyce's *Dubliners* stories can be enriched by placing them in the context of the preoccupation, at times the obsession, with memory and historical consciousness. Joyce, in fact, can be said to have entered the debate on memory and the past with the publication of his fiction: his theory on epiphany, set forth in *Stephen Hero* but already present in *Dubliners*, is his first contribution to such a debate.[3] Joyce's exploration of this topic fits in well with the views expressed by Friedrich Nietzsche, Henri Bergson, and Marcel Proust, partly because like them he reveals an ambivalent attitude toward the past and partly because his use of memory, like that of his male contemporaries, reveals a traditional attitude toward women. A gendered reading of Joyce's contribution to the debate on memory and the past is an attempt to contribute to the wealth of feminist criticism which, as Bonnie Kime Scott has argued, is "writing gender into modernism" (*Gender of Modernism* 7).

In *Dubliners,* memory appears as an essential ingredient for the development of many stories. In particular, a story like "Eveline" is totally constructed around the theme of memory and develops through the protagonist's recollections. Other stories, such as "The Boarding House," "A Painful Case," and "The Dead," present memory as the climactic element in the narrative. Whether memory constitutes the central component of a shorter story or represents the vital part of a longer one, memory is often an agent of recognition for Joyce's characters. For Joyce's Dubliners, memory sets in motion a recognition about themselves and promotes their own understanding of their identity.

However, like most of the aforementioned modernist intellectuals, Joyce shows an ambivalence toward memory in two ways: first, in its link to the forces of paralysis such as family, religion, and habits and second, in its unsettling effect on individuals. In *Dubliners* memory works essentially as an early epiphany with a double function: it is a moment of revelation or insight for his characters, but far from leading toward liberation and action, that insight actually leads them further toward oppression and paralysis. In both cases, as revelation and as oppression, memory unsettles Joyce's characters, leads them to displacement, and makes them exiled from themselves. Thus, memory embodies and anticipates the theme of exile that will be explicitly treated in Joyce's later works at the same time as it reflects the controversial debate on the value of memory and habits that was in progress at that time.[4]

If memory has an unsettling but still positive effect on Joyce's male protagonists, the situation is significantly different for his female characters, because in the author's particular use of memory his female characters are denied subjectivity. Since they remain locked into memory—both in reference to their own lives and as figures of memory for the male characters—unlike men, women in *Dubliners* do not seem to reach a recognition about themselves and an understanding of their identity. Therefore, women in Joyce's stories tend to be important not as much for what they do but rather for what they stand for or what they stimulate, thus continuing to be "the *objects* of male theorizing, male desires, male fears and male representations" (Suleiman 7). Women, therefore, are tied to their place as "bearer[s] of meaning, not maker[s] of meaning" (Mulvey 7).

Memory, in fact, is functional only to men in *Dubliners;* Joyce's women, on the other hand, are figures of memory for men, functional instruments for men's growth and awareness but otherwise incapable of reaching an understanding about themselves and attaining the status of *subjects* of their own lives, whether they are the center of consciousness of a story or not. As embodiments of memory, Polly, Gretta, and Mrs. Sinico are agents of epiphany for Bob Doran, Gabriel, and Mr. Duffy; in Eveline's case, the link between the character and memory is so pervasive that Eveline herself is memory, completely set in and imprisoned by the past. Thus the possibility of revelation and the future are foreclosed for Joyce's female characters.

Joyce's Contribution to the Theory of Memory

"The daughters of memory," states Richard Ellmann, "received regular employment from Joyce . . . [who] was never a creator *ex nihilo;* he recomposed what he remembered, and he remembered most of what he had seen or had heard other people remember" (364-65). In quoting *Ulysses,* Ellmann says that Joyce's "work is 'history fabled'" (364), but his otherwise influential study does not foreground gender issues. Joyce's first contribution to the debate on historical consciousness and memory, which will constitute a privileged theme and a recurrent structure in his writing, appears in *Dubliners,* a work that has not been extensively treated in relation to this issue.[5] Like Nietzsche, Bergson, Proust, and Eliot, Joyce shows ambivalence toward the past and memory. The past is, in fact, often linked to habits and conventions, which in his collection of short stories stand as a prominent source of paralysis.

Joyce's attack on habits and conventions situates him in the twentieth-century attack on memory since it was really an attack on the value of habit, the repetition and remembering of something from the past or, in other words, a "remembering embodied in acts which have become automatic" (Gross 369). While nineteenth-century philosophers had expressed their unconditioned support for the value of habit, modern writers and philosophers did not hesitate to show contempt for it. If for nineteenth-century thinkers habits were essential for a stable social life, for modernists they had to be rejected as they were inextricably linked to societal norms and rules and as such they stifled the individual's potential.[6]

For most of the philosophers and writers who dealt with the issue of memory at the turn of the century, habits hinder individual growth, but memory is nonetheless positive in its association with recognition. They seem to maintain, in fact, a distinction between different types of memories; they distinguished between a less valuable memory and a highly functional one, a distinction that to a certain extent had always been present in the debate on the art of memory.[7] Henri Bergson, for example, distinguishes between a more limited (and limiting) and a spontaneous (almost superior) kind of memory. In *Matter and Memory* (1896), Bergson affirms that *"the past survives under two distinct forms: first in motor mechanisms; secondly, in independent recollections"* (87; emphasis in the original), where by motor mechanisms he means habits, and by independent recollections he means individual acts of recollection that come spontaneously to one's mind. It is clear that for Bergson independent recollections are far superior to habits. Similarly to Nietzsche and to the modernists, for Bergson memory and the past are valuable and functional: they make one's perception understandable; they let one interpret the present or what is about to come; they make a valuable and desirable guide to life.[8]

Likewise, for Joyce memory as habit hinders the individual's growth, but memory as epiphany is positive. The stories collected in *Dubliners* (hereafter cited with page numbers as *D*) describe moments of revelation, "sudden spiritual manifestation[s]," which are similar to the recognition that takes place through memory.[9] With the experience of the epiphanic moment, Joyce's characters come to an understanding of their personal history and, thus, of themselves and their past; because such a discovery reveals their own limitations—a pervasive sense of impotence together with the inability to act or to seize opportunities that distinguish many modernist characters—their revelations last only a few moments. Moreover, these characters break with a mode of being in their past life often through memory of a woman.

Memory and especially the memories of women, then, are the means by which most of Joyce's Dubliners experience an epiphany. Joyce's male characters need to know the past, and although that knowledge leads to displacement, they nonetheless experience a recognition. Women, on the other hand, are only instrumental to men's process of awareness, and therefore they are not only denied revelation but also subjectivity and the possibility to change.[10] Such gender difference emerges in Joyce's stories both thematically and structurally: because his female characters are mostly voiceless and conventional, their point of view, and hence their subjectivity, is hardly revealed.

"The Boarding House" is one such story where memory serves both as a theme and as the prominent structural device of the last pages of the story. After a brief description of the Mooney family (*D* 61-63), the theme of the story—seduction and the need for reparation and, thus, entrapment—is introduced (*D* 63-66) mostly through Mrs. Mooney's considerations, which deal less with the recollection of what has taken place in her boardinghouse between her daughter Polly and Mr. Doran and more with her speculations of how reparation can be made. The last pages of the story, on the other hand, are governed by Doran's and Polly's memories, and while for Doran memory becomes increasingly associated with the physicality of Polly's body, leading him to the recognition of seduction and entrapment, for Polly memory leads her into revery and to no sign of illumination.

From the start, Bob Doran's memories are associated with discomfort: "The recollection of his confession of the night before was a cause of acute pain to him" (*D* 65). Soon, though, his memory goes to his affair with Polly:

> He remembered well, with the curious patient memory of the celibate, the first casual caresses her dress, her breath, her fingers had given him. Then late one night as he was undressing for bed she had tapped at his door, timidly. She wanted to relight her candle at his for hers had been blown out by a gust. It was her bath night. She wore a loose open combing-jacket of printed flannel. Her white instep shone in the opening of her furry slippers and the blood glowed warmly behind her perfumed skin. From her hands and wrists too as she lit and steadied her candle a faint perfume arose.
>
> On nights when he came in very late it was she who warmed up his dinner. He scarcely knew what he was eating, feeling her beside him alone, at night, in the sleeping house. . . .
>
> They used to go upstairs together on tiptoe, each with a candle, and on the third landing exchange reluctant goodnights. They used to kiss. He remembered well her eyes, the touch of her hand and his delirium. . . . [*D* 67]

Doran's recollection of Polly becomes increasingly more physical; by employing all verbs of perception, Joyce turns Polly into physical memory for Doran. At first, Doran remembers well the "casual caresses her dress, her breath, her fingers had given him." His next recollection is of Polly's sight and of her scent: her body, the way she is dressed, but most of all her "perfumed skin." Taste is irrelevant, as he remembers that he "scarcely knew what he was eating, feeling her [presence] beside him." In a crescendo, explicit physical contact is remembered, and all he can recollect is the passion that her kisses and "the touch of her hand" aroused in him.

Polly and her body are one with memory for Bob Doran, and as such they awaken him to an abrupt reality: "But delirium passes. He echoed her phrase, applying it to himself: *What am I to do?* The instinct of the celibate warned him to hold back" (*D* 67). The movement Joyce traces in Bob Doran's mind is one that goes from recall—Polly's body and her seduction—to recognition—seduction as entrapment into marriage, a choice he reluctantly has to accept. It is a recognition that leads to a further feeling of "discomfiture" and displacement, because he lacks the courage to take any action and gives in to Mrs. Mooney's plan (*D* 68). His impotence allows him to escape only through imagination: "He longed to ascend through the roof and fly away to another country where he would never hear again of his trouble" (*D* 67-68).

Polly, on the other hand, is denied any sign of recognition. She is Mrs. Mooney's voiceless daughter who looks like "a little perverse madonna" (*D* 62-63). Her own identification with the body reinforces her voicelessness and denies her subjectivity. Polly, whose voice we never hear except for the clichés "What am I to do . . . O my God!" and that "she would put an end to herself" (*D* 66-67),[11] is mostly described through Doran's perception: until the story's last paragraph where Polly is described sitting patiently in her room while her mother and Doran decide her future for her, what the reader knows of Polly is mainly mediated by Doran's thoughts and memories. She is memory for Bob Doran but incapable herself of having meaningful memories:

> Polly sat for a little time on the side of the bed, crying. Then she dried her eyes and went over to the looking-glass. She dipped the end of the towel in the water-jug and refreshed her eyes with the cool water. She looked at herself in profile and readjusted a hairpin above her ear. Then she went back to the bed again and sat at the foot. She regarded the pillows for a long time and the sight of them awakened in her mind secret, amiable memories. She rested the nape of her neck against the cool iron bed-rail and fell into a revery. There was no longer any perturbation visible on her face.
>
> She waited on patiently, almost cheerfully, without alarm, her memories gradually giving place to hopes and visions of the future. Her hopes and visions were so intricate that she no longer saw the white pillows on which her gaze was fixed or remembered that she was waiting for anything.
>
> At last she heard her mother calling. She started to her feet and ran to the banisters.
>
> —Polly! Polly!
>
> —Yes, mamma?
>
> —Come down, dear. Mr. Doran wants to speak to you.
>
> Then she remembered what she had been waiting for. [*D* 68-69]

Far from leading to an unsettling displacement and a knowledge about oneself, the "secret amiable memories" in Polly's case last only a short time, giving place to a "revery" and "to hopes and visions of the future." Unlike Doran, whose memories bring him to a painful awakening, she "wait[s] on patiently, almost cheerfully, without alarm," to the point that there is no trace of perturbation on her face, and she cannot even remember that she is waiting to know her future. Except for the initial crying, Polly does not show any pain but rather a puzzling sense of appeasement: there is no lingering on the past, no attempt to understand it in order to understand oneself on Polly's part; she immediately proceeds to daydream about her future. The scene depicting her flight back into memories and forward into imagination contributes to showing her in an ambiguous light. On the one hand, she seems the scheming and

manipulative woman who does not "wish it to be thought that in her wise innocence she had divined the intention behind her mother's tolerance" (*D* 64);
on the other, she is the shallow girl who seems to be trapped in romantic notions, incapable of any understanding about herself, and lost in reveries about
a future that has been chosen for her. It is not memory, an understanding of
past events, that leads Polly to a painful awakening; it is her mother's voice that
makes her remember what she had been waiting for.

As in the previous story, in "A Painful Case" memory serves as thematic element and toward the end also as structural pattern. But more than anywhere
else in the collection, this story shows how habits and conventions thwart the
life potential of both Mr. Duffy and Mrs. Sinico, thus revealing to what extent
Joyce will fit in with the twentieth-century attack on the value of habits. The
protagonist's "even . . . life," in fact, "roll[s] out evenly" as an "adventureless
tale" (*D* 112, 109). His life is described by the repetition of habitual, meticu-
lous patterns, as attested by the recurrence of "even," "evenly," "every morning," and "every evening" (*D* 108, 109, 112). Habits are also—literally—deadly
for Mrs. Sinico who, being "in the habit of crossing the lines late at night from
platform to platform" and "in the habit of going out at night to buy spirits," is
killed by a habitual train, the "ten o'clock slow train from Kingstown" (*D* 114,
115, 113).[12]
    As in the other stories, the dichotomy between mind and body/man and
woman shapes the writing. Mr. Duffy lives the life of a quasi misanthropist—
certainly a misogynist—in his self-exile from the rest of society. His condition
is one of displacement: he abhors "anything which betoken[s] physical or
mental disorder" and lives "at a little distance from his body" (*D* 108). If
Mr. Duffy, in his delusional belief that he is a philosopher,[13] is the mind,
Mrs. Sinico is the body and is capable of catching "up his hand passionately and
press[ing] it to her cheek" (*D* 111). Their relationship further suggests this
dichotomy and how traditional Duffy's way of thinking is. In fact, the narrator's voice increasingly fuses with Mr. Duffy's consciousness, so that we see
Mrs. Sinico and their relationship through Duffy's eyes: "Little by little he entangled his thoughts with hers. He lent her books, provided her with ideas,
shared his intellectual life with her. She listened to all. . . . This union exalted
him, wore away the rough edges of his character, emotionalised his mental life.
Sometimes he caught himself listening to the sound of his own voice. He
thought that in her eyes he would ascend to an angelical stature" (*D* 110-11).
    Despite the statement that Mr. Duffy "shared his intellectual life with her,"
what is described does not represent a sharing relationship. Duffy is the master
of language; she listens to him; when she talks, her language only reinforces
the split between body and mind: "in return for his theories she gave out some

fact of her own life" (*D* 110). She is instrumental for him as she "emotion-alise[s]" his mind—a rather traditional view that holds women, and women's bodies in particular, as a source of renewal for men. He actually thinks so highly of himself that he catches "himself listening to the sound of his own voice." Finally, the last remark bears a resemblance to Virginia Woolf's later statement that "women have served all these centuries as looking-glasses possessing the magic and delicious power of reflecting the figure of man at twice its natural size" (*A Room of One's Own* 35). There is a sense, in fact, that if Mr. Duffy ascends to an angelical stature for Mrs. Sinico, he does so even more for himself; it is Mrs. Sinico's respect for him—or perhaps the very way in which he perceives her—that generates such feeling.

These conventional views of women are made possible partly because "A Painful Case," like most of Joyce's stories, is mainly constructed around the male protagonist's center of consciousness. In fact, even if it is true that Joyce wavers, as he often does, between sympathy for and derision of his protagonists, it is also true that in depicting primarily the point of view of his male characters, he displays predominately an interest in them. He certainly cannot be said to approve of Mr. Duffy's way of life or of the other "paralyzed" characters, and yet Mr. Duffy is more memorable than any of Joyce's female characters. By often denying his female characters to be the recognizable center of consciousness of a story, he also prevents them from affirming their actions and their subjectivity.

A visual interruption on the page marks, as often is the case in *Dubliners,* the beginning of the character's recollection. In Mr. Duffy's case, the death of Mrs. Sinico gives place first of all to a selfish reaction that is in line with his characteristics: he lingers in self-absorption and self-commiseration, feels disgusted, and, above all, is only able to think of himself. The language employed in the description of Mr. Duffy's reaction to the death of his acquaintance suggests his misogynist and unfeeling view: words such as "revolted," "vulgar," "degraded," "squalid," "miserable," "malodorous," "unfit," and "sunk" all attest to his inability to feel compassion and to understand (*D* 115).

But Mrs. Sinico's death and his blind, selfish reaction to it give place to memory:

> As he sat there, living over his life with her and evoking alternately the two images in which he now conceived her, he realised that she was dead, that she had ceased to exist, that she had become a memory. He began to feel ill at ease. He asked himself what else could he have done. . . . He had done what seemed to him best. How was he to blame? Now that she was gone he understood how lonely her life must have been, sitting night after night alone in that room. His life would be lonely too until he, too, died, ceased to exist, became a memory—if anyone remembered him. [*D* 116]

This passage as well stresses the shift from recollection to recognition on the part of Joyce's male characters. From verbs that describe mere recall, such as "living over" and "evoking," Joyce moves to the use of verbs such as "realised" and "understood," which underscore Mr. Duffy's epiphanic moment. It is precisely at the moment in which Mrs. Sinico "become[s] a memory" that recognition takes place together with displacement. Right when he is capable of empathizing with Mrs. Sinico, Duffy begins to "feel ill at ease" and "lonely" and is afraid that there will be no one to remember him once he is dead. The passage also suggests a topos of patriarchal culture that feminist critic Teresa De Lauretis has explored in *Alice Doesn't*, namely the idea that woman's absence is paradoxically necessary to man's culture. It is first Mrs. Sinico's absence and then her memory that motivate Duffy's awareness and set the story's ending in motion.

His memory of Mrs. Sinico almost materializes her for him, and he seems to feel her presence "near him in the darkness" (*D* 117). Even in the moment of recognition, Joyce's character is unable to view woman as other than body; in fact, he seems to feel "her hand touch his" and even "her voice touch his ear" (*D* 117). The unusual choice of the verb "to touch" applied to "voice" reinforces the image of Mrs. Sinico as body and as one with memory; through touch, it materializes her voice which, however, does not speak. Mrs. Sinico is denied subjectivity since she is only voiceless body in life, in death, and in Mr. Duffy's memory. Her death and the memory of her are instrumental to Mr. Duffy's awakening; yet, the ending with the repetition of Mr. Duffy's feelings in a negative sense ("He could not feel her near him in the darkness nor her voice touch his ear. . . . He could hear nothing") suggests a bleak future for him (*D* 117). Once again, illumination does not seem to lead to effective change. The final reversal in fact suggests that most likely Mr. Duffy will not seize this opportunity for change; rather, his propensity for self-absorption and self-commiseration will constitute the most obvious way for him to go back to old habits.

In "The Dead," memory figures prominently as well. As a theme and as a structure, it is first introduced when Gabriel remembers his mother, then it becomes one of the topics of Gabriel's speech, and finally at the end of the story Gabriel's memories of his life with his wife develop parallel to Gretta's reminiscences of her dead lover, Michael Furey. Like the previous stories, "The Dead" shows a male character reaching an understanding of himself, while the female character is misread and reduced first to an object of male gaze and desire and then to an instrument of others' epiphanies. Thus, like Polly and Mrs. Sinico before her, Gretta is denied subjectivity even if, unlike them, she does speak; what she says, however—the narrative of her memories—is only functional to her husband's illumination.

Gabriel's speech is important, on the other hand, as it introduces two central issues: past or tradition and memory. The misunderstanding he has with the Irish nationalist Miss Ivors brings him to accentuate in his speech the differences between past and present while emphasizing the superiority of the former over the latter: "A new generation is growing up in our midst, a generation actuated by new ideas and new principles. It is serious and enthusiastic for these new ideas and its enthusiasm, even when it is misdirected, is, I believe, in the main sincere. But we are living in a sceptical and, if I may use the phrase, a thought-tormented age: and sometimes I fear that this new generation, educated or hypereducated as it is, will lack those qualities of humanity, of hospitality, of kindly humour which belonged to an older day" (D 203). The modern generation, with its acceptance of new ideas and principles, is only distancing itself from the past and its values. The only way to counter this inevitable change, Gabriel suggests, is to "cherish in our hearts the memory" of the past (D 203). Gabriel adopts what Nietzsche called, in *The Use and Abuse of History*, the "monumental" attitude toward the past: tradition is the source of heroic models to be imitated. And yet, Gabriel also adopts what the German philosopher called the "critical" attitude by rejecting nostalgia and choosing not to "linger on the past" (D 204). Memory and knowledge then provide modern generations with a link to the better past.

But while, on the one hand, memory and the past serve Gabriel as agents of epiphany, on the other they also come back to haunt and displace him (cf. D 220). In the last part of the story, in fact, memory is used in the usual ambivalent way. Once again, Joyce juxtaposes Gabriel's memory to Gretta's, and again, while Gabriel experiences an epiphany, Gretta is denied the experience. Her memory of Furey's love and death is not accompanied by an illumination about herself. Gabriel's memory is set off by the view of his wife Gretta who is listening to a traditional ballad. Gretta's memory, on the other hand, is stimulated by that very music. The scene is also important as it is another instance where Joyce's women are denied subjectivity in two ways. First, Gretta's experience is not directly described but is mediated by Gabriel's perception; second, the sight of his wife leads Gabriel to imagine himself as the artist and his wife as the model and muse: "There was grace and mystery in her attitude as if she were a symbol of something. He asked himself what is a woman standing on the stairs in the shadow, listening to distant music, a symbol of. If he were a painter he would paint her in that attitude" (D 210).

Like Polly's, Gabriel's recollections waver between the evocation of the past and his desires for the future. The emergence of memories of his past life with Gretta gives place to his desire:[14] "Moments of their secret life together burst like stars upon his memory. . . . A wave of yet more tender joy escaped from his heart and went coursing in warm flood along his arteries. Like the tender fires of stars moments of their life together, that no one knew of or would ever know of, broke upon and illumined his memory. He longed to recall to her those moments, to make her forget the years of their dull existence together and remember only their moments of ecstasy" (D 213-14). Memory and desire mix in the passage, as if to anticipate the famous modernist imperative by Eliot in *The Waste Land*. Gabriel's memories are characterized by silence and passion throughout the description of his feelings (see, for example, the repetition of "silence" and the use of words such as "desire," "pang of lust," "fever of rage and desire," "delight," and "happiness" [D 215, 217]); above all, they stand in stark contrast with Gretta's verbalized and shocking memories. But memory and desire also mix to disclose Gabriel's wish for possession, as the use of "master," "crush," and "overmaster" reveal (D 217). Like Gabriel's earlier gaze, his memory becomes another means of objectifying women, much as it is for Mr. Duffy who tries "to *fix* [Mrs. Sinico] permanently in his memory" (D 109; emphasis mine).

Unlike Gabriel's memories and those of the other characters, Gretta's recollections are spoken. But even if she is granted speech, her words do not stimulate self-illumination; rather, her painful narration results in her falling "fast asleep" (D 222). In fact, Gretta is denied the moment of reflection that accompanies the recollection of most male characters. This gender difference represents another destructive dichotomy: while Gabriel is the intellectual, "country cute" Gretta is the passionate woman incapable of thought (D 187). Gretta thus represents another example of woman as man's memory but whose identification with memory and language does not grant her the status of subject. Her memory, on the contrary, has the power to awaken Gabriel's feelings; her own recollections lead to his recognition: "Gabriel felt humiliated by the failure of his irony and by the evocation of this figure from the dead, a boy in the gasworks. While he had been full of memories of their secret life together, full of tenderness and joy and desire, she had been comparing him in her mind with another. A shameful consciousness of his own person assailed him. He saw himself as a ludicrous figure" (D 219-20). His first recognition brings pain and displacement but, in turn, leads him to compassion and empathy. Unsettled by the revelation he feels that "his own identity [is] fading out into a grey impalpable world" (D 223). Gabriel's self-consciousness seems to give place to his ability to feel for others as well, but the great ambiguity of the story's ending undermines the potential for change and action.[15]

Of all of Joyce's stories in *Dubliners*, "Eveline" is the one most identified with memory. More than anywhere else in the book, in fact, memories shape here the development of the story—a story that unfolds little through the description of Eveline's present life and dreams of her future and much through her recollections. The story mostly consists of long recollections interspersed with brief, sudden flights of imagination. Of eighteen identifiable clusters in the story, five depict Eveline in the present, five in her revery, and eight as she is overwhelmed by memories. Like all other characters, Eveline wavers between memory and speculations about her future while the story evolves, but for Eveline memories do not bring her to any illumination—she is so trapped by the force of recall and the past that she is completely identified with memory. Thus, Eveline epitomizes the female condition in *Dubliners;* her identification with the past and her passivity foreclose any possibility of a future for her. Like the previous female characters, Eveline is denied the experience of illumination, even if, unlike them, she is given the status of protagonist, is the center of consciousness of the story, and is not relegated to being a mere accessory to man. Unlike the male characters, on the other hand, not only does Eveline's memory not bring her illumination, but it actually deceives her.

With the other female characters, in fact, she shares the same traits, although they are all brought to an extreme. She is totally passive and voiceless. All the verbs that refer to her in the present describe her in a static stance, even the ones that describe her in motion: in addition to the often used "remember," "sat," "leaned," "looked," "heard," "continued to sit," "she could hear," "as she mused," "she trembled," "she stood up," "she stood," "she gripped," "her hand clutched," and "she set her white face to him" hardly reveal any movement at all (*D* 36, 37, 39, 40, 41).[16] In fact, when she moves it is only to stand up, and when she moves her hands it is only to fasten herself securely to the past, a point that has led Bernard Benstock, among others, to suggest rightly that Eveline seems physically paralyzed (*James Joyce* 34).

But most of all, Eveline is overwhelmed by the weight of the memories of her family—the tyrannical father and the overbearing dead mother—as well as by her material conditions and her subjugation to societal conventions.[17] Also in her case, it is the memory of a woman, her mother, that seems to suggest the (false) movement from recall to recognition:

> She knew the air. Strange that it should come that very night to remind her of the promise to her mother, her promise to keep the home together as long as she could. She remembered the last night of her mother's illness. . . . As she mused the pitiful vision of her mother's life laid its spell on the very quick of her being—that life of commonplace sacrifices closing in final craziness. She trembled as she heard again her mother's voice saying constantly with foolish insistence:
> —Derevaun Seraun! Derevaun Seraun!
> She stood up in a sudden impulse of terror. Escape! She must escape!
> [*D* 40]

The memory of her ill mother and her crazy, mysterious words generate Eveline's conflicting feelings: she is trapped by the promise to her mother, and yet she feels that keeping that promise means succumbing to the past. The scene can also be seen as an early version of Stephen's "agenbite of inwit" (*Ulysses* 1.481); like Stephen, whose remorse constantly reminds his conscience of his refusal to kneel and pray for his dying mother, Eveline's conscience is reminded of the promise to the dying mother to keep the home together. Like his characters, Joyce will be driven to return with his memory and imagination to the same scene.[18] But the scene also suggests the ambivalence toward the past in that it is seen both as a source of entrapment and of one's rootedness. "To keep the home together" strips Eveline of her identity as she fulfills the selfless woman's lot, but it also gives her a sense of belonging.

Most important, however, is the fact that the memory of Eveline's mother produces a false recognition. Eveline is actually blinded by the belief that she can free herself and pursue her rightful happiness through Frank: "Frank would save her. He would give her life, perhaps love, too" (*D* 40). Eveline's first mistake is one of delusion; she is deluded into believing that she is able to carry through with her plan to elope, while there is no sign in the story that she has freed herself from the constraints of society, religion, and family. Second, she entrusts her liberation to Frank, thus relinquishing any claim to agency. Eveline's belief and choice represent one of the most widespread cultural habits that, far from eliminating dependency, just changes its source. In fact, she moves from the dependency on her family to that on her spouse-to-be. Thus, while memory *as* and *of* women leads male characters from recall to recognition and to self-knowledge, in "Eveline" Joyce adds a perverse twist by showing how in her case it leads her to delusion, deceit, and ignorance of herself.

Ambivalence and gender difference emerge from Joyce's treatment of memory, but while they situate the author in the modernist debate on history and time, they also reveal to what extent that debate is permeated primarily with male texts and theories that negate women's existence. They attest as well to the continuing need to write gender into modernism both through a recovery and reevaluation of women authors' works and through feminist criticism of male texts. For all the characters of Joyce's collection here examined, memory constitutes the very basis of rootedness and belonging: men who know their past also know their places in tradition, thus gaining a knowledge of themselves and having the Nietzschean choice to reject the past—the oppressive, stifling habits—for the future. The theory of memory is, therefore, above all a theory of knowledge, but Joyce, like Proust, adds the unsettling component to it: memory—involuntary memory and epiphany—confounds the individual.

Once Joyce's characters have reached an illumination, they are displaced from their selves as they used to be. Thus recognition opens up the potential for change for Joyce's male characters, an opportunity, however, that does not often seem to be seized.

A gendered reading of Joyce's contribution, though, reveals how different the situation is for his female characters, because through the author's particular use of memory his women are denied subjectivity. Memory and especially the memories of women are the means by which most of Joyce's Dubliners experience an epiphany. But, as Bonnie Kime Scott has also suggested, "unlike some of the men of *Dubliners,* who detect the paralysis of their positions through an epiphany, often touched off by a woman, the women of *Dubliners* are denied such illumination" (*Joyce and Feminism* 16). Joyce's stories display such gender difference both thematically and structurally. Unlike women writers of his time and as feminist critics have uncovered, because he fails to portray women as other than man's instrument and because he often portrays them as voiceless, his female characters are denied their point of view, their plot, and their subjectivity. Feminist critics have extensively discussed women's instrumental function in relation to Stephen's *bildung* as an artist; Joyce's treatment of memory reveals that in *Dubliners* as well women are instrumental to men's growth. His female characters have a long way to go: dismembered of their subjectivities, reconstituted only as body and memory, instrumental to men's epiphanies but not to their own, they would need to claim memory for themselves in order to re-member their selves.

Notes

1. I would like to thank Susan Stanford Friedman for her precious suggestions.
2. Marcel Proust's *Remembrance of Things Past* is the novel of memory par excellence. Poets such as H.D., T.S. Eliot, and Ezra Pound make memory one of their structural devices in modernist masterpieces like *Winter Love, The Waste Land,* and *The Pisan Cantos.* Virginia Woolf's characters in *To the Lighthouse, Mrs. Dalloway,* and *The Waves* seem haunted by their memories, while novelists like Joyce and H.D. have essentially retold the same story again and again: Joyce's different versions of Stephen's narrative in *Stephen Hero, Portrait,* and *Ulysses;* H.D.'s different accounts of her early years in London in her "Madrigal cycle," *Bid Me to Live, Asphodel,* and *Paint It To-Day.*
3. For a discussion of Joyce's views on history in his critical writing, see Robert Spoo's "Tropics of Joycean Discourse"; in *Portrait* and *Ulysses,* see his volume *James Joyce and the Language of History.*
4. The notion that the past, and therefore memory and history, is functional and of use had already been set forth by Friedrich Nietzsche in his "proto-modernist" essay, *The Use and Abuse of History.* According to the German philosopher, the capacity of remembering distinguishes humans from animals, and yet it is also a source of alibis. Through memory we find excuses for doing or not doing what the present demands of

us. It follows that memory is always intentional and functional since we use memory to go back to the past for a certain purpose. There cannot be, therefore, an objective use of the past (preface and §1). It is precisely here that Nietzsche's modernity lies: the issue is not whether we use or abuse the past, but how we do it. Nietzsche's study of memory continues with the identification of three different attitudes toward the past, which he calls the monumental, the antiquarian, and the critical. Monumental historical awareness views the past as a source of models; it turns to the past for imitation of heroic action. The danger implicit in such an attitude, which Nietzsche warns us of, is the tendency to mythologize the past—to look at it with nostalgia. The antiquarian approach to the past shows an indiscriminate reverence for it, while the critical attitude criticizes the past in the name of the present in an attempt to free oneself from its claims (§2 and §3). Nietzsche's final recommendation is to learn to forget: we must first learn the past and then forget it once we have learned it. In light of this argument, Nietzsche appears then as an early representative of the modernist ambivalence toward history and the past. To be modern, one must learn the past in order to reject it. As a consequence of this line of thinking, remembering lost some of its value, and doubts were insinuated as to the capacity of memory to understand the past. According to David Gross, for ages memory "had been indispensable as a guide to life; most people had always found it natural to orient themselves in the world by relying on remembered experiences. By the end of the nineteenth century, however, reliance on such memories was becoming much less serviceable. Economic and social forces were transforming reality so rapidly that resort simply to remembering became 'dysfunctional' for enabling one to adjust to the swirl of modern existence. Faithfulness to memory as a guide only served to make one increasingly incapable of coping with the new forces of modernity" (369).

5. On this matter see the excellent special issue of *James Joyce Quarterly* on Joyce and history edited by Victor Luftig and Mark A. Wollaeger (now revised and expanded as *Joyce and the Subject of History,* ed. Wollaeger, Luftig, and Spoo). Most articles contained in the special issue and in the book only touch upon *Dubliners;* see also Spoo's useful bibliography of criticism on the subject. On *Dubliners,* see Robert Adams Day; and Spoo ("Uncanny Returns in 'The Dead'; *James Joyce and the Language of History*).

6. According to Gross, among supporters and detractors of habits were William James and Henri Bergson. In *Principles of Psychology,* James made an apology of habits by affirming that habit is "the enormous fly-wheel of society, its most precious conservative agent" (quoted in Gross 371). Bergson's position, on the other hand, is more ambivalent, as he distinguished "motor mechanisms," or habits, from "independent recollections" (87). If, on the one hand, Bergson did not deny that good habits produce a kind of moral life in the individual, he nonetheless gave prominence to the other type of memory, independent recollections. Furthermore, in *Creative Evolution,* he claimed that habits should not be viewed as the fulfillment of freedom but as its stifling (Gross 371-73).

7. For a comprehensive analysis of the art of memory up to the Renaissance, see Frances A. Yates. The philosophical tradition has always distinguished recall from recognition: Plato, Aristotle, St. Thomas Aquinas, St. Augustine, for example, have all

identified two types of memory, of which the second involves judgment and leads to knowledge (1-81). On memory, forgetfulness, and the past, see also Paolo Rossi.

8. Although the distinction between voluntary and involuntary memory is not explicitly made, Bergson's theory clearly anticipates Proust's. Like Bergson, Joyce, and other modernist writers, Proust disliked habits and saw them as a paralyzing and stifling force on the individual. But Proust's most famous contribution to the theory of memory is his distinction between voluntary and involuntary memory as stated in *Remembrance of Things Past.* By voluntary memory, he meant a kind of memory deliberately recalled in order to apply it to and interpret a present situation. By involuntary memory, on the other hand, he meant a kind of memory that comes spontaneously, unsolicited from the past, and that usually displaces, unsettles, confounds the individual. For Proust this second type of memory is clearly superior to the first, since while voluntary memory only offers a partial evocation of the past, involuntary memory contributes to its total evocation. An analogous yet different distinction between kinds of memories is also present in Sigmund Freud's essay "Remembering, Repeating, and Working-Through." Like Nietzsche, Freud believed the past could be a burden on the present; like him he worked toward the assumption that the past could be known and transcended—in a certain way forgotten, done away with—through psychoanalytic cure (154-55). And yet in Freud's work as well as in modernists' writing, we find that ambivalent feeling—the disturbing suspicion that we cannot be altogether free of the past. For a brilliant discussion of Freudian "return of the repressed" in Joyce, see Susan Stanford Friedman ("[Self] Censorship"; *Joyce: The Return of the Repressed*).

9. Among the many discussions of Joyce's concept of epiphany, see Morris Beja; Bernard Benstock (*James Joyce* 23-26); Palmira De Angelis; Umberto Eco (44-58); and Lia Guerra. See also Day, who is one of the few critics to link epiphanies to the art of memory.

10. The critical bibliography on *Dubliners* is extensive; see, for example, Benstock's *Narrative Con/Texts* and the following special journal issues: of *James Joyce Quarterly,* edited by Spoo; of *Modern Fiction Studies,* edited by Ellen Carol Jones; and of *Style,* edited by Rosa Maria Bollettieri Bosinelli and Christine van Boheemen. Among the feminist contributions that deal at least in part with Joyce's collection, see in particular Marlena G. Corcoran; Friedman; Suzette Henke; Henke and Elaine Unkeless; Earl G. Ingersoll; Margot Norris; Bonnie Kime Scott (*James Joyce; Joyce and Feminism; New Alliances*); and Trevor L. Williams.

11. On clichés in Joyce's *Dubliners,* see Harold F. Mosher Jr.

12. From the point of view of society, on the other hand, it is Mrs. Sinico's change of habits that leads to her downfall. According to the newspaper report, in fact, she "had lived happily until about two years [earlier] when [she] began to be rather intemperate in her habits" (*D* 115).

13. See, for example, the books by Nietzsche on his shelves (*D* 112).

14. On the issue of desire in Joyce, see Henke.

15. The ending of "The Dead" has produced numerous, divergent readings; on its ambivalence, see Florence L. Walzl's pioneering essay.

16. Eveline's passivity is also extended to the description of her perceptions, so that she sits at the window watching the "evening *invade* the avenue" (*D* 36; emphasis mine).

17. Cf. the recurrent usage of "used to" throughout the story to suggest both memories and habits.

18. For an analysis of the different scenes portraying Stephen and his mother in *Stephen Hero, Portrait,* and *Ulysses,* see Friedman ("[Self] Censorship").

Works Cited

Augustine, St. *The Confessions.* Trans. F.J. Sheed. New York: Sheed, 1943.

Beja, Morris. *Epiphany in the Modern World.* London: Owen, 1971.

Benstock, Bernard. *James Joyce.* New York: Ungar, 1985.

————. *Narrative Con/Texts in* Dubliners. London: Macmillan, 1994.

Bergson, Henri. *Matter and Memory.* Trans. N.M. Paul and W.S. Palmer. 1896. Reprint, London: Allen, 1911.

Bosinelli, Rosa Maria Bollettieri, and Christine van Boheemen, eds. *James Joyce's* Dubliners. Special issue of *Style* 25.3 (1991): 351-516.

Bosinelli, Rosa Maria, Paola Pugliatti, and Romana Zacchi. *Myriadminded Man: Jottings on Joyce.* Bologna: CLUEB, 1986.

Corcoran, Marlena G. "Language, Character, and Gender in the Direct Discourse of *Dubliners.*" In *James Joyce's* Dubliners, ed. Rosa Maria Bollettieri Bosinelli and Christine van Boheemen, 439-52. Special issue of *Style* 25.3 (1991).

Day, Robert Adams. "Dante, Ibsen, Joyce, Epiphanies, and the Art of Memory." *James Joyce Quarterly* 25 (1988): 357-62.

De Angelis, Palmira. *L'immaginazione epifanica. Hopkins, D'Annunzio, Joyce: Momenti di una poetica.* Rome: Bulzoni, 1989.

De Lauretis, Teresa. *Alice Doesn't: Feminism, Semiotics, Cinema.* Bloomington: Indiana Univ. Press, 1984.

Eco, Umberto. *Le poetiche di Joyce.* Milan: Bompiani, 1987.

Eliot, T.S. *Selected Poems.* Boston: Harcourt, 1964.

————. "Tradition and the Individual Talent." In *Selected Prose of T.S. Eliot,* ed. Frank Kermode, 37-44. New York: Farrar, 1988.

————. "*Ulysses,* Order and Myth." In *Selected Prose of T.S. Eliot,* ed. Frank Kermode, 175-78. New York: Farrar, 1988.

Ellmann, Richard. *James Joyce.* New York: Oxford Univ. Press, 1982.

Faulkner, Peter, ed. *A Modernist Reader: Modernism in England, 1910-1930.* London: Batsford, 1986.

Freud, Sigmund. "Remembering, Repeating, and Working-Through." In *The Standard Edition of the Complete Psychological Works of Sigmund Freud,* trans. J. Strachey, 12:147-56. London: Hogarth, 1958.

Friedman, Susan Stanford, ed. *Joyce: The Return of the Repressed.* Ithaca, N.Y.: Cornell Univ. Press, 1993.

————. "(Self)Censorship and the Making of Joyce's Modernism." In Friedman, *Joyce: The Return of the Repressed,* 21-57.

Gross, David. "Bergson, Proust, and the Revaluation of Memory." *International Philosophical Quarterly* 25 (winter 1985): 369-80.

Guerra, Lia. "Fragmentation in *Dubliners* and the Reader's Epiphany." In *Muriad-*

minded Man: Jottings on Joyce, ed. Rosa Maria Bosinelli et al., 41-49. Bologna: CLUEB, 1986.

H.D. [Hilda Doolittle]. *Asphodel.* Durham, N.C.: Duke Univ. Press, 1992.

―――. *Bid Me to Live (A Madrigal).* New York: Dial, 1960.

―――. *Paint It Today.* New York: New York Univ. Press, 1992.

―――. *Winter Love (Esperance). Hermetic Definition.* New York: New Directions, 1972.

Henke, Suzette. *James Joyce and the Politics of Desire.* London: Routledge, 1990.

Henke, Suzette, and Elaine Unkeless, eds. *Women in Joyce.* Urbana: Univ. of Illinois Press, 1982.

Ingersoll, Earl G. "The Gender of Travel in 'The Dead.'" *James Joyce Quarterly* 30 (1992): 41-50.

―――. "The Stigma of Femininity in James Joyce's 'Eveline' and 'The Boarding House.'" *Studies in Short Fiction* 30 (1993): 501-10.

Jones, Ellen Carol, ed. *Feminist Readings of Joyce.* Special issue of *Modern Fiction Studies* 35.3 (1989): 405-635.

Joyce, James. Dubliners: *Text, Criticism, and Notes.* Ed. Robert Scholes and A. Walton Litz. New York: Viking, 1969.

―――. *Finnegans Wake.* New York: Viking, 1939.

―――. A Portrait of the Artist as a Young Man: *Text, Criticism, and Notes.* Ed. Chester G. Anderson. New York: Viking, 1968.

―――. *Stephen Hero.* Ed. John J. Slocum and Herbert Cahoon. New York: New Directions, 1963.

―――. *Ulysses.* New York: Vintage, 1986.

Lewis, Wyndham. "Our Vortex." In *A Modernist Reader: Moderism in England, 1910-1930,* ed. Peter Faulkner, 44-46. London: Batsford, 1986.

Luftig, Victor, and Mark A. Wollaeger, eds. *Papers from the Joyce and History Conference at Yale, October 1990.* Special issue of *James Joyce Quarterly* 28.4 (1991): 745-935.

Mosher, Jr., Harold F. "Clichés and Repetition in *Dubliners:* The Example of 'A Little Cloud.'" In *James Joyce's* Dubliners, ed. Rosa Maria Bollettieri Bosinelli and Christine van Boheemen, 378-92. Special issue of *Style* 25.3 (1991).

Mulvey, Laura. "Visual Pleasure and Narrative Cinema." *Screen* 16 (1975): 6-18.

Nietzsche, Friedrich. *The Use and Abuse of History.* Trans. Adrian Collins. Indianapolis: Bobbs-Merrill, 1957.

Norris, Margot. "Stifled Back Answers: The Gender Politics of Art in Joyce's 'The Dead.'" In *Feminist Readings of Joyce,* ed. Ellen Carol Jones, 479-503. Special issue of *Modern Fiction Studies* 35.3 (1989).

Pound, Ezra. *The Cantos.* New York: New Directions, 1952.

Proust, Marcel. *Remembrance of Things Past.* Trans. C.K. Scott Moncrieff, Terence Kilmartin, and Andreas Mayor. New York: Random, 1981.

Rossi, Paolo. *Il passato, la memoria, l'oblio.* Bologna: Il Mulino, 1991.

Scott, Bonnie Kime, ed. *The Gender of Modernism.* Bloomington: Indiana Univ. Press, 1990.

―――. *James Joyce.* Atlantic Highlands, N.J.: Humanities Press, 1987.

―――. *Joyce and Feminism.* Bloomington: Indiana Univ. Press, 1984.

―――, ed. *New Alliances in Joyce Studies: "When It's Aped to Foul a Delfian."* Newark: Univ. of Delaware Press, 1988.

Spoo, Robert. "A Bibliography of Criticism on Joyce and History." In *Joyce and the Subject of History*, ed. Mark A. Wollaeger, Victor Luftig, and Robert Spoo, 211-39. Ann Arbor: Univ. of Michigan Press, 1996.

―――. *James Joyce and the Language of History. Dedalus's Nightmare.* New York: Oxford Univ. Press, 1994.

―――. "Tropics of Joycean Discourse: Representations of the Historical Process in *The Critical Writings.*" In *Papers from the Joyce and History Conference at Yale, October 1990*, ed. Victor Luftig and Mark A. Wollaeger, 819-25. Special issue of *James Joyce Quarterly* 28.4 (1991).

―――. "Uncanny Returns in 'The Dead': Ibsenian Intertexts and the Estranged Infant." In *Joyce: The Return of the Repressed*, ed. Susan Stanford Friedman, 89-113. Ithaca, N.Y.: Cornell Univ. Press, 1993.

―――, ed. *Dubliners Issue.* Special issue of *James Joyce Quarterly* 28.2 (1991): 335-550.

Suleiman, Susan R. "(Re)Writing the Body: The Politics and Poetics of Female Eroticism." In *The Female Body in Western Culture*, ed. Susan R. Suleiman, 7-29. Cambridge, Mass.: Harvard Univ. Press, 1986.

Vico, Giambattista. *The New Science.* Trans. Thomas Goddard Bergin and Max Harold Fisch. 1774. Reprint, Ithaca, N.Y.: Cornell Univ. Press, 1984.

Walzl, Florence L. "Gabriel and Michael: The Conclusion of 'The Dead.'" *James Joyce Quarterly* 4 (1966): 17-31.

White, Hayden. *Tropics of Discourse.* Baltimore: Johns Hopkins Univ. Press, 1978.

Williams, Trevor L. "Resistance to Paralysis in *Dubliners.*" In *Feminist Readings of Joyce*, ed. Ellen Carol Jones, 437-57. Special issue of *Modern Fiction Studies* 35.3 (1989).

Wollaeger, Mark A., Victor Luftig, and Robert Spoo, eds. *Joyce and the Subject of History.* Ann Arbor: Univ. of Michigan Press, 1996.

Woolf, Virginia. *Mrs. Dalloway.* New York: Harcourt, 1953.

―――. *A Room of One's Own* (1929). New York: Harcourt, 1957.

―――. *To the Lighthouse.* New York: Harcourt, 1979.

―――. *The Waves.* New York: Harcourt, 1959.

Yates, Frances A. *The Art of Memory.* Chicago: Univ. of Chicago Press, 1966.

CHAPTER NINE

Language, Character, and Gender in the Direct Discourse of *Dubliners*

Marlena G. Corcoran

> *He did not question her again for he felt that she would tell him of herself.*
> *[James Joyce, "The Dead"]*

Much goes unsaid in *Dubliners*, and far less is said by women than by men.[1] Nevertheless, an analysis of patterns of direct discourse in the book—with what frequency it occurs and under what circumstances and in what constellations male and female characters speak—is revealing. The terms *men*, *women*, and *speech*, though used with seeming naivete, are not understood here as preexisting categories; the investigation in the first section is rather into the complementary establishment of language, character, and gender as systems of sociotextual practice. In the second, historical section, I contrast these patterns with what is known of certain Dublin discussions in which Joyce took part and with the discourse of Irish nationalism. Finally, a few close readings demonstrate how character and gender are textualized through dialogic exchange.

These last sections of the essay examine two instances of the suppression of direct discourse by the text: the suppression of Tom Kernan's name in "Grace" and Gabriel Conroy's attempts to limit Lily's and Gretta's discourse in "The Dead." In order to see how the factor of gender changes the pattern of direct discourse, I have chosen one case involving only male characters and one case involving female characters as well.[2] Through the initial withholding of his name, Tom Kernan's particular character is problematized but not in ways that eliminate his own or other men's discourse; the story in which he appears abounds with the speech of men to the virtual exclusion of speech by women. In "The Dead," Lily and Gretta engage in direct discourse but against great textual odds: their interlocutor is ignorant or unsympathetic, and to this point there has been little textual space for women's discourse. What indications might we find in these conversations about the suppression of speech in

Original version published in *Style* 25.3 (1991).

ways peculiar to one's standing in the interlocking systems of language, character, and gender?

Analyzing direct discourse by gender reveals other patterns concerning lyric, epic, and dramatic forms; the use of dialogue; and the role of women's speech in framing both the concluding story and *Dubliners* as a whole. *Dubliners* is not a book in which women typically speak among themselves or in mixed groups; rather, they speak most often in a dialogue between one woman and one man. Perhaps most strikingly, *Dubliners* is a book in which women speak at the beginning and again at the end. Furthermore, the distribution of women's direct discourse does not follow the same pattern as men's. This evidence encourages us to qualify by gender such otherwise useful generalizations as that made by Ulrich Schneider about the Joycean trajectory from lyric through epic to dramatic:

> Aber während im *Portrait* diese Perspektive konsequent durchgehalten wird und alle übrigen Figuren nur in der Bewusstseinsspiegelung Stephens erscheinen, kommen in *Dubliners* nach der dritten Erzählung die Dubliner Durchschnittsbürger selbst zu Wort. Der damit verbundene Wechsel von der Ich-zur Er-Erzählung lässt sich in den Begriffen der Aesthetik, wie sie Stephen im *Portrait* entwickelt, als ein Fortschreiten vom Lyrischen zum Epischen und Dramatischen sehen. [*James Joyces* Dubliners 9]

> [But while in *Portrait* this perspective is consistently maintained and all other figures appear only in the mirror of Stephen's consciousness, in *Dubliners,* after the third story, average citizens of Dublin speak for themselves. The associated shift from first-to third-person narration can be seen in terms of the concepts of the aesthetic, developed by Stephen in *Portrait,* as a progression from the lyric to the epic and dramatic. (my translation)]

This may well be true of male characters, but the pattern of female speech in *Dubliners* is rather different. The most dramatic scenes involving women take place in the first and last stories, when women occupy the stage at the end of "The Sisters" and at the Misses Morkans' party. The direct discourse of women provides a remarkable frame for *Dubliners;* in order to see such patterns, we need a brief but exact account of direct discourse contained therein.[3] Though a simple exercise in counting is not enough, it will help ensure the accuracy of further analysis. This is especially important, given how linguistic research has documented that we tend to overestimate, often grossly, the extent of women's participation in conversation; we probably do so in reading as well.[4]

Table 1 documents the instances of direct discourse by story and by gender. There are 960 instances of direct discourse in *Dubliners:* 707 by males, 243 by females, and 10 unmarked for gender.[5] Female speakers thus account

Table 1. Direct Discourse in *Dubliners*

Story	Male	Female	Unmarked	Total
The Sisters	13	31		44
An Encounter	15	0		15
Araby	8	6		14
Eveline	6	3		9
After the Race	6	0		6
Two Gallants	49	1		50
The Boarding House	0	5		5
A Little Cloud	69	3		72
Counterparts	42	1		43
Clay	1	2	1	4
A Painful Case	0	1		1
Ivy Day	167	0		167
A Mother	15	24		39
Grace	194	13		207
The Dead	122	153	9	284
Totals:	707	243	10	960
w/o "The Dead"	585	90	1	676

for almost 25 percent of the total number of instances of direct discourse; another way to put this is that for every time a woman speaks, a man speaks three times. Without "The Dead," the instances of female speech would account for only 13 percent of the total, or one woman speaker for every eight men. In "The Dead," there are 284 instances of direct discourse, and female speakers account for just over half of the direct discourse. To get some understanding of how rare this is in *Dubliners,* consider how sharply the instances of female speech fall from 153 in "The Dead" to 31 in "The Sisters," 24 in "A Mother," and 13 in "Grace."[6] Following that, there are eleven stories in which females speak six times or less, including six stories in which a woman speaks once or not at all. The comparable figures for instances of male speech by story are 194, 167, 122, 69, 49, 42. The figures for the remaining stories descend less abruptly than do those for women, and there are only three stories in which a man speaks once or not at all. The difference between the stories in which no man speaks and the stories in which no woman speaks is that, to put it crudely, if no man speaks, no one speaks at all. More precisely, in the three stories in which a man speaks not at all or only once, the incidence of female speech is also very low: M/F=0/1, 0/5, 1/2. On the other hand, in the stories with no female speaker, male characters manage to continue talking: M/F=6/0, 15/0, 167/0.

It certainly is true, and it is remarkable, that in "A Painful Case" there is only one instance of direct discourse: this is Mrs. Sinico's remark about singing to empty benches. However, her comment might well be construed to mean that when Mrs. Sinico speaks, no one is listening.[7] "A Painful Case" should be considered in the context of the other two stories in which a woman speaks once and only once. In "Counterparts," Annie speaks once, and men speak forty-two times. In "Two Gallants," a "slatternly girl" speaks once, and men speak forty-nine times. The typical case thereafter is a story in which a woman speaks not at all or once, and the text is overwhelmed by male discourse. There is no comparable pattern for male speech being overwhelmed by female speech. The total number of instances of female speech is not achieved by speech scenes in which women dominate a mixed conversation. The raising of the total is typically achieved by a private conversation between one man and one woman in which the two parties speak about an equal number of times. Thus in the opening speech scene of "The Dead," for example, Lily and Gabriel each speak seven times; in their final conversation in the hotel room, Gretta speaks twenty-three times and Gabriel twenty-four times. After "The Dead," the story that contributes the highest number of female speech acts is "The Sisters": the figures are 134 and 13, respectively. "The Sisters" contains an anomalous speech scene: a conversation among women with no (living) adult male present. So we see that among themselves or individually with one other man, the female characters of *Dubliners* speak; it is in public scenes that their speech is not represented.

Joyce's Choices

One reason for the paucity of female speech in *Dubliners* is obvious: Joyce creates a textual Dublin in which women are often absent. However, even in the stories in which women figure prominently, such as "Eveline" and "Clay," the mode of discourse is predominantly indirect. Eveline pronounces not one word in direct speech though she is talked at by her father, her mother, her boss, and Frank; and stretches of Maria's discourse seem to conflate the words of Maria and others.

One might object that the pattern of distribution of direct discourse in *Dubliners* simply reflects the way the world is: the women of Dublin, it is claimed, did not speak much in mixed company or in public. But is this true? At the end of this section, I will consider historical evidence of the vociferous role played by women in Irish politics as Joyce was growing up. First, let us consider Joyce's personal friends, the notoriously opinionated and outspoken Sheehy sisters. These examples of women's voices in both the public and private realms provide a pointed contrast to the paucity of women's discourse in *Dubliners*. Richard Ellmann portrays the Sheehy household as the seeming center of James Joyce's social life around 1896. "James and Stanislaus were there regularly," writes Ellmann, "and at Mrs. Sheehy's invitation James stayed several times overnight" (*James Joyce* 51). Another indication of Joyce's involvement with the family is that "[f]or Mary [Sheehy], Joyce conceived a small, rich passion which, unsuspected by her, lasted for several years" (51).

James Joyce's self-esteemed superiority to the Sheehy household is clear in the depiction in *Stephen Hero* and even in *Portrait* of "the house where young men are called by their Christian names a little too soon."[8] Stanislaus Joyce's condescension toward the Sheehys in his diary (his calling Hanna "a practical animal" [23] sounds a bit like James Joyce's own disparaging descriptions of women) may have helped give Joyce critics a rather partial view of the relative positions of the Sheehy and Joyce families. Consider the ambivalence in Bonnie Kime Scott's *Joyce and Feminism:*

> Joyce may have experienced some discomfort in the Sheehy household. He was a poet among practical people, and his feeling of social inequality may have made him particularly critical of the manners of the young women. The latter he exaggerates to his eventual life-partner, Nora, during their courtship: "I could never speak to the girls I used to meet at houses. Their false manners checked me at once" (*L* II, 237). Stanislaus Joyce suspected that Hanna Sheehy-Skeffington did not "understand those disattached personalities, the world's poets and artists and cranks," whose numbers implicitly contained his brother. She was a "practical animal" who found men who would not serve her purposes "worthless." [28][9]

Scott concludes this very informative chapter on "Early Encounters with Feminism: The Irish Literary Feminist Movement and the Literary Feminism of Moore, Shaw, Hauptmann, and Ibsen" on an optimistic note: "Their nationalism encouraged Joyce to see the women of his day in unconventional ways: in assertive roles, alongside his male peers, or in the context of national history" (28).

Joyce did indeed know feminists both male and female; yet female characters in *Dubliners* are not, it seems to me, represented "in assertive roles, alongside [their] male peers" or as effective nationalists.[10] As the data on direct discourse show, they hardly talk. It seems rather that Joyce's way of dealing with his inability to speak to girls of his own social class ("I could never speak to the girls I used to meet at houses") is to give them little direct voice in his fiction.

It would be hard to exaggerate the paucity of Joyce's social relations with his female peers. In her biography of the loquacious chambermaid preferred by Joyce, Brenda Maddox presents a refreshing overview of the matter: "Given his background, it is not surprising . . . that Joyce found middle-class Dublin girls coy, unattainable and condescending. . . . [The Sheehy salon] was the highest he rose in genteel Dublin society. Yet the four Sheehy sisters thought he was uncouth, if amusing and talented. *'Farouche'* was the word that Hanna Sheehy later chose to describe him—that is, wild and savage. Their mother had to give him a clean shirt when he came to her 'evenings'" (51).[11] Joyce's need to feel that he was doing the rejecting comes through again in Maddox's account of his contact with the Sheehy family during his visit to Ireland in 1909:

> [M]any of [Joyce's] old circle who had remained in Ireland had risen in society, married and prospered. . . . Thomas Kettle, another University College friend, was a Member of Parliament, and about to marry the girl Joyce had so admired, Mary Sheehy. . . . Joyce was invited to dinner by another of the Sheehy girls, Hanna, who had just married his friend, Francis Skeffington. Joyce declined. Yet when Hanna's parents, the senior Sheehys, whose house on Belvedere Place he had so often visited as a young man, did not get in touch with him, he smarted from the slight. [127]

Skeffington's article on behalf of women at the university was privately published together with Joyce's "Day of the Rabblement" in 1901.[12] In 1903, Joyce proposed a further collaboration on a halfpenny daily newspaper. "It would be primarily literary rather than political," Ellmann reports, "although [Joyce] conceded to Skeffington that general issues such as the emancipation of women, pacifism, and socialism might be given some space" (140). I bring this up not to credit Joyce with feminist thinking but to document that Joyce sang, played, published, and presumably also talked with a number of women and men who wrote, and presumably also spoke, for a larger role to be taken by women in both private and public discourse. Given the political positions and practices of Joyce's friends, it is all the more surprising that women as subjects of discourse—both as topic and as speaker—are so circumscribed in *Dubliners*.

Though the Sheehys were particularly outspoken, the voices of other women in public life were certainly not lacking.[13] Around the year of Joyce's birth, women were in the forefront of efforts to aid Irish farmers devastated by the miserable potato harvest of 1879, the worst since the Great Famine. The women were not practicing apolitical charity. The formation of the Ladies' Land League on 31 January 1881 began a period of resistance to rack rents and evictions that was far more fervent and radically nationalist under the direction of the "ladies" and Anna Parnell than it had been under male leadership. Margaret Ward's *Unmanageable Revolutionaries: Women and Irish Nationalism* documents this as well as the vehemence of the women's organization Inghinidhe na nEireann in the years 1900-1914, the period during which Joyce wrote *Dubliners*. Much of the documentation in Ward's book is from Irish newspapers of the time. Joyce's frequent requests for a steady stream of newspapers from Ireland during his residence on the Continent suggests that these same newspaper reports were seen by him. Yet these accounts of Irish women's political activities do not figure in Joyce's fiction. It is not in the world but in Joyce's texts that women are silent; it is Joyce's choices that remain to be explicated.

Tom Kernan: Or, "—Don't Mention It . . ."

A charitable view of the minimal representation of women and their speech in *Dubliners* (hereafter cited with page numbers as *D*) might call Joyce's choices "nonnaturalistic." Men's speech is occasionally also represented nonnaturalistically, as in the case of Tom Kernan. The difference is that this altered speech pattern concerns one individual and not the entire class to which he belongs. Tom Kernan's speech defect is not what one would expect after that particular accident. As A.M.L. Knuth observes: "The only serious [factual error] I noticed in *D* occurs in 'Grace,' when [Joyce] puts into the mouth of Tom Kernan, who has bitten off a piece of his tongue, the words: 'I' 'ery 'uch o'liged to you sir. I hope we'll 'eet again. 'y na'e is Kernan' (*D* 153). It is evident that Kernan is having more difficulty with the labials than with the apical and dorsal consonants. He is admittedly drunk, but even so he should either have skipped the appropriate sounds or else lost part of his lip" (35). Whatever the reason for the gaps in Kernan's speech, these distortions support the critical observation that the missing consonants make a guessing game out of Kernan's discourse. The linguistic deformation inscribes at the level of direct discourse the questions posed by the crowd and the constable: "—Who is the man? What's his name and address?" (*D* 151).

"—Sha, 's nothing" is the only thing the man says, and he says it twice in the first three pages of the story, which are concerned with the efforts of others to find out who he is. His adroit escape from both the questioning and the adventure with the assertion " 's nothing" could be construed as a version of Odysseus's escape from the Cyclops as he replies with "Noman," the gnomon of that Homeric episode, to the Cyclops's question about the name of who blinded him. This is not to draw an Odyssean parallel as a sufficient explanation but to point out that these episodes share a linguistic exploit: they deflect a question of reference onto the plane of language itself, where one of the most intriguing capabilities of language is to assert the negative.

The withholding of Kernan's name is not dismissable as a quirk of the character, though one could certainly understand that under the circumstances a person would be loath to give it; the value of such discretion is confirmed later in the discussion in the bedroom. The direct discourse contrives in the suppression of the name. When this oddly spoken character finally avers, "'y na'e is

Kernan," he is told: "—Don't mention it" (*D* 153). Of course, one could understand the cyclist to mean, "you needn't thank me for the trouble I've taken." Yet the formulaic phrase in its abstraction, brevity, and syntactic placement connects the injunction to silence with the revelation of the name. The reader feels chided for the very curiosity the text has taken such trouble to arouse.

Joyce frustrates the urge to easy characterization by denying us the name of a speaker, which in another construction might have been avowed freely in the first person. Instead, the story asks the reader to build up a third-person view of a character from the guesses or the partial information of those around the speaker. In using third-person rather than first-person perspective, Joyce avoids lyricism in characterization; Kernan is first to us what he is to others. When Kernan finally speaks his own name, his discourse is defective, and he is told not to mention it. Lyricism, or speaking of oneself for oneself, is thereby compromised.

The case of Kernan dramatically enacts a narrative pattern of *Dubliners:* namely, the denial to the reader of a character's name. Significant numbers of characters remain nameless, including the boy of the first three stories, the man of "An Encounter," and Mangan's sister. Sometimes a character is for a significant duration pointedly nameless, as is Tom Kernan. The characters in the story attempt to find out Kernan's name, thereby acting out the reader's own desire to know; when the characters are frustrated, the reader's desire is called into question. This narrative strategy of suppressing the name thwarts our desire to compartmentalize character by drawing a clear boundary around it and tagging it with an individual name. Joyce's own modernist practice calls attention to and qualifies our tendency to use such a compartmentalized model.

Such experimentation with character is already clear in *Dubliners,* and it is singularly interesting here in that *Dubliners* both employs and negates a nineteenth-century model of character. Part of the continuing popularity of *Dubliners,* particularly as a teaching text, is that it toys with our desire to read texts as we have been trained to read persons, and it does this by partially presenting some characters in nineteenth-century realist fashion. It is all the more surprising that a writer engaged in radical rethinking of the conventions of individual identity should so conserve conventions of gender. The female characters of *Dubliners* are stereotypes on their way to becoming archetypes.

Let us consider the formal constraints operating on the direct discourse of Lily and Gretta in "The Dead." Like Tom Kernan, Lily and Gretta are engaged in conversations crucial to the story. Each of these three characters is oddly both encouraged and discouraged from talking. Yet the differences are more important than the similarities, and the differences are linked to gender. It is largely Tom Kernan's own reluctance to speak that limits his participation. For the text as a whole, the result is not a limitation on male discourse as such but the circumscription of the discourse of a particular individual. "Grace" is amply supplied with the words of a curate, a cyclist, a constable, some male friends, and a priest. Their discourse is rendered in various circumstances and combinations of characters. Women's speech in *Dubliners,* however, comes from a limited number of characters and is mainly constrained to conversations between two people. The conversations involving Lily and Gretta are therefore more typical of the limitations on women's speech generally than the restriction on Tom Kernan's is of the discourse of men.

Bonnie Kime Scott suggests that it was Joyce's admiration of Ibsen that prompted Joyce's dialogues in which "both parties (but especially the women) explain their present and remembered frustrations, make charges, and react either with candid truth or renewed questioning—a strategy that evades hypocritical submission to the male's view. This is an aspect of style that Joyce definitely attempted in *Exiles.* . . . He may have tried something similar in the dialogues between Stephen and Emma Clery, which are so deliberately positioned throughout the surviving pages of *Stephen Hero.* Gabriel's exchanges with Gretta and especially with Miss Ivors in 'The Dead' are also reminiscent of the form" (48). Such conversations may be typical of Ibsenite egalitarianism, but let us not hasten to ascribe overly feminist qualities to the pattern of Joyce's direct discourse. The data presented in this essay certainly confirm that there are pockets of dialogue between one man and one woman in *Dubliners,* but they are noteworthy precisely because they are "dramatic" exceptions. The dialogues between Stephen and Emma Clery are edited out of *A Portrait of the Artist as a Young Man.* Gabriel's dialogues with Lily and Gretta in "The Dead" reveal very different formal patterns of discourse for the male partner and the female partner.

Gabriel and Lily

In both the opening conversation between Gabriel and Lily and the closing talk between Gabriel and Gretta, Gabriel tries to speak for the women. He tries to impose on the direct discourse of both Lily and Gretta his preferred version, a generic gendered tale we might call "A Young Woman's Story." How is the suppression of women's discourse achieved? Gabriel's interactions with Lily and Gretta dramatize the fine art of missing opportunities.

In response to Gabriel's questions about school and wedding plans, which were asked "in a friendly tone" and "gaily," Lily delivers a ringing rejoinder: "The girl glanced back at him over her shoulder and said with bitterness:— The men that is now is only all palaver and what they can get out of you" (178). Lily's reply may come as a shock to Gabriel, but the attentive reader will already have noticed that the two speakers are on different wavelengths.

Gabriel has been projecting platitudes onto Lily and risks putting words in her mouth. Gabriel's "friendly tone" in asking first whether she is still in school does not disguise that he is out of touch with Lily; addressing him as "sir," she says she has been out of school for over a year. Continuing his conventional plot of a young woman's life, Gabriel proceeds: "—O, then, said Gabriel gaily, I suppose we'll be going to your wedding one of these fine days with your young man, eh?" (*D* 178).

This rhetorical question contains the platitudes of an inevitable wedding, the cliché "one of these fine days," and an unidentified and interchangeable bit-part player, the presumed "young man." They are tailored to Lily only by the pronoun "your": "your wedding," "your young man." Gabriel's conventional plot remains the same, just waiting for her to step into her projected role. Lily's first response prepares the way for her second bitter reply. She already has had to tell Gabriel that she is not in school. She now disillusions him on the subject of his next set of assumptions about her happy progress toward marriage. Her bitterness suggests she has broken it off with a "young man," and her judgment comes down on all men of today.

These two elements of Lily's surprising rejoinder to Gabriel recur in Gretta's revelation to him at the close of the story. Lily's charge against the men of today is that they are "all palaver," all talk. Gabriel's shortcoming, enacted in both these conversations, is that he talks for women; he does not let them talk for themselves. Rather than ask Lily what happened, or what she meant, "Gabriel coloured as if he felt he had made a mistake and, without looking at her, kicked off his goloshes and flicked actively with his muffler at his patent leather shoes" (*D* 178). The narrative follows Gabriel's gaze: the paragraph after this is a rather self-reflexive description of Gabriel as he would see himself; Lily is left out of the picture.

Lacking conversational transition, the reader must provide one: perhaps Gabriel is one such man of today, all palaver, and the text's occupation with Gabriel himself both as the seer and the seen is a doubling of the lack of dialogue at the level of direct discourse. Rather than exchange words, he proffers a coin, "thrusting it into her hands" over Lily's protests of "—O no, sir!" and "Really sir, I wouldn't take it." Though of course she does, and their only successfully completed exchange is monetary rather than linguistic. That exchange serves to end the interchange, however. As he tenders Lily the coin, Gabriel is on the run, "almost trotting to the stairs and waving to her in deprecation" (*D* 178).

Gabriel and Gretta: "His Voice Would Strike Her"

A false start and talk of monetary exchange similarly mark the beginning of Gretta and Gabriel's private conversation in their darkened hotel room at the end of "The Dead." Gabriel has rehearsed his opening line in the cab on the way there: "He would call her softly:—Gretta!" (*D* 214). But when in their room Gabriel calls her name in just this way, "—Gretta!" (*D* 216), what follows is not what he had imagined. He had thought: "Perhaps she would not hear at once: she would be undressing. Then something in his voice would strike her. She would turn and look at him . . ." (*D* 214; ellipsis in original). Gretta is indeed undressing as Gabriel calls her name in the hotel, but she is looking in the mirror at herself much as Gabriel looked at himself and not at Lily in their aborted conversation. (Gabriel too will see himself in a mirror as he goes to Gretta momentarily.) Gabriel's conversation with his wife falters as the word "tired" passes from him to her. Starting once again, "he said abruptly: —By the way, Gretta!" (*D* 216).

But this beginning is also wrong. And just as he had done in his unsuccessful conversation with Lily, Gabriel diverts the level of exchange to the monetary. His mention of a felicitously completed monetary exchange may be read as a displacement of the verbal exchange, which is not going so well. Gabriel finds himself talking "in a false voice" about a sovereign he had loaned to Freddy Malins, which Malins unexpectedly returned. Finding out about the loan prompts Gretta to exclaim: "—You are a very generous person, Gabriel . . ." (*D* 217). Gabriel swells with the compliment and feels rather sure of himself as he asks, for once, an open question: "—Gretta dear, what are you thinking about?" (*D* 218). The dialogue switches now to question-and-answer format for the duration of this next segment of the conversation. Gabriel "tried to keep up his tone of cold interrogation" (*D* 220), which implies that first he had such a tone and then he had risked losing it, but the question-and-answer format implied throughout is evidence of both the form and tone of sustained interrogation.

I am not concerned here with exactly what Gretta and Gabriel say but with the pattern of direct discourse. In the cab, Gabriel imagines his address to Gretta, but, significantly, he imagines no verbal reply. He carries out his address at the hotel. Subsequently, Gretta replies to a rather relentless series of questions. In short, the interaction is planned, initiated, and sustained by Gabriel. He imagines that only he will have an active, forceful, and, above all, speaking part: "his voice would strike her." Her role is to be responsive and silent: "She would turn and look at him. . . . " But Gabriel's fantasy does not work out; Gretta is not silent and instead says something completely unexpected: "—I think he [Michael Furey] died for me . . ." (*D* 220). Until this point, Gabriel has more or less solicited Gretta's words. But now, "He did not question her again for he felt that she would tell him of herself" (*D* 220). His previous questions must have presumed that in her answers she would not tell him of herself. What kind of questions are they? Rhetorical questions, in which the answers only serve to confirm what the questioner already believes.

But here at the end of *Dubliners,* a woman's voice speaks unbidden. In her longest speech so far, Gretta utters four sentences. She pauses and, though no encouraging remark or leading question is forthcoming, continues with another five sentences. As Gretta finishes the story of herself and Michael Furey, Gabriel speaks three separate lines. Two of them rather pointedly suggest his desire to see Michael Furey gone: "—And did you not tell him to go back? . . . —And did he go home?" (*D* 221). Again Gabriel does not ask her about herself. Gretta concludes the story in tears and a textual blank:

> Gabriel held her hand for a moment, irresolutely, and then, shy of intruding on her grief, let it fall gently and walked quietly to the window.
>
> She was fast asleep. [*D* 221-22]

"It's so hard on people to have to sing to empty benches" (*D* 109), we might remark about the last effort a woman makes to speak in *Dubliners.*

Notes

1. I am grateful to Cheryl Herr and Fritz Senn for helpful criticism of an earlier version of this paper. Most of the work was done while I was in residence as the first Zurich James Joyce Foundation Scholar. I thank the Zurich James Joyce Foundation and the Friends of the Zurich James Joyce Foundation for their warm welcome and generous support.

2. All-female conversations are hardly to be found.

3. I chose to count those instances that are preceded by the dash, which Joyce used instead of quotation marks to indicate direct discourse. This means that songs, poems, and most remembered or imagined speech are not counted; they are interesting in a different way. (An exception is Polly Mooney's song, which I counted because her enunciation of the lyrics is crucial in the establishment of character and gender in "The Boarding House.") It also means that, for example, Gabriel Conroy's dinner speech in "The Dead" might be counted differently. I believe however that such slight variations will not alter the substance of this essay.

4. See Dale Spender. In short, Spender's test subjects respond as if when a woman speaks at all, it is too much.

5. The length of the stories is not calculated because the proportion of most interest to this essay is that of women's to men's speech, not of speech to story length.

6. "The Dead" is of course much longer than the other stories, which tempers any comparison of absolute numbers of instances of direct discourse. Nevertheless, the relative percentage of female to male speech calls for commentary, and the way to get accurate percentages is to first count the instances.

7. Women characters in *Dubliners* tend to remain oddly oblique to a given conversation, understanding little of the dynamics or the content of male conversation. When I presented the first version of this paper at the Eleventh International James Joyce Symposium (Venice, 1988), it was suggested to me that the relative rarity of women's speech makes the little they do say more significant. It remains to be established just what such significance might be.

8. This citation from *Portrait* (219) is preceded by the phrase "he remembered his own sarcasm." The sarcasm is from the description of the Daniels, modeled on the Sheehys, in *Stephen Hero:* "In this house it was the custom to call a young visitor 'by his Christian name' a little too soon" (44). Like James Joyce, Stephen, in both texts, scrupulously observes the distinction in address.

9. The citations from James Joyce are from the *Letters of James Joyce*, 2:237; the citations from Stanislaus Joyce are from *The Complete Dublin Diary*, 23.

10. Miss Ivors, the nationalist university graduate in "The Dead," is remarkable as an exception, and it is debatable whether Joyce's portrayal of Ivors is positive. This essay is about the general patterns of direct discourse in *Dubliners*, which differ considerably from the conversation between Miss Ivors and Mr. Conroy.

11. Maddox also reminds us that Joyce's sexual experience was limited to prostitutes.

12. Joyce was razzed about this essay by Hanna and Maggie Sheehy and by Francis Skeffington. One can hardly imagine that Joyce took it lightly: "Joyce wrote the dialogue down in an epiphany, perhaps to suggest how in Ireland all things are cheapened" (Ellmann 90). It is enlightening to contrast the feminists' fond bantering with the cavernous mysticism of the epiphany. It seems that in this case it was not the feminists who lacked a sense of humor.

13. Again, let us contrast historical evidence of women's voices in Irish politics with their representation in particular literary texts. That most literary critics are more familiar with Yeats's bitter lament over Maud Gonne's speechmaking than with her speeches themselves should not obscure our recognition that one of the strongest of Ireland's public voices at that time was a woman's. Margaret Ward's *Unmanageable Revolutionaries* also gives a very different picture of the tireless labor of the nationalist feminist Hanna Sheehy Skeffington than one could glean from the slighting remarks about her husband and her to be found in the writings of Joyce. Ward's book is also a sobering reminder that women's interests and the nationalist movement are not synonymous. When I presented the first version of this paper at the Eleventh International James Joyce Symposium, a Marxist scholar pointed out that men too were oppressed under imperialist rule in Ireland. With Ward, however, I would say that an analysis of the nationalist struggle alone is not enough and tends to veil the different significance nationalism had for men and women citizens. The establishment of an Irish state did not return Irish society to the oft-invoked golden days of the prestige of women in Celtic culture. In fact, as Ward's book documents, the new state consolidated itself in nudging women out of what political power they had exercised in the days of the Ladies' Land League and Inghinidhe na nEireann. The "protective" labor laws limiting women's legal ability to work are a case in point.

Works Cited

Ellmann, Richard. *James Joyce.* New York: Oxford Univ. Press, 1982.

Joyce, James. Dubliners: *Text, Criticism and Notes.* Ed. Robert Scholes and A. Walton Litz. New York: Viking, 1969.

———. *Letters of James Joyce.* Ed. Stuart Gilbert and Richard Ellmann. 3 vols. New York: Viking, 1966.

———. A Portrait of the Artist as a Young Man: *Text, Criticism, and Notes.* Ed. Chester G. Anderson. New York: Viking, 1968.

———. *Stephen Hero.* Ed. Theodore Spencer, John J. Slocum, and Hebert Cahoon. New York: New Directions, 1944.

Joyce, Stanislaus. *The Complete Dublin Diary of Stanislaus Joyce.* Ed. George H. Healey. Ithaca, N.Y.: Cornell Univ. Press, 1971.

Knuth, A.M.L. *The Wink of the Word: A Study of James Joyce's Phatic Communication.* Amsterdam: Rodopi, 1976.

Maddox, Brenda. *Nora: A Biography of Nora Joyce.* London: Hamilton, 1988.

Schneider, Ulrich. *James Joyce:* Dubliners. Munich: Fink, 1982.

Scott, Bonnie Kime. *Joyce and Feminism.* Bloomington: Indiana Univ. Press, 1984.

Spender, Dale. *Man Made Language.* London: Routledge, 1980.

Ward, Margaret. *Unmanageable Revolutionaries: Women and Irish Nationalism.* London: Pluto, 1964.

CHAPTER TEN

Gendered Discourse and the Structure of Joyce's "The Dead"

David Leon Higdon

"At any rate, very careful composition," wrote Virginia Woolf in her "Dalloway Notebook" on 16 October 1922, "[t]he contrast must be arranged. . . . The design is extremely complicated. The balance must be very finely considered" (quoted in Novak 226-27). She was, of course, mapping the structure of *Mrs. Dalloway* being generated by the eventual intersection of the lives of Clarissa Dalloway and Septimus Smith. However, with equal appropriateness she could have been describing the structural features of James Joyce's "The Dead," for it, too, has an "extremely complicated" binary design whose "contrast . . . must be finely considered." In many ways, though, this design has been inadequately recognized and largely undescribed because the thematic and psychological macrostructures have eclipsed the microstructures of the story, particularly the patterns wherein music and noise images coordinate with female and male worlds, microstructures whose subtleties make the story a rehearsal for the "Sirens" episode in *Ulysses* and for the "[m]elodiotiosities in purefusion by the score" of *Finnegans Wake* (222). Stanislaus Joyce indicated as much when he wrote that "[t]here is a mastery of story telling in the skill with which *a crescendo of noise and jollity* is gradually worked up and then *suddenly silenced* by the ghost of a memory" (527; emphasis added).

Virtually every critical discussion of "The Dead" has taken place within the intellectual boundaries inscribed early by David Daiches and Brewster Ghiselin. In *The Novel and the Modern World* (1939), Daiches very deftly established three guiding principles regarding Joyce's story: its "expansive technique" (73), its self-conscious "working-out . . . of a preconceived theme" (74), and its "lopsided[ness]" (75) set it far apart from the other fourteen stories in the collection and make it a crucially transitional bridge into the ever increasingly complex novels, written "as it was at a time when Joyce was becoming increasingly preoccupied with the problems of aesthetics" (81). Daiches made clear that Gabriel Conroy's encounters with three women—Lily, Molly Ivors, and Gretta Conroy—which mark the several stages in his journey toward self-knowledge, constitute the heart and soul of the story's technique, theme, and pattern. In 1956, in "The Unity of Joyce's *Dubliners*," Ghiselin extended these areas into symbolic structure and "a pattern of correspondences" (75), such as found in *Ulysses*, and thus a critical template was firmly established in place.[1]

At present, most Joyce critics work almost exclusively in terms of these women and their roles in Gabriel's evening. Regardless of the theoretical map, the destination seems the same. The 1994 Lacanian approach of Garry M. Leonard, suggestive and persuasive as it is, sees "the story as three attempts by Gabriel Conroy, with three different women, to confirm the fictional unity of his masculine subjectivity" (289) and differs little from Gerald Doherty's 1989 Bakhtinian untangling of the metaphoric and metonymic dimensions of the text that leads to "Lily's bitter comment about men," "Miss Ivor's aggression," and Gabriel's "brief tiff with Gretta" (227) as features of the metonymic plot line. Richard Brown (1985) and Edward Brandabur (1971) had already reached similar conclusions, the former observing that "the story . . . seems tailor-made for feminist interpretation. Gabriel's evening consists of a succession of significant encounters with women" (92), the latter concluding that "throughout the story, personal encounters disturb [Gabriel's] poise until he finally gives in to the annihilation he has not only anticipated but invited" (116).

The recent Daniel R. Schwarz edition (1994) for St. Martin's very successful series "Case Studies in Contemporary Criticism" also takes us down this same familiar road whether the vehicle is psychoanalytic, reader-response, new historicist, or deconstructionist criticism. Schwarz sounds the familiar call in relating the autobiographies of Joyce and Conroy: "Gabriel expresses Joyce's fear of betrayal—*sexual, political, and personal*" (104, emphasis added)—abstractions of the views of, wounds inflicted by, and temptations posed by the three women. These designs adequately describe the "encounter scenes," but they rarely do justice to the sections separating them. By concentrating on the 618 lines in the encounters and essentially ignoring the structural significances of the remaining 1,042 lines, they fail to account fully for the "considerable formal differences" (O'Connor 305) between "The Dead" and the other stories and also overlook the subtle, complicated interplay of counterpointing rhythms, musical and sexual, among the scenes.

I propose that the Lily, Molly, and Gretta "encounter scenes," dramatizing the comfortable illusions Gabriel harbored about himself and about most other men, alternate with inverted scenes in which individual men threaten to disrupt, if indeed not to overthrow, the harmony and melody usually bodied forth in dance, song, and performance by the women. The main offenders— Freddy Malins, Mr. Browne, and Bartell D'Arcy—are eventually joined by Gabriel himself as the Lord of Misrule dethroning harmony this winter night.[2] Freddy's drunkenness and unzipped fly, Browne's coarseness and defiance,

D'Arcy's rudeness and hoarseness, and Gabriel's smug sense of superiority and condescension threaten the spirited, celebratory world created by the three Misses Morkan, but only Gabriel emerges from the evening enlightened in any way.

In other words, the grand tonal shifts occurring between the endings and beginnings of chapters in *A Portrait of the Artist as a Young Man*, patterns so ably delineated by A. Walton Litz and Hugh Kenner, are fully anticipated and realized throughout "The Dead." Litz argues that "[e]ach chapter ends on a tone of intense lyricism, corresponding to Stephen's new-found hope; but then—as we move into the next chapter—there is an abrupt change in language which reflects the decline in Stephen's resolution" (69), movement from lyrical triumph to Icarian plummet. This is a more sophisticated, more aesthetic observation on structure than Kenner's remarks on the alternations between dream and reality, but both capture the binary clashes that generate structure. Thus, in "The Dead," there is a constant juxtaposition of male/female, past/present, public/private, and other binaries that cluster together around thematic and structural poles as the three scenes in which the female "wounds" the male's self-image, leaving him pondering in silence how to respond and how to defend his ego—a pattern of exclusion, alienation, interior monologue, and silence alternating with a pattern of inclusion (whether in dance, song, or feasting), sharing, and sound. The female rhythm in this story directly points toward Molly Bloom and Anna Livia Plurabelle.

Following the tightly designed opening scene (*D* 175.1-176.33) and Lily "encounter" episode (*D* 176.34-179.20), Joyce's story appears to concentrate randomly for the next few pages on unrelated groups of characters at the party, giving first this man or that woman his or her moment of attention.[3] The story's structure thus alternates between the private moments of Gabriel and a woman (first Lily, then Molly, and finally Gretta) and the public world of the party in which men boorishly endanger the social balances, proprieties, and melodies—perhaps a hostess's most serious but unvoiced fear. Gabriel is, of course, actually alone with both Lily in the "little pantry" (*D* 175) downstairs where he insults her with the improperly given tip and Gretta in the hotel. In one way or another, Gabriel consciously insults each significant woman in the story, and he clearly intends his words to wound, as when he reminds Gretta of her violation of clear social distinctions in her relationship with Michael Furey and even ventures to question her fidelity to him (*D* 219).

It has been less clear, perhaps, how he insults Lily. Of course, the scene lacks the complexity and significance of the other two "encounter scenes," and Gabriel must be quick and more spontaneous in his response. The crux is the coin he gives Lily, which is less a muted sexual insult than it is a gross violation of the etiquette of his class and period. No houseguest would tip his or her hostess's servant unless remaining in the house overnight, and never on the guest's arrival. Redoubtable Elizabeth L. Post still firmly decrees, "No tip—ever—for servants in a private house at a dinner party" (403), and such measures would have been even more pronounced at the time of the Misses Morkans' party, especially given the social pretensions of the family. Gabriel attempts to mask his act as one of generosity authorized by the season, but Lily sees beneath the mask an unmistakable rudeness and insensitiveness.

Although his encounter with Molly takes place on the dance floor, fellow dancers become aware of their conversation only after their voices are raised, an obviously intended effect since Joyce originally had Gretta remarking on "the row" Gabriel had had with Molly (Scholes 29). The private, male, illu-sioned world endangered by the female though is abruptly swept away by the roisterous, good-natured, public, female rhythms, and the two rhythms ulti-mately fuse in the final scene of the story.

In the first of the female-ordered worlds (*D* 179.21-187.18), the females triumph, even though the "pretty waltz" (*D* 183) with its accompanying "stamping and shuffling of feet" (*D* 177), the quadrilles announced by "a red-faced young woman" (*D* 183), and Mary Jane's showy concert piece, designed more to highlight her masterful technique than the work's substance, could at any moment be disrupted. Aunt Kate fears that Freddy Malins is "screwed" (*D* 182), but he seems "hardly noticeable" as he crosses the floor "on rather shaky legs" (*D* 185). Browne threatens more serious disruption as he leads not one but three young ladies "into the back room" (*D* 182), drinks "a goodly measure of whisky" (*D* 183), and attempts "a very low Dublin accent" (*D* 183) in his coarse joke. In the rush to pair men and women for the quadrilles, how-ever, Mary Jane and Aunt Kate avert further disruptions and sweep the guests up in dance, but not before Aunt Kate has satisfied herself that Malins is under control and has chastised Browne "by frowning and shaking her forefinger in warning to and fro" (*D* 185), thus leaving them alone and silenced in their own disorder and evading, for the moment, the disruptions that a habitual drunk and a socially displaced boor could inflict on the party.

Following Gabriel's more serious encounter with Molly Ivors (*D* 187.19-192.27), the story moves to the second female-ordered scene (*D* 192.30-213.30), one much more highly fragmented and potentially disordered than the first; as might be expected, the men are again much more disruptive than the women. Browne escorts Aunt Julia to the piano so that she may treat her guests to a song. After she finishes the song, Freddy Malins continues applaud-ing long after everyone has stopped and further embarrasses Julia with his overeffusive compliments. Unexpectedly, too, a near quarrel erupts among Malins, Browne, Kate, and Mary Jane. At fault is another man, Pope Pius X, who has declared that since "singers in churches have a real liturgical office . . .

women . . . cannot be admitted to form part of the choir or of the musical chapel" (Gifford 119). Aunt Kate "had worked herself into a passion" (*D* 194), we are told, and the group has become "very quarrelsome" (*D* 195). At this point, Molly Ivors says her farewells, though not in the ill humor we might have expected after her exchange with Gabriel.

For a while, "a great deal of confusion and laughter and noise" (*D* 197) reigns as the dinner proceeds, and, as Warren Beck has pointed out, the guests' "nearest approach to a common interest is not Irish nationalism but *music, and more especially singers*" (305; emphasis added). Talk of the Negro tenor at the Gaiety, though, soon has Freddy questioning "sharply" (*D* 198) and Browne speaking "defiantly" (*D* 199) and "incredulously" (*D* 200), as the talk eventually grows "lugubrious" (*D* 201), turns to monks' coffins, and then lapses into silence. Gabriel's speech, with its embedded insult to the now-absent Molly, follows, loudly interrupted several times by Browne's effusive, noisy protestations (*D* 202, 203). Despite all of its compliments to his aunts and his cousin, it harshly judges the moderns for living in "a less spacious age" (*D* 203), and we sense its many hypocrisies because Gabriel had earlier dismissed the company for its low "grade of culture" (*D* 179) and his aunts as "only two ignorant old women" (*D* 192). The revenge Gabriel takes on Lily with his impolite tip and on Molly through insults shows how mean-spirited he can be and just how unfairly his patriarchal values enable him to treat servants, colleagues, and wives. Ruth Bauerle quite rightly perceives that "scarcely a woman has encountered Gabriel without being disdained, overruled, or interrupted" (117).

As the guests leave, again the men threaten disorder: Freddy with his "resounding knock" (*D* 208); Browne by holding the front door open far too long, letting in cold air, and creating confusion in the "cross-directions and contradictions and abundance of laughter" (*D* 209) as the cabdriver attempts to sort out his fares' wishes; Bartell D'Arcy with his shockingly rude, "rough" reply that takes the women "aback": "'Can't you see that I'm as hoarse as a crow?'" (*D* 211). He, of course, also supplies the ultimate thematic and psychological disruption by singing the song, "The Lass of Aughrim," which triggers Gretta's tearful memories of Michael Furey and strips Gabriel of his last marital illusions. In light of these examples, it is difficult not to see Gabriel's "wild impulse of . . . body" (*D* 215), his "desire to *seize*" Gretta (*D* 215; emphasis added), "the thoughts . . . *rioting* through his brain, proud, joyful, tender, valorous" (*D* 213; emphasis added), and his "keen pang of lust" (*D* 215) as being an attack on Gretta—"mate-rape," Bauerle has called it; Gabriel does, after all, long "to be master of her strange mood" (*D* 217) and wish "*to crush* her body against his, to overmaster her" (*D* 217; emphasis added), phrases with very strong connotations of noisy action.

Throughout these six scenes, three voices, fully available to reader and author but not uniformly available to characters and narrator, dominate the story—a point considered in great technical detail by John Paul Riquelme (121-30), who finds in this medley "clearly the stylistic proving ground that makes possible the configuration of technique in the later work" (123). First, there is the voice of the individual character in dialogue, asking, responding, cajoling, offering, in ways that reveal what the character wishes to show forth to the world as well as what the author wishes to unveil. Second, there is the interior monologue voice of the characters, that aspect of the story so inadequately communicated to the audience in John Huston's 1987 film adaptation, which are unavailable to the other characters. Indeed, lack of access to this voice creates some of the key misunderstandings within the story, as when Gabriel blunders so in his reading of Gretta's thoughts and provokes such an "outburst of tears" (*D* 218) that he is left nonplussed by his own reflection in the mirror. The third voice, primarily available to Joyce and his reader, usually appears in such rhetoric as the adverbial speech tags and descriptive passages. For example, Gabriel mentions that the cab window "rattl[ed] all the way" (*D* 180), and the narrator that Gabriel went down the stairs "noisily" (*D* 182) and that Bartell D'Arcy spoke "roughly" (*D* 211), but only Joyce and the reader are intended to discern in these words the gradual evolution of a pattern in which certain actions, certain speeches, certain attitudes are associated with noise. In discussing *Finnegans Wake*, Clive Hart presciently notes that "there are unmistakable signs at least as early as 'The Dead' of the deliberate use of verbal motifs for structural and tonal effects" (162), and we can see that this deliberate use belongs largely to the third voice, which is fully capable of defining and exploiting the unique qualities of "The Dead" and also of creating complex symbolic relationships amongst melody, noise, and silence, available in the traditions of European literature since Pythagoras, who supposed the whole heaven to be a "*harmonia* and a number," a medley fully exploited as early as Geoffrey Chaucer's "The General Prologue."

Numerous unifying patterns of images have been identified in the text of "The Dead," and warnings concerning "denial of proportion" in relating imagery to the totality of the story have been firmly posted. Epifanio San Juan Jr., for example, has raised particularly sound objections against "the mistakes the formalist habitually commits, stemming from the denial of proportion by exaggerating the role of a part and making part and whole somehow equivalent" (215). If one turns to images of sounds, however, of which there are at least 345 in the text, one sees patterns develop in terms of harmony and noise, standing in direct relationship to the female and male divisions of the story.[4] Determining just what constitutes a sound image is, of course, subjective to a degree and thus probably admits no exact count.

Quite obviously, words such as "scraping," "squeaking," "stamping," and "shuffling" (*D* 177) gleaned from early in the story constitute sound images, as do the adverbial constructions "said gaily" (*D* 178) and "laughed heartily" (*D* 180). It is equally obvious that the first three images constitute noise or discord, whereas the latter suggest harmony or melody. Thus such speech tags as "nervously" (*D* 180), "almost testily" (*D* 181), "noisily" (*D* 182), "bluntly" (*D* 187), "lamely" (*D* 188), "warmly" (*D* 190), "moodily" (*D* 191), "coldly" (*D* 191), "loudly" (*D* 197), "defiantly" (*D* 199), "archly" (*D* 206), "roughly" (*D* 211), and "ironically" (*D* 219) have been grouped together as noise images with such verbals as "clanged" (*D* 175), "exploded" (*D* 185), "stuttered" (*D* 190), "tapped" (*D* 192), "coughed" (*D* 201), "puffing" (*D* 208), "shouted" (*D* 209), "muttered" (*D* 216), and "mumbled" (*D* 216) and such substantives as "bitter and sudden retort" (*D* 179), "sidling mimicry" (*D* 183), "habitual catch" (*D* 185), "a kink of high-pitched bronchitic laughter" (*D* 185), "loud applause" (*D* 193), "clatter" (*D* 200), "broken only by the noise of the wine and by unsettlings of chairs" (*D* 201), "shrill prolonged whistling" (*D* 206), "confusion" (*D* 208), "thumping" (*D* 215), and "sobbing" (*D* 221). On the other hand, "peal of laughter" (*D* 180), "lovely voice" (*D* 184), "opening melody" (*D* 187), "soft friendly tone" (*D* 188), "distant music" (*D* 210), "old Irish tonality" (*D* 210), and "merry-making" (*D* 222) have been categorized with the verbals "murmured" (*D* 181), "laughed in musical echo" (*D* 183), "singing" (*D* 199), "strumming" (*D* 206), and "call . . . softly" (*D* 214) as harmonic or melodic images, appropriate to this Twelfth Night celebration.

Consideration of the roles of music in *Dubliners* in general and in "The Dead" in particular would take us in several directions, some already well covered. We could look at the role of music in Joyce's own life, especially as it relates to his great-aunts whose party was the source of the party in the story; we could look at the specific allusions to songs, operas, and composers in *Dubliners,* material already more than adequately catalogued by Matthew J.C. Hodgart, Mabel P. Worthington, Zack Bowen, Timothy Martin, and others; we could look at the uses of music in relation to the characters and themes. All three approaches carry their own satisfactions.

Joyce's contemporaries recall again and again that music reigned in his household. Jacques Mercanton remembered Joyce, sitting at a piano, "carried away by his own delight in [an Irish folksong]," singing and accompanying himself "in a voice melodious and vibrant, though a little ragged" (231). Robert Haas has shown how pervasive musical references are throughout *Dubliners* in the daily lives of the characters, references that finally "serve to enrich" (20) all the stories but especially "The Dead." Bruce Avery has even successfully fused the biographical data with the textual allusions to demonstrate that the numerous "musical references in the text signal that 'The Dead' is concerned with hearing and sound in much the same way that 'Araby' concerns itself with vision and sight" (475). Indeed, Avery anticipated my key point when he wrote that music "even affects the language of the narrator, whose figures compose aural images drawn from the terminology of music" (474). The critical ground has been well prepared for sowing the idea that sounds are key elements in the figurative structures of the story.

Approximately 119 sound images are associated with the men, 137 with the women. (The remainder belong to the company in general, as with "[a]n irregular musketry of applause" [*D* 192], or simply constitute a sound, neither melody nor noise.) Considered more closely, 69 noise images and 50 harmony images are associated with the men's actions, thoughts, and comments—the latter figure slightly unbalanced since so many of the harmony images emanate from Browne while he is discussing opera singers. Specifically, 32 noise images are associated with Gabriel, 15 with Freddy Malins, 8 with Browne, and 6 with Bartell D'Arcy. In sharp contrast, the 137 sound images associated with the women, who are dancing, singing, playing the piano, or chatting pleasantly throughout the story, divide into 104 harmonic images and only 20 clearly noise images, most of which fall within the "encounter scenes." In other words, it is even money that men will produce either harmony or noise; however, women are five times more likely to produce harmony than noise. We do hear Lily respond "with great bitterness" (*D* 178), Molly Ivors speak "bluntly" (*D* 187), "frankly" (*D* 188), and "warmly" (in the sense of annoyed or piqued [*D* 190]), and Gretta burst into tears (*D* 218) and choke with sobs (*D* 221), but these are exceptions to the generally harmonic images accompanying the speeches and actions of the women and do indeed appear in the malice-governed scenes. In her discussion of *Dubliners* criticism, Florence L. Walzl cogently observed that "over half" of the 200 music teachers listed in the 1904 *Thom's Directory* were women and that "no field seemed more promising or safer for young women of talent" (*"Dubliners"* 198), a point most relevant to the lives of the Misses Morkans in Joyce's story.

Perhaps we could expect no more than noise from Freddy Malins, described as he is from the first as a potentially disruptive force: "His face was fleshy and pallid, touched with colour only at the thick hanging lobes of his ears and at the wide wings of his nose. He had coarse features, a blunt nose, a convex and receding brow, tumid and protruded lips" (*D* 184). Freddy may be "laughing heartily" (*D* 184) at times, but usually we hear his "habitual catch" (*D* 185) or "resounding knock" (*D* 208) or find him clapping loudly, speaking "sharply" (*D* 198), or beating time with a pudding fork, perhaps on the table-top or even against his glass (*D* 205). Browne, equally unpromising with his "stiff grizzled moustache and swarthy skin" (*D* 182) and "sidling mimicry" (*D* 183), generates some "mirth" (*D* 185), does "laugh very heartily" (*D* 193), and shows his appreciation of operatic voices, but he also speaks "defiantly" (*D* 199), "warmly" (*D* 199), and "loudly" (*D* 203), asks questions "incredulously" (*D* 200), and creates "a good deal of confused talk" (*D* 208). Donald T. Torchiana has suggested the importance of Browne as a structural device when he observed that Joyce uses Browne "to punctuate almost every scene at the party with something like a full stop" (*D* 226). Bartell D'Arcy, more a presence than a character in the story most of the time, responds to Browne "warmly" (*D* 199) and to his hostesses "roughly" and "rudely" (*D* 211), always speaking "hoarsely."

Even such minor male figures as the four young men with their "vigorous clapping" (*D* 187), the cabman with his "rattling" vehicle (*D* 209), and the hotel porter who "mutters" and "mumbles" (*D* 216) Gretta and Gabriel to their room create noise. Although much is said about the vocal abilities of Michael Furey, the only sound he actually produces in Gretta's narrative comes from the gravel he flings against her bedroom window. The noisiest male, though, is Gabriel Conroy himself. He "scrapes" his shoes "vigorously" (*D* 177); descends the stairs "noisily" (*D* 182); speaks "slightly angered" (*D* 181), "lamely" (*D* 188), "shortly" (*D* 189), "moodily" (*D* 191), "coldly" (*D* 191), "loudly" (*D* 205), "abruptly" (*D* 216), and "ironically" (*D* 219); adopts "a false voice" (*D* 217) and a "tone of cold interrogation" (*D* 220); and once must "restrain himself from *breaking out* into *brutal* language" (*D* 217; emphasis added). Indeed, the story ends with him listening to the "few light taps" (*D* 223) the snowfall makes against the Gresham Hotel window.

In *Joyce, Bakhtin, and Popular Literature*, R.B. Kershner maintains "that within a society in which women are disempowered there should arise an opposing imaginative scenario in which women are omnipotent" (147). Indeed, "The Dead" contains just such a scenario within the three very private scenes when Lily, Molly, and Gretta evade the rhetoric Gabriel has scripted for them and "defeat him," Lily by rejecting his money, Molly by leaving before his insult, Gretta by simply going to sleep. Within the party scenes, the harmonies of the women also overrule the threatened disorder of the men. Margot Norris's feminist discussion makes much of the interplay between "two texts: a 'loud' or audible male narrative challenged and disrupted by a 'silent' or discounted female countertext. . . . 'The Dead' itself thematizes these complicated textual operations in the homely gesture of what I call 'the stifled back answer'" (192), but, as I have shown, the answers given by the women, available through the imagery in Joyce's story, are anything but silent or stifled. Paradoxically, Gabriel becomes threatened not only by his wife's revelations but also by Michael Furey's ghostly presence, thus fusing the male and female patterns and the two strands of intertwined images. The story, however, ends in an ambiguous impasse, as so many of the thematic discussions have concluded; neither noise nor music penetrates the silence of the closing sentences.

Paradoxically, closure in "The Dead" brings images of neither concord nor discord, but rather a profound and ambiguous silence that lends itself to contradictory readings of the story's final page. The reader does not know what will eventually result from Gabriel's silence because the pattern established in his encounters with Lily and Molly remains incomplete and there is no third "party" scene. Women in Gabriel's world both wound and heal, both pet and correct. Gabriel could not be wounded or corrected, however, were there not already some inner vulnerability in his self-image, some inner awareness that he has indeed lightly flirted with Lily, politically compromised himself for a few books, and ungenerously insulted his wife. Gabriel has been a highly disruptive individual in the tightly constituted world of his family and the restrictive world of his culture. His disruptions and noises, however, have been obliterated by the gender-inflected music of independent, capable, and talented women, rhetorical and thematic sisters to Molly Bloom and Anna Livia Plurabella. The noise of the self is ultimately silenced by the music of the group. Only if we cease to let the diachronic action of Gabriel Conroy entice us away from the synchronic structures of the entire story does it become entirely clear to what extent gender has permeated every aspect of "The Dead," from the psychology of the encounter scenes, to the culturally charged public scenes, to the highly gendered discourse patterned by melody and noise attached to the female and male.

Notes

1. I found it very puzzling that in 1982, Florence L. Walzl's insightful "*Dubliners:* Women in Irish Society" would remark that "[i]t is significant that the plot progresses by a series of confrontations Gabriel has with women" (50), adding in a note that "[t]he fact that all the main confrontations of 'The Dead' are with women has not received as much critical attention [as the self-perceived assaults on Gabriel's ego]" (56). Almost more puzzling is that R.B. Kershner could write in 1989 that "[s]urprisingly, few critics have noted that Gabriel's significant encounters in the story are all with women, especially the three encounters with Lily, Molly Ivors, and Gretta" (140).

2. Thomas Dilworth briefly discusses the Mock King of Twelfth Night festivities and concludes that "the resemblance of the Morkans' party to the ancient celebration of the god of sowing and husbandry may have symbolic resonance with the party's occurring in a house shared by the office of a 'cornfactor' . . . a grain and seed merchant" (114).

3. Hereafter cited as *D* followed by page and line numbers, the divisions are as follows: prologue (*D* 175.01-176.33), Lily encounter scene (*D* 175.34-179.20), party scene (*D* 179.21-187.18), Molly Ivors encounter scene (*D* 187.19-192.27), second party scene (*D* 192.28-213.03), Gretta Conroy encounter scene (*D* 213.04-222.02), and Gabriel

Conroy recognition scene (*D* 222.03-224.04). Discussions of "The Dead" mention from two to five "parts" or "divisions." Robert Scholes's edition, used for this essay, prints the story with only one break. The Yale manuscript clearly indicates breaks on page 17 ("Gabriel could not listen while Mary Jane was playing") and page 74 ("She was fast asleep"); the Cornell composite typescript-manuscript indicates the former (page 9) but not the latter and has an additional break on page 31 ("the piercing morning air came into the hall . . ."); see Michael Groden 489, 497, 513, and 535.

4. Late in my work on this essay, I read what I consider to be an exemplary essay relating motifs to gender issues: Earl G. Ingersoll's "The Gender of Travel in 'The Dead.'" Fusing structuralist, psychological, and feminist thought, Ingersoll remarks: "Of particular interest in 'The Dead' is evidence of the metaphor of travel, with its associations of freedom and the phallocentric, and metonymy, with its associations of servitude and the neglected 'feminine'" (42). His success in explicating the implications of the spatial language of the story enforced my belief that sounds in "The Dead" are inextricably intertwined with gender. I found the following critics quite useful for spurring thought about Joyce and women—Richard Brown, Bonnie Kime Scott, Karen Lawrence, Shari Benstock, and Hana Wirth-Nesher—although none of these individuals seemed to make a particularly strong statement about "The Dead" and Gabriel's relationship with women.

Works Cited

Avery, Bruce. "Distant Music: Sound and the Dialogics of Satire in 'The Dead.'" *James Joyce Quarterly* 28 (1991): 473-83.

Bauerle, Ruth. "Date Rape, Mate Rape: A Liturgical Interpretation of 'The Dead.'" In *New Alliances in Joyce Studies,* ed. Bonnie Kime Scott, 113-25. Newark: Univ. of Delaware Press, 1988.

Beck, Warren. *Joyce's* Dubliners: *Substance, Vision, and Art.* Durham, N.C.: Duke Univ. Press, 1969.

Benstock, Shari. "City Spaces and Women's Places in Joyce's Dublin." In *James Joyce: The Augmented Ninth,* ed. Bernard Benstock, 293-307. Syracuse, N.Y.: Syracuse Univ. Press, 1988.

Bowen, Zack. *Musical Allusions in the Works of James Joyce: Early Poetry through* Ulysses. Albany: State University of New York Press, 1974.

Brandabur, Edward. *A Scrupulous Meanness: A Study of James Joyce's Early Work.* Chicago: Univ. of Illinois Press, 1971.

Brown, Richard. *James Joyce and Sexuality.* Cambridge: Cambridge Univ. Press, 1985.

Daiches, David. *The Novel and the Modern World.* Rev. ed. Chicago: Univ. of Chicago Press, 1960.

Dilworth, Thomas. "Sex and Politics in 'The Dead.'" *James Joyce Quarterly* 23 (1986): 157-71.

Doherty, Gerald. "Shades of Difference: Tropic Transformations in James Joyce's 'The Dead.'" *Style* 23 (1989): 225-36.

Ghiselin, Brewster. "The Unity of Joyce's *Dubliners.*" *Accent* 16 (1956): 75-88.

Gifford, Don. *Joyce Annotated.* 2d ed. Berkeley: Univ. of California Press, 1982.

Groden, Michael, ed. Dubliners: *A Facsimile of Drafts and Manuscripts, The James Joyce Archives.* Vol. 4. New York: Garland, 1978.

Guthrie, W.K.C. "Pythagoras and Pythagoreanism." In *The Encyclopedia of Philosophy,* ed. Paul Edwards, 7: 37-39. New York: Macmillan, 1967.

Haas, Robert. "Music in *Dubliners.*" *Colby Quarterly* 28 (1992): 19-33.

Hart, Clive. *Structure and Motif in* Finnegans Wake. Evanston, Ill.: Northwestern Univ. Press, 1962.

Hodgart, Matthew J.C., and Mabel P. Worthington. *Song in the Works of James Joyce.* New York: Columbia Univ. Press, 1959.

Ingersoll, Earl G. "The Gender of Travel in 'The Dead.'" *James Joyce Quarterly* 30 (1992): 41-50.

Joyce, James. *Dubliners.* Ed. Robert Scholes. New York: Viking, 1968.

———. Dubliners: *Text, Criticism, and Notes.* Ed. Robert Scholes and A. Walton Litz. 1969. Reprint, New York: Penguin, 1976.

———. *Finnegans Wake.* New York: Viking, 1959.

Joyce, Stanislaus. "The Background to *Dubliners.*" *Listener* 51 (1954): 526-27.

Kenner, Hugh. "The *Portrait* in Perspective." In *James Joyce: Two Decades of Criticism,* ed. Seon Givens, 81. New York: Vanguard 1948.

Kershner, R.B. *Joyce, Bakhtin, and Popular Literature.* Chapel Hill: Univ. of North Carolina Press, 1989.

Lawrence, Karen. "Gender and Narrative Voice in *Jacob's Room* and *A Portrait of the Artist as a Young Man.*" In *James Joyce: The Centennial Symposium,* ed. Morris Beja, Phillip Herring, Maurice Harmon, and David Norris, 31-38. Urbana: Univ. of Illinois Press, 1986.

Leonard, Garry M. *Reading* Dubliners *Again: A Lacanian Perspective.* Syracuse, N.Y.: Syracuse Univ. Press, 1994.

Litz, A. Walton. *James Joyce.* 2d ed. Boston: Twayne, 1972.

Martin, Timothy. *Joyce and Wagner: A Study of Influence.* Cambridge: Cambridge Univ. Press, 1991.

Mercanton, Jacques. "The Hours of James Joyce." In *Portraits of the Artist in Exile: Recollections of James Joyce by Europeans,* ed. Willard Potts, 206-52. New York: Harcourt, 1986.

Norris, Margot. "Not the Girl She Was at All: Women in 'The Dead.'" In *The Dead,* ed. Daniel R. Schwarz, 190-205. New York: St. Martin's, 1994.

Novak, Jane. *The Razor Edge of Balance: A Study of Virginia Woolf.* Coral Gables: Univ. of Miami Press, 1975.

O'Connor, Frank. "Work in Progress." In Dubliners: *Text, Criticism, and Notes,* ed. Robert Scholes and A. Walton Litz, 304-15. New York: Penguin, 1976.

Post, Elizabeth L. *Emily Post's Etiquette.* 14th ed. New York: Harper, 1984.

Riquelme, John Paul. *Teller and Tale in Joyce's Fiction: Oscillating Perspectives.* Baltimore: Johns Hopkins Univ. Press, 1983.

San Juan, Epifanio, Jr. *James Joyce and the Craft of Fiction.* Rutherford, N.J.: Fairleigh Dickenson Univ. Press, 1972.

Scholes, Robert. *In Search of James Joyce.* Urbana: Univ. of Illinois Press, 1992.

Scholes, Robert, and A. Walton Litz, eds. Dubliners: *Text, Criticism, and Notes.* New York: Penguin, 1976.

Schwarz, Daniel R., ed. *The Dead.* New York: St. Martin's, 1994.

Scott, Bonnie Kime. *James Joyce.* Atlantic Highlands, N.J.: Humanities, 1987.

————. *Joyce and Feminism.* Bloomington: Indiana Univ. Press, 1984.

Torchiana, Donald T. *Backgrounds for Joyce's* Dubliners. Boston: Allen, 1986.

Walzl, Florence L. *"Dubliners."* In *A Companion to Joyce Studies,* ed. Zack Bowen and James F. Carens, 157-228. Westport, Conn.: Greenwood, 1984.

————. *"Dubliners:* Women in Irish Society." In *Women in Joyce,* ed. Suzette Henke and Elaine Unkeless, 31-56. Urbana: Univ. of Illinois Press, 1982.

Wirth-Nesher, Hana. "Reading Joyce's City: Public Space, Self, and Gender in *Dubliners.*" In *James Joyce: The Augmented Ninth,* ed. Bernard Benstock, 282-92. Syracuse, N.Y.: Syracuse Univ. Press, 1988.

Meaning Deferred and Revealed

CHAPTER ELEVEN

Titles in *Dubliners*

Ulrich Schneider

Joyce critics have often been puzzled by the meaning of some of the more enigmatic titles in *Dubliners* but, as far as I know, have never given them their due in the form of a special study. Yet in dealing with the stories as in dealing with other literary texts, we are bound, in Harry Levin's words, "to address ourselves sooner or later to the subject of titology" (xxiii). In the last ten years, research on titles has been promoted energetically by Leo H. Hoek, Arnold Rothe, Gérard Genette, and others.[1] Methodologically different as their studies are, they have all deepened our insight into the important function of titles for literary texts in general. The importance of titles may even have increased in modern literature where, as Wayne C. Booth observes, titles and epigraphs "are often the only explicit commentary the reader is given" (298).

One may ask, though, why Booth's type of modern narrator should be more reliable in the choice of his titles than in the choice of his other devices. Far from making explicit what the cotext means, titles in modern (and postmodern) literature depend to an even higher degree than in traditional literature upon the complete cotext to unfold all their implications. If a Beckett critic asserts that the title *Premier amour* in itself indicates the themes of "love and all forms of physicality, eating, secretion, begetting and birth . . . and in addition the philosophical reflexion about the self and the other, about the kind of love, and dying and decomposing" (Schoell 47), he can discover all these things only after having read the whole story and, in addition, other texts by the same author.

As Hoek claims, the title has priority over the following text (or cotext) in a twofold sense: it is the textual element that we perceive first in the process of reading, and it is also an authoritative element programming everything else that follows (1-2). The relationship between title and cotext has been illustrated with a variety of metaphors. The title has been compared to a menu at the entrance of an inn, to a mustard seed of the whole plant, or to a portal leading into a building (Rothe 174). Let me add another variation by comparing titles

---

Original version published in *Style* 25.3 (1991).

with a revolving door through which we enter and leave the cotext in a circular movement that is characteristic of hermeneutic processes in general.

In Joyce's works we find an abundance of examples of how titles condition our expectations of a text and how, reciprocally, a knowledge of books with similar titles helps us to classify a new title at a glance. Just by looking at titles such as *Fair Tyrants* or *Sweets of Sin,* Bloom "know[s] the kind that is" and what is "more in her line" (*Ulysses* 10.602 and 606; hereafter cited as *U* followed by episode and line numbers). As an adman Bloom also knows how much depends on a catchy title from a commercial point of view, such as "*The Mystery Man on the Beach*" or "*My Experiences,* let us say, *in a Cabman's Shelter*" (*U* 13.1060 and 16.1231), titles he considers for the story contest in *Titbits.* Stephen, on the other hand, demonstrates his scorn for such commercial considerations by his former intention to write books "with letters for titles" (*U* 3.83). He shares the animadversion of most avant-garde writers against sensational or effusive titles and their preference for the shortest and most noncommittal titles possible if they do not jettison titles altogether (cf. Hoek 175 and Rothe 33). If Stephen did not carry out his plan, other writers did after him and called their books *V.* (Pynchon), *S/Z* (Barthes), or *H* (Sollers).

Obviously, the creator of characters like Stephen was equally aware of the significance of titles, and it is well known that Joyce liked to play all kinds of games with them. In the case of *Finnegans Wake,* the title remained a matter of "strictest secrecy" (Ellmann 53), and Joyce kept teasing his friends about it. Perhaps he was already teasing the readers of his first collection of poems published in 1907. Once we find out about Bloom's brainwave ("Chamber music. Could make a kind of pun on that. It is a kind of music I often thought when she" [*U* 11.979-81]), we can never be sure again whether the poems are really "the least ironic of Joycean texts," as Patrick Parrinder believes (24). And what should we make of a book that, as Valéry Larbaud was among the first to ask, "is entitled *Ulysses,* and no character in it bears this name"? Authorized by Joyce himself, he could reveal to the noninitiated that the title was no less than the key to the book, a key in the right place, "in the door, or rather on the cover" (quoted in Deming 258). After the circulation of Joyce's various schemata, it has become such a common habit to call the episodes by their Homeric titles that, in Hugh Kenner's words, "we sometimes forget that they are not part of the text." The highly charged title of the book is for Kenner "a neat instance of Joyce's trust in synecdoche" (22).

In two recent articles, the one on Joyce's first short story, the other on his last work, Leonard Albert and Scott Simpkins shed more light on Joyce's entitling devices. Different as these articles are, both authors appropriate Larbaud's comparison, arguing on the one hand that "Joyce chose his titles with enormous care to be both keys to his 'epiphanies' and traps for the unwary"

(Albert 353) and on the other that "the title . . . may well be the most substantial key to the codings of *Finnegans Wake*" (Simpkins 741). The following remarks will corroborate much of what has been said on Joyce's titles in general and increase our insight into the function of titles in *Dubliners* in particular.

Ulysses, as we know, developed after a long gestation from the idea to write a story about a certain Mr. Hunter to be included in *Dubliners* under the title "Ulysses." We also know that for a while Joyce wanted to call his short story cycle *Ulysses in Dublin* but then put the idea on the shelf (Jacquet 52). Had he stuck to it, the reception of *Dubliners* might well have taken another course, and from the very beginning it would have been hard to read the stories as naturalistic slices of life. We might have even been won over to the view that "*Dubliners* has an architectural unity in a secret technique—that, like *Ulysses,* only far more obviously and demonstrably . . . *Dubliners* is based upon Homer's *Odyssey*," as Richard Levin and Charles Shattuck claimed in 1944 (49). In view of the fact that Joyce, after all, did not adhere to this title, not many critics have been convinced by their argument.

As it turned out, Joyce preferred the shortest, most prosaic, and most noncommittal title possible, a title that does not make a statement in the way George Moore's *The Untilled Field* or Arthur Morrison's *Tales of Mean Streets* do, a title without the fin de siècle touch of *The Portrait of the Artist as a Young Man* either. Joyce's title does not reveal anything about his attitude toward his characters. When Georg Goyert suggested *So Sind Sie in Dublin* for the German translation, Joyce preferred *So Sind Wir in Dublin,* although he added, "but I like neither" (*Letters* 3:164). In the one case the emphasis is on critical detachment, in the other on empathy, whereas in the original no such choice is necessary. Nothing is indicated except that all characters in the stories have one thing in common, their environment.

Titles such as *Dubliners, Winesburg, Ohio, St. Petersburg, Manhattan Transfer,* or *Berlin Alexanderplatz* highlight the urban milieu that conditions the individual, just as narratives entitled after the main characters reflect the individualistic worldview of the bourgeois novel. In *Dubliners* only one out of fifteen stories is given the name of its main character ("Eveline"). In the first three stories the first-person narrators remain anonymous and so little individualized that we may wonder whether or not they are identical. When we come to a story in which a name is announced in the title, we are likely to expect some more fully developed individuality. Which, we may ask, will be stronger: the pressure of Eveline's environment or her individual will? If individualism is defined in terms of a sense of "inner direction" (Riesman 101-3), Eveline must be one of the least individualized characters in all literature. Torn between the expectations of others, she hardly knows what she wants for herself: she can only react, never act. Her lack of individuality is implied by the delay in identifying her by name. For quite a while she remains an anonymous "she"; then she is called "Miss Hill" (*Dubliners* 37; hereafter cited with page numbers as *D*), the name by which she is addressed in the Stores. Only then does Eveline mention her Christian name: "Then she would be married—she, Eveline" (*D* 37), with an odd mixture of pride and disbelief, as if it were quite exceptional that a girl called Eveline should ever get married. Since we rarely address ourselves by names, this remains the only occasion in which Eveline uses her own name. Frank prefers to call her "Poppens out of fun" (*D* 39), and only in the final crisis he calls her "Eveline! Evvy" (*D* 41). Miss Hill, Eveline, Poppens, Evvy—four names are used in four different situations, as if names could not warrant a fixed identity anymore but only different roles of the individual in society.

The pressure to conform to Dublin standards is as strong in the other stories, but once Joyce has brought out the tension between the individuals and their environment through the tension between the generalized title of the whole cycle and the individualized title of a single story, he has made his point and can move to other possibilities of intitulation. One thing all titles in *Dubliners* have in common: they are extremely short and thus appropriate for a genre defined by its shortness. They indicate that Joyce will not waste a single word but instead develop a strategy of omission, which is further suggested by the word "gnomon" on the first page. Nine titles consist of a single noun or name ("The Sisters," "An Encounter," "Araby," "Eveline," "Counterparts," "Clay," "A Mother," "Grace," "The Dead"), one consists of a compound ("The Boarding House"), four just add an adjective, a preposition, or a numeral ("After the Race," "Two Gallants," "A Little Cloud," "A Painful Case"), and only one runs into six words, four of them monosyllabic ("Ivy Day in the Committee Room").

In other respects the story titles are varied and run the whole gamut from the descriptive to the symbolic. Some of them point toward the social roles that the individual characters play ("The Sisters," "Two Gallants," "A Mother"). Short stories as a genre tend toward the typical rather than the individual, as a quick glance at Katherine Mansfield's stories with titles will corroborate: "The Young Girl," "The Stranger," "The Lady's Maid." Even so, Joyce is able with the utmost economy of means in his cotext to differentiate between the drowsy Nannie and the garrulous Eliza or between the obtuse Corley and the nimble Lenehan without help from his titles.

Two titles refer to the setting of the stories but transcend their realistic circumference and point toward qualities that are conspicuous by absence in Joyce's Dublin. "Araby" is much more than a place-name; the word casts "an Eastern enchantment" over the boy (*D* 32), which ends in complete disillusionment. "Ivy Day in the Committee Room" conjures up the committee room in which occurred the fatal split of the Irish Party, and that, through juxtaposition, points to the decline in Irish politics after Parnell's downfall (*D* 132).

The titles that have perplexed readers most in *Dubliners* are probably "Clay" and "A Little Cloud." We can easily relate the title "The Boarding House" to the setting of the story, but what about "Clay"? The word does not recur in the cotext, and we have to read the story very carefully before we find a passage that gives us a clue. Once we have established a connection between the title and the "soft wet substance" from the garden (*D* 105), we still have to work out how it all relates to Maria and to the story as a whole. As an element in the fortune-telling game it forbodes death, but surely the point of the story is not an indication that Maria will die before the year is over. Being offered a glimpse of her life, we may rather surmise that hers is a slow psychic death, a death that has set in a long time ago. But the title could also offer a different insight. Clay, as the raw material for a potter, could support our impression that Maria, like Eveline, is some material in the hands of others, is manipulated by them just as she is blindfolded and pushed around.

In "A Little Cloud," there is only one reference to clouds in the story, to the "clouds of smoke" from Gallaher's cigar. We are told that he uses these clouds as a smokescreen behind which he has "taken refuge" (*D* 78). But why a man like Gallaher, cocksure and on top of the world, should feel the need to take refuge is far from clear. No wonder that most critics have been looking beyond the story for a clue. One tempting option is to see in the title an ironical allusion to 1 Kings 17:1, where "a little cloud out of the sea" heralds the coming of rain after a long drought. Indeed, taken in the biblical sense, the little cloud in the title matches well Little Chandler's "infant hope" on his way to his meeting with Gallaher (*D* 73). The title, understood this way, becomes part of the intertextual network between *Dubliners* and the Bible that I find more relevant than the Homeric parallel favored by Levin and Shattuck.

Titles frequently function as intertextual markers, and the Bible has been perhaps the most important source for titles such as *Gone with the Wind, The Sun Also Rises, Absalom, Absalom!,* or *Si le grain ne meurt.* Such allusive titles have become very common in the nineteenth and twentieth centuries and can, at worst, function as some heavy-handed allegorical overcode, but again Joyce keeps them well under control. In fact, in this case it is so unobtrusive that Charles Peake finds it questionable whether any biblical allusion is intended at all (30). Other critics, also not satisfied with the biblical explanation, have assumed a possible Celtic pun or traced it back to a passage in Guglielmo Ferrero's *L'europa giovane,* which Joyce was reading while he worked on this particular story (cf. Weir 301-2 and Spoo 401-10). No matter how we try to come to grips with the title, we can understand why "A Little Cloud" has been called "the most perplexing title of all the stories in *Dubliners*" (Weir 301), although some other titles come fairly close.

In the other stories the words of the titles are also used very sparsely or avoided completely. A quick glance into Wilhelm Füger's *Concordance* will show that in five stories the nouns in the titles do not recur. Apart from "Clay," this is the case in "An Encounter," "After the Race," "Two Gallants," and "Counterparts." The last mentioned is another striking example of Joyce's tendency to avoid a one-dimensional relationship between title and cotext. The different lexical meanings of the word "counterpart" can be applied to the story and, moreover, to Joyce's narrative strategies in so many ways that one can easily accept Robert Scholes's remark that the story's title offers "a major clue to the whole structure of *Dubliners*" (379).

The word suggests to Scholes that in his work Farrington is "merely a replaceable cog in a mechanical operation" (384), and we may add that in copying out legal documents Farrington has to do with counterparts on a literary level as well. On the level of the characters in the story, employer and employee, father and son, husband and wife can be seen as counterparts. In another sense the title indicates for Scholes the "harmonious balance of counterpointed musical parts" (379) and the "echoes and resonances" (380) within the story and also the whole story cycle. On a metafictional level Scholes reads the title as a subtle hint at the relationship Joyce wants to establish with his readers, inviting them to become participants in the creative process: in other words, his "counterparts" (387).[2]

All these interpretations are made possible through the absence of an explicit reference to the title in the cotext. We cannot put our finger on any particular passage that would provide us with a sufficient explanation of the title. Resisting any fast anchorage within the cotext, titles become, in poststructuralist terms, floating signifiers deferring definite meaning (cf. Leitch 12-17). One thus could claim that Joyce anticipates what in postmodern fiction has been called "floating narration" (Slethaug 647-55). As if to tease us, parts of the titles keep bobbing up to the surface of the text without giving us a steady hold for interpretation.

In the office, Farrington has to lift a "counter" when he wants to leave or to return to his place (*D* 86, 88); Mr. Alleyne and Mrs. Delacour are standing "outside the counter" (*D* 91). In the pub, Farrington puts his money "on the counter" (*D* 89); his cronies form "a little party at the corner of the counter" (*D* 94). Thus the two counters in the office and in the pub form another set of counterparts in the story. When we read that Farrington "counted the sheets which remained to be copied" (*D* 88), we may think of counterparts even if the word is not there. Equally in "A Little Cloud" the title does not recur in its complete form, but we find parts of it in the name of the main character and in the "clouds of smoke" from Gallaher's cigar. At the end of the story we find an accumulation of the adjective. Thus Little Chandler asks himself, "could he not escape from his little house" (*D* 83), and his wife tries to hush the baby by calling him "My little man! My little mannie! . . . Mamma's little lamb of the world!" (*D* 85). Whatever else the title might mean, in retrospect it fits perfectly the belittling going on in the story.

Titles or parts of titles also reverberate outside the stories to which they belong. Thus the word "clay" occurs first in Byron's poem that Little Chandler reads: "*within this narrow cell her clay/That clay where once . . .*" (*D* 84). "A Little Cloud" is not only echoed in the "clouds of smoke" from Gallaher's cigar but more fully anticipated in the "little clouds of smoke" from the priest's snuff in "The Sisters" (*D* 12). The word "committee," used only once in "Ivy Day," turns up ten times in the following story, "A Mother." Hoppy Holohan's constant talk about the committee almost provokes Mrs. Kearney to mimic him to his face, "And who is the *Cometty,* pray" (*D* 141), a question that is also pertinent in the previous story. In "A Mother" we find a committee but never see it in function; in "Ivy Day" we find a committee room that does not serve its purpose. In both cases the word has almost completely lost its referential meaning and exists only in language.

"A Painful Case" is an exceptional story insofar as the title is a quotation from the cotext. First used by the deputy coroner in his report on Mrs. Sinico's death (*D* 115), it becomes the subtitle of the newspaper article read by Mr. Duffy (*D* 113) and then the title of the whole story. As readers we proceed in reverse order until we find out that the title is the quotation of a quotation. Again, the title functions as a floating signifier that refers not only to Mrs. Sinico's death but also more and more to Mr. Duffy's life and eventually to all the painful cases presented in *Dubliners.* Incidentally, the word "painful" occurs only once outside the story, when at a critical moment in "A Mother" "the strain of the silence had become somewhat painful" (*D* 146). This passage leads us back to Mr. Duffy's situation at the end of "A Painful Case": "He waited for some minutes listening. He could hear nothing: the night was perfectly silent. He listened again: perfectly silent. He felt that he was alone" (*D* 117).

"Grace" is the best example for showing how titles can radiate far beyond single stories. In the story itself, "grace" as a noun occurs only three times, twice associated with external things such as manners and clothes. Mr. Kernan is a staunch believer not in divine grace or the articles of the church but in things like silk hats and gaiters: "By grace of these two articles of clothing, he said, a man could always pass muster" (*D* 154). Mr. Fogarty, a failed publican and now a small grocer, bears himself "with a certain grace" (*D* 166) in the hope that his manners will "ingratiate him with the housewives of the district"

(*D* 166). In the story he ingratiates himself with a "gift" of whiskey, and this word is repeated twice within a few lines. Further apart the words "ingratiate" and "gift" may have slipped our attention, but in close vicinity with "grace" we notice their interrelation.

"Grace" in its original meaning of a free gift adds an ironic touch to Mr. Fogarty's ingratiating stratagems. In a world of sharp "modern business methods" (*D* 154), he cannot afford too much generosity: he gives in order to receive. In "Counterparts," Farrington's attention is caught by a seductive woman in the pub, and he gazes "admiringly at the plump arm which she moved very often and with much grace" (*D* 95). In a sense, this is a free gift, which grants Farrington a certain amount of voyeuristic pleasure, but like Mr. Fogarty's whiskey, it is certainly offered in the expectation of some recompense. In a world in which everything has a price tacked on it, grace, too, must turn into a commodity. It is left to Father Purdon to sanction this transformation and to define grace in terms of business ethics based upon correct accountancy.

Grace must have been a very rare and elusive quality at all times, and Joyce approaches it only by indirection, thus avoiding a reification that would run counter to the very idea of grace. Thus the Latin poem on photography mentioned by Martin Cunningham as an example of the wit and erudition of the popes (*D* 168) contains the words "et oris gratiam": "by grace of mouth." Even if the poem is not quoted in the story, once we have discovered it and come across "oris gratiam," we may well ask with Fritz Senn, "And isn't this perhaps what the story may all be about?" ("Rhetorical Account" 128). If nothing else, words are given away overly generously by Joyce's Dubliners, exceptions like Mr. Crofton or Mr. Duffy always granted.

The title of "Grace" highlights an important theme in *Dubliners* and retroactively gives a richer meaning to the previous stories. Once given the cue, the unusual word "inefficacious" (*D* 12), used for describing the priest's red handkerchief in "The Sisters," may remind us of the theological concept of "efficacious grace" and tell us obliquely something about the absence of such a redeeming faculty within the story. The word "grace," however, is not restricted to the sphere of theology but plays an equally important role in aesthetics. A silk hat can be balanced "gracefully" on Mr. Kernan's arm (*D* 156), a poet can have the "*gift of easy and graceful verse*" (*D* 74), and three musical ladies may be called the "Three Graces of the Dublin musical world" (*D* 204). All these passages have some feedback on the title of the story and make us wonder, for instance, whether the German translation as "Gnade" is quite adequate. Unlike English, German has no word that covers the religious and the aesthetic meaning of the word, and we must choose between "Gnade" and "Grazie," the second stemming from the same Latin source as the English word. By linguistic necessity the German title must restrict the semantic potential of the English original.

Many readers must have asked themselves why the first story in *Dubliners* is entitled "The Sisters" when the first-person narrator and the priest are so much more in the foreground of the narration. Leonard Albert builds up a strong case arguing that the function of the two old woman "is not such as to warrant their being assigned the title role." He finds it more plausible that the title hints obliquely but unmistakably at the homosexual relationship between the priest and the young boy (363). Nevertheless, it may be exactly the point of the title to shift to the center two figures who have been pushed to the margins of their society and thus to redress the balance through some act of poetic justice. But perhaps "center" is not the right word for a story that has more foci than one and could in a not-too-strict Euclidian sense be called "elliptical." Ellipsis in dialogue and narration is certainly one of the most striking features of the story.

Focusing on the two sisters in the title also contributes to the structure of the whole story cycle. It has been claimed that titles, like proper names, have something arbitrary about them, and titles in *Dubliners* confirm this to a certain degree. While some titles, "Araby" for instance, could not be shifted to another story, "An Encounter" might do well as a title for the stories in which Little Chandler meets Gallaher or Mr. Duffy meets Mrs. Sinico, just as "A Mother" might do for a story in which Mrs. Mooney holds all the strings in her hand. "A Painful Case" is so generally applicable that it would do for each of the other stories. And the same holds true, of course, for "The Dead," which functions as a retroactive comment on the whole story cycle. The titles of the first and last stories, in particular, could be easily exchanged. The first story, like the last, is much concerned with death and with the interrelation between the living and the dead; the last story, like the first, is partly set in the house of two sisters. Thus the circularity of the stories, which so often move in circles, is emphasized through the titles.

Focusing on the titles in *Dubliners*, I have also moved in circles looking for clues first in the corresponding stories and then in the whole story cycle. Only by such a procedure can we do justice to the dynamic interaction between titles and their cotexts, which has been well expressed by Michel Butor when he speaks of "pôles entre lesquels circule une électricité de sens" ("poles between which circulates an electricity of meaning") (quoted in Rothe 174). Far from offering an "explicit commentary," as Wayne C. Booth claims (198), they depend on the reader's explication just like any textual element. As Fritz Senn points out, the interaction between title and story in *Dubliners* offers some insight into the process of reading Joyce, a process that he describes as "a halting temporal progression with inevitable glances backward that reinterpret what was apprehended before, in perpetual retroactive resemantification" ("Probes" 37). In this virtually endless process, titles, as I hope to have shown, offer valuable clues not so much for a reified "meaning" of the stories in *Dubliners* but for Joyce's strategies of elision, indirection, and destabilization of meaning, which mark his radical departure into modernism.

Notes

1. I am also indebted to Wolfgang Karrer for letting me read his article "Titles and Mottoes as Intertextual Devices."
2. Following Scholes, John Paul Riquelme finds other story titles in *Dubliners* "suggestive" on a fictional and metafictional level (108).

Works Cited

Albert, Leonard. "Gnomonology: Joyce's 'The Sisters.'" *James Joyce Quarterly* 27 (winter 1990): 353-64.

Barthes, Roland. *S/Z*. Paris: Seuil, 1970.

Beckett, Samuel. *Premier amour*. Paris: Minuit, 1970.

Booth, Wayne C. *The Rhetoric of Fiction*. Chicago: Univ. of Chicago Press, 1961.

Deming, Robert H., ed. *James Joyce: The Critical Heritage*. Vol. 1. London: Routledge, 1970.

Ellmann, Richard. *James Joyce*. Rev. ed. Oxford: Oxford Univ. Press, 1983.

Füger, Wilhelm, ed. *Concordance to James Joyce's* Dubliners. Hildesheim, Germany: Olms, 1980.

Genette, Gérard. "Structure and Functions of the Title in Literature." *Critical Inquiry* 14 (summer 1988): 692-720.

Hoek, Leo H. *La marque du titre*. La Haye, The Netherlands: Mouton, 1981.

Jacquet, Claude. "Les plans de Joyce pour *Ulysse*." In Ulysses: *Cinquante ans après*, ed. Louis Bonnerot, 45-82. Paris: Didier, 1974.

Joyce, James. *Dubliners*. Ed. Robert Scholes and A. Walton Litz. Harmondsworth: Penguin, 1976.

———. *Letters*. Ed. Richard Ellmann. Vol. 3. London: Faber, 1966.

———. *Ulysses*. Ed. Hans Walter Gabler et al. New York: Garland, 1984.

Karrer, Wolfgang. "Titles and Mottoes as Intertextual Devices." In *Intertextualität*, ed. Heinrich Plett, Berlin: de Gruyter, 1991.

Kenner, Hugh. *Ulysses*. London: Allen, 1980.

Leitch, Vincent B. *Deconstructive Criticism: An Advanced Introduction*. New York: Columbia Univ. Press, 1983.

Levin, Harry. "The Title as a Literary Genre." *Modern Language Review* 72 (1977): xxiii-xxxvi.

Levin, Richard, and Charles Shattuck. "First Flight to Ithaca: A New Reading of Joyce's *Dubliners*." In *James Joyce: Two Decades of Criticism,* ed. Seon Givens, 47-94. New York: Vanguard, 1948.

Mansfield, Katherine. *The Garden Party*. 1922. Reprint, Harmondsworth: Penguin, 1981.

Parrinder, Patrick. *James Joyce.* Cambridge: Cambridge Univ. Press, 1984.

Peake, Charles. *James Joyce: The Citizen and the Artist.* London: Arnold, 1977.

Pynchon, Thomas. *V.* 1963. New York: Bantam, 1968.

Riesman, David. *Individualism Reconsidered.* New York: Free, 1964.

Riquelme, John Paul. *Teller and Tale in Joyce's Fiction.* Baltimore: Johns Hopkins Univ. Press, 1983.

Rothe, Arnold. *Der literarische Titel.* Frankfurt: Klostermann, 1986.

Schoell, Konrad. "Becketts Beschreibungen." In *Beckett und die Literatur der Gegenwart,* ed. Martin Brunkhorst, Gerd Hofmann, and Konrad Schoell, 45-59. Heidelberg: Winter, 1988.

Scholes, Robert. "'Counterparts' and the Method of *Dubliners.*" In Joyce, *Dubliners.* 379-87.

Senn, Fritz. "Anagnostic Probes." In *Modernity and Its Mediation.* European Joyce Studies 1, ed. Christine van Boheemen, 37-61. Amsterdam: Rodopi, 1989.

————. "A Rhetorical Account of James Joyce's 'Grace.'" *Moderna Språk* 74 (1980): 121-28.

Simpkins, Scott. "The Agency of the Title: *Finnegans Wake.*" *James Joyce Quarterly* 27 (summer 1990): 735-43.

Slethaug, Gordon E. "Floating Signifiers in John Barth's *Sabbatical.*" *Modern Fiction Studies* 33 (1987): 647-55.

Sollers, Philippe. *H.* Paris: Seuil, 1973.

Spoo, Robert E. "'Una Piccola Nuvoletta': Ferrero's *Young Europe* and Joyce's Mature *Dubliners* Stories." *James Joyce Quarterly* 24 (1987): 401-10.

Weir, David. "'A Little Cloud': New Light on the Title." *James Joyce Quarterly* 17 (1980): 301-2.

CHAPTER TWELVE

"A Very Fine Piece of Writing"

An Etymological, Dantean, and Gnostic Reading of Joyce's "Ivy Day in the Committee Room"

Michael Brian

Joyce's familiarity with etymology preceded the writing of *Dubliners* by several years. About 1898 to 1899, the college student Stephen, of Joyce's semiautobiographical novel, *Stephen Hero*, "read Skeat's Etymological Dictionary by the hour and his mind, which had from the first been only too submissive to the infant sense of wonder, was often hypnotised by the most commonplace conversation. People seemed to him strangely ignorant of the value of the words they used so glibly" (32). Joyce wrote about the same time an essay that stresses the centrality and pervasiveness of etymology in writing. He claimed: "The Grammar of a language, its orthography and etymology are admitted as known. They are studies in the same manner as tables of Arithmetic, surely and accurately" (*Critical Writings* 27). He argued further that a knowledge of the derivations of words gives us "a truer meaning" (29). If one takes Joyce at his word, then etymology would be as basic to a reading of *Dubliners* as arithmetic is to the understanding of mathematics. In this essay I explore the implications of this approach in "Ivy Day in the Committee Room," Joyce's favorite story, which was written in 1905.

Etymology has been with us from the beginning of writing; Plato (perhaps ironically) and Genesis testify to this. It was an essential part of Stoic philosophy and found sanctuary in the church; it is central to an understanding of such writers as St. Augustine and Isidore of Seville. The discovery of the connection between Sanskrit and the European languages began a new era that led to "scientific etymology," and it is out of this tradition that Joyce's essay was written. However, a reaction set in. In *Peculiar Language: Literature as Difference from the Renaissance to James Joyce*, Derek Attridge points out that Saussure's theories repudiated etymology as significant for an understanding of meaning. I think this is one of the reasons why those of us who were educated when Saussure's influence was at its height resist interpretations based on

Original version published in *Style* 25.3 (1991).

etymology. However, Jacques Derrida has restored interest in etymology, not as meaning but as rhetoric: "But having banished etymology from the realms of logic and science, he welcomes it instead into a different realm of rhetoric, where it has a subtle and scintillating role to play" (Attridge 108).

The publication of Joyce's *Stephen Hero* in 1944 with its reference to Skeat's *Etymological Dictionary* encouraged an etymological approach to his work. At first it was mentioned merely as an indication of his interest in words. In the second stage (with reference to *Dubliners*), various obscure words derived from Latin (and occasionally from Greek or Hebrew) received attention. The *gnomon, paralysis, simony* triad in "The Sisters" received particular attention. The structural significance of gnomon was increasingly explored and eventually a reference to it became almost mandatory. *Epiphany* is another one of the few words that received considerable attention. Few critics went beyond this and limited themselves to obscure words that needed to be explained or words that were obviously derived from Latin. Examples of critics who are the exceptions to this approach are Fritz Senn, who recognized the significance of the etymology of *sherry*, which links it to *Caesaris*, arguing that it represents "a secularization of the spiritual" (72); and Epifanio San Juan Jr., who explores the derivation of *palaver* from *parable* (196-97).

After this attention to etymology, even the formerly obligatory reference to the etymology of *gnomon* is dropped. Works whose titles might suggest they would include a discussion of etymology omit it. *Joyce's Voices* by Hugh Kenner ignores the voices of etymology. "Crosslocution in *Dubliners*" by Wilhelm Füger merely refers to the etymology of *dismal* (97) and has a note on the "etymological handicap of this neologism" (i.e., his title). Although *A Companion to Joyce Studies* (edited by Zack Bowen and James F. Carens) runs to 800-odd pages, it neglects etymology, and Florence L. Walzl's lengthy article on *Dubliners* within it makes only one tangential reference to etymology (204), even though she has made significant contributions in this area.

Recently there have been signs of a revival of interest in the significance of Skeat to *Dubliners* (hereafter cited with page numbers as *D*). Stephen Whittaker optimistically claims that "many readers routinely consult the listings in Skeat's *Etymological Dictionary*" (177). He notes that from "the beginning of *Dubliners* the roots of language (etymologies, ambiguities, and polysemantics) riddled the reality presented" (178). (The pun on *riddled* is appropriate.) He is one of the few who are aware of the implications of the etymology of ordinary words: "Skeat's etymology links not only souls and umbrellas, but also hats, flowers, ghosts, clouds, shadows, covers of all kinds, and surfaces" (180). Unfortunately, the shortness of his article precludes him from further developing this point.

Meanwhile work on Irish etymologies continues: a reading of "Ivy Day" by Sylvia Huntley Horowitz uses the Irish etymology of Hynes's name to link him with ivy and interprets him as the risen saviour at the Pentecost (151). Thomas Dilworth demonstrates the significance of the false etymology (son of the king) of Gabriel Conroy's surname and its real Irish derivation from "hound of the plain" (163), and Cóilín Owens reveals a punning etymological link between Irish *clé* and the title "Clay" (607). Such readings are complex and illuminating. Etymology reveals unexpected meanings and connections between the words of a text, sometimes confirming, reinforcing, extending, and modifying patterns discernible on the surface even to the point of contradicting them. Etymology also reveals new, unsuspected patterns and new themes.

An etymological reading of "Ivy Day in the Committee Room" reinforces and extends several obvious themes such as those of guardianship, paternity, and manhood. Joyce seems to have set up words related to man as guardian as a clue to an etymological reading because he draws unique attention to some of them, and their etymological relationship is likely to be recognized by the reader. Next the incessant repetition of *man* calls for an investigation of its etymology, which shows it is closely linked to such words as *mind* and *money*. This clarifies the definition of manhood through the polarity of spirituality and simony. Men betray each other and themselves through simony, a form of treachery. Treachery dominates the story and is further extended in the unexpected guise of words such as *little* and *trick*. Treachery occurs between mastered and masters, and another group of cognates emerges as significant: *Mayor, Major, master,* and *Mr.,* for example. The etymology of a word distinguished by its isolation, such as *velvety,* is one of many details that confirm the links to *The Divine Comedy* and places the scene in the final circles of hell, where those who have betrayed family, state, and masters are punished. Once such an etymological link to Dante has been established, other references become evident. It is here we find Satan himself in various disguises. Finally, etymology shows that the ambiguous Hynes is described in words that unexpectedly identify him as a manifestation of the serpent, and a Gnostic interpretation of the story emerges.

Although Skeat is useful to guide us through the murkier circles of the hell of Dublin, I shall discuss first some key words whose etymology is fairly well-known. The presence of words that are etymologically significant is often indicated by patternings such as incessant repetition, alliteration, or other forms of emphasis. One such passage occurs on the second page of "Ivy Day" when we read:

He selected one of the cards and read what was printed on it:

MUNICIPAL ELECTIONS

ROYAL EXCHANGE WARD

Mr Richard J. Tierney, P.L.G., respectfully solicits the favour of your vote and influence at the upcoming election in the Royal Exchange Ward. [*D* 119]

The words "Royal Exchange Ward" are highlighted by being in upper case and centered in the text as they would have appeared on the card itself. This alone throws the words into a prominence that one cannot miss. Joyce then repeats the phrase "Royal Exchange Ward." We are also presented with an acronym: when we solve this particular riddle, it turns out "P.L.G." stands for Poor Law Guardian, giving us another repetition of *ward* with a variation. The etymological relation of *ward* and *guard* is fairly common knowledge. (English contains several examples of doublets beginning with *g* and *w*. Common instances are *warranty* and *guaranty, gage* and *wage, guile* and *wile,* and so on.) The story continues with another repetition of *ward:* "Mr O'Connor had been engaged by Tierney's agent to canvass one part of the ward" (*D* 119). Thus, three *wards* and one related *guardian* are found in very close proximity. Such a repetition of a word with grammatical and etymological variations is the classical rhetorical scheme polyptoton. Now that the reader has been sensitized to the word *ward,* its appearance elsewhere catches the attention. Not only is there a character called Ward in the story, but he is told that Mr. Tierney is a Poor Law Guardian. *Ward* appears once again. Much of the crisis in the story develops from the projected arrival of the king of England in Dublin. His name, of course, is Ed*ward.* The story is almost entirely concerned with wards and guardians in the form of fathers, masters, and kings who betray their wards and wards who betray their kings, masters, and fathers.

Among fathers may be counted old Jack, drunkenly brutalizing his drunk son (*D* 120); comments on Hynes's father (*D* 124); the reference to "the City Fathers" (*D* 127), who back only those who borrow money from them; the black sheep, Father Keon; and so on: vicious circles that form and reform kaleidoscopically throughout. Henchy in his inimically treacherous and devilish way explains the lineal descent of their immediate employer, Tierney: "Mean little tinker! 'Usha, how could he be anything else? . . . Mean little shoeboy of hell! I suppose he forgets the time his little old father kept the hand-me-down shop in Mary's lane" (*D* 123). Or take another ancestral hand-me-down, which is a dazzling tour de force, for nearly every word points in the same direction through double entendre, pun, repetition, etymology, and ambivalence: "But there's a certain little *nobleman* with a *cock*-eye. . . . There's a *lineal descendant* of *Major Sirr* for you if you like! O, the heart's blood of a *patriot!*" (*D* 125; emphasis mine). Family and its extension into city and state have gone awry through the corruption of this baleful paternal influence.

The boy bringing the bottles is corrupted by his masters with what he brings: the source of false spirit produces a "drunken bowsy" (*D* 127); the bottle of stout becomes "this lad" (*D* 130). The church, having abandoned its spiritual mission and turned to secular power and money, produces a Father Keon who is regretfully mistaken for the dozen of stout. These forces cannot produce men but only ambiguous boy-men like the "grey-haired young man"

(*D* 118) with his "husky falsetto" (*D* 119), Mr. O'Connor. The cockeyed Major Sirr is only one of many such father figures, malformed and malforming. If we examine his title of "Major" (*D* 125), we see that he is linked through etymology to the doublet of *major, mayor,* the center of Dublin's problems and the subject of the caretaker's story about his friend's story against his master.

All of these words—*major, mayor, master*—can be traced back to the same Aryan root. Suddenly the text becomes illuminated with further signals. The constantly recurring *Mr* is revitalized from bland title to significant comment, for *Mr* too is one of this family of words that carry the weight of the story about fathers and sons, masters and mastered. And what about those innocent syllables in the names of the characters? The *O* of *O'Connor* and even the *son* of *Dawson street* (*D* 131) relate to paternity or tribal affiliations, as does the Anglo-Saxon element of *ing* in *Fanning* (*D* 123) and *Wilkins* (*D* 131). *At-kin-son* (*D* 131) provides three significant elements, as it means the son of the son of Adam. Appropriately, *Tierney* means descendant of a lord. It begins to become clear what Joyce meant when he said that he could do anything with words.

Out of these families comes betrayal, and ironically those who betray others betray themselves. Hynes, perhaps the only moral person in this farce, describes the corruption of politics: "The working-man is not looking for fat jobs for his sons and nephews and cousins. The working-man is not going to drag the honour of Dublin in the mud to please a German monarch" (*D* 121). It is in exactly these terms that Henchy betrays others and himself even in his ideals:

> You must owe the City Fathers money nowadays if you want to be made Lord Mayor. Then they'll make you Lord Mayor. By God! I'm thinking seriously of becoming a City father myself. . . . Driving out of the Mansion House . . . in all my vermin, with Jack here standing up behind me in a powdered wig—eh?
> —And make me your private secretary, John.
> —Yes. And I'll make Father Keon my private chaplain. We'll have a family party. [*D* 127]

We would seem to be already in Mary T. Reynolds's Dantean world, which she applies to *Ulysses:*

> Dante uses the idea of fatherhood poetically as a central principle of order. Paternal imagery begins in the *Inferno* and continues through the three divisions of the *Commedia*. By its use Dante expresses the condition of people under civil government as brothers under the rule of their sire. Ultimately the vision extends to the family of Man, as brothers under the rule of God the Father. Within this pattern Dante explores the mystery of generation, the inheritance of intelligence and talent. The negative image also is sharply

and subtly drawn; not only the benevolent ruler but the tyrant is shown. The simoniac priest and corrupt pope are an aspect of the configuration, as are also the teacher and the poet who misuse their trust. [34]

Reynolds's phrase "the family of Man" is appropriate because the word *man* occurs incessantly in the story as it deals with a small group of men hired to persuade another larger group of men to vote for their man from among a few men to take municipal office and guard them and their interests. Their conversation takes in a wide range of men from the king of England and the mayor of Dublin to the caretaker's drunken son. *Man* is one of the most constantly repeated words in the story: *Working-man* occurs five times in Hynes's praise of Colgan alone (*D* 121), and in the same passage we find "One *man* is a plain honest *man*" (*D* 121); "Our *man* won't vote for the address," "If this *man* were alive" (*D* 122). And elsewhere: "I think he's a *man* from the other camp," "His father was a decent respectable *man*," "Couldn't he have some spark of *man*hood about him?" "I think Joe Hynes is a straight *man*" (*D* 124); "It was impossible to say whether he wore a clergy*man*'s collar or a lay*man*'s," "He's an unfortunate *man* of some kind" (*D* 125); "till the *man* was grey," "are we going to insult the *man*?" "I admire the *man* personally . . . he's a good sports*man*," "Why would he welcome a *man* like that?" "Do you think now after what he did Parnell was a fit *man* to lead us?" (*D* 132); "he was a gentle*man*," "he was the only *man* that could keep that bag of cats in order," "You stuck to him like a *man*!" "Out with it *man*" (*D* 133); "Good *man*, Joe" (*D* 135; emphasis mine). That is an awful lot of manpower, or rather lack of it, for no one in the story seems to be working effectively. (*Hand, handle* have a similar frequency and irony.) The story defines what a man should be by showing the negation: what a man should not be. The image of fire clarifies this technique as the fire burns low in a room in *Wicklow* street in which two candles are lit. Such candles, we learn from "The Sisters," are placed at the head of a corpse (*D* 9). Anecdotes about seeing the light and having a spark of manhood are all negated by the setting.

But it is the etymology of the word *man* in Skeat's *Etymological Dictionary* that provides the arithmetical tables of manhood:

MAN, . . . The sense is "thinking animal"; from √MAN, to think; cf. Skt. *man*, to think; and see *Mind.*

MIND, the understanding, intellect, memory . . . all from √MAN, to think. From the same root, *man, mental, mentor . . . money, mint, mendacious, comment. . . .*

√253. MA, to think, more commonly MAN . . . Skt. man, to think, to mind, to believe, to understand, know . . . Ex. *mental . . . meditate, comment, reminiscence, man, mind, mood, mean.* [emphasis mine]

Although it could be argued that such "mean" words would naturally appear in any text, it should not be forgotten that we are dealing with a story of less than twenty pages. There is also an exceedingly odd distribution of such words, for with one exception and putting aside the ubiquitous word *man*, the derivatives of root "253. √MA. MAN" are centered on O'Connor and Henchy. It is as if they are having a particular battle of manhood between themselves. For example, here are such words as *money, mentioned, mind,* and *means* from the same root as *man* and used with frequent repetition by Henchy: "—No money, boys" (*D* 122); "I mentioned Father Burke's name" (*D* 123); "Couldn't he pay up like a man instead of: " ... *I've spent a lot of money?*" (*D* 123); "Do you mind now?" (*D* 123); "He means well, you know" (*D* 129); "Look at all the money there is in the country" (*D* 131); "He's a man of the world, and he means well by us" (*D* 132). Men can use their "minds" and escape, or they can take the "money" and perish.

The word *boy* also appears frequently because how boys are treated determines what men they will become. We have already seen several boy-men such as O'Connor and King Edward ("come to the throne after his old mother keeping him out of it till the man was grey" [*D* 132]) and the caretaker (a guardian who does not take care), who early in the story bemoans his son's drunkenness but offers a drink to the boy who brings the dozen of stout. The vicious circle of betrayal is led up to by a series of *man/boy* repetitions, which are interwoven with the false spirit in the "bottles":

> At this point there was a knock at the door, and a boy put in his head.
> —What is it? said the old man.
> —From the *Black Eagle,* said the boy, walking in sideways and depositing a basket on the floor with a noise of shaken bottles.
> The old man helped the boy to transfer the bottles from the basket to the table and counted the full tally. After the transfer the boy put his basket on his arm and asked:
> —Any bottles?
> —What bottles? said the old man.
> —Won't you let us drink them first? said Mr. Henchy.
> —I was told to ask for bottles.
> —Come back to-morrow, said the old man.
> —Here, boy! [*D* 128]

and:

> —Would you like a drink, boy?
> —If you please, sir, said the boy.
> The old man opened another bottle grudgingly, and handed it to the boy.

—What age are you? he asked.
—Seventeen, said the boy. [*D* 129]

If patterns of repetition, alliteration, typography, and etymology can act as markers for underlying meanings, so can placing key words in key positions. For example, the interference of the state in the affairs of the church and vice versa, which was such anathema to Dante and Joyce, relates to the analogy between the promiscuity of Edward VII, who is about to be welcomed to Dublin, and the one sexual indiscretion of Parnell, which led to his political downfall at the instigation of the church and delayed Home Rule in Ireland. Henchy denies the key analogy between the sexual escapades of Edward and Parnell but does admit that Edward is "a bit of a rake" (*D* 132). The word *rake* appears in another key position in the story, its beginning, and is later repeated.

The story begins: "Old Jack raked the cinders together" (*D* 118). The word *rake*, as applied to Edward and to the caretaker's act of raking, is connected through an error of folk etymology, which may well have appealed to Joyce. The *rake*, meaning "a wild disolute fellow," is a perversion of the Middle English *rakel*, meaning *rash*. However, as Skeat notes, "This word was corrupted into *rake-hell* . . . and then shortened to *rake*." It is not difficult to see how this came to be identified with the implement. Attridge discusses the assumption of "connections between signifiers on the basis of a similarity of sound" (112) in folk etymology and also points out that etymology's "rhetorical partner, from which it is sometimes indistinguishable, is the *calembour* or *paronomasia*, the play on words" (108). Old Jack rakes the fire: he rakes in hell; Edward is a rake-hell in the same circle of hell.

Although Reynolds is not centrally concerned with works as early as *Dubliners* in the schema she presents ("The Dantean Design of Joyce's *Dubliners*"), she does place "Ivy Day in the Committee Room" in the circle in hell of the "Grafters and Barrators" (159). This classification applies to what the story is about on the surface, but I shall try to show that Joyce is already roaming much more widely through the circles of hell in this story and that the center is elsewhere.

We should also investigate a possible connection between the caretaker, who "set himself to fan the fire" (*D* 118), and Mr. Fanning, who seems in control of the political corruption. Fanning is an action of Dante's Satan, and when Dante catches his first sight of him in the foggy distance, he seems to see a windmill blown by the wind (*Inferno* 34.4-7). A few lines later, and closer to Satan, he sees that what he took for the arms of a windmill are huge bat wings: "And he was flapping, so that three winds went forth from him whereby Cocytus was all congealed" (*Inferno* 34.49-52). Dante spares little over fifty lines on Satan, whom he calls Dis,[1] but much of the detail has striking analogies to the details of Joyce's story. A study of Dis's attributes will reveal that Joyce has, like a Cubist, shattered his subject and redistributed the fragments among various characters and images in the story.

The most obviously Dis-like is Father Keon, who arrives appropriately looking for Mr. Fanning. Dis's three tear-stained faces are respectively red,[2] black, and a color between white and yellow. Keon wears "a round hat of hard black felt. His face, shining with raindrops had the appearance of damp yellow cheese save where two rosy spots indicated his cheekbones" (*D* 125). Dante's description of Dis reveals the resemblance:

> Lo Dis ... The Emperor of the woeful realms stood forth from mid-breast out of the ice. ... Oh how great a marvel it was to me when I saw three faces on his head; one in front and it was red, and the other two joined to this just over the middle of each shoulder, and all were joined at the crown. The right one seemed between white and yellow, and the left one was such in appearance as are those who come whence the Nile descends. From under each there came forth two mighty wings, of a size befitting such a bird. ... They had no feathers but were like a bat's. And he was flapping them, so that three winds went forth from him, whereby Cocytus was all congealed. With six eyes he was weeping, and down over three chins dripped tears and bloody foam. In each mouth he champed a sinner with his teeth. [*Inferno* 34.20-55]

Keon's "velvety voice" (*D* 126) is particularly suggestive, for *velvety* is a word with a particular etymological history and derives directly from the word Dante used in describing Dis. Skeat says:

> This word is interesting as being almost the only Ital. word (in E.) of so early a date; it may have been imported directly from Italy. The Ital. velluto answers to a Low Lat. form villutus; shaggy ... —Lat. villus, shaggy hair, a tuft of hair, so that velvet means "woolly" or shaggy stuff.

The passage where it occurs in Dante shows where Joyce may have learned the art of significant repetition. It describes Dante and Virgil climbing out of hell, using the shaggy flanks of Dis as a sort of ladder:

> a le *vellute* coste,
> di *vello* in *vello* giu discese poscia
> tra 'l *folto pelo* e le gelate croste. ... [*Inferno* 34.73-75; emphasis mine]

> [He caught hold of the shaggy flanks;
> down from shag to shag he descended
> between the matted hair and frozen crusts.]

The analogy continues as Joyce now moves with both Dante and Skeat as inspiration. Even though Father Keon is a man of the cloth, he is a discredited one and must cut his coat according to his cloth. Velvet as a material would be far too luxurious for the meanness of his "shabby frock coat." Instead Joyce has transferred it to his voice. (Similarly, in "The Sisters," velvet appears in a satanic context but only in a dream.) The second phrase describing Dis's fur, "matted hair" ("folto pelo"), resembles Skeat's definition of *felt* as "cloth made by matting wool together": "folto pelo" suggests Keon's "hat of hard black felt." The woolliness of Keon fragments further. He is called a "black sheep" (*D* 126), and his "shabby frock-coat" (*D* 125) supplies us with the word *frock*, which Skeat derives from "Flock:" "Probably so called because woollen." The third phrase describing Dis's fur is "le gelate croste" ("frozen crusts"). "Frozen scabs" would be another possible translation, and Skeat connects this word with *shabby*. Many words describing Dis and many of the images have been transferred to Keon. Even the rain on Keon's face resembles Dis's tears. O'Connor sums it up nicely: "Fanning and himself seem to be very thick" (*D* 126). Joyce uses the images and words associated with Dis to suggest the satanic in several other characters. Dis's mouths chew sinners; similarly Old Jack, the caretaker's "moist mouth fell open at times, munching once or twice" (*D* 118).

It should not be forgotten that Joyce is also a comic writer and that there is a long tradition of mocking devils even in Dante. After all, the Devil is an ass. Mary Reynolds's identification of this story as being in the circle of grafters and barrators is particularly significant here, for it contains the most farcical of all Dante's writings. Dorothy L. Sayers in her translation of the relevant cantos 21 and 22 notes that "the mood of these two cantos—a mixture of savage satire and tearing high spirits—is unlike anything else in the *Comedy,* and is a little disconcerting to the more solemn-minded of Dante's admirers. Artistically, this grim burlesque is of great value as an interlude" (205).

Perhaps another indication of the element of farce is the fact that the door opens and closes as rapidly as in a French farce: opening to disclose a burlesque character and closing to allow backbiting behind the back of the character who has just exited. It opens and closes thirteen times, suitable to a dismal day and one on which there is a reenactment of the betrayal mentioned at the Last Supper.

Given the detailed analogy between Keon and Dis, I would suggest that it is no accident that Keon expresses "*dis*appointment" (*D* 125), just as Father Flynn of "The Sisters" was a "*dis*appointed man" (*D* 17). Keon, with the same possible sense in "Ivy Day," does not want to "*dis*turb" (*D* 126), while his velvety voice is "*dis*creet" (*D* 126) and the day is "*dis*mal" (*D* 119; emphasis mine). The pun seems to be too available for Joyce to have been able to resist it.

A detail not yet accounted for is Dante's reference to Dis as a bird. May this be why Mr. Fanning is to be found at the Black Eagle? This image effectively imputes satanic qualities to the emblem of the "German monarch" (*D* 121), Edward. As the black eagle is also a symbol of the Roman and Holy Roman Empires, it symbolizes all of these, pointing to the lost integrity and the lost autonomy of such institutions. The imperial eagle as a symbol of justice takes up three whole cantos in Dante's *Paradiso,* but the image is formed of lights (*Paradiso* 18-20). The black eagle also returns us to the circle of hell of the barrators, which ends with the image of winged fiends entangled in the black pitch (*Inferno* 22). Oliver St. John Gogarty was not exaggerating when he called Joyce the Dante of Dublin (quoted in Ellmann 75).

Joyce did not limit himself to Dante's portrayal of Dis but ranged through much of the rest of the tradition. For example, Satan as Lucifer—the light bearer—may explain why Father Keon's buttons "reflected the candle-light" (*D* 125). This reflection is also of two candles traditionally set at the head of a corpse. Furthermore, Keon, as if in Milton's "darkness visible," can see in the dark. Satan as the great naysayer ("Non Serviam") is reflected in Father Keon, who manages to say "no" ten times in half a page (*D* 126). Another example of Milton's influence is seen, for example, in Old Jack's chewing over the cinders, for this reenacts the events of the Miltonic Satan's return to hell.

As we have seen, the story is much concerned with betrayal and treachery and, centering on Parnell, deals with those who have betrayed their master. Hynes's poem has linked them to the betrayal of Judas. If we focus on Dante's Dis, reflected from various angles in the slivers of the cracked looking glass, we can appreciate the significance of the various characters in this story. "Ivy Day" is firmly placed in the final circles of hell, where those who have betrayed family, state, and master are frozen in ice around the figure of the archbetrayer, Dis. The great contemporary betrayal is that of those who betrayed Parnell. The irony results from the setting being in the Royal Exchange Ward (here barrators exchange power for money) where Parnell is exchanged for the rake, Edward VII, that "German monarch" (*D* 121). A further irony is derived from the building after which the ward is named, which by a change analogous to those of etymology was at one time the City Hall and at another the Royal Exchange, a fitting place for barrators. Edward is truly represented by Richard Tierney, for the *Ed* of Edward means "rich" and is thus a form of the *Rich* of Richard Tierney.

But the "Exchange" of the Royal Exchange Ward is even more—as we might expect—complicated. An exchange is a financial and capitalistic institution. Henchy argues in his dismissal of the memory of Parnell and the welcoming of Edward VII that "what we want in this country, as I said to old Ward, is capital. The King's coming here will mean an influx of money into this country. . . . It's capital we want" (*D* 131). *Capital*, as in *capital punishment*, is fairly obviously a word of Latin derivation meaning "head." And what was Parnell's informal title, the title given to the "Uncrowned King" of Hynes's poem (*D* 134)? Mr. O'Connor is allowed to use this phrase that was so significant to Parnell's supporters: "the Chief" (*D* 133). This word is merely the French form of the Latin *capital*. In turn, the English *head* is cognate with both *chief* and *capital:* that is, it is related etymologically. So the Irish in the story are depicted as having lost their heads and lost their Head; of having exchanged their uncrowned king (their Chief) for the money (capital) they expect from the British Empire under its head (King Edward), a very *poor* law guardian. In a word, this is the ultimate betrayal (in its secular form), the final circle of hell.

There are many other intriguing references in the story that point in this same direction. The words repeated in the story—*treachery, traitor, trick, tricky*—reiterate the crime of this icy region. The word *kowtow,* in the line "What do we want kowtowing to a foreign king?" (*D* 122), is only one of many clues that indicate exactly where we are in hell, for *kowtow* is Chinese for *head-banging,* an occupation of those traitors to family imprisoned in hell's ice (*Inferno* 32.40-51). The frozen victims surrounding Dis are embedded in the ice and wear visors of ice over their faces. Keon, who is seen as "a poor actor" (*D* 125), quite suitably is also a "person" (*D* 125), for that word derives from *persona,* which, as Skeat explains, is "a mask worn by an actor."

But although the story is mainly set in these circles of traitors, Joyce allows himself flashes of other parts of hell. "It did not appear whether he was a layman or cleric" could easily be mistaken for Joyce's comment on Father Keon: "It was impossible to say whether he wore a clergyman's collar or a layman's" (*D* 125). The earlier version is Singleton's translation of Dante (*Inferno* 18.117) in the hell of flatterers. Keon, in "pursing" (*D* 126) his mouth, punningly suggests one of the simoniacs who are ubiquitous in Joyce's Dantean Dublin. The phrase "stump up" (*D* 123), that is pay up, refers to *Inferno* 28.104, the circle of dissension. It is in this circle that we meet Mosca, who had the distinction of instigating the great Guelf-Ghibelline feud in Florence: "And one who had both hands lopped off, raising the stumps through the murky air" (*Inferno* 28.103-4). Hynes's "very cold ears" (*D* 122) link him to the circle of those who betrayed their kindred, to Camicion de' Pazzi, who has lost his ears in the circle of ice (*Inferno* 32.52-53). As the aspects of Dis can be fragmented and distributed through several characters, similarly one character can have a basic reference to one sin but include variations from several others.

The sinners in Dante's hell either condemn others or, inadvertently, themselves. Henchy is outstanding in this respect. Joyce's use of Skeat's *Etymological Dictionary* reveals a classic combination of repetition and word history in the description of Henchy. As a self-betraying betrayer, he uses the word *little* incessantly about others. For example: "—It's no go. . . . I asked the little shoeboy. . . . Mean little tinker!" (*D* 123); "He hasn't got those little pigs' eyes for nothing. . . . Mean little shoeboy of hell! I suppose he forgets the time his little old father kept the hand-me-down shop in Mary's Lane" (*D* 123); "But Tricky Dicky's little old father always had a tricky little black bottle up in a corner" (*D* 123); "Do you know what my private and candid opinion is about some of those little jokers?" (*D* 125); "But there's a certain little nobleman with a cock-eye" (*D* 125); "—I asked that little shoeboy three times" (*D* 127); "—I just waited till I caught his eye, and said: *About that little matter I was speaking to you about.* . . . Yerra, sure the little hop-o'-my-thumb" (*D* 127); "—I think I know the little game they're at" (*D* 127); "Did you ever see this little trick?" (*D* 130).

Henchy diversifies his constant criticism of littleness with words like "tinpot," "not worth a damn," "the thin edge of the wedge" (*D* 129), "a stroke above that," "a bit too clever" (*D* 125), "a bit of coal" (*D* 123), and "a spark of manhood" (*D* 124). Even his praise is belittling. He refers to King Edward in these words: "I admire the man personally. He's just an ordinary knockabout like you and me" (*D* 132). Certainly the theme is insistent. But the littleness of which he constantly accuses others is his own main attribute, revealed by the words that introduce him: "Then a bustling little man with a snuffling nose and very cold ears pushed in the door" (*D* 122). And what is the etymology of *little*? According to Skeat, "LITTLE, . . . All [cognates] from base LUT, to deceive, in connection with which we also find A.S. *lytig*, deceitful . . . also A.S. *lot*, deceit, and the Goth. *liuts*, deceitful, *liuta*, dissembler, *luton*, to betray. Thus the old sense of *little* is 'deceitful' or 'mean'; a sense still retained."

Not all those in the committee room are treacherous and imprisoned in their own hell. The depiction of Hynes and his poem present us with many surprises. It is generally agreed that there is some sort of ambivalence here if only in the relation between the faithful writer and his terrible poem. But it is unlikely that Joyce would be quite so simple. Hynes's poem is well prefaced with O'Connor's "Fire away, Joe" (*D* 133), for it presents the apotheosis of the fire imagery presided over by the feeble fire in the committee room. The fire sinks even lower to the infernal snakes: "Mr Henchy snuffled vigorously and spat so copiously that he nearly put out the fire which uttered a hissing protest" (*D* 124). Later, given its feebleness, the poem presents a fitting and ironic image for the manhood of the story: "Couldn't he have some spark of manhood about him?" (*D* 124). Parnell is resurrected from his funeral "pyre" and eventually

> . . . his spirit may
> Rise, like the Phoenix from the flames,
> When breaks the dawning of the day. [*D* 135]

The Parnell of Hynes's verse shows clearly these contrasting poles each attracting the other into the dynamic tension of unity. The analogy to Christ is evident:

> Shame on the coward caitiff hands
> That smote their Lord or with a kiss
> Betrayed him to the rabble-rout
> Of fawning priests—no friends of his. [*D* 134]

For whatever Christ symbolism Parnell reenacts, he is also depicted in satanic terms:

> . . . th' exalted name
> Of one who spurned them in his pride.
>
> He fell as fall the mighty ones. . . . [*D* 135]

The pyre, Phoenix, and dawn would seem now to be also the light of the herald of light, Lucifer the light bearer. Even *calm* in the poem etymologically means "heat."

Hynes too seems to be presented ambivalently. He is accused of sponging and of lacking a spark of manhood, is said to be not nineteen carat, although all these are phrases of Henchy, who is hardly an objective critic. The fulcrum is Henchy's comment: "I think he's a man from the other camp. He's a spy of Colgan's if you ask me" (*D* 124). A spy at first would seem ignoble, but if he is from "the other camp" and the scene is set in hell, he must be from heaven. If he is from heaven, he must be a blessed soul, an angel, or God. If he is in hell, he must be there for some purpose. Could it be to deliver a message, his poem?

The etymologies of several words applied to Hynes suggest positive, heavenly qualities: "splendid" (*D* 133) comes from the Latin ("to shine"); he is "bareheaded" (*D* 135), and "bare" comes from the Sanskrit "to shine." This is an extraordinary conjunction. He is "clever" (*D* 125), which is related to the word "deliver, meaning to set free." He is clever with his "pen" (*D* 125), which rises from the root meaning "to fly." He is a flying, shining deliverer. But other words associated with him seem to contradict this. The etymologies of these require extended tracing. Hynes is "slender" (*D* 120); he leaves the room "slowly" (*D* 124) and later reenters "slowly" (*D* 133). From Skeat's entry, *slender* is "also used as a sb., meaning a water-snake . . . *slinder* is a long snake." What can we find in *slow*? Its derivatives include *slip*, a word that takes us back through Skeat's own labyrinth to "Aryan √SARP, to creep; whence E. *Serpent* q. v."

Hynes, who on the surface is honest, loyal, intelligent, and angelic on the etymological level, is a snake and seems to be no different from the other hellish snakes who surround him. The elucidation, I hope, of this epiphany is not too far away. He is the Gnostic savior-serpent. He brings a message from the supreme God that will free mankind from the tyranny of the Demiurge creator. (This notion represents the doctrine of the Ophite sect; *Ophite* can be translated as "snake men.") The fire and snake imagery, which surrounds Hynes, is thus resolved. His message (the poem) is of "Freedom's reign" (*D* 135) that "spirit may / Rise . . ." (*D* 135) and redeem the failure or perversion of fire and spirit in the committee room into a triumph of liberty:

> But Erin, list, his spirit may
> Rise, like the Phoenix from the flames,
> When breaks the dawning of the day,
>
> The day that brings us Freedom's reign.
> And on that day may Erin well
> Pledge in the cup she lifts to Joy.
> One grief—the memory of Parnell. [*D* 135]

The portrait of the virtuous Hynes challenges the mockery of the fiends in the circle of the barrators, for the evil do not have a monopoly on humor. Hynes's father, "Larry," who "did many a good turn" (*D* 124), thus resembles St. Lawrence in more than name. St. Lawrence, noted for his care of the poor, was martyred by being roasted on a grill and "is said to have triumphed over the tyrant by the famous ironical speech—'Assatus est, jam versa et manduca'" (*Encyclopedia Britannica* 14:371) ("I am roasted on this side, turn me around, and eat"). Humor is not confined to hell, and of course neither are fire and hot air.

I have tried to show the dominance of Skeat's *Etymological Dictionary* in "Ivy Day in the Committee Room," which one could say is written in Skeatish. Several other questions immediately present themselves: Is there evidence of much significant etymology other than Skeat's in the story? How much of *Dubliners* is Skeatish? How significant is Gnosticism to *Dubliners*? Where did Joyce get his knowledge of Gnosticism? The answer to the last question is the simplest. The key authority of Gnosticism is the second-century St. Irenœus, whose work was accessible to Joyce at the National Library. Various reference works such as *The Encyclopedia Britannica* were also available. Joyce's contemporaries, especially Yeats, also could have been his sources.

It would be strange if Joyce limited himself to Skeat's etymology, although it seems to be by far the most influential in his early writing. Etymology was in the air at the turn of the century. Several etymological works were available to him at the National Library in Dublin, and many standard reference books included etymology as a normal aspect of definition. For example, it would have been atypical of Joyce if he had overlooked P.W. Joyce's *The Origin and History of Irish Names of Places*. His knowledge of Latin would have alerted him to etymological connections with words derived from it in modern English. As he absorbed modern languages, his knowledge would have been further developed. Etymology may even have formed the mnemonic matrix that underlay his skills as an accomplished linguist.

It has long been argued that Joyce manipulates the etymology of the names of the places and people in *Dubliners*. The names of various characters extend the same themes across several stories through etymological links. Thus Frank, whose name means "free" and who offers *Eveline* escape—"He would save her" (*D* 40)—is an obvious savior figure. "He had fallen on his feet" (*D* 39) reveals his Lucifer/Vulcan aspect. Eveline, who wonders "where on earth all the dust came from" (*D* 37) (the answer is that it comes from the earth), never does find out just how good the air is in Buenos Aires (*D* 39) and returns to her dusty cretonne and a plethora of negative air and heart imagery. "The man from Belfast" (*D* 36) carries on her father's bad work, as a very Blakean Gnostic Demiurge, and builds houses in the field where she used to play. Earlier "Her father used often to hunt them out of the field with his blackthorn stick" (*D* 36), and he behaves badly throughout, giving her "the palpitations" (*D* 38).

The drunk Freddy of "The Dead" is another potential savior. *Freddy* contains a punning element of "free," but his name means "peace," a fitting variant, as the Magi gather together at the Epiphany to celebrate the angels' message "Peace on Earth." Freddy's habit of wiping his left eye with his left hand is corroborated as the act of a savior by reference to Dante: "He was clearing that gross air from before his face, often moving his left hand before him, and only with that annoyance did he seem weary. Well did I perceive that he was a messenger from Heaven" (*Inferno* 9.82-85). Browne constantly misnames Freddy as Teddy, and if we can assume that Teddy is a contraction of Theodore (God's gift), the angelic messenger role is patent.

These are only some of the many clues that link these "characters" to such "messengers" as Hynes with his poem announcing freedom. The "telegram [distant letter] boy" (*D* 12) in "The Sisters" is joined outside the dead priest's house by two women, and they form a tableau of the angel and the women at Christ's tomb. The identity of all these messengers is clear, for "messenger" is the meaning of *angel*, derived from Hebrew. Their nature, however, is suitably puzzling. As St. Irenœus informs us that one of the names of the Gnostic redeeming serpent is Michael, Michael Furey of "The Dead" presents himself as another candidate for such a role (Irenœus 109).

The evil Creator/Demiurge/Jehovah can also be traced throughout *Dubliners* without too much difficulty. He is fragmented into the various negative father figures in "Ivy Day" and in "Eveline." He can also be seen in the perverted "queer old josser" (*D* 26) of "An Encounter" (*Joss* means God in Pidgin English, an etymology not to be found in Skeat, however); in the drunk Joe; in the sinister "gentleman" of "Clay"; and in the rage-filled Farrington of "Counterparts," who ends the story beating his little son. They are all manifestations of the malicious Demiurge of Gnosticism. In some Gnostic systems, this figure is not malevolent but merely incompetent. The paralytic Father Flynn, whose actions are "inefficacious" in "The Sisters" (*D* 12); the drunk, forgetful uncle of "Araby"; and even Gabriel of "The Dead" are representatives of this aspect. Michael Furey is a fitting opponent to Gabriel's ineffective bossiness and false sense of superiority. Gabriel stands apart from the other representatives in that he gains some degree of self-knowledge and seems very much like Joyce rather than those whom Joyce observed.

Men like Hynes, Frank, and Freddy are bound together throughout *Dubliners* by the presence of a man who does not appear: Simon Magus. It is standard criticism that simony, derived from the name Simon Magus and mentioned on the first page of "The Sisters," defines the dominant sin of *Dubliners*. But equally significant is his role as a Gnostic. "There can be little doubt, however, that Simon must be placed in the very front of the history of Gnosticism" (*Enclopedia Britannica* 10:702).

Gnosticism adds the missing element to the *gnomon* of "The Sisters," for it is derived from the same root, "$\sqrt{GNA}$," and joins *gnomon*'s cognates and synonyms that define the intellectual black hole engulfing everyone except the priest who embodies it and the boy who reports it, the author, and the reader. Derivations for the name Simon include "famous," "hearkener," and "snubnosed" (a feature Freddy Malins shares). But the "hearkener" element meets with "catechism" in "The Sisters," for it derives from the word for "loudshouting." Nannie's deafness, the whispering, the gossip, the gestures that pervade the story, are all aspects of the angelic message or the lack of it. *Magus* comes from the root meaning "power," taking in *magic* along the way together with all the *master/mayor* words that dominate "Ivy Day."

Dante's great subject of the correct and incorrect actions of the two arms of government, the church and state, is often presented by Joyce through etymology. Thus while Eliza "sits in the chair of state," Nannie pours "sherry" (*D* 15), which is etymologically derived by Skeat from the town "Xerex" (formerly "Caesaris"), which in turn is derived from "Caesar," Dante's archetypal secular ruler. "The Sisters" is as heavily etymologized as "Ivy Day," but space permits me only to add one more key phrase from the story. The first paragraph ends with the boy's comment on the word *paralysis,* which he associates with *simony* and *gnomon.* "But now it sounded to me like the name of some maleficent and sinful being" (*D* 9). Skeat derives *sin* from *being.* If Joyce thought this was the "truer meaning" of the word, it is of great significance for an understanding of his writing. Whatever the truth about this idea, it certainly provided him with a useful system. It also fits in with the belief of many Gnostics that the creation (being) was totally evil.

From another viewpoint it is the "sin" identified by Christians that is life and being. Mrs. *Sinico's* name in "A Painful Case" takes on new Gnostic and Dantean significance just as does the train at the end of the story: "like a worm with a fiery head winding through the darkness . . . the laborious drone of the engine reiterating the syllables of her name" (*D* 117). The worm is a common name for Satan. Sinico sounds like the institution (*Co*) of sin. Her Eve-like tempting fails, but after her death, her biblical associate, the snake/worm, haunts the protagonist, Mr. Duffy. He is reminded that what he has rejected is life and that finally takes on a positive form: "he saw the squalid tract of her vice," "unfit to live" (*D* 115); "As he sat there, living over his life with her," "how lonely her life must have been," "His life would be lonely too" (*D* 116); "had he withheld life from her?" "he felt that he had been an outcast from life's feast" (*D* 117). Once again we see in *Dubliners* the tension between Gnostic and Christian interpretations of sin, being, God, the serpent, and the savior.

"The Sisters," "Ivy Day," and "The Dead" seem to me to be the most heavily dependent on etymology. Joyce called his last story a coda and as usual he is accurate, for it contains almost all the themes of the rest of *Dubliners* with a complex mixture of elements from Dante's *Inferno, Purgatorio,* and *Paradiso,* juggling from farce to tragedy. Old Cotter in the first story tells "endless stories about the distillery" (*D* 10) where mode and subject observe decorum: not only do the stories form a circular repetition—a pattern repeated throughout Joyce's work—but the dominant image of distillation is endless, for it is itself a circulatory process. Stephen/Joyce seems never to have really turned off the valve of the circulatory process of the "refrigerating apparatus, invented and patented in all countries by Dante Alighieri" (*Portrait* 252). (Refrigerators, of course, also produce heat.) "The Dead" is crammed with the circulatory processes of distillation, hot and cold, macrocosmic and microcosmic. The falling/dropping aspect in particular seems to have fascinated Joyce, and indeed that is the etymological foundation of *distill.*

"The Dead" is an endless story told about the distillery, the maker and manipulator of spirits human and otherwise. The waltzes in three-time mix with the four-time "quadrilles" (etymologically "squares") together with many other military connotations that sum up Dante's vision of the spiritual (Trinity as three-time) and the secular (military as four-time) in *Paradiso.* The triplicities, which are climaxed by the vision of the trinity as intertwining spheres, are present as the three potatoes in the cloth offered to Gabriel (*D* 198) and in the demonic inversion of the three-headed coach: "There was a good deal of confused talk, and then Mr Browne got into the cab. The cabman settled his rug over his knees, and bent down for the address. The confusion grew greater and the cabman was directed differently by Freddy Malins and Mr Browne, each of whom had his head out through a window of the cab. . . . —Well, drive bang up against Trinity College gates, said Mr Browne" (*D* 208-9).

Etymology increases the identification with triple-headed Dis; the rug stands in for Dis's shaggy covering, which Joyce has already used elsewhere. Furthermore, Skeat defines *rug* as related to *rough,* which in turn is defined as "shaggy." The confusion speaks for itself, but the repeated *cab* points in the same satanic direction, for Skeat links it to the *caper* of a goat—a word insistently associated with Freddy, who "will have all the cabs in Dublin out" (*D* 206)—and traditionally associates it with Satan particularly in his nether regions, presenting a standard shaggy image. The repetitions of *cab* (six times) and *cab-man* (five times) in a short passage (*D* 208-9) signal the importance of this word. That they are driving "bang up against Trinity" suggests that they are part of a burlesque on the satanic inversion of the Trinity.

How profound etymology is in the story is indicated by Gabriel's reiteration: "She was leaning on the banisters listening to something. . . . There was grace and mystery in her attitude as if she were a symbol of something. He asked himself what is a woman standing on the stairs in the shadow, listening to distant music, a symbol of" (*D* 209-10). On the surface the question remains unanswered, but Skeat provides the clue that takes us to the heart of this labyrinth. He tells the reader under his entry for "SYMBOL" to see "Baluster," which includes the information that this word is related to Sanskrit "*gal,* to trickle down, fall away" and derives from "√GAR." The root itself also supplies the word used by Lily when dismissing men, "palaver" (*D* 178), which foreshadows the later development of words and ideas that are related to it. Skeat's entry under "BANISTER" refers the reader to "Balusters," of which it is a corruption. We are back in one way to the "endless stories about the distillery" (*D* 10), for Skeat defines "distil" as "to fall in drops, flow slowly" and traces it back to the Latin with the same meaning.

The theme of the fall is central to all Joyce's work, but there are many ways of interpreting this concept. The fall of Satan and of Adam and Eve are reversed by the doctrines of the Gnostic heresy (especially by the Cainites) and can also include the descent of the Holy Ghost. As Gretta in "The Dead" is surrounded with words that relate etymologically to fire, wind, and dove, all symbols of the Holy Ghost, this would seem to be part of her role. Putting the fall element of *banisters* and *symbol* together with these symbols, we arrive at an image of the descent of the Holy Ghost. Nor is it startling to find a female Holy Ghost because that was precisely the role that the Gnostic Simon Magus claimed for his female companion. From the very beginning Joyce had his techniques, his vocabulary, and his themes firmly under control.

Dubliners shows Joyce's detailed and profound knowledge of Skeat's *Etymological Dictionary,* Christianity (mainly represented by Dante's *Divine Comedy*), and the Gnostic heresy; these three form major aspects of his art. The hell imagery in "Ivy Day" drew early attention, but its importance has not been developed fully. The Gnostic element clarifies the significance of the other two factors, but despite its links to Simon (simony) Magus—one of the Magi but not one of the three wise men—and its etymological links to *gnomon,* Gnosticism has been neglected. The major significance of Skeat's *Etymological Dictionary* and especially its information on Aryan roots has not been recognized. Skeat sees the Aryan root words as the original ideas of the race. The ablaut of their development through time and space records the history of the race. Apparently heterogeneous modern words conceal what is left of their original unity and significance.

This evolution allows Joyce to write colloquially but convey profound meaning. He leaves clues in his stories to lead the reader through the labyrinth of etymology back to fundamental concepts. The clues can be the constant repetition of a word illustrating the lack of comprehension in the present. But such words, when investigated, lead back to key concepts. *Man* is an example of this. Joyce also links unusual words (*gnomon, paralysis,* and *simony*) whose denotation invites investigation and whose etymology leads back, as a first step, to the languages of those nations whose contribution to European culture is generally recognized. *Gnomon, simony,* and *paralysis* received a great deal of early critical attention, but their etymologies have not been investigated beyond the classical and biblical languages. Heterogeneous groups of words with a common Aryan root have been rarely investigated; common words incessantly repeated have been ignored.

By confronting Christianity and Gnosticism, Joyce produces a richly ambiguous scheme, for the serpent-savior of the Gnostics is the satanic tempter of Christianity; the loving creator, Jehovah, is the Gnostic creator-Demiurge, who entraps mankind through malice or stupidity; and the descent of the Holy Ghost is the Gnostic fall of spirit into matter. Mankind moves through these conflicting systems seeking freedom to love, which brings with it danger: freedom gives the freedom to choose wrongly. Freedom and love are achieved through the full exploitation of the forces of the spirit, the mind, and the body, forces usually presented in their negative forms. This trinity is introduced in the first paragraph of *Dubliners,* in "The Sisters," and its significance and interconnections are highlighted. *Gnomon* represents the intellect by a geometrical figure with something missing; *paralysis* represents the body that has lost its full powers; and *simony* represents the perversion of spirit by matter. In "Ivy Day in the Committee Room," the social aspects of these interconnections are presented: treachery replaces love; Hynes, with his poem, brings a message of freedom but is misunderstood through a failure of the intellect of his audience, which is the culmination of a failure to understand social ties; the spirit becomes degraded into beer (simony); the body of the "working man" does not work.

Joyce's essay on "The Study of Languages" claims, "In the history of words there is much that indicates the history of men, and in comparing the speech of to-day with that of years ago we have a useful illustration of the effect of the external influences on the very words of the race" (*Critical Writings* 28). I have tried to show how Joyce restored that history to the mean words of his stories. It was not Hynes's work that was "a very fine piece of writing" but Joyce's.

Notes

1. Joyce uses the form *Dis* although it never occurs in Dante, who uses the form *Dite*. English usually adopts the nominative of proper nouns, while Italian uses the ablative. Joyce would have been familiar with *Dis* from the translations of Dante available to him and from its occurrence in *Paradise Lost*. Both the infernal god Dis and its homonym, the prefix *dis,* are particularly appropriate. This Roman god of the infernal regions is also the Celtic god of night. That, however, is not the end of the matter, for Skeat directs us from the prefix *dis,* which originally meant "two," to its homonym, which means the "devil," and in turn traces this to the Latin *Deus* ("God").

2. The word Dante uses for the red face of Dis is "vermiglia" ("vermilion"), which was made from insects and worms, hence the name and etymology; he uses it again in the form *vermo* ("worm") to describe Dis himself. Worms occur naturally in depictions of the dead and the damned. Probably Mr. Henchy's fantasy of being mayor ("Driving out of the Mansion House . . . in all my vermin" [*D* 127]) relates to both of them. Henchy's attempt to be funny—for a malapropism here would be unlikely at a time and place in which vermin were common and commonly referred to as such—indicates the truth more than he realizes and is particularly applicable to himself.

Works Cited

Attridge, Derek. *Peculiar Language: Literature as Difference from the Renaissance to James Joyce.* Ithaca, N.Y.: Cornell Univ. Press, 1988.
Bowen, Zack, and James F. Carens. *A Companion to Joyce Studies.* Westport, Conn.: Greenwood, 1984.
Dante Alighieri. *The Divine Comedy.* Trans. and ed. Charles S. Singleton. Princeton, N.J.: Princeton Univ. Press, 1973.
Dilworth, Thomas. "Sex and Politics in 'The Dead.'" *James Joyce Quarterly* 23 (1986): 157-71.
Ellmann, Richard. *James Joyce.* Rev. ed. Oxford: Oxford Univ. Press, 1983.

Encyclopedia Britannica. 9th ed. 1879.

Füger, Wilhelm. "Crosslocution in *Dubliners.*" *James Joyce Quarterly* 27 (1989): 87-99.

Horowitz, Sylvia Huntley. "More Christian Allegory in 'Ivy Day in the Committee Room.'" *James Joyce Quarterly* 21 (1984): 145-54.

Irenœus. *The Writings of Irenœus.* Trans. and ed. Rev. Alexander Roberts and W.H. Rambaut. Edinburgh, 1868.

Joyce, James. *The Critical Writings.* Ed. Ellsworth Mason and Richard Ellmann. New York: Viking, 1966.

————. *Dubliners.* New York: Viking, 1967.

————. *A Portrait of the Artist as a Young Man.* Ed. Chester G. Anderson. New York: Viking, 1968.

————. *Stephen Hero.* Ed. Theodore Spencer. London: Cape, 1944.

Joyce, P.W. *The Origin and History of Irish Names of Places.* Dublin: Gill, 1869.

Kenner, Hugh. *Joyce's Voices.* Berkley: Univ. of California Press, 1978.

Owens, Cóilín. "'Clay' (2): The Myth of Irish Sovereignty." *James Joyce Quarterly* 27 (1990): 603-14.

Reynolds, Mary T. *Joyce and Dante.* Princeton, N.J.: Princeton Univ. Press, 1981.

San Juan, Epifanio, Jr. *James Joyce and the Craft of Fiction: An Interpretation of Dubliners.* Rutherford, N.J.: Farleigh Dickinson Univ. Press, 1972.

Sayers, Dorothy L., trans. *The Divine Comedy,* by Dante Alighieri. Harmondsworth, Middlesex: Penquin, 1969.

Senn, Fritz. "He Was Too Scrupulous Always." *James Joyce Quarterly* 2 (1965): 66-72.

Skeat, Walter W. *An Etymological Dictionary of the English Language.* Oxford: Clarendon Press, 1882.

Walzl, Florence L. "Dubliners." In *A Companion to Joyce Studies,* ed. Zack Bowen and James F. Carens, 157-228. Westport, Conn.: Greenwood, 1984.

Whittaker, Stephen. "Joyce and Skeat." *James Joyce Quarterly* 24 (1987): 177-92.

CHAPTER THIRTEEN

The Artist Paring His Quotations

Aesthetic and Ethical Implications of the Dantean Intertext in *Dubliners*

Lucia Boldrini

"There was no hope for him this time: it was the third stroke" (*Dubliners* 9; hereafter cited with page numbers as *D*). The opening sentence of "The Sisters," much quoted and much commented on, has been analyzed brilliantly by John Paul Riquelme in *Teller and Tale in Joyce's Fiction* to show how it can be recognized only retrospectively as first-person narration (a fact generally unnoticed by even the most skilled readers) and can be defined as a rare instance of "self-narrated interior monologue" (101). Despite Riquelme's convincing arguments against fusing boy and narrator in the story (98), some critics have identified the young boy as the narrator of the story, pointing out his "precociousness" (Bremen 61; Albert 359) and charging him with the accusation of unreliability (an accusation already made by Fischer). The critics who identify the boy *in* the story with the narrator *of* the story find themselves (understandably) ill at ease with the difficult words and sophisticated constructions he uses, generally put down to the influence of the priest's vocabulary and teachings and sometimes taken as indices of the inevitability of the boy's own "paralysis" in the "hemiplegia of the will" (Richard Ellmann 140) of Dublin city.

The first sentence of the story also has been interpreted as a direct allusion to one of the terrible lines that Dante reads above the portal of Hell as he enters the land of the dead: "Lasciate ogne speranza, voi ch'intrate" ("Abandon every hope, you who enter")[1] (*Inferno* 3.9; hereafter cited as *Inf* followed by canto and page number) an epigraph of damnation for the entire collection and for the city of Dublin itself with all its inhabitants (Cope, "Epigraph" 364).[2] The recognition of a precise literary allusion in these words—and, as we shall see, of a dense, pervasive pattern of Dantean echoes and "twisted misquotations" (Senn, "Scrupulous" 66)[3]—raises the question of the relationship between the status of the "allusion" and the position of the narrator in the

---

Original version published in *Style* 25.3 (1991) as "'The Sisters' and the *Inferno:* An Intertextual Network."

story, a question that concerns issues both of attribution (who is quoting or alluding to previous texts?) and of narrative and ethical responsibility (who is judging the characters and the narrators, and from what position?). In this essay I shall follow up some Dantean allusions in "The Sisters" and "The Dead" and with their help try to address the general and complex issue of the relationship between the artist, his characters and narrators, and his sources.

> There was no hope for him this time: it was the third stroke. Night after
> night I had passed the house (it was vacation time) and studied the lighted
> square of window: and night after night I had found it lighted in the same
> way, faintly and evenly. If he was dead, I thought, I would see the reflection
> of candles on the darkened blind for I knew that two candles must be set at
> the head of a corpse. He had often said to me: *I am not long for this world,*
> and I had thought his words idle. Now I knew they were true. Every night as I
> gazed up at the window I said softly to myself the word *paralysis*. It had
> always sounded strangely in my ears, like the word *gnomon* in the Euclid and
> the word *simony* in the Catechism. But now it sounded to me like the name
> of some maleficent and sinful being. It filled me with fear, and yet I longed to
> be nearer to it and to look upon its deadly work. [*D* 9]

The heavy atmosphere of darkness and sin that "The Sisters" opens on does corroborate Jackson Cope's identification of the incipit of "The Sisters" with Dante's definitive denial of hope, and his extension of the scope of the allusion to the whole of *Dubliners* also may be seen as constituting a warning for the reader at the outset of his journey through the dark and "paralysed" world of *Dubliners*. However, the reference to canto 3 of the *Inferno* may allow for a double interpretation: while the terrible words written on the portal of hell signal the entrance into the "cieco mondo" ("blind world" [*Inf* 4.13]; see also Joyce's parallactic use of "darkened blind" in the opening paragraph), admonishing the souls of the dead to abandon every hope of spiritual redemption, the entrance into hell through that very door marks for Dante the beginning of a pilgrimage of redemption and the hope—indeed the certainty—of salvation. Thus the literary allusion may also convey the hint of a possible positive interpretation for the story and the collection.

When Dante reads the stern inscription on the door he is frightened and finds the meaning of the words obscure: "Queste parole di colore oscuro / vid'io scritte al sommo d'una porta; / per ch'io: "Maestro, il senso lor m'è duro" (These words of obscure color I saw inscribed over a portal; whereupon I said, "Master, their meaning is hard for me") (*Inf* 3:10-12). The rhyming words, "oscuro" and "duro," are ambiguous: they mean "dark" and "hard" respectively, but both also can mean "difficult to understand" and "menacing." Dante is almost paralyzed with fear when he sees them, and his reaction can be compared to the attitude of the young protagonist of "The Sisters." The boy too has to face a similar situation in which he observes words whose meaning elude and frighten him, but his position is more complex that Dante's. The boy's first reaction to words is a wrong evaluation of the priest's warning ("I had thought his words idle"), which he now has to revise ("Now I knew they were true"). It is not the priest's words, however, that make him afraid, but the word he has heard and not fully understood: "paralysis," which he links with other words, "gnomon" and "simony," divorcing them from their context and associating them through their sound, thus transforming this link into a semantic and symbolic one.[4]

By means of a "grammatical and logical mistake of actually confusing the word with what it stands for" (Senn, "Scrupulous" 67), the boy now transforms the word into the "maleficent and sinful *being*" (my emphasis), which frightens but also fascinates him: "I longed to be nearer to it and look upon its deadly work." The boy looks upon the word in his mind just as Dante observed the obscure, hard words written above the gate of hell: like Dante, he finds the words puzzling and fearful; unlike Dante, he longs to be nearer to the name of this maleficent and sinful being in order to observe it at work. In his fear, Dante appeals to Virgil, calling him "Maestro," and Virgil rescues him by leading him through that very gate: "E poi che la sua mano a la mia puose/con lieto volto, ond'io mi confortai,/mi mise dentro a le segrete cose" (And when he had placed his hand on mine, with a cheerful look from which I took comfort, he led me into the secret things) (*Inf* 3.19-21).

The boy, on the contrary, cannot appeal to his "maestro," the priest, because the master is the very object of the "deadly work" of that maleficent and sinful being which attracts and frightens him. An implicit comparison is developed between Father Flynn and Virgil: the fatherly figure of the priest (the spiritual guide of the boy as well as of the Christian flock and a substitute for the youth's missing biological father) may recall Dante's relationship with Virgil, whom the younger poet sees as his master and guide—"tu duca, tu segnore, e tu maestro" ("you my leader, you my master, and you my teacher") (*Inf* 2.140)—and on one occasion in the *Inferno* explicitly designates as "sweet father" ("lo dolce padre") (*Inf* 8.110). However, the priest's failure as a spiritual father makes the comparison ironical, and his teachings about the mysteries of the church's institutions and the "secrecy of the confessional" appear very inadequate and misleading when weighed against the salvation that Virgil helps Dante to achieve by means of the pilgrimage through the "secret" other world ("mi mise dentro a le segrete cose") (*Inf* 3.21).

In fact, the boy's teacher recalls another "maestro" of Dante's, Brunetto Latini, met by the two pilgrims among the sodomites of the seventh circle. Thematic, situational, and linguistic elements link the episode of Brunetto in canto 15 of the *Inferno* with the first story of *Dubliners*. At the beginning of the canto the souls try to see the pilgrim and his guide through the darkness: " . . . e ciascuna / ci riguardava come suol da sera / guardare uno altro sotto nuova luna; / e sì ver' noi aguzzavan le ciglia / com 'l vecchio sartor fa ne la cruna" (. . . and each looked at us as men look at one another under a new moon at dusk; and they knit their brows at us as the old tailor does at the eye of his needle) (*Inf* 15.17-21).

In the darkness, they "sharpened their eyes" (their "eyelashes" in Dante's synecdoche: "aguzzavan le ciglia"), just as the boy in the street sharpened his eyes to discern the light of candles behind the blinds.

One of the souls recognizes Dante: it is Brunetto, who pulls the hem of Dante's robe to attract his attention. Dante, recognizing his old master in spite of his "baked features," bends down in order to bring his face nearer to that of Brunetto and addresses him with affection and surprise: "Siete voi qui, ser Brunetto?" ("Are you here, sir Brunetto?) (*Inf* 15.30). The relationship between master and disciple is treated in similar ways in "The Sisters" and in the *Inferno*. Both disciples show affection for their one-time teachers, but the latter are condemned for their sins: Dante places Brunetto in hell, while in "The Sisters" a context is created in which the priest's illness, "paralysis," is associated with the sin of simony and transformed into a "maleficent and sinful being" (later, in the dream, the boy smiles "as if to absolve the simoniac of his sin" [*D* 11]).

The attribute of "sweet father" in *Inferno* is reserved for Virgil but the relationship between Brunetto and Dante is also treated as one of father and son: Brunetto calls Dante "figliuol mio" ("my son") (*Inf* 15.31), and Dante reveals that he still keeps in his mind "la cara e buona imagine paterna / di voi quando nel mondo ad ora ad ora / m'insegnavate come l'uom s'etterna" ("the dear, kind, paternal image of you, when in the world hour by hour you taught me how man makes himself eternal") (*Inf* 15.83-85). Brunetto's teaching in his lifetime was in the art of eloquence and rhetoric, that is, in the art of words and their performative value—an interesting detail in the context of "The Sisters," where the value of words and their action are foregrounded.[5]

Let us pause for a moment and ask, who is making these allusions to the *Inferno*? We certainly cannot attribute to the young boy so consummate a literary expertise as would enable him to allude to the *Divine Comedy,* since his literary background seems at the moment to be limited to such schoolbooks as "the Euclid" and "the Catechism." Even in "Araby," another first-person story where the protagonist is slightly older and somewhat more experienced, such sophisticated literary attributions would seem, to say the least, improbable. The boy in this later story casts himself into a role that may owe a lot to a reading of chivalric romances; this feature, consistent with his age (although the several echoes from the *Vita Nuova*[6] would already suggest a more unlikely reading for a young Dubliner at the turn of the century), would also justify, to a point, the use of echoes and intertextual references in the narrative through a first-person version of what Kenner has termed the Uncle Charles Principle (*Joyce's Voices* 15-38) and which could in this case be described as a cunning oscillation between first-person narrated monologue and the later consciousness of the grown-up narrator.[7] The child in "The Sisters," on the contrary, does not seem to cast himself into any explicit literary role, and his knowledge of the *Divine Comedy* no doubt can be ruled out. The voice is clearly that of an adult narrator who tries to reproduce in his own words the sensations, thoughts, and fears of his younger self, at times striving to recapture his puzzlement and naivete and underlaying them with an intertextual, interlinguistic web of meanings that would have been inaccessible to the child. However, the semantic and symbolic value of the Dantean subtext may even go beyond the understanding that the narrator himself has of his story as well as beyond his capability to see the larger project of *Dubliners* as a book, its relation to the other stories in the collection (to which the subtext also extends), and the larger, symbolic implications that it has for the city and its inhabitants, unless we understand all the stories to be told by one and the same narrator—a possibility that nothing in the text allows us to reject a priori but for which there is no textual evidence.[8]

The literary allusions in "The Sisters," in fact, form a tightly knit subtext, a discourse that *also* underlies that of the narrator(s) of the other stories. To whom, then, or to what textual agency besides the narrator can this other discourse, which unobtrusively makes its appearance from the very first line of "The Sisters" and continues until the very end of "The Dead," be attributed? We may be authorized to hear in this voice that of James Joyce himself (significantly called by his friends "the Dante of Dublin" [Richard Ellmann 75]), but if we want to explore the projection of the artist in his own work without committing ourselves to a biographical interpretation, we might paraphrase instead Wayne Booth's canonical definition of the "implied author" by using the figure of a very specific "implied artist" who, in Stephen Dedalus's words, "like the God of the creation, remains within or behind or beyond or above his handiwork, invisible, refined out of existence, indifferent, paring his fingernails" (*A Portrait of the Artist as a Young Man* 215; herafter cited with page numbers as *P*). That is, the artist, invisible, writing parallel texts to the ones spun by his own narrators, remaining behind his personae, above his stories, beneath them with his subtexts, and always within them, perhaps not so indifferent after all, but slaving away at his books, paring his quotations into "mere" allusions that testify, first and foremost, to his own invisible presence. In casting this image of the artist, Joyce constructs for himself the ideal role of the upbraider of society[9] who can claim that his writings provide a "nicely polished looking-glass" for the conscience of the Irish people (*Selected Letters* 90); to create this "looking glass" will be the task of his artistic alter ego in *A*

Portrait ("forge in the smithy of my soul the uncreated conscience of my race" [*P* 253]).

The wider context of the encounter between Dante and Brunetto in the *Inferno* confirms this ethical vocation. During his dramatic dialogue with his former disciple, Brunetto speaks in stern, passionate tones of the moral and political decadence of Florence (*Inf* 15.61-78) and admonishes Dante against the evil customs of the Florentine people: "dai lor costumi fa che tu ti forbi" ("look that you cleanse yourself of their customs") (*Inf* 15.69). Brunetto's words provide what we can describe as "a chapter of the moral history of [his] country" (*Letters* 134); for Dante this country is Florence, for Joyce it is Ireland and, in particular, Dublin, which he "chose . . . for the scene because that city seemed to [him] the centre of paralysis" (*Letters* 134). Later, in canto 16 of the *Inferno*, Dante identifies the Florentines' appetite for money and material values at the expense of matters spiritual as the main cause for their corruption (*Inf* 16.67-68)—another form of simony, in the literal sense a traffic of sacred things but in a wider meaning the barter of spiritual for material values.

The "invisible" and apparently "silent" artist—whose biographical counterpart was in "exile" in Trieste when he revised "The Sisters" into the final form that contains the Dantean echoes analyzed here[10]—shows an instance of his literary "cunning" when he postpones the expected references to the canto of the simoniacs until a later episode in the story, the boy's dream of the old priest:

It was late when I fell asleep. Though I was angry with old Cotter for alluding to me as a child I puzzled my head to extract meaning from his unfinished sentences. In the dark of my room I imagined that I saw again the heavy grey face of the paralytic. I drew the blankets over my head and tried to think of Christmas. But the grey face still followed me. It murmured; and I understood that it desired to confess something. I felt my soul receding into some pleasant and vicious region; and there again I found it waiting for me. It began to confess to me in a murmuring voice and I wondered why it smiled continually and why the lips were so moist with spittle. But then I remembered that it had died of paralysis and I felt that I too was smiling feebly as if to absolve the simoniac of his sin. [*D* 11]

Dante meets the simoniacs in canto 19, their heads stuck in narrow holes in the ground and their feet kicking up in the air. As he bends down beside one of them, Pope Nicholas III, he describes his position as that of a priest during confession: "Io stava come 'l frate che confessa" ("I was standing there like the friar who confesses") (*Inf* 19.49). There is a similar reversal of the normal situation in both Dante's and Joyce's stories: Dante, the pilgrim, hears the confession of the Pope, and in "The Sisters" the old priest confesses to the little boy.

Thematic and linguistic repetitions tighten the connection between the first paragraph of the story and the dream episode (death, darkness, the puzzlement of the child over words and sentences, the syntactic structure of "some pleasant and vicious region" that echoes "some maleficient and sinful being"), and the boy's imagination works in similar ways in both instances. In the incipit it extracts words from their contexts, linking them in new associations and transforming them from sound into being, whereas in the dream a human being is transformed into an object, first with Father Flynn becoming only a face, and then with the face becoming only "it"—an "it" that murmurs, desires to confess, waits, smiles, and finally dies ("it had died of paralysis"). Like the words, the face is decontextualized; severed from the body, it develops into an independent entity, but as soon as "paralysis" is mentioned, simony is evoked too, and the face, "it," reverts again to its human qualities: "the simoniac of *his* sin."[11] The priest's association with Brunetto Latini is also strengthened by the insistence on his face (in canto 15 Dante recognizes Brunetto in spite of the "baked features" of his "scorched face": "ficcai li occhi per lo cotto aspetto,/sì che 'l viso abbrusciato non difese/la conoscenza sua al mio 'ntelletto" ["I fixed my eyes on his scorched face, so that the baked features did not prevent my knowing him"] [*Inf* 15.26-28]).

Although the sin that old Father Flynn is tainted with is not sodomy but simony, there have been suggestions of the priest's homosexual desire for the young man,[12] and several critics have pointed out the connections that can be made between the two words and the sins of sodomy and simony.[13] Moreover sodomy and simony are pieced together in the figure of Father Flynn by the allusions to Dante's cantos of Brunetto and of the simoniacs. Dante himself—who regarded both sins as unnatural practices—establishes a connection between them by having Brunetto explain that all the sinners who share his penance in this section of hell (the sodomites) are clerics and well-known men of letters: "In somma sappi che tutti fur cherci/e litterati grandi e di gran fama" ("In brief, know that they were all clerks, and great men of letters and of great fame") (*Inf* 15.106-7).

Joyce used the Brunetto episode of the *Divine Comedy* in other works and linked it again to the sin of simony. Mary Reynolds has shown how Dante's encounter with his master of rhetoric is recalled in *Stephen Hero* when Stephen meets his old schoolmate Wells, now preparing for the priesthood, that is, to become a spiritual father (*Joyce and Dante* 46). As Reynolds comments, "Wells sees the priesthood as his best road to an easy life. He is thus marked as a simoniac, a fraudulent father" (47). A situational analogy reinforces the connection: "Joyce's chapter and Dante's Canto 15 both begin with a pattern of continuous movement" (48).[14] This movement is not only continuous but also circular, and the same situation can be found at the beginning of "The Sisters," where the boy keeps returning to the house of the dying priest.[15] The echo of Brunetto's tirade against the decayed morals of the city and its undue attachment to money and material values reverberates throughout the rest of the collection and is illustrated for instance in "After the Race," "The Boarding House," and "A Mother," where dignity, honesty, art, "those qualities of humanity, of hospitality, of kindly humour which belonged to an older day" (*D* 203), have given way to crass, mean, material concerns. The last quotation is from Gabriel Conroy's after-dinner speech in "The Dead," an address whose spirit in a milder form may vaguely echo Brunetto's sad prospects for the future of his own town and his nostalgic remembrance of times past.[16]

Dantean echoes cluster toward the end of this last story, forming a thick web that also recirculates back to the beginning of "The Sisters," confirming and giving deeper meaning to the situational, thematic, and linguistic links between the two stories.[17] In the partial darkness of the third canto ("fioco lume" ["dim light"] [*Inf* 3.75]), the souls cross the river Acheron in Charon's boat, leaving the shore one by one like leaves falling from a tree in autumn:

> Come d'autunno si levan le foglie
>   l'una appresso de l'altra, fin che 'l ramo
>   vede a la terra tutte le sue spoglie,
> similemente il mal seme d'Adamo
>   gittansi di quel lito ad una ad una. . . .

> (As the leaves fall away in autumn, one after another, till the bough sees all its spoils upon the ground, so there the evil seed of Adam: one by one they cast themselves from that shore. . . .) [*Inf* 3.112-16]

Many details from these lines are echoed in Gabriel's thoughts: "*One by one* they were all becoming shades . . . in the *partial darkness* he imagined he saw the form of a young man standing under a *dripping tree*. Other forms were near. His soul had approached that region where dwell the vast hosts of the dead" (*D* 223).[18]

The region of the dead approached by Gabriel's soul is also the country Gabriel is ready to travel to on his journey westward. He looks at the snow falling "farther westward, softly falling into the dark mutinous Shannon waves . . . faintly falling, like the descent of their last end, upon all the living and the dead" (*D* 223-24). The "dark mutinous Shannon waves," which recall the Acheron's "onda bruna" ("dark wave") (*Inf* 3.118), flow westward toward the ocean where Dante situated Mount Purgatory (*Inf* 26). To reach it, Dante has to cross the Acheron and travel through the world of the dead. Likewise, Gabriel's journey westward will take him to the region of the dead but also across it to the sea beyond that region, and his journey toward death may turn out to be, like Dante's, a journey through death toward salvation.[19]

At the outset of "The Sisters," Dantean references point to the beginning of a journey (the entrance to hell) that is also the beginning of a journey through the text for the reader. Later the references to *Inferno* 3 in "The Dead" point again to another threshold (the crossing of the Acheron), but the snow "general all over Ireland" (*D* 223) also reminds us of the last cantos of the *Inferno* where the sinners are plunged into ice, showing that this in fact may be the end of the journey—or rather the end of one of its stages: when Dante gets to the frozen wastes ("la ghiaccia") (*Inf* 32.35; 34.29), he still needs to complete two thirds of his pilgrimage. The references at the end of "The Dead" to the beginning of "The Sisters" and the allusions to the *Inferno* in both stories can therefore be seen as pointing to a pattern of circularity in *Dubliners,* confirming that the journey will have to start again—this time, however, with a difference. When Dante passes through the portal of hell, he is frightened and needs Virgil's judgement and encouragement in order to proceed further. This will happen time and time again in the course of their journey through the other world, until Dante is finally cleansed of all sin by the fire in *Purgatorio* 27. As he advances in his pilgrimage through hell, however, his understanding of sin and of divine justice increases; when he crosses the Acheron, he has already witnessed one instance of sin punished, and, however slightly, his awareness has started to improve. In the final pages of "The Dead," Gabriel too becomes aware of a sin: his own. The sin that he has been guilty of and the one Dante observes before crossing the Acheron are the same, *ignavia,* such an extreme form of sloth that in Dante's poem neither heaven nor hell want to receive the souls of these sinners, who must remain eternally in the vestibule of hell:

> .... l'anime triste di coloro
> che visser sanza 'nfamia e sanza lodo.
> Mischiate sono a quel cattivo coro
> de li angeli che non furon ribelli
> né fur fedeli a Dio, ma per sé fuoro.
> Caccianli i ciel per non esser men belli,
> né lo profondo inferno li riceve,
> ch'alcuna gloria i rei avrebber d'elli.

(... the sorry souls of those who lived without infamy and without praise. They are mingled with that base band of angels who were neither rebellious nor faithful to God, but stood apart. The heavens drive them out, so as not to be less beautiful; and deep Hell does not receive them, lest the wicked have some glory over them.) [*Inf.* 3:35-42]

Questi non hanno speranza di morte,
   e la lor cieca vita è tanto bassa,
   che 'nvidiosi son d'ogne altra sorte.
Fama di loro il mondo esser non lassa;

(These have no hope of death, and their blind life is so abject that they are envious of every other lot. The world does not let any report of them live.) . . .
[*Inf* 3:46-49]

. . . questa era la setta d'i cattivi,
a Dio spiacenti e a' nemici sui.
Questi sciaurati, che mai non fur vivi . . .

(. . . this was the sorry sect of those who are displeasing to God and to his enemies. These wretches, who never were alive . . .) [*Inf* 3: 62-64]

Realizing at last that his life has been that of an *ignavo,* Gabriel now thinks: "Better pass boldly into that other world, in the full glory of some passion, than fade and wither dismally with age" (*D* 223); only a short time before, he suddenly had become aware of the shame of his own condition: "A shameful consciousness of his own person assailed him. He saw himself as a ludicrous figure . . . the pitiable fatuous fellow he had caught a glimpse of in the mirror" (*D* 219-20). Suddenly confronted with his sin, he turns away from the light so that Gretta would not see "the shame that burned upon his forehead" (*D* 220) (cf. "vergognosa fronte" ["my brow covered with shame"] [*Inf* 1.81]). Seized by a "vague terror," Gabriel feels "some impalpable and vindictive being . . . coming against him" (*D* 220), a phrase that recalls Dante's difficult predicament in the first canto of the *Inferno,* when his path out of the dark forest is blocked by the three beasts, a leopard, a lion and a she-wolf. Dante sees them coming against him: the lion "seemed to be coming at me" ("parea che contra me venisse") (*Inf* 1.46), and the she-wolf was "coming on against me" ("venendomi 'ncontro") (*Inf* 1.59). Although these beasts are described in very concrete, physical terms, they have the "impalpable" nature of symbols, unexpectedly appearing on his path and just as suddenly disappearing when Virgil rescues him and explains that in order to exit the dark forest of sin they shall have to embark on a journey of salvation through the world of the dead.

Gabriel's thoughts and the allusions to the *Divine Comedy* also enable us to discover other Dantean echoes in the first story and to throw some more light on their meaning and symbolic implications. Gabriel's "some impalpable and vindictive being" recalls both the name and the cadence of "some maleficent and sinful being," as well as the dream of "some pleasant and vicious region." This phrase brings to mind the line where Dante describes the she-wolf's "nature so vicious and malign" ("natura sì malvagia e ria") (*Inf* 1.97), but it is only after reading of Gabriel's "vague terror" (parallel to Dante's "hopelessness": "perdei la speranza dell'altezza" ["I lost hope of the height"] [*Inf* 1.54]) of the impalpable, vindictive being that he feels "coming against him" that we can identify the source and more fully understand the subtle implications of the dangers the boy is facing (the identification of the she-wolf with the sin of *cupiditas* makes the allusions to Brunetto's speech more cogent in this context).

When the phrase returns two pages later as "some pleasant and vicious region," one of the adjectives ("vicious") still echoes Dante, while the other ("pleasant") recalls the ambiguous mixture of fear and attraction with which the boy considers in his mind the word "paralysis" and its deadly work. When it finally resurfaces, at the other end of the book, in the early stages of the reflection that leads Gabriel Conroy to the full realization of his "sin," it is part of a context that alludes to a further stage in Dante's journey (the crossing of the Acheron), and the wording of the phrase in the boy's dream ("pleasant and vicious *region*") still can be heard in Gabriel's thought that "his soul had approached that *region* where dwell the vast hosts of the dead." The region Gabriel's soul approaches is the world of the dead as well as the region of his own sin, the "*impalpable* world" in which his own identity is "fading out" (*D* 223) (the "*impalpable* and vindictive being" was "gathering forces against him in his *vague world*," [*D* 220]). The boy "recedes" into the region he dreams of, whereas Gabriel's soul "approaches" it: his attitude is no longer that of the *ignavo* and he is now ready to "set out on his journey westward" (*D* 223).[20] The concealed implication of a positive outcome contained in the ambivalent beginning of *Dubliners* spreads out to the end of "The Dead" and only then does its relevance for the whole collection become more explicit. The paradoxically hopeful "There was no hope for him this time" (*D* 9) is indeed an "Epigraph for Dubliners," as Jackson Cope has defined it (364).[21]

Bruce Avery has argued in "Distant Music: Sound and the Dialogics of Satire in 'The Dead'" that the ironic dialogics between the character's and the narrator's voices in the story makes the reader oscillate between an aural perspective, when we are made to listen to the character's voice paraphrased by the narrator, and a visual one, when the narrator takes over again and makes us see the character's actions. Avery formulates an extension of Kenner's Uncle Charles Principle, which he calls the "Aunt Kate Principle" and explains as follows: "if the narrator is employing an idiom other than his own one should suspect he has a satiric purpose" (478). Building on Riquelme's analysis of how the distance between the narrator's and the character's voices is blurred at the end of "The Dead," Avery furthermore argues that the narratorial voice at the end of the story shifts from its ironical, distanced position to one of identification with the character's thoughts, thereby showing a sort of "repentance," an awareness that if it had kept its distance and its superiority over the character's voice, it could have been tainted with the same accusation of presumption and elitism to which Gabriel is liable. Thus the conflation of voices, which can be seen as a sympathetic attitude to the character, comes at the moment when Gabriel himself has discovered the capacity for sympathy toward others.

In other words, this fusion of voices implies an ethical stance on the part of the narrator and of that subtle manipulator of narrators who stands behind the curtain, pretending to pare his fingernails, as it is concerned both with choosing (taking positions) and judging (exposing public and private sins or vices) and extends also to the artist's narratorial, literary practice. While withdrawing his narrator and letting dialogic voices speak in unison, the artist still weaves the web of references, sending his readers back to the beginning of the text and thus reminding them of lessons learned in matters of poetics and rhetoric but also in matters of judgment, as in the first story the experience of death also means for the young boy the need to revise his mistaken judgment of the words he had heard from the priest ("I had thought his words idle. Now I knew they were true" [*D* 9]).[22]

This furthermore may remind us that the other two "childhood" stories in *Dubliners* end on a note of repentance, on the boy-narrator's realization of his mistakes: "And I was penitent; for in my heart I had always despised him a little" ("An Encounter" *D* 28); "Gazing up into the darkness I saw myself as a creature driven and derided by vanity; and my eyes burned with anguish and anger" ("Araby" *D* 35). These endings, by comparison with the third-person stories, mark the young protagonists as the only ones in the book capable of some form of redemption, and this possibility finally seems to come nearer to its realization with the "generous tears" that filled Gabriel's eyes (*D* 223). Gabriel's tears and the general pattern of revising one's positions and "righting" one's judgments[23] point to an analogous process that takes place throughout the whole of Dante's journey in the other world, where Dante has to cleanse himself of his sins and to review his positions, misconceptions, and mistakes in spiritual, intellectual, doctrinal, and also literary matters.

Two of the most dramatic and cogent moments in this process of growth develop through Dante's confrontation with two women: one is in the second canticle, when, having reached Eden, he is questioned and harshly reprimanded by Beatrice (*Purgatorio* 30). The other episode, more relevant for us, is in *Inferno* 5 (a canto Joyce kept going back to throughout his literary career), when Dante meets Paolo and Francesca and hears from her the tale of their sinful and ill-fated love. The parallels with the moments in "The Dead" when Gabriel listens to Gretta's story of love and death are striking. The context is, in both cases, one of lust: this is the sin punished in the first circle of hell, and Gabriel's desire for his wife is explicitly described as "lust."[24]

Dante weeps copiously, like both Paolo and Francesca (*Inf* 5.126, 139-40), as he reflects on the intensity of the passion that brought about the lovers' death; he almost swoons on hearing the names of ancient ladies and knights and their loves (*Inf* 5:72), and, overcome by emotion, does actually faint at the end of the canto (*Inf* 5.140-42). Likewise, Gabriel, overcome by the intensity of a love that he has never experienced, weeps copious and "generous" tears until his soul "swooned slowly" into sleep at the end of the story (*D* 224). Both male characters ask to know more about the story and in both cases a kiss is exchanged: between Paolo and Francesca in the *Inferno* (5.132-36) and between Gretta and Gabriel in "The Dead." However, what brings about the exchange of the kiss in Joyce's text is not a book or the story of a literary love (*Inf* 5.127-38) but a pound lent by Gabriel to Freddy Malins (*D* 217); thus Gretta's words "You are a very generous person, Gabriel" ironically anticipate Gabriel's "generous tears" (*D* 223).[25]

Francesca speaks of love in the manner of the "dolce stil novo," whose doctrine Dante himself adhered to in his earlier poetry. The episode of Paolo and Francesca and her manner of speech provide an occasion for Dante to think about his own literary activity and the possible implications of a poetics that celebrates Love as an absolute value, constituting an ethics in itself and remaining foreign to any other moral principle. Love rules over the poet's heart and style (see esp. *Purgatorio* 24.49-63) in what could be seen as a version of the "impersonality" of the artist, who, according to this ethics, declines any merit but also any responsibility for the poetry dictated by Love. One may reasonably wonder whether the parallel episode in "The Dead" may imply similar considerations about the artist's responsibility, not to "institutional" moral concerns but to truth and to what his own heart and artistic disposition dictate.[26]

While Gabriel's feigned distance from his wife's story suggests the narrator's analogous difficulty in keeping up his ironic position ("He tried to keep up his tone of cold interrogation but his voice when he spoke was humble and indifferent" [*D* 220]), the word "indifferent" may be evocative of the description of the artist that Stephen Dedalus would later give in *A Portrait* and which is already foreshadowed in Joyce's early essay "Drama and Life" (1900). In drama, Joyce writes, "the artist forgoes his very self and stands as a mediator in awful truth before the veiled face of God" (*Critical Writings* 42); in a later review of Arnold Graves's *Clytaemnestra*, the concept crystallizes as "indifferent sympathy" (*Critical Writings* 127).

If we look back at *Dubliners* from the context of Stephen's theory of literature in *A Portrait*, the shift from first-person to third-person narration in the stories (also signaled by the shift from "I imagined I saw" [*D* 11] to "he imagined he saw" [*D* 223]²⁷) seems to represent what Stephen defines as a progress from the lyrical to the epical form:

> The simplest epical form is seen emerging out of lyrical literature when the artist prolongs and broods upon himself as the centre of an epical event and this form progresses till the centre of emotional gravity is equidistant from the artist himself and from others. The narrative is no longer purely personal. The personality of the artist passes into the narration itself, flowing round and round the persons and the action like a vital sea. This progress you will see easily in that old English ballad *Turpin Hero* which begins in the first person and ends in the third person. [*P* 214-15]

However, the distance between the narrator and the represented thoughts of the characters in *Dubliners* makes it impossible to apply Stephen's definition rigidly to the stories, and at any rate, the ironic attitude of the narrator of the later novel toward the character Stephen, as well as the significant shift from third-to first-person narration in the last pages of the novel, discourages any acritical acceptance of the theory. The artist's vigilance over his "handiwork" is never, and can never be, abdicated, whether it seeks the mediation of a narrator's ironic stance or whether, as in the case of Gabriel's final monologue, the character is more sympathetically presented. In other words, whereas characters and narrators may be made to take positions and therefore more explicit moral stances, the artist "remains . . . invisible" (*P* 215), although "like the god of creation" everywhere present ("remains" clearly indicates that the presence, however unnnoticed, is necessarily presupposed "within or behind or beyond or above" the creation).

The artist's "indifference" is clearly not a lack of care for the creation or for its moral implications, and the amoral²⁸ conception of art that it conveys signifies not immorality (such as the one that Ibsen is accused of by Stephen's myopic opponents in *Stephen Hero*) but the almost scientific detachment with which he can perform the literary act, refraining from showing himself but taking an omnipresent position in the text.²⁹ Thus, Gabriel's "indifferent" voice signals the moment when he almost unwillingly gives up his pretense of superiority and prepares to listen to Gretta's story with equanimity³⁰ rather than in order to judge her, and it can be contrasted with Mr. Duffy's "strange impersonal voice" ("A Painful Case" [*D* 111]), which, belonging to a character whose personal voice we hear through the narration of his thoughts, is exposed as an index of his insensitivity and moral aridity. The artist's lack of involvement in the narration can only indicate, therefore, his refraining from taking explicit visible narratorial or moralistic positions, and it cannot be an act of renunciation of his ethical stance. If it were, the artist would be tainted with the same sin of *ignavia* of which Gabriel is learning to cleanse himself.

In *Dubliners*, Joyce's relationship with Dante—a Dante who discourses with his masters and reflects on the ethics of his own aesthetic creation—is already much more problematic than simple parody, the borrowing of a structure, or a humble following in literary footsteps.[31] It creates a rich substratum that gives greater depth to the symbolic and semantic web of the stories but that is erased in the process and refined out of visibility, although it always *remains* present in vestigial traces that can be recovered by careful textual archaeology. It also betrays the omnipresence of the artist who imprints his seal on the text while pretending to be paring his fingernails, thus revealing the ethical dimension of his aesthetic project, his responsibility toward his creation, and the need for the critic to redefine the traditionally clear-cut distinction between omnipresence and impersonality.[32]

Notes

1. Singleton's translation; some translations have been silently amended.

2. See also Cope, *Joyce's Cities* 15-16.

3. Fritz Senn's essay, still one of the most stimulating on "The Sisters," picks up several biblical allusions and echoes and follows up the semantic implications of the etymologies of some of the key words in the story. In this article Senn also voices one of the problems that beset (especially) Joycean critics, that of the hazy borderline between quotations, allusions, and the unspecific but definite evocation of literary asociations in the attentive reader (66).

4. Many essays written on "The Sisters" explore the semantic connections that can be established between these three puzzling words and their symbolic meaning; see, for instance, Senn, "Scrupulous"; Donald Torchiana; Florence L. Walzl; Jean-Michel Rabaté, "Silence"; Phillip F. Herring 3-18; Albert; and David Weir.

5. But see also the performative value that silence too has in *Dubliners* and in the rest of Joyce's works; Hugh Kenner, "Rhetoric"; Herring esp. 3-18; and Rabaté, "Silence."

6. The references have been pointed out by several critics; a useful list can be found in Mary T. Reynolds, *Joyce and Dante* 238-40.

7. See Riquelme 94-108.

8. The option of a single narrator for the collection has been supported by some critics; this implies that the young protagonists of the first three stories are one and the same person. It also has been suggested that Gabriel *is* the boy of the first stories. This involves a shift from the first to the third person, which may anticipate Stephen's later theory of the progression of literature from the lyrical to the dramatic (which Joyce however treats ironically; see my discussion of this issue below) but which also would make Gabriel tell his story in the same way as the arid Mr. Duffy imagines doing in "A Painful Case."

9. In *Stephen Hero* Stephen defends the greatness of Ibsen's drama before the President, who finds fault with the notion that art should be concerned with an examination of the corruption of society, a task that according to him should be limited to

scientists; Stephen retorts: "Why not for the poet too? Dante surely examines and upbraids society" (85). Howard Helsinger explores the significance of the Dantean model for the character of Stephen in *Stephen Hero* and *A Portrait*: "Dante served Joyce as a model of the artist who, wishing to speak trenchantly about his own time, must, like the intellectual and the critic, be always at war with his society. . . . If the risk of suffocation is real, if the artist's integrity is threatened in the establishment, he must, to preserve it, hold himself aloof. This Joyce recognized, and he suggests as much by casting Stephen Dedalus as an Irish Dante" (591).

10. For a history and evaluation of the successive revisions of the story, see Walzl and Fischer.

11. My emphasis; all emphases in subsequent quotations are mine.

12. John Kuehl (5) was the first, as far as I am aware, to interpret the priest's "great wish" for the boy (*D* 10) as homosexual attraction. Albert (359ff.) explains the title of the story as a reference to the slang word "sisters" used in male circles to denote homosexuals and as a hint at the homosexual relationship that was being developed between the two characters. The allusions to the canto of Brunetto might bear out these hypotheses.

13. See, for instance, Walzl 392-93, and for a more recent treatment of the relationship between sodomy, simony, and paralysis, Rabaté, *James Joyce* 31-36.

14. Reynolds discusses two more episodes of *Ulysses* where Joyce refers to *Inferno* 15: one is the portrait of John Eglinton in "Scylla and Charybdis" (a literary environment), and the other is in Stephen's meeting with his music teacher Armidano Artifoni in "Wandering Rocks" (*Joyce and Dante* 51-53). Reynolds notes that in the library chapter Stephen is described as "battling against hopelessness," and she rightly identifies Stephen's subsequent quotation of the first line from the first canto of the *Inferno*, where Dante is lost in the dark forest and despairs. As I hope to have shown, a precedent for a context that brings together a Brunetto Latini figure and an expression of hopelessness can already be found in "The Sisters."

15. See also the implicit circularity of the paragraph with its shift from sight (the boy looking at the window) to sound (of words) and back to sight (the boy looking upon the "deadly work" of the word).

16. A more precise reference, if any, may be to Cacciaguida's long speech in *Paradiso* 16, when he lists the names of the old worthy families of Florence and contrasts the past cheerful honesty of the city with its present moral decadence.

17. These have been pointed out by several critics. To recapitulate: the situation of the boy looking through a window from the dark outside into the lighted inside, trying to discover whether an old man has died, is reversed into a middle-aged man looking out through a window from the dark inside to the lighted outside, imagining that he sees a young man, now dead, standing under a tree. The element of death and words and phrases in "The Dead" that closely echo, or even repeat, words and phrases from "The Sisters": "some impalpable and vindictive being" (*D* 220), "blinds," "no longer" (222), "darkness," "near," "time," "softly," "window" (223), and "some maleficent and sinful being," "blind," "not long," "I longed," "darkened," "nearer," "time," "softly," "window" (*D* 9).

18. See also "he imagined he saw" echoing "I imagined that I saw" (*D* 11).

19. But could one detect instead in this parallel the possibility of an ineluctable condemnation to death? The character in the *Divine Comedy* who tried to reach Purgatory by traveling westward across the ocean is Ulysses, and his ship sank as the crew tried to approach the mountain (*Inf* 26).

20. Compare Gabriel's changed attitude with Eveline's immobility both at the beginning of the story that bears her name, when she passively "*watched* the evening *invade* the avenue" (*D* 36), and at its end, when she stands still "passive, like a helpless animal" at the North Wall station (*D* 40). Indeed, *ignavia* may be another name for "paralysis."

21. The web of references to the episode of the three beasts that cause Dante to lose any residual hope of salvation in *Inferno* 1 before Virgil's intervention may add another intertextual layer to the opening sentence of "The Sisters," where hopelessness follows the "third stroke." Thus, this sentence too would conflate references to cantos 1 and 3.

22. The hypotactic sentences that describe the boy's attempt to organize his sensorial perceptions in hypotheses that have to be checked against his previous knowledge stand out in the generally paratactic structure of the paragraph: "[I] studied the lighted square of window" (empirical observation); "If he was dead, I thought, I would see the reflection of candles" (hypothesis); "for I knew that two candles must be set at the head of a corpse" (previous knowledge). There follows the need to review his wrong assumption about the priest's words, and these two patterns are next brought together in an internalized process in which his previous attempt to organize his sensorial perceptions into connected wholes ("It had alway sounded . . . like the word . . . and the word") has to be revised ("But now it sounded").

23. A principle that Fritz Senn has shown to be constantly at work in Joyce's writing as well as in the reading process; see "Righting Ulysses."

24. "But now, after the kindling again of so many memories, the first touch of her body, musical and strange and perfumed, sent through him a keen pang of lust"; "He could have flung his arms about her hips and held her still for his arms were trembling with desire to seize her" (*D* 215); "He longed to cry to her from his soul, to crush her body against his, to overmaster her" (*D* 217); "the dull fires of his lust began to glow angrily in his veins" (*D* 219).

25. See Riquelme 127.

26. In *Stephen Hero,* written in the same years as Joyce revised the *Dubliners* stories, Stephen enthusiastically defends Ibsen's drama because it depicts society as it is and does not dutifully try to "improve" it by conventionally pious, edificatory examples. See also *Paradiso* 27.124ff.

27. My thanks to Laurent Milesi for bringing this to my attention.

28. One is tempted here to pun on the word *amore* (love) to point out that Stephen's villanelle (the poetic attempt following the expounding of the theory), Gabriel's "indifference," and Dante's poetics are all inspired by forms of love.

29. See also *Stephen Hero,* when Stephen says that he can feel Ibsen's "spirit" behind his creation (41).

30. See also Bloom's "equanimity" in "Ithaca" (*Ulysses* 692-94).

31. Cope writes, for instance, that had Joyce concluded *Dubliners* with "Grace,"

"the book would have stood as a complicated parody of Dante expressing Joyce's disdain for ... Dublin. ... It would have been a parody on a large scale. ... But ... in 1907 his more developed sensibilities demanded modest emulation rather than parody of the great Italian" (Cope, *Joyce's Cities* 9-10). It was Stanislaus Joyce ("Background"; *My Brother's* 228) who first suggested that Joyce's "Grace" is a parody of the *Divine Comedy*, and this parallel has been expanded by William York Tindall 38, Robert Boyle, and Francesco Gozzi 195-204. Gozzi writes, "When [Joyce] resorts to the structural framework of the *Commedia*, his attitude becomes increasingly more ambiguous as we proceed from the sphere of damnation to that of expiation and then salvation" (195); Joyce's attitude to Dante is in fact as complex and ambivalent even in relation to the *Inferno*. For a useful tabulation of parallels between the *Inferno* and *Dubliners*, see Reynolds, *Joyce and Dante* 124-30 and "Dantean Design."

32. For a fascinating discussion of the contradictions and complexities of the modernist myth of impersonality in the poetry of Pound and Eliot, see Maud Ellmann.

Works Cited

Albert, Leonard. "Gnomonology: Joyce's 'The Sisters.'" *James Joyce Quarterly* 27 (1990): 353-64.

Avery, Bruce. "Distant Music: Sound and the Dialogics of Satire in 'The Dead.'" *James Joyce Quarterly* 28 (1991): 473-83.

Boyle, Robert. "Swiftian Allegory and Dantean Parody in Joyce's 'Grace.'" *James Joyce Quarterly* 7 (1969): 11-21.

Bremen, Brian. "'He Was Too Scrupulous Always:' A Re-examination of Joyce's 'The Sisters.'" *James Joyce Quarterly* 22 (1984): 55-66.

Cope, Jackson. "An Epigraph for Dubliners." *James Joyce Quarterly* 7 (1970): 362-64.

———. *Joyce's Cities: Archaeologies of the Soul*. Baltimore: Johns Hopkins Univ. Press, 1981.

Dante Alighieri. *The Divine Comedy*. Trans. Charles S. Singleton. 3 vols. Princeton, N.J.: Princeton Univ. Press, 1970.

Ellmann, Maud. *The Poetics of Impersonality: T.S. Eliot and Ezra Pound*. Sussex: Harvester, 1987.

Ellmann, Richard. *James Joyce*. Rev. ed. Oxford: Oxford Univ. Press, 1982.

Fischer, Therese. "From Reliable to Unreliable Narrator: Rhetorical Changes in Joyce's 'The Sisters.'" *James Joyce Quarterly* 9 (1971): 85-92.

Gozzi, Francesco. "Dante nell'Inferno di Joyce." *English Miscellany* 23 (1972): 195-229.

Helsinger, Howard. "Joyce and Dante." *English Literary History* 35 (1968): 591-605.

Herring, Phillip F. *Joyce's Uncertainty Principle*. Princeton. N.J.: Princeton Univ. Press, 1987.

Joyce, James. *Critical Writings of James Joyce*. Ed. Ellsworth Mason and Richard Ellmann. New York: Viking, 1959.

———. *Dubliners: Text, Criticism, and Notes*. Ed. Robert Scholes and A. Walton Litz. New York: Viking, 1969.

———. *Letters of James Joyce*. Ed. Richard Ellmann. Vol. 2. London: Faber, 1966.

———. A Portrait of the Artist as A Young Man: *Text, Criticism, and Notes.* Ed. Chester G. Anderson. New York: Viking, 1968.

———. *Selected Letters of James Joyce.* Ed. Richard Ellmann. London: Faber, 1975.

———. *Stephen Hero.* London: Granada, 1977.

———. *Ulysses.* London: Bodley Head, 1937.

Joyce, Stanislaus. "The Background to *Dubliners.*" *Listener* 60 (March 1954): 526.

———. *My Brother's Keeper: James Joyce's Early Years.* New York: Viking, 1957.

Kenner, Hugh. *Joyce's Voices.* Berkeley: Univ. of California Press, 1978.

———. "The Rhetoric of Silence." *James Joyce Quarterly* 14 (1977): 382-94.

Kuehl, John. "A la Joyce: The Sisters Fitzgerald's Absolution." *James Joyce Quarterly* 2 (1964): 2-6.

Rabaté, Jean-Michel. *James Joyce.* Paris: Hachette, 1993.

———. "Silence in *Dubliners.*" In *James Joyce: New Perspectives,* ed. Colin MacCabe, 43-72. Sussex, England: Harvester; Bloomington: Indiana Univ. Press, 1982.

Reynolds, Mary T. "The Dantean Design of Joyce's *Dubliners.*" In *The Seventh of Joyce: Essays from the 7th International James Joyce Symposium, Frankfurt,* ed. Bernard Benstock, 124-30. Bloomington: Indiana Univ. Press, 1982.

———. *Joyce and Dante: The Shaping Imagination.* Princeton, N.J.: Princeton Univ. Press, 1981.

Riquelme, John Paul. *Teller and Tale in Joyce's Fiction: Oscillating Perspectives.* Baltimore: Johns Hopkins Univ. Press, 1983.

Senn, Fritz. "'He Was Too Scrupulous Always': Joyce's 'The Sisters.'" *James Joyce Quarterly* 2 (1965): 66-72.

———. "Righting *Ulysses.*" In *James Joyce: New Perspectives,* ed. Colin MacCabe, 3-28. Sussex, England: Harvester; Bloomington: Indiana Univ. Press, 1982.

Tindall, William York. *A Reader's Guide to James Joyce.* London: Thames, 1959.

Torchiana, Donald. "The Opening of *Dubliners:* A Reconsideration." *Irish University Review* 1.2 (1971): 149-60 (reprinted in Torchiana, *Backgrounds for Joyce's Dubliners,* 18-35. Boston: Allen, 1986).

Walzl, Florence L. "Joyce's 'The Sisters:' A Development." *James Joyce Quarterly* 10 (1973): 375-421.

Weir, David. "Gnomon Is an Island: Euclid and Bruno in Joyce's Narrative Practice." *James Joyce Quarterly* 28 (1991): 343-60.

New Directions

CHAPTER FOURTEEN

Gnomon Inverted

Fritz Senn

Few of Joyce's own embedded cues have been as provocative as the triad of strange words that trouble the young boy in "The Sisters": *paralysis, gnomon, simony.* In their privileged position, closing the initial paragraph, they are lexical irritants or intriguing, efficient signposts. They have been amply commented on and their alleged directions have been avidly followed.

Euclid defined *gnomon* as what is left once one small parallelog is subtracted from a larger one. Euclid (incidentally the first name offered in the story[1]) gave the geometrical form a name, perhaps after one of its previous meanings as a carpenter's tool. Therefore gnomon, The Figure with Something Missing, The Gap to Be Filled, has symbolically meant deficiency, whatever is lacking, and a lot is indeed lacking in those stories, not only corkscrews or some bicycle to match a rusty bicycle pump but also parents, spiritual values, you name it. It has been named, and the deficiency trail has been one profitable approach to *Dubliners* and, by extension, has been applied as a skeleton key to all of Joyce: the impact of what is potently not there yet perhaps should be. Framed absences early on begin to raise their vigorous metaphysical heads.

A gnomon seen in the context of a vacancy demands supplementation. We are also puzzling our heads "to extract meaning from . . . unfinished sentences" (*Dubliners* 11; hereafter cited with page numbers as *D*): the first story has conversations full of ellipses, and an ellipsis ends it. Filling out sentences or the boxing of Euclidean corners has become a worthwhile critical occupation. It is certain to continue. The analogy has been inspiring and satisfactory, and many of us have reiterated or expanded its application (I have). So it may be that the time has come to suggest alternative applications. One such welcome change is David Weir's "Gnomon Is an Island: Euclid and Bruno in Joyce's Narrative Practice."[2] The following sketch is much less sophisticated and geometrically non-Euclidean.

It seems evident that seen as a shape, a gnomon is more interesting, more challenging, more complex, than a straitlaced parallelogram: it has more delineation, more character, more sides and corners, for instance, more scope for variation. In itself a gnomon is *not* a failed parallelogram; by nature it is not intrinsically inferior to its Euclidean parent. In fact it represents a move, which also happens to be a Joycean proclivity, from the simple toward the intricate. In its own right, it is not at all deficient. It is its classical origin via the *Elements of Geometry*—as a process of breaking a piece off something larger—that makes it appear incomplete. But it might have been defined just as well as an addition: if you take one parallelogram and join a smaller one to its corner (with parallel sides) you get the same result: a construction of *both and*.

Accretion is also a typically Joycean experience. Take your choice: a smaller shape is taken away from a bigger one, or else it is implanted on it. But then, the Euclidean subtraction is implied in the first paragraph, and so the taking away has a certain authorial priority: Joyce does direct us to the Euclidean deficiency. The subtractive view, valid as well as serviceable, is just not the whole story. The perspective can be changed: from impoverishment to artistic expansion. The three strange-sounding words at the beginning of "The Sisters" in themselves are such an expansion. Thoughts about a moribund person and funereal customs give way to verbal associations that momentarily take on a life of their own, a sudden move away from streets and windows or candles toward exotic and conspicuous signifiers that point to their own lexical existences as well as what they designate: from things to words—a transition from reality to verbal oddities that roughly mirrors trends in Joyce criticism.

So I am merely pointing out that the renewed perpetuation of incompleteness, though far from futile, has become a little worn and shows signs of diminishing perceptive invigoration. Gnomon need not automatically or mechanically spell deprivation. This note then is nothing more than a descriptive possibility to see *Dubliners* on occasion as complexity brought about by unforeseen augmentations that can be disruptive and unsettling. So in "An Encounter," an excursion to the Pigeonhouse is planned but not achieved (gnomonic failure in the conventional sense), but the appearance of the mysterious man with a stick (though his life, to judge from the symptoms, is characterized by emotional deficiencies) toward the end is an unexpected supplement, something not bargained for in the original strategy of the outing. The man is also acting in a startling way ("I say! Look what he is doing!"), and if we want to overuse Euclidean imagery, the old man's second parallelogram, his treatise on whipping, certainly differs from his first ("liberal") one. In some analogous way, more corners keep being added to the figure envisaged at the outset.

We might adduce the small gold coin that closes "Two Gallants." It gives the preceding shabby love affair (if that's what it is) a mercenary twist (simony may be evoked), but it also opens another door toward a minor mystery. Or consider that poem by Hynes on the death of Parnell: a small analogous shape appended to the prevailing pattern, it entails a change of tone and atmosphere. Cheap muses have descended into the committee room. In the Hallow Eve game played in "Clay," something not part of the rules is furtively substituted, upsetting the traditional course of events. Quite literally, the children provide an extension that is not part of the game rules. The "soft wet substance" that Maria touches (with next to no surprise) can be linked to the story's title. If we did not have that title, we would be at a loss: it is a (geometrical) figure that is tacked on.

Some of the titles in *Dubliners* are gnomonically extraneous, not quite within the confines of what is to follow. "Counterparts" seems to point in many directions (no wonder, for example, that translations of that title vary considerably). "A Little Cloud" is an accessory; as something not inherent in the narrated events it stimulates readers into excursions, a biblical little cloud that promises rain but does not seem to enlighten the story at all. Those many early interpretations often used symbolic extensions to prove once more the moral or spiritual gnomonic shortcomings of the characters involved and never ran out of evidence, but by their procedure they tacitly admitted gnomonic radiation *of* the symbols that were invoked.

"Grace" at first remains outside the story that sails under this heading. Here we can demonstrate the sleight of hand that we call interpretation: the title "Grace" points toward something that is manifestly lacking, the traditional absence of a spiritual gift. On the other hand the titular term, which adds a great deal of resonance to the next-to-last sentence ("But with God's grace, I will rectify this and this" [*D* 174]), introduces an element hardly contained in the first two sections of the story. The title might promise something like poise or elegance ("the plump arm she moved very often with much grace" [*D* 95]) or turn out to be a name (like "Eveline"), but once "Grace" manifests itself as a theological notion, we get a different focus on all events. Some phrases—"By grace of these two articles of clothing" (*D* 154); "He bore himself with a certain grace" (*D* 166)—acquire a different, ironical ring. "Grace" in the story so named is mathematically plus/minus: its overtone introduces alineations or even requirements that then allow us to notice an absence that otherwise would not even exist. It opens the way to speculations.

Since "Grace" was once designed to be the last story and its close would have been a peroration, we might notice all the more that "grace" is sandwiched between "my accounts." A gift of the Holy Ghost is parenthesized in bookkeeping. (In a similar vein, music, which ought to be the main concern of the series of concerts, is practically absent in "A Mother.") Father Purdon's wording, the Parable of the Unjust Steward (Luke 16:1-18), is prefigured in the Gospel, where a steward is asked "to give an account" of his stewardship (Luke 16:2).

Interestingly enough, the word for "account" is *logos* ("*apodos ton logon*"), the same term that also signifies the Divine Word that St. John puts at the beginning (parenthetically, the first paragraph in *Dubliners* highlights "words" idle or true, "the word *paralysis*... the word *gnomon*... the word *simony*," and then the word itself grammatically becomes something capable of "deadly work," not divine work).

This New Testament gloss is not thrown in as a meaningful expansion or even one intended by the author, who may have been as little concerned about the Greek basis of the Gospel as most of his commentators. It is offered as a textual possibility that is enabled almost exclusively by the radiance of a title. At the least, both a religious and a literary text show how words change in different contexts: just as *logos* can mean word, talk, speech, announcement, doctrine, affair, reason, or the Divine Word, "grace" can do multiple duty in several contexts. The point of the above digression is that many of our explicative glosses or interpretations consist of positive gnomonic supplementations. *Dubliners* is also a series of gratuities.

On occasion an alternating series of gnomonic removal and enlargement may be appropriate. Take a painful case in point: Mr. Duffy's geometrically bare life is thrown out of gear when Mrs. Sinico introduces a disturbing note. Both of them briefly add something to each other's lives. Then he breaks out of the affair, more pieces are broken out, there is disintegration, Mrs. Sinico "[begins] to be rather intemperate in her habits" and soon is removed entirely. When Mr. Duffy learns of her death, he righteously thinks she had degraded herself as well as him. He also feels "his moral nature falling to pieces," a series of subtractions until toward the end another mood creeps in, even if it were nothing less than that he "felt" what he had always been—"alone." Gnomonic reversal, a balance of not enough and too much, can be exemplified by Mr. Duffy's two gnomic sentences: "Love between man and man is impossible because there must not be sexual intercourse and friendship between man and woman is impossible because there must be sexual intercourse" (*D* 112).

Finally, "The Dead": without question there are many deficiencies, lives lacking in wholeness, the story negatively gnomonic. (There is no dearth of criticism, discriminating or plain censorious, to rub this in.) But you also might characterize the events as a sequence of (mainly unwanted) adjuncts to something that should be as smooth, regular, and four-cornered as either a party ("it was always a great affair, the Misses Morkans annual dance") or the festive outing of a married couple. The aunts are afraid that something unsuitable might be added: "Freddy Malins might turn up screwed." In fact there are several unplanned increments. Lily adds uncalled-for bitterness in her retort and ruffles the even surface of Gabriel's parallelogram, and we may consider Gabriel's embarrassed attempt to smooth it over with a monetary gift as one more instance of simony. The hidden plot of Lily's disappointment is an extension that we only notice in passing. Miss Ivors with her taunts and challenges is another threat, one more piece broken out of Gabriel's complacency; yet it also introduces the Irish past, nationalism, and the rural West and so adds depth to the painting. In other words, each episode that decomposes Gabriel is also an opening into another dimension. Above all, the entirely unsuspected yet consequential past existence of a former admirer of Gretta drastically changes the shape of Gabriel's evening.

In his after-dinner speech Gabriel refers to the hostesses as "the Three Graces of the Dublin musical world" (*D* 204). The mythological attribute can be seen as a mixture of gallantry, irony, cliché, and whatever else, and we are invited to speculate on its appropriateness: in many respects the aunts and Mary Jane are not goddesses dispensing charm and beauty. The figure of speech also retroactively adds another potential facet to the previous story (and so does "grace notes," the "grace and mystery" in Gretta's attitude [*D* 193, 210, 213, 215]). But when Gabriel moves on, changing mythological tracks, to "the part that Paris played on another occasion" (*D* 204), a new theme is gratuitously inserted that might *potentially* provoke links to an apple (or, if you want, "apple sauce" [*D* 197]) of discord with subsequent calamities or at least the intervention of another man (Paris) in a married couple (Menelaos and Helen). Such an interpretation might develop into gross exaggerations and stray far afield, but these (examples abound) are also the results of Joyce's technique of surplus signification.

Gabriel's speech abounds in stereotypes, phrases that have lost their original edge. Meaning is taken away; some phrases are empty shells and social currency. Lily is right: "The men that is now is only all palaver" (*D* 178). Against such overt vacuities we find that words that at first appear to be casual throwaways acquire meaning in the course of the story. Gabriel's conversational remark "I think we're in for a night of it" (*D* 177) will become much more widely pertinent. The Misses Morkans' annual dance was "always a great affair" (*D* 175). So, we gather, would people refer to it, in part out of a sense of courtesy. But this particular dance is going to trigger memories of what might be termed an affair, and the harmless, social epithet "great" will resurface in Gretta's simple and reverberating "I was great with him at that time" (*D* 220). Such simple words are filled with new, unanticipated meaning. Routine phrasing from a weather forecast, "the snow is general all over Ireland" (*D* 211), will come to have almost haunting reverberations when Gabriel repeats it later to himself. The title itself seems to undergo metamorphoses: most of us would take it to be a vague plural at first, it may become more concrete when there is talk about famous figures of the past, at one point it seems to narrow to Michael Furey and his powerful spectral reappearance,[3] but in the final cadence, "upon all the living and the dead," we may sense eschatological vibrations.

Gnomonic applications of the story's climax could go in several directions. If connubial harmony and revived desire correspond to an intact parallelogram, a part of it, Gretta's affection, is removed, similar to what happened when Gretta's frail admirer had died years ago. But Gabriel entered Gretta's life, and now, out of the dead past, Michael Furey's specter and its momentary abduction of Gabriel's wife is something wholly unforeseen. A vacuum has opened, and both Gretta and Gabriel are momentarily alone, deprived, but they are now also part of a triangle. We have an interplay of vacuums and unsuspected appearances.

The movement is a constant diminishing: the noisy crowd of the party dwindles to a few persons standing in the hall, soon only a few people are together in the cab, in the hotel only Gretta and Gabriel are left, and finally he is alone and feels even more isolated, almost at a vanishing point. But then the story widens out again. "The Dead" ends with a paragraph of another dimension ("the universe") and a different register, cadences not part of the original framework. Critical evaluations of the outcome ("all is and remains vanity" or else some powerful epiphanic turning point) could be rephrased as pointing toward gnomonic lack or else a gnomonic bonus. The believers in epiphany as a general insightful device, incidentally, could claim that each final unexpected twist causes changes that were not part of any original expectation.

Joyce revised his works by deleting little and putting a lot in. It is a commonplace that Joyce worked by amplification; he kept adding, he kept changing tracks. The genetics of Joyce's works consist of reconfigurations. Come to think of it, Joyce's procedures were additively gnomonic throughout. Excrescence is a key feature. If the basis of *Ulysses* is the *Odyssey* (or for that matter, any other pretext), its Dublin or metropolitan avatar is characterized by multiple supplementation, as it was all those seeming oddities that caused such a stir in 1922 (as well as difficulties for all later readers). If there were Homeric parallels in *Ulysses* (there aren't; nothing runs strictly parallel as deemed by Euclid who surfaces so early in the canon), the book would be, literally, a parallelogram, but it turned into something much more labyrinthine as new sides, corners, angles, or perspectives kept being added. Within a purely Homeric framework a Penelopean monologue amounts to a surplus. "Wandering Rocks," which in the prototype was an alternative route merely sketched, has become a full-fledged part. Each new "style" is a lateral enlargement of the preceding ones; some are blatant transgressions of the genre. Headlines were imposed on "Aeolus," an episode like "Circe" played havoc with the proportions of the whole novel, or, if you prefer, the work at hand deviated at this point from being a novel. Metatextual concerns put the apparent ultrarealism of earlier chapters in doubt. No one, including the author, could have guessed after the first, say, six episodes how the book was going to turn out, while at the same time, the old, mainly negative radiations of gnomon or paralysis are still in operation.

Joyce worked by leaving out and putting in. It is a common place that he proceeded by amplification, he kept adding, he kept changing tracks. The genetics of Joyce's works consist of reconfigurations. The geometrical figures, in our guiding metaphor here, became more and more intricate. The genetics of Joyce's works consist of reconfigurations. The gnomon patterns can explain *Finnegans Wake* oddities as less than or more than. Almost any sample will do. Take "etym" (*FW* 353.22), which falls short of its Greek parent, an adjective "etymos" or a noun "etymos," and even shorter of "etymology," though all these meanings are conjured up. Wake words tend to be incomplete parts for divergent wholes. But the overtone "atom" (which word it adumbrates even less obtrusively than the others) is a powerful and miraculous expansion as well as the basis for dynamic molecular links. In some way such a paradigm "simply" escalates an uneducated mistake in "The Sisters," where Eliza's "*Freeman's General*" (*D* 16) is an obvious failure, but where the lapsed "General" generates reverberations (and, for example, teams up with the snow at the end of the book that "was general all over Ireland").

If "Nomon" (*FW* 374.23) is to signal our word *gnomon* in the *Wake*, it is insufficient, and it would be inaccurate to do duty for *Noman* or Latin *nomen*, which it may suggest (as an accusative form of Greek "nomos," "law," it would be lexically correct but not grammatically). So the word is a series of Wakean incompleteness, unless we turn the tables and say that each possible meaning is grafted on every other as a fringe benefit, quite apart from the peculiarity of "Nomon" as a palindrome, equally accessible from either side. *Finnegans Wake* is patently more than any of the models we try out to describe its whatness: more than a dream, a Viconian perpetuum mobile, a kaleidoscope, a History of Mankind, an Irish myth, or whatever we think up (just as it is far less than any of these).

Geometrical correspondences, in other words, need not be limited to insufficiency. Addition and subtraction may be two sides of the same coin. The gnomonic signal at the opening of *Dubliners* may show something more basic. Euclid's classic sample of construction helped numerous readers to see and give focus to the stories. The inversion suggested above is merely a change of outlook. Approaches are definitional, our concepts shape what we are going to discover. A reader who focuses on gnomon as, primarily, someone or something that knows (the original meaning from which others like sundial derived) would emphasize knowledge (deficient or unwanted). If the sundial aspect is dominant, chronology and the workings of time can be foregrounded and detected all the more easily ("it was the third time"). Another stress could be put on Euclidean geometry as an exact science: shapes are ideally predictable and truths are known (because self-created); conclusions about a gnomon's sides and angles can be drawn with certainty. This serves as a contrast to Joyce's inauguration story; though Old Cotter has his own "opinion" and his own "theory" (neither ever stated)[4] and Father Flynn seems to know the correct answers to the most intricate questions he puts to the boy, we cannot construct anything remotely compelling from the fragments of information. In fact, even Old Cotter sets out with a denial of geometrical kinds of truth: "No, I wouldn't say he was exactly . . . " (first words ever uttered). Those, finally, who ignore the term entirely will find other inspiratorial blinders to guide them in their searches.

We, the Joycean readers, are also gnomonically minus/plus: we never know or understand enough, we see but in a glass darkly, but in compensation we bring to bear more and more on the texts by expanding their presumed potential. We produce ample superfluities. The present note may be an example of leaving out essential elements and exaggerating minor ones. Each interpretation in its nature is inadvertence combined with lateral excrescence. Each predisposition sets up a bundle of expectations (partly self-fulfilling) and will both sharpen and obstruct observation as well as speculation. Nothing new in this, but double-edged *gnomon* can bring it home once more.

Notes

1. "by Neuclidius and Inexagoras" (*Finnegans Wake* 155.32; hereafter cited as *FW* followed by page and line numbers): Euclid is the first name in *Dubliners*. Isn't it intriguing that in a story where we'll never learn who tells it, and where the main character's name is withheld until we see it on a death notice (and to understand his misfortunes we have to rely on doubtful clues or keys), the first name given is of a wholly subsidiary figure, but this name appears to contain the Greek for key, *kleis* (its root is *kleid–*)? Euclid's concept is in fact being used as a key. A warning is called for, however. If the name indeed implies how good ("eu") it is to handle keys ("kleidas"), we may keep in mind that "me elementator joyclid" (*FW* 302.12) also maintained that "there is no royal road to geometry." There we have a key and the assurance that there is no road—as Joycean a constellation as one could want.

2. Weir stresses the possible formation of any number of either smaller or larger gnomons. His quotation from Giordano Bruno's *De Triplici Minimo*, "The *gnomon* is that which, added or subtracted, enlarges or diminishes a figure without changing its form" (548), indicates alternatives that I am also going to work out but is still based on the Euclidean premise.

3. Translators have to make up their minds whether to use a singular or plural equivalent. Most of them, but not all, opt for the plural.

4. Interestingly enough, opinion is paired with doubt—"no doubt arranging his opinion in his mind"—in a passage that expresses the boy's own speculation, not knowledge. In the New Testament the related word *gnome* (also linked to *know*) could mean opinion of judgment (1 Cor. 7:25, 40, and so on).

Works Cited

Joyce, James. *Dubliners.* Ed. Robert Scholes. New York: Viking, 1967.

————. *Finnegans Wake.* London: Faber, 1939.

Weir, David. "Gnomon Is an Island: Euclid and Bruno in Joyce's Narrative Practice." *James Joyce Quarterly* 8 (1991): 343-60.

Contributors

Raffaella Baccolini is assistant professor of English at the University of Bologna, Italy. She is the author of *Tradition, Identity, Desire: Revisionist Strategies in H.D.'s Late Poetry* and has published several articles on modernist writers (H.D., Pound, Ford, Loy), women's writing (Levertov, women's theater, female autobiography), and dystopian literature (Atwood, Orwell, Burdekin). She is currently working on the function of memory and the past in twentieth-century women's literature.

Sonja Bašić is professor of English at Zagreb University. She has published studies on Joyce, Faulkner, and Hemingway in Italian, German, and Croatian publications. Her *Modernist Subversions: Joyce and Faulkner* (in Croatian) was published in Zagreb in 1996.

Lucia Boldrini is lecturer in English Literature at Goldsmiths College, University of London. She holds a Ph.D. from the University of Pisa (Italy) and one from the University of Leicester (U.K.). Her *Biografie fittizie di personaggi storici: (Auto)biografia, soggettività, teoria nel romanzo inglese contemporaneo* is forthcoming with ETS, Pisa. She is currently editing *Middayevil Joyce: A Forum on Joyce's Medieval Cultures* (Rodopi, "European Joyce Studies" series) and completing *In Dante's Wake: The Dantean Poetics of* Finnegans Wake.

Rosa Maria Bollettieri Bosinelli is professor of English at the University of Bologna, Italy, and has been vice-president of the James Joyce International Foundation since June 1994. She has published extensively on metaphor, translation, the language of politics, advertising, and Joyce. Her recent publications include *Anna Livia Plurabelle di James Joyce nella traduzione di Samuel Beckett e altri* (editor, 1996); *Myriadmindedman: Jottings on Joyce,* (coeditor, with P. Pugliatti and R. Zacchi, 1986), *The Languages of Joyce* (coeditor, with C. Marengo and C. van Boheemen, 1992). She has published a number of articles on James Joyce in national and international journals.

Michael Brian is associate professor of English at Concordia University, Montreal. He is currently doing research on the influence of such systems as alchemy, astrology, heresy, and rhetoric on literature. His most recent publication is "The Rhetoric of *Urn Burial:* The Decomposition of a Text" in *English Renaissance Prose* (Purdue, 1989).

Marlena G. Corcoran is assistant director of the university honors program at the University of Iowa. She is the author of over fifty scholarly and literary essays. "Material Ideals," her series of Joycean personal essays, appeared in *The James Joyce Literary Supplement* for seven years. She is coeditor of a collection of essays, *Gender in Joyce* (University Press of Florida, 1997). Her recent interest in multimedia has led to exhibitions and performances of her writings in Paris, New York, and on the Internet.

Claire A. Culleton is associate professor of English at Kent State University. She has published a number of articles on Joyce, on Irish and British modernism, and on women and the First World War. Her book *Names and Naming in Joyce* (University of Wisconsin Press) appeared in 1994.

David Leon Higdon, author of *Time and English Fiction* and *Shadows of the Past in Contemporary British Fiction* and editor of Joseph Conrad's *Almayer's Folly* and *Under Western Eyes* for the Cambridge University Press Joseph Conrad Edition, is the Paul Whitfield Horn Professor of English at Texas Tech University. His current projects include a study of textual revision in Graham Greene's novels and a census of gay and lesbian modernist fiction.

Patrick A. McCarthy, professor of English at the University of Miami, has written or edited nine books on modern literature, including four on James Joyce: *The Riddles of* Finnegans Wake (Fairleigh Dickinson University Press, 1980), Ulysses*: Portals of Discovery* (Twayne, 1990), *Critical Essays on James Joyce's* Finnegans Wake (G.K. Hall, 1992), and *Joyce/Lowry: Critical Perspectives,* coedited with Paul Tiessen (University Press of Kentucky, 1997).

Harold F. Mosher Jr., former editor of *Style,* has written often on *Dubliners* and was coeditor of the *Style* special issue on *Dubliners.* He is the coeditor of an anthology of American literature and author of a monograph on rock-music lyrics. In addition to publishing poetry and translations, he has written over sixty articles, reviews, and papers on English, American, and French literature.

Thomas Jackson Rice, professor of English at the University of South Carolina, is the author of eight books and over fifty articles and papers on nineteenth-and twentieth-century English literature. He is best known for his guides to research on modern English fiction, Charles Dickens, D.H. Lawrence, Virginia Woolf, and James Joyce. *Joyce, Chaos, and Complexity* (1997), his most recent book, studies the intersections among mathematics, physics, and Joyce's fiction.

John Paul Riquelme is professor and former chairman of English at Boston University. He has published widely on Joyce, and his *Teller and Tale in Joyce's*

Fiction: Oscillating Perspectives appeared in 1983. His most recent book is *Harmony of Dissonances: T.S. Eliot, Romanticism, and Imagination.*

Ulrich Schneider taught English at the University of Erlangen-Nürnberg, Germany. He has published the following monographs on Joyce and the British music hall: *Die Funktion der Zitate im* Ulysses *von James Joyce* (Bonn, 1970), *James Joyce:* Dubliners (Munich, 1982), *Die Londoner Music Hall und ihre Songs* (Tübingen, 1984), and, together with Laurence Senelick and David F. Cheshire, *British Music-Hall 1840-1923: A Bibliography and Guide to Sources* (Hamden, 1981).

Fritz Senn is in charge of the Zurich James Joyce Foundation. As an amateur scholar he has written essays, articles, and notes mainly on Joyce or translation problems (with forays also on Ochlokinetics). Some of his writings are collected in *Nichts gegan Joyce: Joyce versus Nothing* (1983), *Joycean Dislocutions* (1985), and *Inductive Scrutinies: Focus on Joyce* (1995).

Jolanta W. Wawrzycka is associate professor of English at Radford University in Virginia. In 1989 she was a recipient of the National Endowment for the Humanities stipend to attend the NEH Translation Institute. Her publications include works on Joyce, Milan Kundera, Roland Barthes, and Roman Ingarden as well as translations from Polish. She is coeditor of *Gender in Joyce,* a collection of essays published by the University Press of Florida in 1997.

Trevor L. Williams teaches at the University of Victoria, British Columbia. He has published articles on Joyce in *Modern Fiction Studies, Canadian Journal of Irish Studies,* and *The Ninth of Joyce.* Articles on Joyce are forthcoming in *Twentieth Century Literature* and *James Joyce Quarterly.* His book *Reading Joyce Politically* (University Press of Florida) was published in 1997.

Index

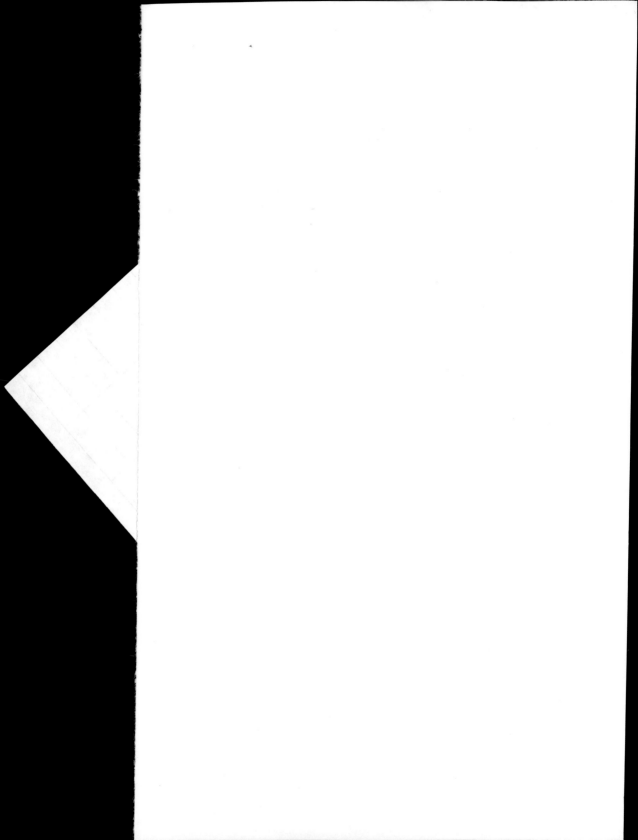

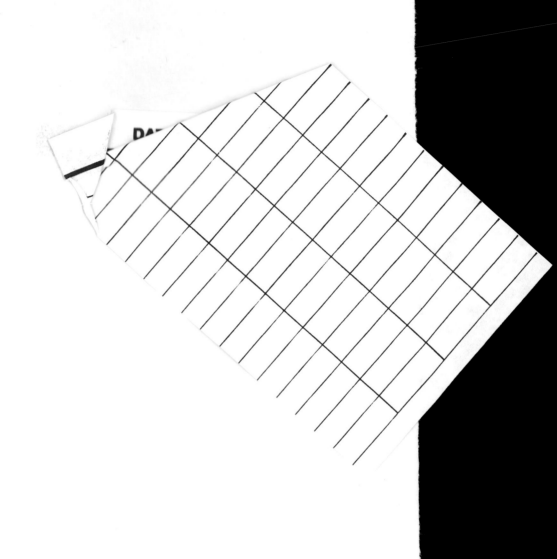